WORLD BOOK
FOCUS ON
TERRORISM

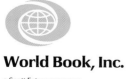

World Book, Inc.

a Scott Fetzer company

Chicago

Staff

**Executive Vice President
and Publisher**
Michael Ross

Editorial

Editor in Chief
Dale W. Jacobs

Managing Editors
Sara Dreyfuss
Warren Silver
Howard Timms

Assistant Managing Editors
Timothy Falk
Lloyd Lindo
Michael B. Schuldt

Subject Editors
Sarah Bright
Brad Finger
Nicholas Kilzer
Barbara Lanctot
Mike Lewis
Jay Myers
Mike Noren
Jay Powers
Thomas J. Wrobel
Daniel O. Zeff

Associate Production Editors
Megan Caras
Dawn Krajcik

Production Editors
Daniel J. Marotta
Cortez McKinney
Alana Papernik

Media Editor
Anne Mrozek

Head, Indexing Services
David Pofelski

Staff Indexer
Tina Trettin

Head, Statistical Services
Kenneth J. Shenkman

Head, Cartographic Services
H. George Stoll

**Manager, Cartographic
Database**
Wayne K. Pichler

Staff Cartographer
Kari Burnett

Staff Services Coordinator
Rose M. Barberio

Support Staff
Teresa Dunne
Carmen Jusino

Art

Executive Director
Roberta Dimmer

Art Director
Wilma Stevens

Senior Designers
Don Di Sante
Isaiah W. Sheppard, Jr.

Photography Manager
Sandra M. Dyrlund

Photographs Editor
Sylvia Ohlrich

Production Assistant
John Whitney

Cover Design
Norman Baugher

Research

**Executive Director of Research
and Product Development**
Paul Kobasa

Editorial Research Manager
Loranne K. Shields

Senior Researchers
Lynn Durbin
Cheryl Graham
Karen McCormack

Staff Researchers
Madolynn Cronk
Thomas Ryan Sullivan

Head, Library Services
Jon M. Fjortoft

Permissions
Janet T. Peterson

Production

Manufacturing/Pre-Press
Carma Fazio, *Director*
Justin Bigos
Audrey Casey
Debra Gill
Janice Rossing

Proofreading
Anne Dillon

Text Processing
Curley Hunter
Gwendolyn Johnson

Library of Congress Cataloging-in-Publication Data

World Book focus on terrorism.
   p. cm.
  Summary: A compendium of articles which deal with aspects of terrorism, including its history, the September 11, 2001 attacks, balancing civil rights and national security, and terrorist methods and weapons.
  Includes bibliographical references and index.
  ISBN 0-7166-1295-X
  1. Terrorism--Juvenile literature. 2. Terrorism--United States--Juvenile literature. 3. National security--United States--Juvenile literature. 4. Terrorism--Religious aspects--Juvenile literature. 5. Civil rights--Juvenile literature. [1. Terrorism. 2. National security. 3 Civil rights.] I. World Book, Inc. II. Title: Focus on terrorism.

HV6431.W634 2002
303.6'25--dc21

2002028854

About this book

The events of September 11, 2001, continue to haunt us. On that day, two airplanes hijacked by terrorists destroyed the twin towers of the World Trade Center in New York City. Another plane smashed into the Pentagon Building near Washington, D.C. And a fourth hijacked jet crashed into rural Somerset County, Pennsylvania, after brave passengers, having learned what had happened at the World Trade Center and the Pentagon, reportedly stormed the cockpit to try to wrest control of the plane from the terrorists.

The tragedy of September 11 shocked the nation and filled Americans with grief and anger. But the hijackings and their aftermath also raised many questions. Who were the hijackers? Why did they act as they did? What weapons and methods do terrorists use? How does the government fight terrorism? How does a democratic government strike the balance between civil rights and the need for security?

World Book Focus on Terrorism is designed to answer those questions and many others. The volume is divided into seven sections. The first section begins with an expanded version of the *World Book* article on the September 11 terrorist attacks. This longer version includes two maps that were specially prepared for this volume by World Book's award-winning Cartography Department. The maps show Ground Zero and the flight paths of the hijacked planes. The article also has a special sidebar feature with the complete text of President George W. Bush's address to the nation on the night of September 11. The rest of the section includes articles on Osama bin Laden, the Saudi-born millionaire and terrorist believed to be behind the attacks; the al-Qa`ida terrorist organization; and the Taliban, the extremist Afghan regime that harbored bin Laden and al-Qa`ida. This section also features a map of suspected al-Qa`ida cells around the world—from a government report dated September 10, 2001—and a table of some restrictions under the Taliban.

The attacks of September 11 were, in some ways, an extension of the Arab-Israeli conflict in the Middle East. The second section of *World Book Focus on Terrorism* concentrates on that troubled part of the world. It includes a collection of articles from *The World Book Encyclopedia* on the conflicts, religions, peoples, and political leaders of the Middle East and surrounding areas. This section also features *Facts in brief* pages for all the countries of the region except Afghanistan, which receives full-article treatment. Overall, the second section of *World Book Focus on Terrorism* serves as a "mini-almanac" of the Middle East and surrounding areas.

The book then presents an essay on the conflicts within Islam between moderates and extremists. The next two sections consist of articles from *The World Book Encyclopedia* that focus on terrorist methods and weapons and on homeland security. Following these pieces are an essay on civil rights and security in times of crisis and a collection of articles on civil rights. The book concludes with a brief history of terrorism around the world.

World Book Focus on Terrorism includes several features that help students develop their thinking and research skills. For example, topics for study suggest ideas for school assignments that require students to seek out, analyze, and evaluate information. Web sites provide additional direction for research.

The events of September 11, 2001, will be analyzed, interpreted, and debated a great deal in the coming years. *World Book Focus on Terrorism* is a comprehensive, authoritative, richly detailed, and easy-to-read reference work that helps provide a framework for understanding those events. As such, *World Book Focus on Terrorism* is equally suited for the general reader or student, and for home or school.

The editors

Table of contents

Focus on
TERRORISM

The Attacks of September 11

Within days after the September 11, 2001, terrorist attacks, the United States government laid the blame for them on the al-Qa`ida terrorist network, which was headed by the Saudi-born millionaire Osama bin Laden. At the time, bin Laden was living in Afghanistan and al-Qa`ida training camps were operating there under the protection of the Taliban regime. This section features expanded *World Book* articles on the September 11 terrorist attacks, al-Qa`ida, bin Laden, and the Taliban.

The terrorist attacks of Sept. 11, 2001, killed about 3,000 people and destroyed the World Trade Center towers in New York City and part of the Pentagon Building near Washington, D.C. New York City firefighters, *left,* searched through the twisted steel and debris of *Ground Zero,* the site of the World Trade Center attacks. The Pentagon Building, *right,* suffered major structural damage to its west side. A section of the building collapsed completely.

September 11 terrorist attacks

September 11 terrorist attacks were the worst acts of terrorism ever carried out against the United States. On Tuesday, September 11, 2001, terrorists in hijacked commercial jetliners slammed into the two towers of the World Trade Center in New York City and into the Pentagon Building near Washington, D.C. Another hijacked jet crashed in rural Pennsylvania. About 3,000 people were killed, and the World Trade Center towers and part of the Pentagon were destroyed. United States officials soon concluded that the Saudi millionaire Osama bin Laden and his *al-Qa'ida* (also spelled *al-Qaeda)* terrorist organization had been behind the attacks.

United States President George W. Bush called the attacks "acts of war" and launched a "war on terrorism." This war led to the overthrow of Afghanistan's rulers, the Taliban, who had sheltered bin Laden since 1996.

The attacks

The terrorist attacks involved four hijacked airplanes. The planes left airports on the East Coast within about 40 minutes of one another on the morning of September 11. The aircraft were headed across the country to

---

Barbara Lanctot, the contributor of this article, is Senior Area Studies Editor, The World Book Encyclopedia.

California and, as a result, were carrying thousands of gallons of fuel. Among the people aboard the four planes were 19 al-Qa'ida terrorists secretly carrying knives and box-cutters, tools with sharp blades. Shortly after departure, the terrorists took over the planes. At least some of them had had pilot training, investigators later learned, and they probably flew the planes.

The World Trade Center. American Airlines Flight 11, bound for Los Angeles, took off from Boston's Logan International Airport at about 8 a.m. (All times of day in this article are in Eastern Daylight Time.) There were 92 people aboard. Soon afterward, at a nearby gate, United Airlines Flight 175 left for Los Angeles with 65 people.

At about 8:45 a.m., Flight 11 crashed into the north tower of the World Trade Center. Less than 20 minutes later, Flight 175 hit the south tower. The 110-story twin towers ranked among the world's tallest skyscrapers and were the most famous part of the World Trade Center, a complex of seven buildings. The complex contained offices of a number of U.S. government agencies and many businesses and organizations involved in finance and international trade. About 50,000 people worked in the complex.

Flames and smoke engulfed the towers after the fuel-laden planes crashed into them. People raced to escape the buildings and the area. Police, fire, and medical personnel rushed to the site. About an hour after being struck, the south tower, weakened by fire, collapsed. About a half-hour later, the north tower collapsed. Other buildings in the area were also destroyed or heavily damaged. The attacks left about 2,800 people dead or missing, including 157 dead on the two hijacked planes.

The Pentagon. American Flight 77 left Dulles International Airport in Virginia at about 8:20 a.m. on September 11, headed for Los Angeles. It carried 58 people. At about 9:40 a.m., Flight 77 crashed into the west side of the Pentagon Building, the nation's military headquarters near Washington, D.C. A section of the building collapsed shortly afterward, leaving 189 people dead or missing, including the people on the hijacked plane.

Pennsylvania. United Flight 93 left Newark International Airport at 8:01 a.m., headed for San Francisco. There were 44 people on the plane. Shortly after 10 a.m., Flight 93 crashed in a field in Somerset County in southwestern Pennsylvania. All aboard were killed.

Reports of what occurred on Flight 93 were drawn from phone calls passengers made before the crash. Several passengers, aware of the other attacks, said they would try to overcome the hijackers. The intended target of the terrorists on Flight 93 is not known.

The aftermath

The immediate reactions to the terrorist attacks included evacuating the White House and offices of the federal government and halting all nonmilitary air traffic over the nation. The major United States stock exchanges stopped trading, and a large number of businesses and public landmarks closed early and sent employees home.

In a televised speech Tuesday evening, President Bush said, "Today, our nation saw evil." He said, "These acts of mass murder were intended to frighten our nation into chaos and retreat. But they have failed. Our country is strong."

The United States government launched a massive investigation to find those responsible for the attacks. Government leaders also worked to increase national security and to strengthen the nation's weakened economy.

Increased national security. In mid-September, President Bush announced the creation of a federal Office of Homeland Security to improve the nation's defense against future terrorist attacks. Bush appointed Pennsylvania Governor Thomas J. Ridge to head the office. Ridge resigned as governor and took responsibility for overseeing and coordinating national efforts to protect against, and respond to, attacks of terrorism.

In the weeks following the September 11 attacks, several U.S. business and government offices received mail that contained anthrax bacteria. Anthrax is an infectious disease that can be fatal if not treated promptly. Five people died from exposure to the bacteria, and fear of anthrax spread across the country. Investigators initially looked for evidence linking the terrorists to the anthrax mailings but found no connection. They then came to believe the source was within the United States.

In October, the U.S. Congress passed an antiterrorism bill giving the government expanded investigative powers against suspected terrorists. For example, the law allows greater scope in conducting electronic surveillance and in detaining immigrants without charges. Some people criticized the act, fearing that such measures would limit civil liberties. The law also aims to help prevent funds from reaching terrorists. It permits the Department of the Treasury to require banks to make greater efforts to determine the sources of large overseas private banking accounts.

After the attacks, Bush also called for increased aviation security. In November, Congress passed legislation that gave the federal government a central role in security measures in airports. The legislation required that all workers who screen travelers and baggage in airports

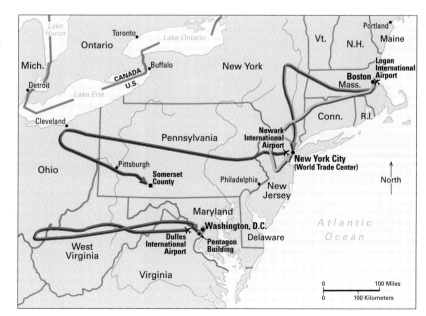

The flight paths of the four hijacked airplanes show the points at which each plane diverted from its intended course. Three of the flights—American Airlines Flights 11 and 77 and United Airlines Flight 175—were bound for Los Angeles. United Airlines Flight 93 was bound for San Francisco.

Flight paths

← American Airlines Flight 11

← United Airlines Flight 175

← United Airlines Flight 93

← American Airlines Flight 77

WORLD BOOK map

President Bush's television address

AP/Wide World

President George W. Bush addressed a grieving and angry nation on the evening of September 11, 2001, offering words of comfort and vowing to punish those responsible.

Good evening. Today, our fellow citizens, our way of life, our very freedom came under attack in a series of deliberate and deadly terrorist acts. The victims were in airplanes or in their offices: secretaries, business men and women, military and federal workers, moms and dads, friends and neighbors. Thousands of lives were suddenly ended by evil, despicable acts of terror.

The pictures of airplanes flying into buildings, fires burning, huge structures collapsing have filled us with disbelief, terrible sadness and a quiet, unyielding anger.

These acts of mass murder were intended to frighten our nation into chaos and retreat. But they have failed. Our country is strong. A great people has been moved to defend a great nation.

Terrorist attacks can shake the foundations of our biggest buildings, but they cannot touch the foundation of America. These acts shatter steel, but they cannot dent the steel of American resolve.

America was targeted for attack because we're the brightest beacon for freedom and opportunity in the world. And no one will keep that light from shining.

Today, our nation saw evil, the very worst of human nature, and we responded with the best of America, with the daring of our rescue workers, with the caring for strangers and neighbors who came to give blood and help in any way they could.

Immediately following the first attack, I implemented our government's emergency response plans. Our military is powerful, and it's prepared. Our emergency teams are working in New York City and Washington, D.C., to help with local rescue efforts.

Our first priority is to get help to those who have been injured and to take every precaution to protect our citizens at home and around the world from further attacks.

The functions of our government continue without interruption. Federal agencies in Washington which had to be evacuated today are reopening for essential personnel tonight and will be open for business tomorrow.

Our financial institutions remain strong, and the American economy will be open for business as well.

The search is underway for those who are behind these evil acts.

I've directed the full resources for our intelligence and law enforcement communities to find those responsible and bring them to justice. We will make no distinction between the terrorists who committed these acts and those who harbor them.

I appreciate so very much the members of Congress who have joined me in strongly condemning these attacks. And on behalf of the American people, I thank the many world leaders who have called to offer their condolences and assistance.

America and our friends and allies join with all those who want peace and security in the world and we stand together to win the war against terrorism.

Tonight I ask for your prayers for all those who grieve, for the children whose worlds have been shattered, for all whose sense of safety and security has been threatened. And I pray they will be comforted by a power greater than any of us spoken through the ages in Psalm 23: "Even though I walk through the valley of the shadow of death, I fear no evil for you are with me."

This is a day when all Americans from every walk of life unite in our resolve for justice and peace. America has stood down enemies before, and we will do so this time. None of us will ever forget this day, yet we go forward to defend freedom and all that is good and just in our world.

Thank you. Good night and God bless America.

---

be federal employees. Before then, the airlines had hired the screeners. The bill specified that the transition to federal employees be completed within a year.

War on terrorism. United States leaders became convinced that the September 11 attacks were the work of the extremist Muslim leader Osama bin Laden and his al-Qa'ida terrorist network. Bin Laden and al-Qa'ida were known to strongly oppose United States policies in the Middle East, particularly United States support for Israel and the presence of United States troops in Saudi Arabia. Bin Laden's headquarters and terrorist training camps were in Afghanistan. Bush called upon the Taliban, the rulers of Afghanistan, to turn over bin Laden and close down the training camps. The Taliban refused.

Meanwhile, Bush worked to form a coalition of countries to wage what he called a "war on terrorism." Bush said the war would include such measures as tightened security, efforts to cut off funds to terrorists, and military action against terrorists and the countries that harbored them.

On October 7, the United States and its allies launched a military campaign in Afghanistan against the Taliban and al-Qa'ida. The campaign included massive air strikes in support of the Northern Alliance and other Afghan rebel groups who opposed the Taliban. This support enabled the rebels to overthrow the Taliban in December. The United Nations brought together representatives of Afghanistan's leading factions to discuss

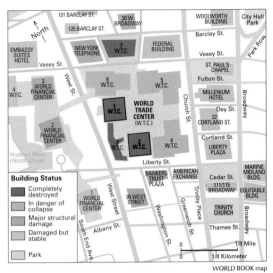

WORLD BOOK map

The World Trade Center complex originally consisted of seven buildings. This map shows the degree of damage to the buildings within and around the center after the attacks.

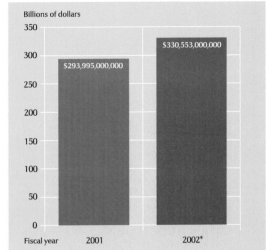

*Proposed

Improving national defense was a top priority of the U.S. government following the September 11 attacks. This graph shows the significant increase in defense spending proposed for 2002.

the formation of a new national government. In early December, the members of the group agreed on a plan for a new government.

Weakened economy. In November 2001, economic data showed the United States economy had been in a recession since March. After the events of September 11, unemployment increased and the recession worsened. Among companies hit hardest by the economic slowdown were a large number of airlines. Some airlines faced bankruptcy. After the attacks, their insurance costs greatly increased, and they had to undertake costly overhauls of their security systems. At the same time, their incomes dropped sharply because many people

were afraid to fly. Congress passed a $15-billion package of cash and loan guarantees to support the failing airlines.

Moving forward. New York City, which had suffered the greatest loss of life and physical damage, faced severe challenges. After the attacks, Mayor Rudolph W. Giuliani helped guide the city through a difficult recovery period. He was widely praised for his leadership. Workers toiled around the clock to clean up the mountain of twisted steel and other debris from *Ground Zero,* the site of the Trade Center attacks. At the Pentagon, the ruins of the shattered section were cleared away and rebuilding began.   Barbara Lanctot

AP/Wide World

A solemn ceremony held on May 30, 2002, marked the official end of more than eight months of cleanup and recovery efforts at the World Trade Center site. An American flag, draped on a stretcher, was carried from the site as part of the ceremony.

Bin Laden, Osama (1957?-   ), is a Saudi-born millionaire and radical Muslim who supports international terrorism. He opposes United States policies in the Middle East, particularly U.S. support for Israel and the presence of U.S. troops in the Arabian Peninsula. He also opposes governments in the Islamic world that are allied to the United States. Bin Laden was the founder and leader of al-Qa`ida, a global terrorist organization that is allied with other Muslim extremist groups worldwide.

United States and other Western intelligence officials believe that bin Laden was the mastermind behind a number of terrorist attacks against U.S. targets. The U.S. government named him as the prime suspect in the Sept. 11, 2001, attacks on the World Trade Center in New York City and the Pentagon Building near Washington, D.C. Officials also believe he was behind the 1998 bombings of U.S. embassies in Kenya and Tanzania.

Bin Laden was born in Riyadh, Saudi Arabia, to a wealthy family. In 1979, he joined the *mujahideen* (Muslim holy warriors) in Pakistan who were fighting against the Soviet occupation of Afghanistan. During much of the 1980's, he collected money and materials to support the mujahideen. In the late 1980's, he established al-Qa`ida to resist the Soviet occupation. After the Soviets withdrew from Afghanistan in 1989, bin Laden reportedly returned to Saudi Arabia.

In 1990, Iraq invaded Kuwait, sparking the Persian Gulf War. A U.S.-led military coalition sent troops to Saudi Arabia to protect that country from Iraqi invasion and to drive the Iraqis out of Kuwait. Bin Laden opposed the Saudi government's decision to allow U.S. troops in Saudi Arabia, where the holiest Muslim sites are located. The Persian Gulf War prompted bin Laden and al-Qa`ida to dramatically expand their goals. They called for removal of foreign influence in Muslim countries and began to oppose governments of Muslim countries allied to the United States. Because of bin Laden's activities against the Saudi government, he was forced to leave the country. From 1991 until 1996, bin Laden lived in Sudan. In 1996, the Sudanese government, under pressure from the United States and Saudi Arabia, expelled him. He then moved to Afghanistan, where he lived under the protection of the Taliban, a conservative Islamic group that controlled most of that country.

In 1998, following the terrorist bombings of the U.S. embassies in Kenya and Tanzania, the United States launched missile strikes against al-Qa`ida training camps in Afghanistan. In 1999 and 2000, the United Nations imposed sanctions against Afghanistan for refusing to surrender bin Laden.

After the September 2001 terrorist attacks, the United States demanded that the Taliban hand over bin Laden. The Taliban refused. The United States and its allies, including Afghan opposition rebels, began a military campaign against the Taliban. The Taliban government fell in late 2001, but the fate of bin Laden and several other al-Qa`ida leaders remained unknown.   Christine Moss Helms

**Qa`ida,** *KAH ihd uh,* **Al-,** also spelled al-Qaida and al-Qaeda, is a terrorist organization that supports the activities of Muslim extremists around the world. Its founder and leader is Osama bin Laden, a Saudi-born millionaire. *Al-Qa`ida* is an Arabic term that means *the base.* The United States government has blamed al-Qa`ida for the Sept. 11, 2001, terrorist attacks against the World Trade Center in New York City and the Pentagon Building near Washington, D.C. Al-Qa`ida also is believed to have aided other attacks against U.S. targets, including the 1998 bombings of U.S. embassies in Kenya and Tanzania.

Al-Qa`ida believes that governments of Muslim countries that fail to follow Islamic law should be overthrown. Al-Qa`ida also considers the United States to be a primary enemy of Islam. It opposes the presence of U.S. troops in Saudi Arabia, where the holiest Muslim sites are located. In 1996, bin Laden called upon Muslims to topple the Saudi government and liberate Islamic holy sites from foreign influence. Two years later, he also said it was the duty of Muslims to kill U.S. citizens, both civilian and military, and their allies.

AP/Wide World

Osama bin Laden, *second from left,* became a terrorist leader in the late 1980's. The United States government concluded that bin Laden and his al-Qa`ida network were responsible for the September 11 terrorist hijackings. This picture shows a scene from a videotaped statement less than a month after the attacks.

The al-Qaʾida network of terrorist *cells* operates in numerous countries throughout the world. A cell is a small group of terrorists that carry out the plans of the larger organization. This map shows the countries in which al-Qaʾida cells have been discovered or suspected to exist. This map is based on a U.S. government report issued on Sept. 10, 2001, the day before the al-Qaʾida terrorist attacks in the United States.

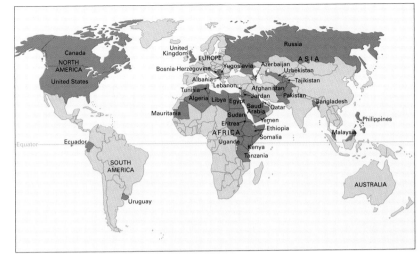

◼ Countries with known or suspected al-Qaʾida cells

WORLD BOOK map

In 1979, bin Laden reportedly joined the *mujahideen,* the Muslim resistance movement that was fighting against the Soviet occupation of Afghanistan. He spent much of the 1980's raising funds to help the mujahideen. In the late 1980's, bin Laden founded al-Qaʾida to resist the Soviets. During the 1990's, al-Qaʾida expanded its goals. It opposed foreign influence in Muslim countries and called for the overthrow of Muslim governments allied to the United States. Al-Qaʾida is believed to support other Islamic extremist groups throughout the world.

In 1996, bin Laden and other al-Qaʾida leaders moved to Afghanistan. There, they lived under the protection of the Taliban, a conservative Islamic group that controlled most of the country. After the September 2001 attacks, the United States and its allies launched a military campaign against the Taliban. The Taliban government fell in late 2001. U.S. and allied forces continued to search for bin Laden and other al-Qaʾida leaders. But the fate of many of them remained unknown.   Christine Moss Helms

Taliban are a militant Islamic political group that gained control of most of Afghanistan beginning in the mid-1990's. The Taliban sought to turn Afghanistan into a united Islamic state. In 2001, the United States and its allies helped Afghan rebels force the Taliban from power. The word *taliban* (also spelled *taleban*) means *seekers after knowledge* and refers to the group's origin in Islamic schools.

The Taliban enforced strict adherence to their interpretation of Islamic laws. These laws included restrictions on most modern forms of entertainment, and personal restrictions on dress and grooming. For example, the Taliban forced men to wear beards and women to wear veils. Those who violated the Taliban's law were punished severely.

The Taliban formed in Pakistan in 1994. The group sought to end the lawlessness and suffering that had re-

AP/Wide World

Captured Taliban fighters are escorted by a Northern Alliance soldier to a prison in Taloqan, Afghanistan, in November 2001. Massive air strikes by U.S. and British armed forces helped the Northern Alliance and other Afghan rebel groups drive the Taliban from power.

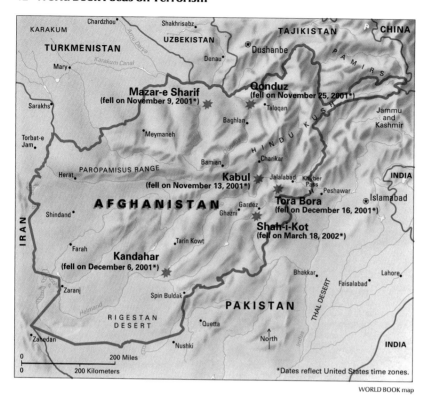

Military strikes against al-Qa'ida and the Taliban in Afghanistan began in October 2001. The United States and its allies launched a powerful air campaign and supported Afghan rebel groups to drive the Taliban from power. This map shows the locations of major battles in Afghanistan.

WORLD BOOK map

sulted from years of civil war in Afghanistan, which had been torn since 1989 by bitter struggles for power. The Taliban drew their forces from Afghan and Pakistani Muslim students, Afghan refugees who had fled to Pakistan, former rebel fighters, and former Communist soldiers. Most of the group's members belonged to Afghanistan's dominant Pashtun ethnic group. The Taliban established their power base in southeastern Afghanistan near the border with Pakistan, where Pashtuns form the majority.

The Taliban captured Afghanistan's second largest city, Kandahar, in November 1994. In January 1995, the Taliban captured the province of Ghazni, northeast of

Some restrictions under the Taliban

Afghanistan's Taliban regime sought to impose its strict and harsh interpretation of Islamic laws on the country. Some Taliban restrictions are listed below.

- Girls were formally forbidden from attending school.
- Women were required to wear a *burqa*–a hooded garment that covers the body from head to toe—when in public.
- Men were required to wear beards a certain length or longer.
- Music, motion pictures, and videos were prohibited.
- With extremely few exceptions, women were not permitted to work outside the home.
- Women were not allowed in public unless they were accompanied by a male relative.
- Conversion from Islam to another religion was punishable by death.
- Homes with female occupants were required to have their windows painted over so that women would not be visible from the street.
- Women were forbidden to be treated by male doctors or to deal with male shopkeepers.

Kandahar. Throughout 1995, the Taliban rebels strengthened their position in southern Afghanistan. In September 1995, they took the western city of Herat. A year later, they seized the capital city, Kabul. The government forces retreated to the northeastern part of Afghanistan.

In 1997, Taliban authorities changed the official name of the country to the Islamic State of Afghanistan. But only three countries recognized the Taliban as a legal government—Pakistan, Saudi Arabia, and the United Arab Emirates.

In 1998, the United States accused the Taliban of harboring the Saudi millionaire Osama bin Laden, wanted in connection with terrorist attacks against two U.S. embassies in Africa. The United States launched missile strikes against suspected terrorist training camps in Afghanistan. A Taliban spokesman acknowledged that bin Laden was in Afghanistan under Taliban protection. In 1999, the United Nations imposed trade sanctions against Afghanistan for refusing to surrender bin Laden.

In 2001, the United States accused bin Laden and his terrorist organization of carrying out attacks that year against the World Trade Center in New York City and the Pentagon Building near Washington, D.C. The attacks killed thousands of people from many different countries. The United States demanded that the Taliban hand over bin Laden and shut down terrorist training camps in Afghanistan. The Taliban refused to do so, and the United States and its allies launched a military campaign against the Taliban. The campaign included massive air strikes in support of Afghan rebels who opposed the Taliban. This support enabled the rebels to drive the Taliban from power later in 2001.

Abraham Marcus

Focus on
TERRORISM

Section Two

Region of Conflict: The Middle East and Surrounding Areas

The September 11 attacks were, in some ways, an extension of the Arab-Israeli conflict in the Middle East. This four-part section looks at that troubled part of the world. The first part features articles on the Arab-Israeli conflict and the Persian Gulf War. The second part includes articles on the Middle East and Afghanistan, followed by "Facts in brief" pages on various countries in the region. The third part (starting on p. 57) consists of articles on peoples and religions. Part four looks at the region's political leaders.

Arab-Israeli conflict is a struggle between the Jewish state of Israel and the Arabs of the Middle East. About 90 percent of all Arabs are Muslims. The conflict has included several wars between Israel and certain Arab countries that have opposed Israel's existence. Israel was formed in 1948. The conflict has also involved a struggle by Palestinian Arabs to establish their own country in some or all of the land occupied by Israel.

The Arab-Israeli conflict is the continuation of an Arab-Jewish struggle that began in the early 1900's for control of Palestine. Palestine today consists of Israel and the areas known as the Gaza Strip and the West Bank. The Palestinians lived in the region long before Jews began moving there in large numbers in the late 1800's.

The Arab-Israeli conflict has been hard to resolve. In 1979, Egypt became the first Arab country to sign a peace treaty with Israel. Jordan, another Arab country, signed a peace treaty with Israel in 1994. But Israel has not made final peace agreements with Syria or with the Palestine Liberation Organization (PLO). The PLO is a political body that represents the Palestinian people.

Historical background. In the mid-1800's, Jewish intellectuals in Europe began to support the idea that Jews should settle in Palestine, which the Bible describes as the Jews' ancient homeland. The word *Palestine* does not appear in the Bible. But it has long been used to refer to the area the Bible describes. The idea that Jews should settle in Palestine became known as Zionism. In the 1800's, Palestine was controlled by the Ottoman Empire, which was centered in present-day Turkey.

Zionism became an important political movement among Jews in Europe because of increasing *anti-Semitism* (prejudice against Jews) there. The anti-Semitism resulted in violent attacks on Jews and their property. In the 1800's, the immigration of European Jews to Palestine accelerated. At first, many of the immigrants and the Palestinian Arabs lived together peacefully. But as more Jews arrived, conflicts increased.

After World War I ended in 1918, the United Kingdom gained control of Palestine from the Ottoman Empire. In the Balfour Declaration of 1917, the United Kingdom had supported creating a national homeland for the Jews.

Under British rule, the Jewish population of Palestine continued to grow.

During World War II (1939-1945), German dictator Adolf Hitler tried to kill all of Europe's Jews. Thus, about 6 million Jews were murdered. After the war, most of the countries that defeated Germany supported the idea of creating a new Jewish state where Jews would be safe from persecution.

The 1948 war. In November 1947, the United Nations (UN) approved a plan to divide Palestine into two states, one Jewish and the other Palestinian. Zionist leaders accepted the plan. But Arab governments and the Palestinians saw the division as the theft of Arab land by Zionists and the governments that supported them.

British rule over Palestine ended when Zionists proclaimed the state of Israel on May 14, 1948. The next day, armies of Egypt, Syria, Lebanon, Transjordan (which became known as Jordan in 1949), and Iraq attacked Israel. Israel fought back. In the war, Israel absorbed much of the land the UN had set aside for the Palestinians. Egypt and Jordan occupied the rest of the area that was assigned to the Palestinians. Egypt held the Gaza Strip, a small area between Israel and the Mediterranean Sea. Jordan held the West Bank, a territory between Israel and the Jordan River. By August 1949, Israel and all five Arab states had agreed to end the fighting. Because of the war, about 700,000 Palestinians became refugees. Most fled to Jordan—including the West Bank—or to the Gaza Strip. Others went to Lebanon and Syria.

The Suez crisis of 1956. During the 1950's, nationalism spread among the Arab countries of the Middle East. Egyptian President Gamal Abdel Nasser and his followers sought to rid Arab lands of the influence of Western nations. On July 26, 1956, Nasser took control of the Suez Canal from its British and French owners. The canal connects the Mediterranean and Red seas and is a key shipping route between Europe and Asia.

Many countries protested Nasser's action. France, Israel, and the United Kingdom secretly plotted to end Egypt's control of the canal. On October 29, Israel attacked Egyptian forces in Egypt's Sinai Peninsula and quickly defeated them. The Sinai lies between Israel and the canal. Israel, with British and French help, occupied most of the peninsula. The UN called a cease-fire on November 6. By early 1957, Israel, under international pressure, returned the Sinai to Egypt. The canal reopened under Egyptian management in April of that year.

After the Suez crisis, Arab guerrillas launched small-scale attacks inside Israel, and Israel responded with raids into Arab territory. At the same time, the Arab nationalist movement began receiving financial and military support from the Soviet Union. The United States, fearing the spread of Soviet-sponsored Communism, gave financial and military aid to Israel.

In 1964, the PLO was formed to represent the Palestinians. The PLO included guerrilla groups dedicated to defeating Israel and creating an independent Palestinian state.

The 1967 war. In May 1967, Nasser closed the Gulf of Aqaba to Israeli shipping. The gulf was Israel's only access to the Red Sea. By June 5, Egypt had signed defense agreements with Syria, Jordan, and Iraq, creating a joint military command.

These apparent preparations for war alarmed the Is-

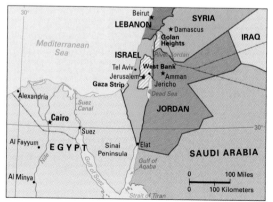

WORLD BOOK map

Israel and its Arab neighbors lie at the eastern end of the Mediterranean Sea. Arab countries that have fought wars against Israel include Egypt, Iraq, Jordan, and Syria.

raelis. On June 5, they launched a surprise attack on Egypt. Syria, Jordan, and Iraq joined Egypt in fighting Israel. Within hours, Israeli warplanes destroyed almost all the Arab air forces. Israeli tanks then retook the Sinai Peninsula. Israel also gained control of the West Bank, the Gaza Strip, and East Jerusalem. It had taken West Jerusalem in the 1948 war. In the north, Israel took Syria's Golan Heights, an area bordering Israel. The fighting ended on June 10. Israelis call this conflict the Six-Day War. Arabs call it the June War. After the war, Israel decided it would return the territories it had taken only if the Arab countries recognized its right to exist.

Also after the 1967 war, the PLO sought to become the representative of the Palestinians in world politics. It developed educational and social service organizations for Palestinians, mainly in the West Bank and Gaza Strip and in refugee camps in Lebanon and Jordan.

The PLO also began to take independent military action. In the late 1960's, PLO groups began to attack Israelis both inside and outside Israel. In response, Israel attacked Palestinian refugee camps in Jordan and Lebanon, in which many guerrillas were based. The Israelis also assassinated a number of PLO leaders.

The 1973 war. After the 1967 war, Egyptian and Israeli troops continued to attack each other across the western border of the Sinai Peninsula. On Oct. 6, 1973, Egypt and Syria launched a massive assault on Israeli forces in the Sinai Peninsula and Golan Heights. The attack took Israel by surprise, in part because it came on Yom Kippur, the holiest day in Judaism.

At first, Egypt drove Israel's forces out of the western Sinai, and Syria pushed Israeli troops from the eastern Golan Heights. However, the United States gave Israel large amounts of military equipment. By October 24, Israeli forces crossed the Suez Canal and surrounded the Egyptian army. They also defeated the Syrian army in the Golan Heights. Israelis call this war the Yom Kippur War. Arabs call it the October War or the Ramadan War.

The Camp David Accords. In 1978, Egyptian President Anwar el-Sadat joined Israeli Prime Minister Menachem Begin and U.S. President Jimmy Carter in signing the Camp David Accords. Under these agreements, Egypt recognized Israel's right to exist. In return, Israel agreed to give back to Egypt the part of the Sinai it still occupied. Israel had returned the far western part of the Sinai in 1975. In talks leading up to the accords, Egypt and Israel were promised large amounts of U.S. economic and military aid. In 1979, Egypt and Israel signed a treaty that confirmed their new peaceful relationship.

Most Arab leaders strongly opposed the Camp David Accords and the 1979 treaty. The Arab League, an organization of Arab countries, expelled Egypt in 1979.

The Israeli invasion of Lebanon. After the signing of the Camp David Accords, the PLO continued to launch guerrilla attacks on Israel, especially from southern Lebanon. In 1982, Israel invaded Lebanon and drove the PLO out of the southern part of the country. Israeli forces remained in southern Lebanon until 2000.

The first intifada. In 1987, Palestinians in the West Bank and Gaza Strip began an uprising against Israel's military rule of those territories. During this *intifada* (an Arabic term meaning *uprising* or *shaking off),* demonstrations occurred throughout the occupied territories. Most demonstrations were peaceful, but a few became

AP/Wide World

The 1967 war was one of several fought between Arab countries and Israel. In this photograph, an Israeli guard watches over Jordanian prisoners shortly after the 1967 war ended.

violent. The intifada grabbed international attention and triggered criticism of Israel for its extensive use of force in trying to control the Palestinians.

Peacemaking. In 1988, the PLO recognized Israel's right to exist. It also declared its readiness to negotiate with Israel for peace in return for the creation of an independent Palestinian state. In addition, it declared it would no longer use violence against Israel. But some PLO members continued to attack Israeli targets.

In 1993, Israel and the PLO, aided by Norway, began secret peace talks. As a result, the PLO and Israel signed an agreement in Washington, D.C., in September 1993. Under the agreement, the PLO again stated its recognition of Israel's right to exist. Israel, in turn, recognized the PLO as the representative of the Palestinian people. It also promised to withdraw from part or all of the West Bank and Gaza Strip and to consider allowing the creation of a Palestinian state in those lands. In 1994, Israel gave the PLO control of the Gaza Strip and the West Bank city of Jericho. In 1995 and 1996, Israel gave the Palestinians control of most West Bank cities and towns.

Jordan signed a peace treaty with Israel in 1994. Peace discussions between Israel and Syria, however, broke down in 1996. Talks resumed in December 1999 but stopped the next month because of continuing disagreement over the Golan Heights.

The second intifada. Peace talks between Israeli and Palestinian leaders continued in 2000. However, the two sides were unable to agree on key remaining issues, especially those involving the final status of Jerusalem. In September 2000, Palestinians began a second intifada against Israeli security forces. Numerous attacks by Palestinian militias and suicide bombers took place throughout Israel, the West Bank, and the Gaza Strip, killing hundreds of Israelis. Israeli forces repeatedly bombed and invaded the West Bank and Gaza Strip, killing more than 1,700 Palestinians. In 2002, Israel reoccupied much of the West Bank.   William B. Vogele

Web site

© Sipa Press

© Corbis/Sygma

© J. Langevin, Corbis/Sygma

Allied forces attacked from the air, sea, and land during the Persian Gulf War. In January 1991, allied aircraft, including the French warplane above, began bombing military targets in Iraq and Kuwait, while U.S. ships in the Persian Gulf launched cruise missiles, *top right.* In February, allied ground forces, including Saudi tanks, *bottom right,* quickly defeated Iraq.

Persian Gulf War, sometimes called *Operation Desert Storm,* was fought in early 1991 between Iraq and a coalition of 39 countries organized mainly by the United States and the United Nations (UN). The war took place chiefly in Iraq and the tiny oil-rich nation of Kuwait. These two countries lie together at the northern end of the Persian Gulf. Leading members of the coalition against Iraq included Egypt, France, Saudi Arabia, Syria, the United Kingdom, and the United States.

The coalition had formed after Iraq invaded Kuwait on Aug. 2, 1990. Iraq's invasion followed unsuccessful attempts to resolve several disputes between the two countries. After quickly gaining control of Kuwait, Iraq moved huge numbers of troops to Kuwait's border with Saudi Arabia, triggering fears that Iraq would invade Saudi Arabia next. Iraq's actions were viewed with alarm by the world's industrialized countries, which relied on Kuwait and Saudi Arabia as a primary source of petroleum. A number of coalition members sent troops to Saudi Arabia to protect it from possible attack.

On Jan. 17, 1991, after months of pressuring Iraq to leave Kuwait, the coalition began bombing Iraqi military and industrial targets. In late February, the coalition launched a massive ground attack into Kuwait and southern Iraq and quickly defeated the Iraqis. Coalition military operations ended on February 28.

The Persian Gulf War was the first major international crisis after the end of the Cold War. It severely tested cooperation between the United States and the Soviet Union, as well as the ability of the UN to play a leading role in world affairs. The war also split the Arab world between coalition members and supporters of Iraq's president, Saddam Hussein.

Background to the war

Competition for Arab leadership. Saddam Hussein's ambition for power and leadership in the Organization of the Petroleum Exporting Countries (OPEC) and in the Middle East was a central cause of the invasion of Kuwait. Besides Iraq, OPEC members also included Kuwait and Saudi Arabia. Like those countries, Iraq was a major oil-exporting nation. But from 1980 to 1988, Iraq had fought a drawn-out war with its neighbor Iran. Iraq suffered serious economic damage in the Iran-Iraq War. Nevertheless, it emerged from that conflict as the second-strongest military power in the Middle East. Only the Jewish state of Israel was stronger.

Hussein argued that Iraq had become the region's chief power opposed to Israel and should thus be recognized by other Arab countries as leader of the Arab world. Many Arabs wanted to abolish Israel and place its lands under the control of Palestinians and other Arabs.

Hussein claimed that, as leader of the Arab world, Iraq should receive help from other Arab countries in rebuilding its economy. According to Hussein, Iraq needed help from OPEC in raising world oil prices, along with the cancellation of debts that Iraq had incurred to Kuwait and other Arab countries to fight the Iran-Iraq War.

Disputes between Iraq and Kuwait. After the Iran-Iraq War, Hussein had disagreed with Kuwait's leaders over how much debt-cancellation and other financial aid Kuwait should provide for Iraq's economic recovery. Hussein also accused Kuwait of exceeding oil production limits set by OPEC and thus lowering world oil prices. In addition, Hussein claimed that Kuwait was taking Iraqi oil from the Rumaila oil field, a large field that lay beneath both Iraq and Kuwait.

Iraq had often claimed that Kuwait should be part of Iraq. Iraq based its claim on the fact that, in the 1800's and early 1900's, Kuwait had been part of a province of the Ottoman Empire, called Basra, which later became part of Iraq. But Kuwait was no longer part of the province when Iraq was formed in the early 1920's. By the early 1920's, Britain controlled Kuwait and what became Iraq. Iraq became an independent nation in 1932, and Kuwait in 1961. But Iraq did not recognize Kuwait's independence until 1963. After 1963, Iraq and Kuwait still disputed the location of their common border.

What Hussein hoped to gain by taking Kuwait. Saddam Hussein was encouraged by a number of factors to consider an invasion of Kuwait. For example, by seizing Kuwait, Iraq could acquire that country's oil wealth and eliminate the Iraqi debt to Kuwait. Also, Iraq's control of Kuwaiti oil could have greatly increased Iraq's power within OPEC.

Hussein also sought better access to the Persian Gulf. Iraq's gulf coastline was extremely short. Kuwait's was much longer and included an excellent harbor. In addition, Hussein probably hoped that an invasion would keep Iraq's military occupied and so end a series of attempts by the military to force him out of power.

Iraq's invasion of Kuwait

At 2:00 a.m. on Aug. 2, 1990, hundreds of tanks and

WORLD BOOK map

The Persian Gulf War was fought mainly by air and land forces in Iraq, Kuwait, and Saudi Arabia and by naval forces in the Persian Gulf. Iraq also launched missile attacks against Israel. Most ground fighting occurred in desert regions.

other Iraqi forces swept across the Kuwaiti border. Within 24 hours, Iraq had complete control of Kuwait. Thousands of Iraqi troops then moved to Kuwait's border with Saudi Arabia. To some, this movement signaled that Iraq might invade Saudi Arabia. On August 8, Iraq announced that it had annexed Kuwait.

Under international law, none of Iraq's claims against Kuwait justified its invasion of that country. The United Nations, as well as the United States and many other countries, condemned the Iraqi invasion. Hussein, however, accused the United States and other nations of following a double standard in their reaction. According to Hussein, if these nations condemned the Iraqi invasion, they should also condemn Israel's continuing occupation of lands it had won from Arab nations in the Arab-Israeli wars. Since the 1970's, the United States had been Israel's chief ally.

Arabs in many countries supported Iraq's invasion of Kuwait—particularly poor Arabs and Palestinians. Hussein became a hero to numerous Arabs by confronting Israel and the United States. He gained additional support from poor Arabs by calling for the redistribution of the vast wealth of Kuwait, Saudi Arabia, and certain other Arab oil-exporting nations.

The world's reaction

On August 2, at UN Headquarters in New York City, the UN Security Council issued a resolution condemning Iraq's invasion. Soon after the invasion, U.S. President George H. W. Bush and other world leaders began working to form an anti-Iraq coalition. The coalition eventually grew to include Afghanistan, Argentina, Australia, Bangladesh, Belgium, Canada, Czechoslovakia, Denmark, France, Germany, Greece, Honduras, Hungary, Italy, the Netherlands, New Zealand, Niger, Norway, Pakistan, Poland, Portugal, Senegal, Sierra Leone, Singapore, South Korea, Spain, Sweden, Turkey, the United Kingdom, and the United States. Arab members of the coalition were Bahrain, Egypt, Kuwait, Morocco, Oman, Qatar, Saudi Arabia, Syria, and the United Arab Emirates. South Korea was the only coalition member that was not also a member of the UN. The Arab countries of Jordan, Libya, and Yemen opposed the involvement of non-Arab countries but did not fight against the coalition. China and the Soviet Union, at that time the world's most powerful Communist countries, did not join the coalition. But their cooperation as members of the UN Security Council allowed the UN to play a leading role in the crisis.

Measures against Iraq. On August 6, the UN Security Council imposed an embargo that prohibited all trade with Iraq except for medical supplies and food in certain circumstances. Nearly all of Iraq's major trading partners supported the embargo. As a result, Iraq's foreign trade all but ended. On August 7, the United States announced that it would send troops to the Persian Gulf to defend Saudi Arabia from possible attack by Iraq.

In mid-August, Iraq began detaining various foreign citizens who had been living in Iraq or Kuwait. These hostages included foreign diplomats in Kuwait. Hussein later ordered these people moved to military and industrial sites in Iraq, where they would serve as "human shields" to discourage attacks by coalition members. By mid-December, however, Iraq had released all the hostages under pressure from other countries, including several key Arab nations.

On August 25, the UN Security Council authorized the use of force to carry out the embargo against Iraq. On November 29, the council gave coalition members permission "to use all necessary means" to expel Iraq from Kuwait if Iraq did not withdraw by Jan. 15, 1991. Iraq chose to stay in Kuwait.

The opposing forces. By mid-January, the coalition had about 670,000 troops, 3,500 tanks, and 1,800 combat aircraft in the Persian Gulf region. The troops came from 28 coalition members and included about 425,000 troops from the United States. Many of the rest of the troops came from the United Kingdom and France and such Arab countries as Egypt, Saudi Arabia, and Syria. Coalition members that did not send troops provided equipment, supplies, or financial support. The coalition also had about 200 warships in the Persian Gulf region, including 6 U.S. aircraft carriers and 2 U.S. battleships. Iraq had between 350,000 and 550,000 troops in Kuwait and southern Iraq, with about 4,500 tanks and 550 combat aircraft. It also had a small navy.

The coalition takes military action

The air war began at 3 a.m. on Jan. 17, 1991. The coalition aimed first to destroy Iraq's ability to launch attacks. Other goals included eliminating Iraq's biological, chemical, and nuclear weapons facilities; gaining superiority over Iraq's air force; disrupting Iraq's ability to gather information about coalition forces and to communicate with its own forces; and reducing the readiness of Iraqi troops in Kuwait and southern Iraq. Allied aircraft first bombed Baghdad, the capital of Iraq, and then attacked targets throughout Iraq and Kuwait. The allies gradually focused heavy bombing on Iraqi troops; artillery and tanks; transportation routes; and supplies of ammunition, food, fuel, and water.

The coalition achieved many of its objectives in the air war, in part due to the use of such high-technology equipment as night-vision systems and precision-guided weapons. These weapons included cruise missiles launched from U.S. ships in the gulf.

Iraq's response. Iraq responded to the start of the air war by launching "Scud" missiles at populated areas in Israel and Saudi Arabia. The Scuds were crude and inaccurate by Western standards. But they terrorized the populations of targeted cities and killed a number of people in both Israel and Saudi Arabia.

Analysts believe that Iraq used the attacks on Israel to try to draw it into the war. Had Israel struck back, Iraq might have succeeded in forcing Arab countries out of the coalition by portraying the war as an Arab-Israeli conflict. However, Israel did not enter the war, thus making it easier to keep the coalition together.

The ground war. The first major ground battle occurred at Khafji, a small Saudi Arabian coastal town near Kuwait. The Saudis had deserted the town before the war. On January 29, Iraqi troops occupied Khafji. With U.S. help, Saudi and Qatari troops recaptured the town on January 31. By late February, the air war had reduced, through casualties and desertions, the number of Iraqi troops in Kuwait and southern Iraq to about 183,000.

At about 4 a.m. on February 24, coalition forces launched a major ground attack into Iraq and Kuwait.

© Noel Quidu, Getty Images

Weeks of bombing by allied aircraft left much of Baghdad, Iraq's capital, in ruins. Residents of the city lacked electricity and running water during most of the war.

The attack consisted of several large operations carried out at the same time. U.S. and French troops invaded Iraq from Saudi Arabia, west of Iraqi fortifications in Kuwait. They moved rapidly north into Iraq and toward the Euphrates River to cut off Iraqi supply lines and to prevent an Iraqi retreat. U.S. and British troops also crossed into Iraq from Saudi Arabia. They moved north into Iraq and then swept east to attack the Iraqi troops.

In another operation, coalition troops assaulted Iraqi forces at several points across southern Kuwait. These coalition troops consisted of U.S. marines and troops from Egypt, Kuwait, Saudi Arabia, and Syria. The troops

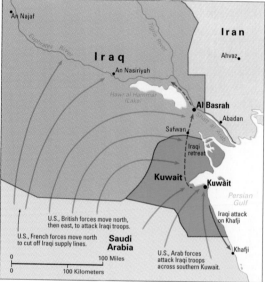

WORLD BOOK map

The allied ground attack included three major movements. In two of them, coalition forces attacked Iraqi troops in Kuwait or southern Iraq. In the other, allied forces charged north into Iraq to cut off Iraqi supply lines.

Oil wells burned out of control in Kuwait after retreating Iraqi troops set fire to hundreds of wells. The dense smoke from the fires darkened the skies in Kuwait and caused serious air pollution in Iran, Iraq, Kuwait, and other parts of west and southwest Asia.

© Noel Quidu, Getty Images

quickly broke through Iraqi fortifications, and about 63,000 Iraqi soldiers surrendered. On February 26, Hussein ordered his troops to leave Kuwait. But by that time, the Iraqi forces had been surrounded. The coalition ended all military operations at 8 a.m. on February 28, about 100 hours after the ground attack had begun.

The war ends. Iraq accepted the terms of a formal cease-fire agreement on April 6. On April 11, the United Nations Security Council officially declared an end to the war. In the cease-fire agreement, Iraq promised to pay Kuwait for war damages. Iraq also agreed to the destruction of all its biological and chemical weapons, its facilities for producing such weapons, and any facilities or materials it might have for producing nuclear weapons. Iraq did not yet have nuclear weapons, but it was trying to produce them. Iraq stockpiled chemical weapons in Kuwait before the ground war, but there is no evidence that either side used chemical weapons during the war. Neither side used biological or nuclear weapons.

After the formal cease-fire, the UN continued the embargo to pressure Iraq to carry out its promises. However, Iraq stubbornly resisted complying with the terms of the cease-fire agreement.

Consequences of the war

As many as 100,000 Iraqi troops may have died as a result of the war, but some experts believe the total is much lower. Deaths of coalition troops totaled only about 370. Thousands of civilians in Iraq and Kuwait probably were also killed during the war. Many other Iraqi civilians later died as a result of wartime destruction or because of revolts triggered by Iraq's defeat.

Coalition bombing severely damaged Iraq's transportation systems, communication systems, and petroleum and other industries. Coalition attacks also wiped out much of Iraq's ability to provide electric power and clean water. As a result, many civilians died after the war from disease or a lack of medicine or food.

In Kuwait, Iraqi troops looted the country and damaged many of Kuwait's oil wells, in most cases by setting them on fire. In addition, Iraq dumped an estimated 465 million gallons (1.75 billion liters) of Kuwaiti crude oil into the Persian Gulf, killing wildlife and causing long-term harm to the environment.

After the war, Saddam Hussein continued to rule Iraq. But revolts broke out among Kurds in northern Iraq and, in southern Iraq, among Arabs of the Shiah division of the Muslim religion. Both groups had long opposed Hussein's rule. Iraq's army swiftly put down most of the rebellions. Hundreds of thousands of Shiite Arabs then fled to Iran. Thousands of others hid in the marshlands of southern Iraq. More than a million Kurds fled to the mountains of northern Iraq and to Turkey and Iran. Tens of thousands of Kurds and Shiites were killed in the revolts or died later of disease, exposure, or hunger.

In April 1991, the United States and other coalition members established a safety zone in northern Iraq to protect the Kurdish refugees from Iraqi troops. Coalition forces remained in northern Iraq until July. But coalition aircraft continued to patrol northern Iraq as part of an effort to enforce a ban on Iraqi aircraft flights and troop movements there. In 1992, to protect the Shiite population, coalition forces imposed a ban on Iraqi aircraft flights over southern Iraq. In 1996, Iraqi troops attacked Kurds in northern Iraq. The United States responded with missile attacks against Iraqi military targets.

The Persian Gulf War also focused world attention on the Arab-Israeli conflict. Soon after the war, the United States renewed diplomatic efforts to resolve disputes between Israel and the Arab countries. These efforts helped lead to the signing of several peace agreements between Israel and the Palestine Liberation Organization, a group that represents Palestinian Arabs.

The war also proved that significant new forms of international cooperation were possible in the post-Cold War era. Cooperation between the United States and the Soviet Union, along with China's support, allowed the UN to take effective action against Iraq.

After the war, some veterans complained of physical and psychological ailments that they believed were related to their service. Their symptoms, sometimes referred to together as Gulf War syndrome, included memory loss, fatigue, and joint pain. Some people believed that exposure to dangerous chemicals when U.S. troops destroyed a chemical weapons depot in Iraq may have affected the troops. Others argued that the syndrome was not a single illness and that the symptoms resulted from the stress of war or other factors.

David A. Deese

Web site

Frontline: The Gulf War
http://www.pbs.org/wgbh/pages/frontline/gulf/index.html
Companion Web site to the Public Broadcasting System (PBS) television series that features transcripts of interviews with key players in the war and war stories of pilots and soldiers. Includes maps, a chronology, and a guide to weapons and technology used in the war.

© Dallas and John Heaton, Getty Images

© Richard Lobell

Ways of life in the Middle East range from modern cities to traditional farms. The city scene above shows a square in Istanbul, Turkey, dominated by a huge *mosque*—an Islamic house of worship. The farming scene shows traditional farming methods being used in southern Lebanon.

Middle East

Middle East is a large region that covers parts of northern Africa, southwestern Asia, and southeastern Europe. Scholars disagree on which countries make up the Middle East. But many say the region consists of Bahrain, Cyprus, Egypt, Iran, Iraq, Israel, Jordan, Kuwait, Lebanon, Oman, Qatar, Saudi Arabia, Sudan, Syria, Turkey, United Arab Emirates, and Yemen. These countries cover about 3,743,000 square miles (9,694,000 square kilometers) and together have a population of about 262 million.

Two of the world's first great civilizations—those of Sumer and Egypt—developed in the area after 3500 B.C. The region also is the birthplace of three major religions—Judaism, Christianity, and Islam.

Since the birth of Islam in the A.D. 600's, Islamic powers have dominated the Middle East. Over 90 percent of the region's people are Muslims—followers of Islam. Most of the region's people are Muslim Arabs. Other religious and ethnic groups include black Africans, Armenians, Copts, Greeks, Iranians, Jews, Kurds, and Turks.

The Middle East is an area of great economic importance as one of the world's major oil-producing regions. It is also a scene of much political unrest and conflict.

People

Ancestry. The people of the Middle East belong to various ethnic groups, which are based largely on culture, language, and history. Ethnically, more than three-fourths of the Middle Eastern people are Arabs. Although they live in different countries, the Arabs share a common culture and a common language, Arabic. Iranians and Turks also form major ethnic groups in the region. Smaller groups in the Middle East include Armenians, Copts, Greeks, Jews, Kurds, and various black African groups.

Way of life. Until the 1900's, most Middle Eastern people lived in villages or small towns and made a living by farming. Only a small number lived in cities. Since World War II (1939-1945), many people have moved to urban areas. Today, in most Middle Eastern countries, more than half the people live in cities. Middle Eastern people have strong ties to their families and to their religious and language groups.

In general, city dwellers in the Middle East have a more modern way of life than the rural villagers. In the cities, cars and people move about at a fast pace. People hold jobs in business, education, government, and the media. Television, which is widely viewed, introduces Western ideas and tastes.

In rural areas of the Middle East, the way of life is slowly changing. Better fertilizers, irrigation methods, and machinery have made life easier for some farmers. But many Middle Eastern farmers still use the same kinds of tools and methods their ancestors used hundreds of years ago. Some people of the Middle East are nomads. They live in the desert and herd cattle, goats, and sheep.

Since the mid-1900's, changes have occurred in the status of urban women in the Middle East. Women in rural areas have always done farm work alongside their husbands, but most urban women were confined to their home. Today, many women in the cities have jobs in business, education, and government.

Religion and language. The Middle East is the birthplace of Judaism, Christianity, and Islam. More than 90 percent of the area's population, including most Arabs, Iranians, and Turks, are Muslims. Christians make up about 7 percent of the population. The largest Christian groups are the Coptic, Melkite, and Maronite denominations. Jews, who make up only 1 percent of the population, live in Israel.

The chief language of the region is Arabic. Written Arabic is the same throughout the region, but the spo-

Middle East

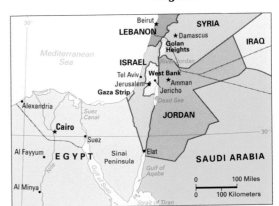

Within the inset map:

SYRIA
Beirut
LEBANON
★Damascus
Golan Heights
IRAQ
ISRAEL
Mediterranean Sea
Tel Aviv
Jerusalem★ West Bank
★Amman
Gaza Strip
Jericho
Dead Sea
Alexandria
Suez Canal
JORDAN
Cairo
Suez
30°
Al Fayyum
EGYPT
Sinai Peninsula
Elat
SAUDI ARABIA
Nile
Al Minya
Gulf of Suez
Gulf of Aqaba
Strait of Tiran

0   100 Miles
0   100 Kilometers

Europe
Asia
MIDDLE EAST
Africa
Equator

★ National capital
• Other city or town
— International boundary
—·— Major oil pipeline
Disputed territory fully or partly controlled by Israel

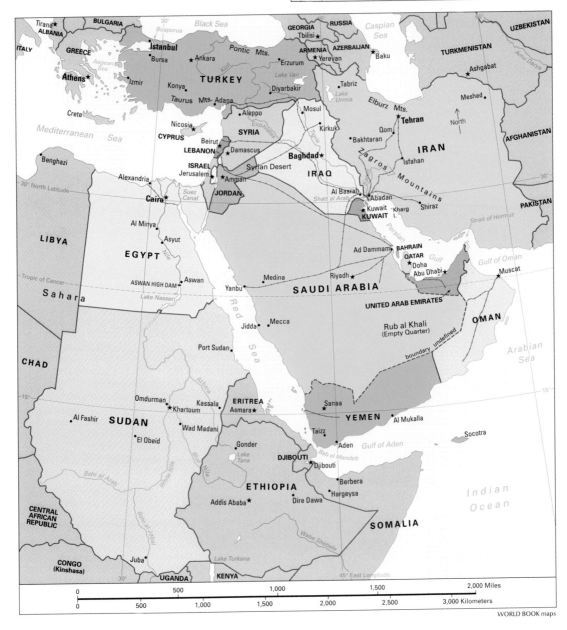

Tirana★
ALBANIA
ITALY
BULGARIA
Black Sea
Bosporus
GEORGIA
Tbilisi★
RUSSIA
Caspian Sea
UZBEKISTAN
GREECE
Istanbul
Pontic Mts.
ARMENIA
AZERBAIJAN
Bursa
★Ankara
Erzurum
Yerevan★
Baku
TURKMENISTAN
Ashgabat
Athens★
Aegean Sea
Izmir
TURKEY
Lake Van
Tabriz
Amu Darya
Konya
Taurus Mts.
Adana
Diyarbakir
Lake Urmia
Elburz Mts.
Meshed
Crete
Aleppo
Mosul
Tehran★
AFGHANISTAN
Nicosia
Euphrates
Kirkuk
Qom
North
CYPRUS
Beirut
SYRIA
Bakhtaran
IRAN
Mediterranean Sea
LEBANON
Damascus
Baghdad★
Isfahan
Benghazi
ISRAEL
Syrian Desert
Tigris
Zagros Mountains
30°
30° North Latitude
Alexandria
Jerusalem★
★Amman
IRAQ
PAKISTAN
Cairo★
JORDAN
Al Basrah
Abadan
Shatt al Arab
Strait of Hormuz
Suez Canal
★Kuwait
Kharg I.
Shiraz
Al Minya
KUWAIT
LIBYA
Asyut
Ad Dammam
BAHRAIN
QATAR
Gulf
Gulf of Oman
EGYPT
★Doha
Abu Dhabi★
Muscat
Medina
Riyadh★
UNITED ARAB EMIRATES
Tropic of Cancer
ASWAN HIGH DAM
Aswan
Yanbu
SAUDI ARABIA
OMAN
Sahara
Lake Nasser
Red Sea
Rub al Khali (Empty Quarter)
Arabian Sea
Jidda
Mecca
boundary undefined
CHAD
Port Sudan
15°
15°
Omdurman
Kassala
ERITREA
Sanaa
Khartoum★
Asmara★
★
YEMEN
Al Mukalla
Al Fashir
SUDAN
Taizz
Socotra
El Obeid
Wad Madani
Aden
Gulf of Aden
Gonder
Lake Tana
Bab el Mandeb
Djibouti
Berbera
DJIBOUTI
Djibouti
Bahr al Arab
Blue Nile
White Nile
ETHIOPIA
Dire Dawa
Hargeysa
Indian Ocean
CENTRAL AFRICAN REPUBLIC
Addis Ababa★
Bahr al Jabal
Wabe Shebele
SOMALIA
CONGO (Kinshasa)
Juba
Lake Turkana
45° East Longitude
UGANDA
KENYA
30°

0   500   1,000   1,500   2,000 Miles
0   500   1,000   1,500   2,000   2,500   3,000 Kilometers

WORLD BOOK maps

© Hutchison Library

Oil is the Middle East's most important mineral product. These workers at Port Rashid in the United Arab Emirates are loading barrels of oil onto oil tankers.

ken language differs from country to country. Persian is the official language of Iran. People in Turkey speak Turkish. Most Israelis speak Hebrew. Other languages of the Middle East include Baluchi, Greek, and Kurdish.

The land

In the northern part of the Middle East, mountains border interior plateaus. The Pontic Mountains and the Taurus Mountains rise in Turkey, and the Elburz and Zagros mountains extend across Iran.

The southern part of the Middle East is a vast arid plateau. Several large deserts lie in this area. The Western and Eastern deserts of Egypt are part of the Sahara. The Rub al Khali, known in English as the Empty Quarter, stretches across southern Saudi Arabia.

The Middle East has two major river systems—the Tigris-Euphrates and the Nile. The Tigris and Euphrates begin in the mountains of Turkey and flow through Syria and Iraq. In Iraq, the rivers meet and form the Shatt al Arab, which empties into the Persian Gulf. The Nile flows north through Sudan and Egypt to the Mediterranean Sea.

Economy

Agriculture has long been the Middle East's most important economic activity. More than half the people are farmers. But the discovery of oil in the Middle East in the early 1900's radically changed the economy of some countries. Oil production became a major industry. Manufacturing increased, particularly the manufacture of products made from oil. In some countries, especially Egypt, tourism is a major industry.

Agriculture. The chief crops of the Middle East include barley, cotton, oranges, sugar cane, tobacco, and wheat. Many Middle Eastern farmers do not own their land, but an increasing number have become owners of the small farms they work. In such countries as Egypt and Iraq, the amount of farmland has doubled since the

late 1800's. The use of fertilizers, improved equipment, and better irrigation methods have helped bring about the increase. But many farmers continue to use traditional machinery and methods. They cannot afford tractors and other heavy equipment.

Mining. Oil is by far the most important mineral product of the Middle East. The region has about three-fifths of the world's known oil reserves. The major oil producers are Iran, Iraq, Kuwait, Oman, Qatar, Saudi Arabia, and the United Arab Emirates. Most of the oil is sold to European countries and Japan.

In 1960, some oil-producing countries formed the Organization of the Petroleum Exporting Countries (OPEC) to gain more control over oil prices. During the Arab-Israeli War of 1973, some Arab members of OPEC stopped or reduced oil shipments to countries supporting Israel. Prices of oil in those countries rose sharply.

Other minerals mined in the Middle East include coal, iron ore, and phosphates. Coal mines operate in Iran and Turkey. Egypt and Turkey produce iron ore. Jordan supplies a fifth of the world's phosphates.

Manufacturing. The major manufacturing countries of the Middle East are Egypt, Iran, and Turkey. Together, these three countries produce 6 percent of the world's refined sugar and 5 percent of its cement and cotton cloth. The Middle East also produces small amounts of fertilizers, paper, and steel. Israel manufactures a variety of specialized technological products, such as computer parts and fighter aircraft. The oil-producing countries have developed industries that make use of oil. These industries include the manufacture of chemicals and plastics.

History

Early civilizations. People lived in parts of the Middle East as early as 25,000 B.C. It was in this region that agriculture began around 8000 B.C. Between 3500 and 3100 B.C., two of the world's earliest great civilizations— those of Sumer and Egypt—developed in the region. The Sumerian civilization developed on the fertile plain between the Tigris and Euphrates rivers. It was later absorbed by the Babylonian Empire. The Egyptian civilization arose in the Nile Valley. About 1900 B.C., a people called the Hittites came to power in what is now Turkey. Other peoples, such as the Hebrews and the Phoenicians, also organized societies in the region.

Beginning in the 800's B.C., a series of invaders conquered these civilizations. The invaders included the Assyrians, the Medes, the Persians, and, finally, Alexander the Great. Alexander conquered the Middle East in 331 B.C. and united it into one empire. He died in 323 B.C. The next 300 years, called the *Hellenistic Age,* brought great achievements in scholarship, science, and the arts.

Topic for study

During the 1900's, the Middle East changed rapidly from an area of Islamic empires and colonial territories into a collection of modern nation-states. Choose one Middle Eastern country and briefly trace its national status from the end of World War I until the present. How did the nation gain its independence, what type of government was established, and what is the chief economic activity? Describe any unresolved ethnic, religious, or territorial disputes.

By 30 B.C., the Romans had conquered much of the Middle East. During Roman rule, Jesus Christ was born in Bethlehem and died in Jerusalem. Christianity spread throughout the Roman Empire, replacing pagan cults. Christianity was the major religion of the Middle East until the rise of Islam in the A.D. 600's.

Islamic empires. Muhammad, the prophet of Islam, was born in Mecca in about 570. In 622, he moved to the oasis of Medina, where he became the head of a small religious and political community. After his death in 632, his followers, called Muslims, conquered what are now Egypt, Iraq, and Syria. Many of the conquered people adopted Islam and the Arabic language. By 711, Arab Muslim rule extended from what is now Spain in the west to Iran in the east. Muslims of the Umayyad family ruled these lands from the city of Damascus. In 750, the Abbasid family overthrew the Umayyads and made Baghdad the capital of the Islamic Empire.

During Abbasid rule, groups of Muslim Turks invaded from central Asia. The most important were the Seljuk Turks. They took over Baghdad in 1055, and soon after, they conquered what are now Syria and Palestine. By the end of the 1000's, the Abbasid Empire was declining, and independent *dynasties* (families of rulers) were emerging. In 1258, Mongols from China conquered Baghdad and destroyed the remains of the Abbasid government.

In the 1300's, the dynasty of the Ottomans became established in Anatolia (now Turkey). In the early 1500's the Ottomans added the Arab lands of the Middle East to their empire. By that time, they had also advanced into the Balkan Peninsula and had become a military threat to Europe. In the 1700's and 1800's, the Ottoman Empire declined in power and size in the face of new, strong states that developed in Europe. By World War I (1914-1918), some European countries had gained much economic and political influence in the Middle East.

World War I. During World War I, the Ottoman Empire joined with Germany against the United Kingdom, France, Italy, and Russia. Arabs who hoped to win independence from the Ottoman Empire supported the European Allies. The United Kingdom promised to help create independent Arab governments in the Middle East after the war. But they also agreed with France to divide the Middle East into zones of British and French rule and influence. In 1917, the United Kingdom issued the Balfour Declaration, which supported the creation of a Jewish homeland in Palestine—but without violating the civil or religious rights of the Arabs there.

In 1923, the defeated Ottoman Empire became the Republic of Turkey. The League of Nations divided most of the Arab lands of the Middle East into mandated territories. France took control of Lebanon and Syria. The United Kingdom received the mandates for Iraq, Jordan (called Transjordan until 1949), and Palestine. The British also kept control over Egypt, which it had conquered in 1882. The Arabs conducted a struggle for independence in the years after the war. Many territories gained independence in the 1930's and 1940's.

Palestine. In Palestine, Arab mistrust of the United Kingdom grew during the 1930's. Between 1933 and 1935, more than 100,000 Jewish refugees fled to Palestine from Nazi Germany and Poland. The Jewish immigration alarmed the Palestinian Arabs, who wanted

Topic for study

How has Arab oil production affected the foreign policies of the major industrialized countries of the world? How has Arab oil production influenced the balance of power among the nations of the Middle East?

Palestine to become an independent Arab state. In 1936, they called a general strike that almost paralyzed Palestine. They declared the strike would last until the British halted Jewish immigration. But after about five months, the Arabs ended the strike without achieving their goals. However, they continued to oppose British control.

In 1947, the United Kingdom asked the United Nations (UN) to deal with the Palestine problem. The UN voted to divide Palestine into two states, one Arab and one Jewish. The Jews accepted this solution and established the state of Israel on May 14, 1948. The Arabs, who made up about two-thirds of the population of Palestine, rejected the plan. The next day, five Arab states—Egypt, Jordan, Iraq, Lebanon, and Syria—attacked Israel. The Israelis defeated the Arabs.

When the war ended in 1949, Israel had about half the land that the UN had assigned to the Arab state. Egypt controlled the Gaza Strip, and Jordan occupied and later annexed the West Bank of the Jordan River. The city of Jerusalem was divided between Israel and Jordan. About 700,000 Palestinian Arabs had fled or been driven out of the land that was now Israel. They became refugees in Gaza, the West Bank, Syria, and Lebanon.

Continuing conflict. The 1950's and 1960's were years of radical change in the Middle East. A new generation led by young army officers took over the governments of many Arab states. They overthrew leaders who had cooperated with the United Kingdom and France. They hoped to bring about a political unification of the Arab world and to remove any European influence. Gamal Abdel Nasser, the leader of Egypt, became the symbol of these hopes. In 1956, Nasser seized the Suez Canal in Egypt from its British and French owners. In response to Nasser's action, France, Israel, and the United Kingdom invaded Egypt. Pressure from the United States, the Soviet Union, and other nations forced the invaders to withdraw.

In May 1967, the Arabs believed Israel was planning a major attack on Syria. Nasser sent Egyptian troops into the Sinai Peninsula and closed the Straits of Tiran, the entrance to the Israeli port of Elat. On June 5, the Israeli air force retaliated by destroying most of the air forces of Egypt, Syria, and Jordan. In the following six days, Israel seized the Sinai Peninsula and the Gaza Strip from Egypt, the Golan Heights from Syria, and the West Bank (including East Jerusalem) from Jordan. Almost 1 million Palestinian Arabs came under Israeli rule.

After the Six-Day War, no solution was reached in the Arab-Israeli conflict. The Arabs wanted Israel to withdraw from the land it had conquered. Israel demanded negotiations and Arab recognition of its right to exist.

The Palestine Liberation Organization (PLO), founded in 1964, became an important force in the Middle East after the 1967 war. The PLO is a confederation of Palestinian Arab groups that wants to establish an Arab state in Palestine. It includes associations of lawyers, teachers,

Suicide bombings by Palestinian extremists became a prominent form of terrorism in the early 2000's. This picture shows the aftermath of a suicide bombing at a Jerusalem bus stop on April 12, 2002.

AP/Wide World

laborers, and other groups, as well as guerrilla fighters who staged terrorist attacks and commando raids against Israel. The Arab nations recognized the PLO as the representative of the Palestinian people.

In October 1973, Egypt and Syria launched a surprise attack against Israel. They were driven back by the Israelis. Most of the fighting ended by November.

Attempt at peace. In 1977, Egyptian President Anwar el-Sadat declared his willingness to make peace. In 1978, Sadat, Israeli Prime Minister Menachem Begin, and U.S. President Jimmy Carter held discussions at Camp David in the United States. The discussions resulted in an agreement called the Camp David Accords. Israel agreed to withdraw from Egypt's Sinai Peninsula. Egypt and Israel pledged to negotiate with Jordan and the Palestinians to grant some form of self-rule to the West Bank and the Gaza Strip. Egypt and Israel signed a peace treaty in 1979, and Israel withdrew from the Sinai. But no immediate progress was made in deciding the future of the Gaza Strip and the West Bank.

More conflict. In the 1970's in Lebanon, an uneasy balance between the Muslim and Christian communities collapsed. The conflict was sparked by the presence of armed PLO members in the country. The Muslims supported the PLO fighters, and the Christians opposed them. But at the heart of the conflict was the fact that Lebanon's growing Muslim population demanded more power in the government. The Christians opposed Muslim demands for increased power. In 1975, civil war broke out between various Muslim and Christian forces. Most of the fighting in Lebanon ended in 1991.

A revolution occurred in Iran in 1979. Muslim religious leader Ayatollah Ruhollah Khomeini and his followers took control of the government. Khomeini declared Iran to be an Islamic republic. From 1980 until 1988, Iran and Iraq fought a war over territorial disputes and other disagreements.

The Arab-Israeli conflict flared up again at the end of 1987. Arabs in the Gaza Strip and the West Bank began demonstrating against Israel's occupation. Violence erupted between Israeli troops and the demonstrators.

In August 1990, Iraq invaded Kuwait. The United States and other nations sent military forces to Saudi

Arabia to defend that country against a possible Iraqi invasion. These nations and Saudi Arabia formed an allied military coalition. In January 1991, war broke out between Iraq and these nations. In February, the allied coalition defeated Iraq and forced its troops to leave Kuwait.

Recent developments. In October 1991, a peace conference began between Israel on one side, and Middle Eastern Arab nations and Arab residents of the Gaza Strip and the West Bank on the other. In separate talks in 1993, Israel and the PLO agreed to recognize each other.

Beginning in 1993, Israel and the PLO signed several agreements that led to the withdrawal of Israeli troops from the Gaza Strip and portions of the West Bank. As the Israelis withdrew, Palestinians took control of these areas. In 1996, Palestinians in these areas elected a legislature and a president.

In 1994, Israel and Jordan signed a peace treaty. This treaty formally ended the state of war that had technically existed between the two countries since 1948.

In 2000, peace talks between Israeli and Palestinian leaders failed to produce a final peace settlement. In September of that year, violence broke between Palestinians and Israeli security forces. Numerous attacks by Palestinian militias and suicide bombers took place throughout Israel, the West Bank, and the Gaza Strip, killing hundreds of Israelis. Israeli forces repeatedly bombed and invaded the Palestinian territories, killing more than 1,700 Palestinians. In 2002, Israel reoccupied much of the West Bank.   Dina Le Gall and Michel Le Gall

Additional resources

Lewis, Bernard. *The Middle East: A Brief History of the Last 2,000 Years.* Scribner, 1995. *The Multiple Identities of the Middle East.* 1999. Reprint. Schocken, 2001.
Middle East and North Africa. Europa, published annually.
Simon, Reeva S., and others, eds. *Encyclopedia of the Modern Middle East.* 4 vols. Macmillan Lib. Reference, 1996.

Topic for study

In recent years, there has been a resurgence of Islamic conservatism throughout the Middle East. Explain the cultural, economic, and political causes of this movement. What have been some of the results?

AP/Wide World

Kabul, Afghanistan's capital and largest city, has both traditional and modern buildings. Traditional mud-brick dwellings, such as those on the hillside, are found throughout Afghanistan. Some modern buildings rise in downtown Kabul. Parts of the city are being rebuilt after decades of war.

Afghanistan

Afghanistan, a nation in southwestern Asia, has towering mountains, scorching deserts, fertile valleys, and rolling plains. Afghanistan is surrounded by six other countries and so does not have a seacoast. The country is bordered by Turkmenistan, Uzbekistan, and Tajikistan on the north, China on the far northeast, Pakistan on the east and south, and Iran on the west.

Afghanistan is one of the world's least developed countries. Most Afghan workers farm the land, and many use old-fashioned farming tools and methods. Some of the people are nomads, who roam the country with their herds of sheep or goats. Kabul is the capital and largest city of Afghanistan.

Almost all the people of Afghanistan are Muslims. The religion of the Muslims, Islam, is the chief common link among them. The population of Afghanistan consists of about 20 ethnic groups, most of which are divided into several tribes. Most of the ethnic groups have distinct languages and cultures. The variety of ethnic groups has made it difficult for Afghanistan to develop into a unified, modern nation.

Afghanistan has a long and troubled history. In early days, Persians, Greeks, Mongols, and other peoples conquered the region. In modern times, Afghanistan has

The contributor of this article, Thomas E. Gouttierre, is Director of the Center for Afghanistan Studies and Dean of International Studies and Programs at the University of Nebraska, Omaha.

continued to suffer foreign interference. The Soviet Union sought to occupy Afghanistan in a war that lasted from 1979 to 1989.

In the 1990's, a conservative Islamic group called the Taliban came to power. The Taliban allowed international terrorist organizations to run training camps in Afghanistan. After terrorist attacks against the United States in 2001, the United States and anti-Taliban forces within Afghanistan drove the Taliban from power. A transitional government was set up to rule the country.

Facts in brief

Capital: Kabul.
Official languages: Pashto (also called Pakhto) and Dari.
Official name: *Da Afghanistan Dowlat* (in Pashto) or *Dowlati Afghanistan* (in Dari), both meaning State of Afghanistan.
Area: 251,773 mi² (652,090 km²). *Greatest distances*—east-west, 820 mi (1,320 km); north-south, 630 mi (1,012 km).
Elevation: *Highest*—Nowshak, 24,557 ft (7,485 m) above sea level. *Lowest*—In Sistan Basin, 1,640 ft (500 m) above sea level.
Population: *Estimated 2002 population*—24,977,000; density, 99 persons per mi² (38 persons per km²); distribution, 80 percent rural, 20 percent urban. *1979 census*—13,051,358.
Chief products: *Agriculture*—barley, corn, cotton, fruits, Karakul skins, mutton, nuts, rice, vegetables, wheat, wool. *Manufacturing*—jewelry, leather goods, rugs. *Mining*—coal, lapis lazuli, natural gas.
Money: *Basic unit*—afghani. One hundred pule equal one afghani.

Noreen S. Ahmed-Ullah © *Chicago Tribune*

A *jirga* (council) is a traditional Afghan community meeting. This jirga near Khowst, in eastern Afghanistan, met in 2002 to choose delegates to send to a national *loya jirga* (grand council) in Kabul.

Government

In the late 1990's, the Taliban controlled most of Afghanistan, including Kabul. The Taliban imposed their harsh interpretation of Islamic law on the country. However, few nations recognized the Taliban government as the legal government of Afghanistan.

The United States and its Afghan allies drove the Taliban from power in 2001. The United Nations then brought together the leaders of Afghanistan's main ethnic and regional groups, who organized a temporary government. These leaders also developed a plan for creating a permanent, more democratic government. Hamid Karzai, head of the Popalzai, an important clan of the Pashtun ethnic group, became head of the temporary government.

In June 2002, Afghan leaders held a *loya jirga* (grand council) to create a transitional government. Loya jirgas are held at times of crisis or when major political or social changes need consideration. Loya jirgas attempt to include representatives of all of Afghanistan's many regional and ethnic groups. In 1964, Afghan women attended a loya jirga for the first time. Afghan tribes and communities often hold smaller *jirgas* (councils) to decide matters of local importance. Local jirgas include all of a single community's adult men or the leaders from several neighboring communities.

In 2002, the loya jirga created a transitional government to lead the country for up to two years. During that time, it would work to establish a commission to create a new constitution and then hold democratic elections for a permanent government. The loya jirga chose Karzai as president of the transitional government. To gain national support for the government, Karzai selected Afghans from a variety of regions and ethnic groups to serve in his cabinet.

People

Ancestry. Most Afghans are a blend of early peoples who came to the country as invaders or settlers. These groups included Aryans, Persians, Arabs, Turkish-

speaking people from central Asia, Mongolians, and people from the Xinjiang region of western China.

Ethnic groups and languages. Afghanistan has about 20 ethnic groups, most of which have their own language and culture. Most ethnic groups consist of several tribes, many of which speak their own dialect of the ethnic language. Many Afghans feel greater loyalty to their ethnic group or tribe than to their country.

The largest ethnic groups are the Pashtuns (or Pakhtuns) and the Tajiks. *Pashtuns* and *Pakhtuns* are also spelled *Pashtoons* and *Pakhtoons*. The Pashtuns and Tajiks make up more than 60 percent of the population. Most Pashtuns live in the southeast, near the Pakistan border. Their language, *Pashto* or *Pakhto,* is one of Afghanistan's two official languages. Most Tajiks live in northeastern Afghanistan and speak *Dari,* the other official language. Dari is also known as Afghan Persian. Most of the country's other ethnic groups speak Dari as either their first or second language.

Way of life. Most of Afghanistan's rural people live in homes made of sun-dried mud bricks. City dwellers live in homes and apartment buildings made of baked brick, concrete, or both. Most of the country's nomadic and seminomadic people live in tents made of goat hair.

Most Afghans wear traditional clothing. In winter, the people wear a heavy coat made of sheepskin, quilted

Symbols of Afghanistan. Afghanistan's flag has black, red, and green vertical stripes and the nation's coat of arms in the center. The coat of arms bears four Arabic inscriptions: at the top, *There Is No God but Allah and Muhammad Is the Prophet of Allah;* near the top, *God Is Great;* near the bottom, the Islamic year *1380* (2001-2002 in the Gregorian calendar); and at the bottom, *Afghanistan.*

WORLD BOOK map

Afghanistan is a landlocked country in southwestern Asia. It is surrounded by six other countries.

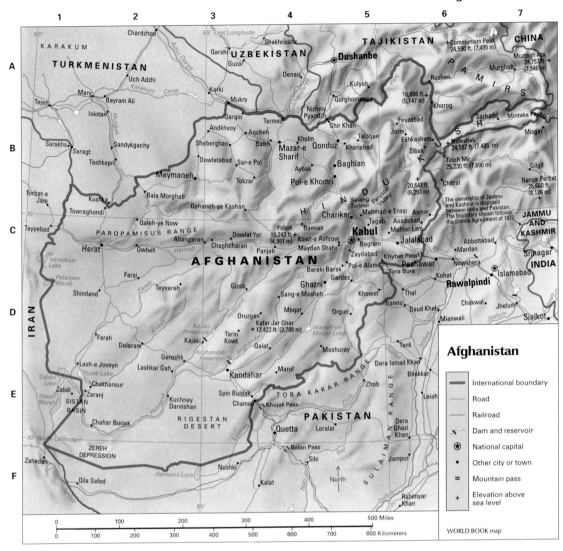

Afghanistan map index

*Does not appear on map; key shows general location.
Source: 1982 official estimates.

Islam greatly influences family and community relationships and almost all other aspects of Afghan life. This beautiful blue *mosque* (Islamic house of worship) is in Mazar-e Sharif.

© John Siceloff

fabric, or felt. Many rural men wear a turban, which may be tied in a certain way to indicate their ethnic group. Most Pashtun women wear a *burqa*, also called a *chadri*, which is a full-length hooded garment that covers the body from head to toe. The Pashtuns believe a woman must not be seen by any men outside of her family. Some rural women in Afghanistan cover their heads with a shawl.

Afghans serve flat loaves of whole-grain, sourdough bread at every meal. They also enjoy vegetables, yogurt, chicken, beef, mutton, and rice. Popular desserts include nuts and fruits. Tea is the favorite drink.

Women have traditionally played a secondary role in Afghan society. Their opportunities for education and careers have been limited, especially in rural areas. Men dominate women in many ways. For example, some Afghan tribes do not allow women to leave their homes without a male relative.

During the 1900's, several Afghan governments at-

tempted to give women more rights. In 1964, for example, a new constitution gave Afghan women equal status with men, and the social and economic position of some women improved. However, most women in rural areas never gained more rights.

In the 1990's and early 2000's, the Taliban greatly limited the freedom of women. For example, the Taliban required all women to cover themselves completely when in public. They also made it illegal for women to work outside their homes. Women who violated Taliban laws were punished severely.

After the Taliban were driven from power in 2001, many Afghan women hoped to reclaim their lost rights. In 2002, several women played significant roles in the national council that created a transitional government and helped decide the country's future.

AP/Wide World

The blue *burqa* (or *chadri*) is a full-length hooded garment worn by most Pashtun women in Afghanistan. Some Afghan women drape a shawl over their heads.

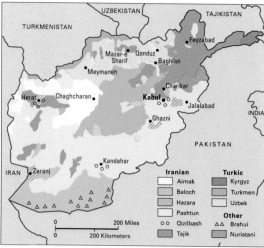

WORLD BOOK map

Afghanistan's major ethnic groups inhabit various parts of the country. The map key arranges the ethnic groups by their language types. For example, the language spoken by the Pashtuns is an Iranian language, but that spoken by Uzbeks is Turkic. Stripes indicate areas shared by more than one ethnic group.

Goat herders lead their herd over an arid mountain path. Afghanistan's economy depends heavily on agriculture. Many of the country's farmers practice sheep and goat herding.

© SuperStock

Religion. About 99 percent of all Afghans are Muslims. Their religion strongly influences family and community relationships and most other aspects of life. Almost every Afghan village or nomadic group has a religious leader called a *mullah.* Mullahs lead prayer services and educate the young. They sometimes have great influence in their communities.

Education. Only about 31 percent of Afghanistan's people 15 years of age or older can read and write. Many children cannot attend school because the country does not have enough schools or teachers. This lack of educational facilities is due largely to the upheaval caused by decades of war. Afghanistan has two universities—Kabul University and Ningrahar University in Jalalabad.

The arts. Because so many of the people of Afghanistan cannot read and write, folklore, folk songs, and folk dances play an important part in Afghan life. They enable the people of Afghanistan to pass their values and traditions on from one generation to the next. The *attan* (also spelled *atan)* is an energetic folk dance. Pashtuns dance the attan at weddings and other community celebrations.

Recreation. Afghans enjoy sports and games, such as soccer, volleyball, and basketball. Many men in Afghanistan like to hunt, and some of them use the famous Afghan hounds as hunting dogs. Men of the northern plains play a game called *buzkashi.* In the game, dozens of horsemen try to grab a headless calf and carry it across a goal.

The land and climate

Afghanistan is made up of three main land regions. These regions are, from north to south: (1) the Northern Plains, (2) the Central Highlands, and (3) the Southwestern Lowlands.

The Northern Plains stretch across northern Afghanistan and consist of mountain plateaus and rolling hills. The soil is fertile in the Northern Plains but can be cultivated only where water is available. Large irrigation systems have been built along the Harirud, Helmand, Qonduz, and other rivers. Nomadic and seminomadic people raise sheep and goats on the vast grasslands.

Temperatures in the Northern Plains of Afghanistan average about 38 °F (3 °C) in January and approximately 90 °F (32 °C) in July. The average annual precipitation in the region totals about 7 inches (18 centimeters).

The Central Highlands cover about two-thirds of Afghanistan. They consist of the towering Hindu Kush mountain range and its branches. Snow-capped peaks rise about 25,000 feet (7,620 meters) along the Pakistani border in the east. The range gradually descends to a rolling plain in the southwest. Most Afghans live in the high, narrow valleys of the Hindu Kush.

The Central Highlands have an average temperature of about 25 °F (–4 °C) in January and about 75 °F (24 °C) in July. The region receives about 15 inches (38 centimeters) of precipitation yearly.

The Southwestern Lowlands lie in southwestern Afghanistan and consist mainly of desert or semidesert land. The region is crossed by the Helmand River, which flows from the Hindu Kush to the Sistan Basin on the Iranian border. The basin has several slightly salty lakes and marshes. Barley, corn, fruits, and wheat are grown in the Helmand Valley.

Temperatures in the lowlands of Afghanistan average about 35 °F (2 °C) in January and about 85 °F (29 °C) in July. The average annual precipitation ranges from 2 to 9 inches (5 to 23 centimeters).

Economy

Afghanistan's economy once benefited from the country's location along the Silk Road and other ancient trade routes. As these routes died out, the country became isolated. In the mid-1900's, Afghan governments attempted to develop the country's economy and to improve educational opportunities. But decades of war and internal struggles at the end of the 1900's reversed most of these advances. A severe drought in the late 1990's and early 2000's further weakened Afghanistan's economy. However, economic aid flowed into the country following the defeat of the Taliban in 2001.

Agriculture. About 85 percent of all Afghan workers earn their living in agriculture. Wheat is the chief crop of Afghanistan. Other crops include barley, corn, cotton, fruits, nuts, rice, sugar beets, and vegetables. Production is limited by a shortage of modern machinery, fertilizer, and high-quality seeds.

During the late 1900's, Afghanistan became one of the world's leading producers of opium, which is used to make the illegal drug heroin. Many Afghan farmers raised opium poppies because it was more profitable than growing wheat and other food crops. In 2000, the Taliban began enforcing a strict ban on poppy farming, but the practice resumed after the Taliban were driven from power in 2001. The governments that have ruled Afghanistan since then have also tried to stop farmers from growing opium poppies.

Afghanistan's nomadic and seminomadic people raise most of the country's livestock. The chief livestock products are dairy items, mutton, wool, and animal hides. The skins of Karakul sheep, a fat-tailed sheep known for its silky pelt, are especially valuable.

Mining. Afghanistan is rich in minerals, but most of the deposits are largely undeveloped. In the 1960's, large deposits of natural gas were discovered in Afghanistan. Since then, the production of natural gas has become an important part of the nation's economy. Afghanistan also produces some coal, copper, gold, and salt. The country has huge deposits of iron ore, but because of Afghanistan's rugged terrain and frequent conflicts, they remain undeveloped.

Afghanistan has deposits of the world's finest lapis lazuli, a valuable azure-blue stone. Other gemstones mined in the country include amethysts and rubies.

Manufacturing. Afghanistan has little industry. Skilled craftworkers in their homes or small shops make gold and silver jewelry, leather goods, rugs, and other handicraft items. A few mills produce textiles, and small factories turn out such products as cement, matches, and processed foods.

International trade. Afghanistan's leading exports are cotton, fruits and nuts, natural gas, rugs, and Karakul sheep skins. Imports include machinery, motor vehicles, petroleum products, and textiles. Afghanistan conducts its international trade mainly over land, through the neighboring countries of Iran and Pakistan.

Transportation and communication. Afghanistan has about 11,700 miles (18,800 kilometers) of roads. However, decades of war heavily damaged most paved roads, making many of them unusable. The country has no railroads.

Afghanistan's most famous transportation route is the Khyber Pass, which crosses the border between Afghanistan and Pakistan. The pass cuts through the Safid Kuh mountains, which are part of the Hindu Kush range. Conquerors, such as Alexander the Great of Macedonia, crossed the pass to invade South Asia. The Khyber Pass has been an important trade route for centuries.

Several newspapers are published in Afghanistan. The country has one national television station and one national radio station. Both stations broadcast from Kabul.

History

Prehistoric hunting people lived in what is now Afghanistan as early as 100,000 years ago. After many thousands of years, the people learned how to farm and to herd animals. Agricultural villages then developed. By about 4000 to 2000 B.C., a number of these villages had grown into small cities.

Early invasions. About 1500 B.C., the Aryans, a central Asian people, invaded the region. They killed many of the area's inhabitants and intermarried with others. In the mid-500's B.C., Persians invaded northern Afghanistan, a region then called Bactria. The Persians ruled Bactria until about 330 B.C., when Greeks and Macedonians led by Alexander the Great conquered the region and much of the rest of Afghanistan.

About 246 B.C., the Bactrians revolted. They eventually conquered Bactria and other parts of Afghanistan. They formed a kingdom that lasted about 150 years, until the Kushans of central Asia seized Afghanistan. Sasanians from Persia invaded in the A.D. 200's, and White Huns from central Asia defeated the Kushans and Sasanians in the 400's.

The coming of Islam. Arab Muslim armies swept into parts of what is now Afghanistan during the late 600's. Three Muslim dynasties—the Tahirid, the Samanid, and the Saffarid—controlled much of the region during the 800's and 900's. Under these dynasties,

© Hulton/Getty Images

The Anglo-Afghan wars of the 1800's resulted largely from the United Kingdom's desire to protect its Indian empire. This photograph shows British troops at a fort in Kabul in 1879.

most local inhabitants became Muslims.

Turkic-speaking peoples from eastern Persia and central Asia ruled Afghanistan from about 900 to 1200. Afghanistan was conquered by Mongols led by Genghis Khan in the 1200's and led by Timur, also called Tamerlane, in the 1300's. Safavids from Persia and Mughals from India struggled for control of Afghanistan from the mid-1500's to the early 1700's.

United Afghanistan. In 1747, Ahmad Khan came to power. He took the title *shah* (king) and adopted the name *Durrani* (Pearl of the Age). Ahmad Shah Durrani united the many Afghan tribes for the first time, marking the beginning of modern Afghanistan. He gained control of territory stretching far beyond the country's current borders.

Ahmad Shah was succeeded by his son Timur Shah. Around 1775, Timur Shah moved the capital from Kandahar to Kabul. Timur Shah and his successors struggled to keep the Afghan tribes united and lost control of most of the territory beyond the current borders of Afghanistan.

In 1819, civil war broke out among rival tribes that wanted to rule the country. The war lasted until 1826, when Dost Muhammad Khan gained control. He took the title of *amir* (prince). Dost Muhammad's descendants ruled the country for the next 150 years.

The Anglo-Afghan wars. During the 1800's, the United Kingdom and Russia competed for control of Afghanistan. Russia wanted an outlet to the Indian Ocean and began to expand toward Afghanistan. The United Kingdom wanted to protect its empire in India, which was threatened by Russia's expansion. In 1839, British troops invaded Afghanistan to reduce Russia's influence in the region. The invasion set off the First Anglo-Afghan War, which lasted until the British withdrew in 1842. Russian influence near Afghanistan increased during the mid-1800's.

In 1878, the United Kingdom invaded the country again, starting the Second Anglo-Afghan War. The British found it difficult to establish control of Afghanistan. In 1880, Abdur Rahman Khan became amir. The British agreed to recognize his authority over the country's internal affairs. In return, Abdur Rahman accepted the United Kingdom's control of Afghanistan's foreign relations. During his reign, Abdur Rahman worked to strengthen the national government and to reduce the power of tribal leaders. After he died in 1901, his policies were continued by his son Habibullah Khan.

Independence. Early in 1919, Habibullah Khan was assassinated. One of his sons, Amanullah Khan, then became amir and attacked British troops in India, beginning the Third Anglo-Afghan War. The United Kingdom had just finished fighting in World War I (1914-1918). It decided to end its involvement in Afghanistan rather than fight another war. In August 1919, Afghanistan became fully independent.

Amanullah began many reforms to modernize Afghanistan, rapidly sweeping away centuries-old traditions and customs. The nation's first constitution was adopted in 1923, and Amanullah changed his title from amir to shah in 1926. But tribal and religious leaders resisted the reform movement and forced Amanullah Shah to give up the throne in 1929.

Late in 1929, Muhammad Nadir Shah became king. In 1931, Afghanistan adopted a new constitution. Under the new Constitution, Nadir Shah began a program of gradual reform. But he was assassinated in 1933, before many of the reforms were begun. Muhammad Zahir Shah, Nadir Shah's son, then became king.

The mid-1900's. By early 1950's, Afghanistan had developed good relations with the United States and many Western European nations. But the Afghans feared the intentions of the Soviet Union, their country's powerful Communist neighbor. In 1953, Muhammad Daoud Khan, the king's cousin and brother-in-law, took control of the government and made himself prime minister. Under Daoud, Afghanistan took no side in the Cold War, a period of hostility between Communist and non-Communist nations, and it received aid from both the United States and the Soviet Union.

Border disputes with Pakistan and other problems led to pressures that forced Daoud to resign in 1963. In 1964, under the leadership of Zahir Shah and Western-educated scholars and thinkers, Afghanistan adopted a constitution that provided for a democratic government. But many problems arose. Zahir Shah and the legislature could not agree on the role of political parties within the reform program. Parliament often deadlocked on

key issues. In addition, the Afghan people had little experience with, or understanding of, democratic government. As a result, the new democratic system failed to bring about the progress that the framers of the Constitution had hoped for.

In 1973, Daoud led a military revolt that overthrew Zahir Shah. Afghanistan's military, aided by Afghan Communists, took control of the government and established the Republic of Afghanistan with Daoud as president and prime minister.

The Soviet invasion. In 1978, rival left-wing military leaders and civilians in Afghanistan staged another revolt, during which Daoud was killed. This group, which received much financial and military aid from the Soviet Union, took control of the government and established policies that had some features of Communism.

Many in Afghanistan opposed the new government. They believed the government's policies conflicted with teachings of Islam. In addition, they resented Soviet influence on the government. Large numbers of Afghan people joined in a rebellion against the government shortly after it came to power. Widespread fighting broke out between the rebels, who called themselves *mujahideen* (holy warriors), and government forces.

The Soviet Union became concerned that the rebels might defeat the Afghan government forces. In 1979 and 1980, the Soviet Union sent thousands of troops to join the fight against the rebels. The Soviets had far better equipment than their opponents. But the rebels, supplied by countries opposed to the Soviet Union, used guerrilla tactics to overcome the Soviet advantage. The Soviets and Afghan government forces bombed many villages.

In 1988, the Soviet Union began withdrawing its troops from Afghanistan. The withdrawal was completed in February 1989. But the fighting between the mujahideen and government forces continued until 1992, when the rebels overthrew the government.

Afghanistan under the Taliban. After 1992, Afghanistan had several governments made up of various combinations of mujahideen groups. Continued fighting among the groups prevented the establishment of a stable government. In the mid-1990's, a new group,

Soviet troops retreated from Afghanistan in 1989. The Soviet Union invaded Afghanistan in 1979 and 1980 to support the Communist government there. Despite their superior military strength, the Soviets failed to defeat the Afghan rebels, known as *mujahideen*.

AP/Wide World

Hamid Karzai, *left,* led Afghanistan after the fall of the Taliban in 2001. The former king of Afghanistan, Muhammad Zahir Shah, *right,* supported Karzai and helped unify the country.

a conservative Islamic organization known as the Taliban, rose to power.

Pashtun religious students who had fled to Pakistan during the Soviet invasion started the Taliban movement. The Taliban were supported by Pakistan's military and by militant Arab Islamic groups. By the late 1990's, the Taliban gained control of most of Afghanistan. They established a body called the Council of Ministers to rule the country.

The Taliban imposed their strict interpretation of Islam on the nation. For example, they banned television, popular music, and most other modern forms of entertainment, and they established rules for dress and grooming. All women were forced to cover themselves completely when in public, and men were required to grow beards. The Taliban also prohibited girls from attending school and forbade women from working outside the home.

The Taliban destroyed many artifacts of the country's heritage because they claimed they were anti-Islamic. For example, they demolished two ancient statues of Buddha carved into a mountainside near Bamian, Afghanistan. The Taliban also destroyed many works of art in the country's museums.

Through the decades of war in the late 1900's, millions of Afghans fled to neighboring Pakistan and Iran, and thousands more became refugees in their own country. Years of drought in the late 1990's and early 2000's left many Afghans in danger of starvation.

Recent developments. In 2001, members of a terrorist organization called al-Qa'ida attacked the World Trade Center in New York City and the Pentagon Building near Washington, D.C. The United States accused the Taliban of harboring and assisting al-Qa'ida, which

was led by the Saudi-born millionaire Osama bin Laden. The United States demanded that the Taliban arrest bin Laden and the other terrorists and shut down their training camps. The Taliban refused to do so, and the United States and its allies launched a military campaign against the Taliban.

The campaign included air strikes in support of Afghan rebels who opposed the Taliban. This support enabled the rebels to drive the Taliban from power in late 2001. Meanwhile, the United Nations brought together representatives of Afghanistan's leading groups to discuss the formation of a new and stable national government. The conference agreed on a plan that included the appointment of a temporary government and the eventual creation of a new constitution and a democratically elected government.

An international peacekeeping force arrived in Kabul in late 2001 and early 2002. In the absence of a strong central government, however, warlords and tribal groups continued to compete for territory and power. Also, small groups of Taliban and al-Qa'ida forces continued to battle U.S. and allied troops.

In April 2002, the former king of Afghanistan, Muhammad Zahir Shah, returned to the country. He did not resume his role as king but attended a *loya jirga* (grand council) of Afghan leaders. In June, the loya jirga met in Kabul and chose Hamid Karzai, leader of the Popalzai clan, as the country's transitional president.

Thomas E. Gouttierre

Outline

I. Government
II. People
    A. Ancestry
    B. Ethnic groups and languages
    C. Way of life
    D. Women
    E. Religion
    F. Education
    G. The arts
    H. Recreation
III. The land and climate
    A. The Northern Plains
    B. The Central Highlands
    C. The Southwestern Lowlands
IV. Economy
    A. Agriculture   D. International trade
    B. Mining   E. Transportation and
    C. Manufacturing   communication
V. History

Questions

What are the largest ethnic groups in Afghanistan?
What is a *loya jirga?*
What valuable stones are found in Afghanistan?
What led to the Anglo-Afghan wars?
What is the Hindu Kush? The Sistan Basin?
How do most Afghan workers earn their living?
What is a *burqa?*
Who first united the Afghan tribes?
What is the chief common link among Afghans?
What country attempted to occupy Afghanistan from 1979 to 1989?

Additional resources

Ewans, Sir Martin. *Afghanistan.* HarperCollins, 2002.
Rashid, Ahmed. *Taliban.* Yale, 2000.
Rubin, Barnett R. *The Fragmentation of Afghanistan.* 2nd ed. Yale, 2002.
Vogelsang, Willem. *The Afghans.* Blackwell, 2002.

Topic for study

Discuss the impact of Taliban rule on Afghanistan. For example, how did day-to-day life change for the Afghans after the Taliban took power? What influence did the Taliban have on Afghanistan's economy? How did Taliban rule affect relations between Afghanistan and other countries?

Bahrain in brief

General information

Capital: Manama.
Official name: Al-Mamlaka Al-Bahrayn (Kingdom of Bahrain).
Official language: Arabic.
Largest city: Manama (pop. 121,986).
Country flag: A red field covers about three-fourths of the flag of Bahrain and adjoins the jagged edge of a vertical white stripe. The five white triangles formed by the junction of the red and white sections of the flag represent the Five Pillars of Islam—*shahada* (the act of bearing witness), prayer, almsgiving, fasting, and pilgrimage.

Land and climate

Land: Bahrain is an island country in the Persian Gulf. Most of Bahrain consists of desert. The island of Bahrain makes up almost the entire country. Other islands include Al Muharraq and Sitrah. Bridges connect the main islands. A causeway links Bahrain to the Saudi Arabian mainland. Many freshwater springs provide drinking water for the northern coast of the island of Bahrain.
Area: 268 mi² (694 km²). *Greatest distances*—north-south, 50 mi (80 km); east-west, 26 mi (42 km). *Coastline*—78 mi (126 km).
Elevation: *Highest*—Jabal ad Dukhan, 443 ft (135 m) above sea level. *Lowest*—sea level.

WORLD BOOK map

Climate: Bahrain has hot, humid summers. The temperature often rises above 100 °F (38 °C) from June to September. Winter temperatures in Bahrain are mild, ranging from about 50 °F (10 °C) to about 80 °F (27 °C). Northern Bahrain receives most of the little rain that falls on the country. The rainfall averages only about 3 inches (8 centimeters) a year. Most of the rain falls during the winter months.

Government

Form of government: Constitutional monarchy.
Head of state: King.
Head of government: Prime minister appointed by the king.
Legislature: National Assembly of two houses—the Chamber of Deputies (40 members elected by the people to four-year terms) and the Consultative Council (40 members appointed by the king) .
Executive: King, prime minister, and Council of Ministers appointed by the king.
Judiciary: The highest court is the Constitutional Court.
Political subdivisions: Five governorates.
Suffrage: All Bahrainis 18 years of age or older may vote.
Armed forces: About 11,000 people serve in Bahrain's army, navy, and air force.

People

Population: *Estimated 2002 population*—636,000. *1991 census*—508,037.
Population density: 2,373 per mi² (916 per km²).
Distribution: 88 percent urban, 12 percent rural.
Life expectancy: *Male*—68. *Female*—71.
Major ethnic groups: About 60 percent of the people are Bahraini Arabs; about 40 percent are non-Bahrainis, including other Arabs, Asians, and Iranians.
Major religions: Islam is the official religion, and nearly all the people are Muslims. About 60 percent belong to the Shiah branch of Islam, and approximately 40 percent belong to the Sunni branch.
Literacy rate: About 88 percent of Bahrain's adult population can read and write.

Economy

Chief products: *Agriculture*—dates, tomatoes. *Fishing*—shrimp, crab, rabbit fish, perch, sea bream, grouper. *Manufacturing*—aluminum and aluminum products, ammonia, iron, liquid natural gas, methanol, refined petroleum products. *Mining*—natural gas, petroleum.
Money: *Basic unit*—dinar. One hundred fils equal one dinar.
International trade: *Major exports*—petroleum, primary metals. *Major imports*—chemicals, electrical equipment and machinery, food products, textiles, transportation equipment. *Major trading partners*—Australia, Japan, Saudi Arabia, United States.

Important dates in Bahrain

c. 2000 B.C.-1800 B.C. Dilmun, a prosperous trading civilization, occupied Bahrain.
A.D. 1500's Portugal controlled Bahrain.
1602-1782 Persia (now Iran) ruled Bahrain.
1782 The Al Khalifah clan, a group of Arabs from what is now Saudi Arabia, drove the Persians from Bahrain.
1861 Bahrain became a British protectorate.
1932 Petroleum was discovered in Bahrain.
1971 Bahrain became independent.
1973 Bahrain adopted a constitution that created a national assembly made up of elected representatives .
1975 Sheik Isa Khalifah, the emir of Bahrain, disbanded the assembly.
1991 During the Persian Gulf War, Bahrain took part in the allied operation to free Kuwait from Iraqi control.
Mid-1990's Shiite-led antigovernment protesters called for the national assembly to be restored and for free elections.
2001 Bahraini voters overwhelmingly approved a National Action Charter that would make Bahrain a constitutional monarchy with an elected legislature.
2002 Bahrain became a constitutional monarchy.

Cyprus in brief

General information

Capital of the Republic of Cyprus: Nicosia.

Official name: Republic of Cyprus.

Official languages of the Republic of Cyprus: Greek and Turkish.

National anthem of the Republic of Cyprus: "Imnos pros tin Eleftherian" ("The Hymn to Liberty").

Largest city: Nicosia (pop. 163,700).

Country flag for the Republic of Cyprus: The flag is white with a map of Cyprus in copper-yellow (for copper) in the center above two green crossed olive branches (for peace).

Land and climate

Land: Cyprus is an island in the Mediterranean Sea. Two mountain systems dominate the landscape. The rugged Kyrenia range stretches along the northern coast. Parts of the Troodos Massif, in the southwest, are thickly forested. Mount Olympus, the range's highest peak, rises 6,403 feet (1,952 meters) above sea level. Between the two systems lies the Mesaoria Plain, the chief agricultural region.

Area: 3,572 mi² (9,251 km²). *Greatest distances*—east-west, 138 mi (223 km); north-south, 60 mi (97 km).

Elevation: *Highest*—Mount Olympus, 6,403 ft (1,952 m) above sea level. *Lowest*—sea level.

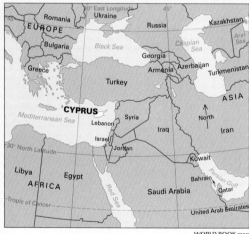

WORLD BOOK map

Climate: Cyprus has a pleasant, sunny climate. Snow falls high in the Troodos Massif early in the year. Winters are mild in the Mesaoria Plain, but in summer, temperatures may rise above 100 °F (38 °C). The plain receives from 12 to 16 inches (30 to 41 centimeters) of rainfall a year. Parts of the Troodos receive over 40 inches (100 centimeters).

Government

Note: Cyprus is divided politically into two sections: the Republic of Cyprus in the south and the Turkish Republic of Northern Cyprus (TRNC). The government of the Greek Cypriot section is recognized by all countries except Turkey as the legal government of the entire island. This section provides information on that government.

Form of government: Republic.

Head of state: President elected by the people to a five-year term.

Head of government: President.

Legislature: House of Representatives with 80 members—56 for Greek Cypriots, 24 for Turkish Cypriots. Only the seats for Greek Cypriots are filled. Members are elected to five-year terms.

Executive: President and Council of Ministers.

Judiciary: The highest court is the Supreme Court.

Political subdivisions: 6 districts.

Suffrage: All Cypriots 18 years of age or older may vote.

Armed forces: About 10,000 people serve in the National Guard.

People

Population: *Estimated 2002 population*—798,000. *1992 census for the Republic of Cyprus only*—602,025.

Population density: 223 persons per mi² (86 per km²).

Distribution: 64 percent urban, 36 percent rural.

Life expectancy: *Male*—74. *Female*—79.

Major ethnic groups: About 78 percent of the people of the island of Cyprus are Greek, and about 18 percent are Turkish.

Major religions: About 78 percent of the people of the island of Cyprus belong to the Greek Orthodox Church. About 18 percent are Muslims.

Literacy rate: About 97 percent of the adult population of the island of Cyprus can read and write.

Economy

Chief products: *Agriculture*— grapes, lemons, oranges, potatoes. *Manufacturing*—cement, cigarettes, clothing, shoes, textiles, wines. *Mining*—asbestos, chromium.

Money: *Basic unit*—Cyprus pound (Republic of Cyprus); Turkish lira (Turkish Republic of Northern Cyprus).

International trade: *Major exports*—clothing, pharmaceutical products, potatoes. *Major imports*—electrical equipment and machinery, food products, motor vehicles. *Major trading partners for the Republic of Cyprus*—Greece, Italy, United Kingdom, United States.

Important dates in Cyprus

1100's B.C. Greek settlers arrived on the island.

A.D. 395 Cyprus became part of the Byzantine Empire.

1570-1571 The Ottomans added Cyprus to their empire.

1925 Cyprus became a British crown colony.

1950's Greek Cypriots, under the leadership of Archbishop Makarios III, started an active campaign for *enosis* (union with Greece).

1961 Cyprus became independent with Makarios as president.

1963 Fighting erupted between Greek and Turkish Cypriots.

1967 The Turkish-controlled areas of the island set up new, separate governing bodies.

1974 On July 4, Greek officers overthrew Makarios. On July 20, Turkey sent troops to Cyprus. In August, a cease-fire was declared.

1975 Turkish Cypriot leaders declared the northeastern territory an *autonomous* (self-governing) region.

1983 The Turkish Cypriots declared their territory an independent nation.

Egypt in brief

General information

Capital: Cairo.

Official name: Jumhuriyat Misr al-Arabiyah (Arab Republic of Egypt).

Official language: Arabic.

National anthem: "Beladi, Beladi" ("My Country, My Country").

Largest city: Cairo (pop. 6,800,000).

Country flag: Egypt's flag has red, white, and black horizontal stripes. The eagle in the center is a symbol of Saladin, a Muslim leader who lived during the 1100's.

Land and climate

Land: Egypt lies mainly in the northeast corner of Africa. A small part of Egypt, the Sinai Peninsula, is in Asia. Dry, windswept desert covers most of the land. But the Nile River flows northward through the desert and serves as a vital source of life for most Egyptians. Almost all of Egypt's people live near the Nile or along the Suez Canal.

Area: 386,662 mi² (1,001,449 km²). *Greatest distances*—east-west, 770 mi (1,240 km); north-south, 675 mi (1,086 km). *Coastline*—Mediterranean Sea, 565 mi (909 km); Red Sea, 850 mi (1,370 km).

Elevation: *Highest*—Jabal Katrinah, 8,651 ft (2,637 m) above sea level. *Lowest*—Qattara Depression, 436 ft (133 m) below sea level.

WORLD BOOK map

Climate: Egypt has a hot, dry climate with only two seasons—scorching summers and mild winters. Summer lasts from around May to October, and winter lasts from around November to April. North winds from the Mediterranean Sea cool the coast during the summer. Around April, a hot windstorm called the *khamsin* sweeps through Egypt. Most of Egypt receives very little rain.

Government

Form of government: Republic.

Head of state: President nominated and confirmed by People's Assembly; then elected by a public referendum to a six-year term.

Head of government: Prime minister appointed by the president.

Legislature: People's Assembly with 444 members elected by the voters and as many as 10 members appointed by the president.

Executive: President, prime minister, and Council of Ministers appointed by the president.

Judiciary: The highest court is the Supreme Constitutional Court.

Political subdivisions: 27 governorates.

Suffrage: All citizens 18 years of age or older may vote.

Armed forces: About 450,000 people serve in Egypt's army, navy, air force, and air defense command.

People

Population: *Estimated 2002 population*—70,818,000. *1996 census*—59,272,382.

Population density: 183 per mi² (71 per km²).

Distribution: 56 percent rural, 44 percent urban.

Life expectancy: *Male*—64. *Female*—67.

Major ethnic groups: Most Egyptians consider themselves Arabs. Bedouins make up a distinct cultural minority among the Arab population. Nubians make up the largest non-Arab minority.

Major religions: About 94 percent of Egypt's people belong to the Sunni branch of Islam. Coptic Christians make up the largest religious minority group in Egypt.

Literacy rate: 51 percent of Egypt's adult population can read and write.

Economy

Chief products: *Agriculture*—corn, cotton, oranges, potatoes, rice, sugar cane, tomatoes, wheat. *Manufacturing*—chemicals, cotton textiles, fertilizers, processed foods, steel. *Mining*—petroleum.

Money: *Basic unit*—pound. One hundred piasters equal one pound.

International trade: *Major exports*—cotton fibers and products, fruits, and petroleum. *Major imports*—food, machinery, and transportation equipment. *Major trading partners*—France, Germany, Italy, Japan, United States.

Important dates in Egypt since A.D. 639

A.D. 639-642 Muslim Arab armies conquered Egypt.

969-1171 The Fatimid dynasty ruled Egypt.

1171-1250 Egypt was governed by the Ayyubid dynasty.

1250-1517 The Mamelukes ruled Egypt.

1517 The Ottoman Empire invaded and occupied Egypt.

1882 British troops occupied Egypt.

1948-1949 Egypt and other Arab countries went to war against Israel, but the Arab armies were defeated.

1953 Egypt became a republic.

1954 Gamal Abdel Nasser came to power in Egypt.

1956 Egypt seized the Suez Canal. Israeli, French, and British forces invaded Egypt, but the UN ended the fighting.

1967 Egypt and other Arab nations lost a war against Israel.

1970 Nasser died. Anwar el-Sadat became president.

1973 Egypt and Syria fought another Arab-Israeli war.

1978 Egypt and Israel reached a major agreement designed to end the disputes between the two countries.

1981 Islamic fundamentalist extremists assassinated Sadat. Hosni Mubarak succeeded him as president.

1991 Egypt participated in a military coalition that defeated Iraq in the Persian Gulf War.

India in brief

General information

Capital: New Delhi.

Official name: Bharat Ganarajya (Republic of India).

Principal official language: Hindi. *Other languages with official status:* English, Sanskrit, and 16 regional languages.

National anthem: "Jana-gana-mana" ("Thou Art the Ruler of the Minds of All People").

Largest city: Mumbai (pop. 9,925,891).

Country flag: India's flag has horizontal stripes of orange-yellow, white, and green. The wheel is an ancient symbol called the *Dharma Chakra* (Wheel of Law).

Land and climate

Land: India lies in southern Asia. Most of northern India is a low-lying plain that includes the valleys of the Ganges and Brahmaputra rivers. The Himalaya rises in the far north. Southern India is a plateau bordered on the east and west by mountains that drop down to coastal plains.

Area: 1,269,346 mi² (3,287,590 km²). *Greatest distances*—north-south, about 2,000 mi (3,200 km); east-west, about 1,700 mi (2,740 km). *Coastline*—4,252 mi (6,843 km), including 815 mi (1,312 km) of coastline of island territories.

Elevation: *Highest*—Kanchenjunga, 28,208 ft (8,598 m) above sea level. *Lowest*—Sea level along the coast.

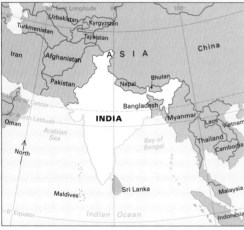

WORLD BOOK map

Climate: Northern and central India have mild, cool temperatures from October to February. Southern India lacks a true cool season, but the period from October to February is not as hot as the rest of the year. The entire country, except the mountains, is hot from March to June. From June to September, rains brought by seasonal winds called *monsoons* bring relief from extreme dry heat. The country's northeastern and western coasts receive heavy rainfall.

Government

Form of government: Federal republic.

Head of state: President.

Head of government: Prime minister.

Legislature: Parliament of two houses—Lok Sabha (545 members) and Rajya Sabha (a maximum of 250 members).

Executive: President and prime minister. The prime minister selects the members of the Council of Ministers, who are then appointed by the president.

Judiciary: The highest court is the Supreme Court.

Political subdivisions: 28 states and 7 territories.

Suffrage: All Indians 18 years of age or older may vote.

Armed forces: More than a million people serve in India's army, navy, and air force.

People

Population: *Estimated 2002 population*—1,042,449,000. *1991 census*—846,302,688.

Population density: 821 per mi² (317 per km²).

Distribution: 72 percent rural, 28 percent urban.

Life expectancy: *Male*—60. *Female*—61.

Major ethnic groups: 72 percent Indo-Aryan, 25 percent Dravidian.

Major religions: 82 percent Hindu, 12 percent Muslim, 2 percent Christian, 2 percent Sikh.

Literacy rate: About 52 percent of India's adult population can read and write.

Economy

Chief products: *Agriculture*—bananas, chickpeas, coconuts, cotton, jute, mangoes, onions, oranges, peanuts, pepper, potatoes, rice, sesame seeds, sugar cane, tea, wheat. *Manufacturing and processing*—bicycles, brassware and silverware, cement, chemicals, clothing and textiles, fertilizer, food products, iron and steel, jute products, leather goods, machinery, medicines, motor vehicles, paper, petroleum products, rugs, sewing machines, sugar, wood products. *Mining*—coal, iron ore, limestone, petroleum.

Money: *Basic unit*—rupee. One hundred paise equal one rupee.

International trade: *Major exports*—chemicals, cotton textiles and clothing, cut diamonds and jewelry, engineering goods, handicrafts, iron ore, leather goods, tea. *Major imports*—chemicals, fertilizer, industrial machinery, pearls and gemstones, petroleum products. *Major trading partners*—Japan, United Kingdom, United States.

Important dates in India

c. 2500 B.C. The Indus Valley civilization began to flourish.

c. 1500 B.C. The Aryans invaded India.

326 B.C. Alexander the Great reached what is now India.

A.D. 320 - c. 500 The Gupta dynasty unified northern India.

1526 The Mughal Empire was established.

1774 Warren Hastings, the first British governor general of India, took office.

1857-1859 The British put down the Indian Rebellion, an uprising in northern and central India.

1858 The British government took over the direct rule of India from the East India Company.

1947 India became independent on August 15, the day after Pakistan was created.

1947-1949 India and Pakistan fought over Kashmir.

1965 India and Pakistan fought a second war over Kashmir.

1971 India assisted East Pakistan in a war against West Pakistan. The West was defeated, and East Pakistan became the independent nation of Bangladesh.

1996 The Congress Party, which had ruled India for all but four years since 1947, was voted out of office, and India entered a period of coalition governments.

Iran in brief

General information

Capital: Tehran.

Official name: Jomhuri-ye Eslami-ye Iran (Islamic Republic of Iran).

Official language: Persian, also called Farsi.

Largest city: Tehran (pop. 6,758,845).

Country flag: The inscription *God Is Great* appears in Arabic 11 times on both the green stripe and the red stripe of the flag. The white stripe bears the coat of arms, which is the word *Allah* (the Arabic name for God) drawn in formal Arabic script.

Land and climate

Land: Iran lies in southwestern Asia. Iran's Interior Plateau lies in the central and eastern part of the country and is largely surrounded by mountains. Much of the plateau consists of two immense deserts. The Caspian Sea Coast is a narrow strip of lowland in the north.

Area: 630,577 mi² (1,633,188 km²). *Greatest distances*—northwest-southeast, 1,375 mi (2,213 km); northeast-southwest, 850 mi (1,370 km). *Coastline*—1,650 mi (2,655 km).

Elevation: *Highest*—Mount Damavand, 18,386 ft (5,604 m) above sea level. *Lowest*—92 ft (28 m) below sea level along the Caspian Sea.

WORLD BOOK map

Climate: The mountainous areas of the northwest have long, severe winters and mild summers. Most of the Interior Plateau has an extremely dry climate. An average of about 2 inches (5 centimeters) of rain falls on the deserts yearly. Average temperatures in Tehran range from 35 °F (2 °C) in January to 85 °F (29 °C) in July. The Caspian Sea Coast receives about 40 inches (100 centimeters) of rain a year.

Government

Form of government: Islamic republic.

Head of state: Supreme Guide, or Leader of the Islamic Revolution. The Supreme Guide is appointed for life by the Assembly of Experts.

Head of government: President elected by the people to a four-year term.

Legislature: Islamic Consultative Assembly, or Majlis, with 290 members elected by the voters.

Executive: Council of Ministers chosen by the president.

Judiciary: The highest court is the Supreme Court.

Political subdivisions: 24 *ostans* (provinces).

Suffrage: All citizens 15 years of age or older may vote.

Armed forces: Over 500,000 people serve in Iran's army, navy, air force, and Revolutionary Guards.

People

Population: *Estimated 2002 population*—69,049,000. *1996 census*—60,055,000.

Population density: 110 per mi² (42 per km²).

Distribution: 63 percent urban, 37 percent rural.

Life expectancy: *Male*—68. *Female*—71.

Major ethnic groups: Persians make up about 60 percent of Iran's population. Other ethnic groups include Arabs, Azerbaijanis, Baluchis, Kurds, and Turkomans.

Major religions: About 99 percent of the Iranian people are Muslims. About 95 percent of them belong to the Shiah branch of Islam.

Literacy rate: About 72 percent of Iran's adult population can read and write.

Economy

Chief products: *Agriculture*—wheat, sugar beets, rice, barley, nuts. *Fishing*—caviar. *Manufacturing*—petroleum products, textiles, cement, brick, food products. *Mining*—petroleum.

Money: *Basic unit*—rial. Ten dinars equal one rial.

International trade: *Major exports*—petroleum, caviar, cotton, dried fruits, mineral ores, nuts, and spices. *Major imports*—electric appliances, food, industrial machinery, medicine, and military equipment. *Major trading partners*—Germany, Italy, Japan, Spain, Turkey, United Arab Emirates, United Kingdom.

Important dates in Iran

1500's B.C. Aryans began migrating to Iran and split into two groups, the Medes and the Persians.

550 B.C. The Persian king Cyrus the Great overthrew the Medes and founded the Achaemenid (Persian) Empire.

331 B.C. Alexander the Great conquered the Achaemenid Empire.

250 B.C. Parthian armies seized control of Iran.

A.D. 224 The Persians overthrew the Parthians.

Mid-600's The Muslim Arabs conquered Iran.

1220 The Mongols invaded Iran.

1501-1722 The Safavid dynasty governed Iran.

1794 The Qajars, a Turkoman tribe, set up a new dynasty that ruled Iran until 1925.

1925 Reza Khan became shah.

1941 Mohammad Reza Pahlavi succeeded to the throne.

1951 The Majlis nationalized the oil industry.

1979 Revolutionaries took control of Iran's government.

1980 War broke out between Iran and Iraq. A cease-fire was declared in 1988.

1997 Mohammad Khatami was elected president.

2000 Reform groups won a majority of seats in the Majlis.

2002 U.S. President George W. Bush declared Iran to be part of an "axis of evil"—along with Iraq and North Korea—that seeks weapons of mass destruction and exports terrorism.

Iraq in brief

General information

Capital: Baghdad.
Official name: Al-Jumhuriya Al-Iraqiya (Republic of Iraq).
Official language: Arabic.
National anthem: "Al-Salam Al-Jumhuri" ("Salute to the Republic").
Largest city: Baghdad (pop. 5,908,000).
Country flag: Iraq's flag was adopted in 1991. The Arabic inscription on the white stripe means "God is great."

Land and climate

Land: Iraq lies in southwestern Asia. The northern plain, a region of dry, rolling land, lies between the Tigris and Euphrates rivers north of the city of Samarra. The southern plain begins near Samarra and extends southeast to the Persian Gulf. It includes the fertile delta between the Tigris and Euphrates rivers. The Tigris and Euphrates meet at the town of Al Qurnah and form the Shatt al Arab river, which empties into the gulf. The Zagros Mountains rise in northeastern Iraq. Desert covers the southwest and west.
Area: 169,235 mi² (438,317 km²). *Greatest distances*—north-south, 530 mi (853 km); east-west, 495 mi (797 km). *Coastline*—40 mi (64 km).
Elevation: *Highest*—about 11,840 ft (3,609 m) in Zagros Mountains. *Lowest*—sea level.

WORLD BOOK map

Climate: Iraq's climate ranges from moderate in the north to semitropical in the east and southeast. The west and southwest have a desert climate. Summer high temperatures average more than 100 °F (38 °C) throughout much of Iraq. Winter low temperatures may drop to around 35 °F (2 °C) in the desert and in the north. In general, little rain falls in Iraq. Most of the precipitation falls between November and April.

Government

Form of government: According to the Constitution, a republic; in reality, a dictatorship.
Head of state: President elected by the Revolutionary Command Council.
Head of government: Prime minister appointed by the president.
Legislature: National Assembly with 250 members elected by the voters to four-year terms.
Executive: President and Council of Ministers.
Judiciary: The highest court is the Court of Cassation.
Political subdivisions: 13 provinces and the city of Damascus.
Suffrage: All Iraqi citizens 18 years of age or older may vote.
Armed forces: Over 420,000 people serve in Iraq's army, navy, and air force.

People

Population: *Estimated 2002 population*—24,451,000. *1987 census*—16,335,199.
Population density: 144 per mi² (56 per km²).
Distribution: 68 percent urban, 32 percent rural.
Life expectancy: *Male*—58. *Female*—60.
Major ethnic groups: Arabs make up about 75 percent of Iraq's population. About 20 percent of Iraq's people are Kurds, the nation's largest ethnic minority.
Major religions: About 95 percent of Iraq's people are Muslims. Of those, about 60 percent belong to the Shiah branch of Islam.
Literacy rate: About 71 percent of Iraq's adult population can read and write.

Economy

Chief products: *Agriculture*—barley, dates, grapes, rice, tomatoes, and wheat. *Mining*—petroleum. *Manufacturing*—building materials, chemicals, flour, iron and steel, leather goods, petroleum refining, textiles.
Money: *Basic unit*—dinar. One thousand fils equal one dinar.
International trade: *Major exports*—petroleum. *Major imports*—food, manufactured goods, medicine. *Major trading partners*—Egypt, France, Russia, Vietnam.

Important dates in Iraq

3500 B.C. The world's first known civilization developed in Mesopotamia, now Iraq.
539 B.C. The Persians conquered Mesopotamia.
331 B.C. Alexander the Great seized Mesopotamia.
A.D. 227 The Sassanid dynasty of Persia conquered Mesopotamia.
637 Arab Muslims overthrew the Sassanids.
1258 The Mongols invaded Mesopotamia.
1500's The Ottoman Empire began to establish control over Mesopotamia.
1920 The League of Nations gave the United Kingdom a mandate (order to rule) over Mesopotamia.
1932 Iraq became independent.
1958 Army officers overthrew the Iraqi government.
1968 The Baath Party took control of Iraq's government.
1973 The Iraqi government completed its take-over of foreign oil companies in Iraq.
1979 Saddam Hussein became president of Iraq.
1980 Iraq declared war on Iran.
1988 Iraq and Iran agreed to a cease-fire.
1990 Iraq invaded Kuwait.
1991 A coalition of 39 nations, including the United States and Canada, defeated Iraq in the Persian Gulf War.
2002 U.S. President George W. Bush declared Iraq to be part of an "axis of evil"—along with Iran and North Korea—that seeks weapons of mass destruction and exports terrorism.

Israel in brief

General information

Capital: Jerusalem.
Official name: State of Israel.
Official language: Hebrew and Arabic.
National anthem: "Hatikva" ("The Hope").
Largest city: Jerusalem (pop. 567,100).
Country flag: Israel's flag shows the Star of David, an ancient Jewish symbol. The colors are those of a *tallit* (prayer shawl).

Land and climate

Land: Israel lies on the eastern shore of the Mediterranean Sea. A narrow strip of fertile land, called the Coastal Plain, runs along the Mediterranean. The Judeo-Galilean Highlands stretch from Galilee—the northernmost part of Israel—to the edge of the Negev Desert in the south. Much of the Rift Valley, in far eastern Israel, lies below sea level.
Area: 8,130 mi² (21,056 km²), not including 2,700 mi² (7,000 km²) of Arab territory occupied since 1967. *Greatest distances*—north-south, 260 mi (420 km); east-west, 70 mi (110 km). *Coastline*—170 mi (273 km).
Elevation: *Highest*—Mount Meron, 3,963 ft (1,208 m) above sea level. *Lowest*—shore of the Dead Sea, about 1,310 ft (399 m) below sea level.

WORLD BOOK map

Climate: Israel has hot, dry summers and cool, mild winters. The climate varies somewhat from region to region, partly because of altitude. Temperatures are generally cooler at higher altitudes and warmer at lower altitudes. Israel has almost continuous sunshine from May through mid-October. Almost all of Israel's rain falls between November and March, much of it in December. Brief snowfalls sometimes occur in the hilly regions.

Government

Form of government: Parliamentary democracy.
Head of state: President elected by the Knesset to a seven-year term.
Head of government: Prime minister.
Legislature: A parliament called the Knesset, which consists of 120 members elected by the voters to four-year terms.
Executive: Prime Minister and Cabinet.
Judiciary: The highest court is the Supreme Court.
Political subdivisions: six districts.
Suffrage: All Israelis 18 years of age or older may vote.
Armed forces: About 175,000 people serve in Israel's army, navy, and air force.

People

Population: *Estimated 2002 population*—6,425,000. *1995 census*—5,548,523. Figures do not include people living in occupied Arab territories, except for Israeli citizens.
Population density: 790 per mi² (305 per km²).
Distribution: 90 percent urban, 10 percent rural.
Life expectancy: *Male*—76. *Female*—80.
Major ethnic groups: About 80 percent of Israel's people are Jews. Nearly all the rest are Arabs.
Major religions: About 80 percent Jews; about 15 percent Muslims; about 2 percent Christians.
Literacy rate: About 96 percent of Israel's adult population can read and write.

Economy

Chief products: *Agriculture*—citrus and other fruits, cotton, eggs, grains, poultry, vegetables. *Manufacturing*—chemical products, electronic equipment, fertilizer, finished diamonds, paper, plastics, processed foods, scientific and optical instruments, textiles and clothing. *Mining*—potash, bromine, salt, phosphates.
Money: *Basic unit*—shekel. One hundred agorot equal one shekel.
International trade: *Major exports*—chemical products, citrus fruits, clothing, electronic equipment, fertilizers, polished diamonds, and processed foods. *Major imports*—chemicals, computer equipment, grain, iron and steel, military equipment, petroleum products, rough diamonds, and textiles. *Major trading partners*—Belgium, Germany, Italy, Luxembourg, the Netherlands, Switzerland, United Kingdom, United States.

Important dates in Israel

1948 Israel came into existence on May 14.
1948 Israel defeated the invading forces of Egypt, Syria, Lebanon, Iraq, and Jordan in the first Arab-Israeli war and gained much territory.
1967 Israel defeated Egypt, Jordan, and Syria in the Six-Day War. Israel captured the Sinai Peninsula, Gaza Strip, West Bank, and Golan Heights.
1972 Palestinian terrorists killed 11 Israeli athletes at the Summer Olympic Games in Munich, West Germany.
1973 Israel defeated Egypt and Syria in the Yom Kippur War.
1978 Israel and Egypt signed the Camp David Accords, an agreement to end the dispute between the two countries.
1979 Egypt and Israel signed a peace treaty.
1982 Israel withdrew from the Sinai Peninsula.
1993 Israel and the Palestine Liberation Organization (PLO) signed an agreement to work to end their conflicts.
1994 As part of the 1993 PLO agreement, Israel withdrew from most of the Gaza Strip and the West Bank city of Jericho. Israel and Jordan signed a peace treaty.
1995 Prime Minister Yitzhak Rabin was assassinated.
2000-2002 Violence between Palestinians and Israelis killed hundreds of people and interrupted the peace process.

Jordan in brief

General information

Capital: Amman.
Official name: Al-Mamlakah Al-Urdiniyah Al-Hashimiyah (Hashemite Kingdom of Jordan).
Official language: Arabic.
National anthem: "Al-Salam Al-Malaki" ("The Royal Salute").
Largest city: Amman (pop. 969,598).
Country flag: Jordan's flag features a seven-pointed star. The points of the star stand for the first seven verses of the Qur'ān, the holy book of Islam.

Land and climate

Land: Jordan lies on the East Bank of the Jordan River in southwest Asia. The Jordan River Valley cuts through the country from just south of the Sea of Galilee to the Dead Sea. The Transjordan Plateau rises steeply from the Jordan River Valley and the Dead Sea. The plateau begins at the Syrian border and narrows as it extends southward. It consists of broad, rolling plains. The Syrian Desert is a vast wasteland to the east and south of the plateau.
Area: 37,738 mi² (97,740 km²).
Elevation: *Highest*—Jabal Ramm, 5,755 ft (1,754 m) above sea level. *Lowest*—shore of the Dead Sea, about 1,310 ft (399 m) below sea level.

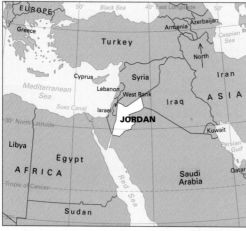

WORLD BOOK map

Climate: Jordan has a warm, pleasant climate but receives little rain. Summer temperatures in the Jordan River Valley regularly exceed 100 °F (38 °C). Average temperatures on the Transjordan Plateau range between 64 and 86 °F (18 and 30 °C) during the summer and between 40 and 52 °F (4 and 11 °C) during the winter. Summer temperatures in the Syrian Desert sometimes reach 120 °F (49 °C). Annual rainfall in the desert is less than 10 inches (25 centimeters).

Government

Form of government: Constitutional monarchy.
Head of state: King.
Head of government: Prime minister appointed by the king.
Legislature: National Assembly of two houses—Chamber of Deputies (88 members elected by the voters to four-year terms) and Senate (40 members appointed by the king to four-year terms).
Executive: Prime minister and Council of Ministers appointed by the king.
Judiciary: The highest courts are the Court of Cassation and the Supreme Court.
Political subdivisions: Eight governorates.
Suffrage: All Jordanians 20 years of age or older may vote.
Armed forces: About 103,000 people serve in the army, navy, and air force.

People

Population: *Estimated 2002 population*—6,639,000. *1994 census*—4,095,579.
Population density: 176 per mi² (68 per km²).
Distribution: 78 percent urban, 22 percent rural.
Life expectancy: *Male*—68. *Female*—70.
Major ethnic groups: About 98 percent of Jordan's people are Arabs. The country also has small numbers of Armenians and Circassians.
Major religions: About 92 percent of the people are Sunni Muslims; about 6 percent are Christians.
Literacy rate: About 86 percent of Jordan's adult population can read and write.

Economy

Chief products: *Agriculture*—barley, cabbages, citrus fruits, cucumbers, eggplants, grapes, melons, olives, tomatoes, wheat. *Manufacturing*—batteries, cement, ceramics, detergents, fertilizer, petroleum products, pharmaceutical products, shoes, textiles. *Mining*—phosphates, potash.
Money: *Basic unit*—dinar. One thousand fils equal one dinar.
International trade: *Major exports*—phosphates, chemicals, potash, fruits and vegetables, manufactured products. *Major imports*—machinery, petroleum, grain, meat. *Major trading partners*—Germany, India, Italy, Japan, Saudi Arabia, United Kingdom, United States.

Important dates in Jordan

c. 2000 B.C. Semitic nomads entered what is now Jordan.
900's B.C. The Israelites conquered and ruled the region.
331 B.C. Alexander the Great conquered the region.
60's B.C. The Romans took control of Jordan.
A.D. 300's Jordan became part of the Byzantine Empire.
636 Arab Muslims conquered the northern Jordan region.
Late 1000's European Crusaders conquered parts of Jordan.
1187 The Muslim leader Saladin drove out the Crusaders.
1250 Egyptian Mamelukes overthrew Saladin's successors.
1517 Most of Jordan became part of the Ottoman Empire.
1921 Territory east of the Jordan River became an emirate called Transjordan.
1946 Transjordan became independent.
1948-1949 Jordan and other Arab countries lost a war with the newly created state of Israel.
1949 Transjordan was renamed Jordan.
1950 Jordan officially annexed the West Bank.
1952 Hussein became king of Jordan.
1967 Israel defeated Jordan, Egypt, and Syria in the Six-Day War. Jordan lost East Jerusalem and the West Bank to the Israelis.
1994 Jordan and Israel signed a peace treaty.
1999 King Hussein died. His son became king as Abdullah II.

Kuwait in brief

General information

Capital: Kuwait.
Official name: Dawlat al Kuwayt (State of Kuwait).
Official language: Arabic.
Largest city: Kuwait (pop. 44,335).
Country flag: The Kuwaiti flag has horizontal green, white, and red stripes that join a black, vertical stripe at the flagstaff.

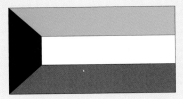

Land and climate

Land: Kuwait lies in southwestern Asia, at the north end of the Persian Gulf. Most of the country consists of waterless desert. The country includes several islands. Faylakah, the most important island, lies about 12 miles (19 kilometers) off the coast. Bubiyan, the largest island, is uninhabited. The city of Kuwait lies on the southern side of Kuwait Bay, which is an excellent harbor. Kuwait has no rivers or lakes.

Area: 6,880 mi² (17,818 km²), including offshore islands. *Greatest distances*—east-west, 95 mi (153 km); north-south, 90 mi (145 km). *Coastline*—120 mi (193 km).

Elevation: *Highest*—1,004 ft (306 m) above sea level in far western Kuwait. *Lowest*—sea level along the coast.

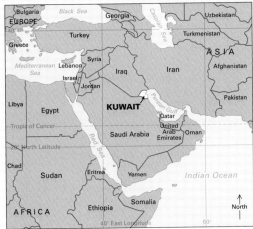

WORLD BOOK map

Climate: From April to September, Kuwait is very hot. Temperatures often exceed 120 °F (49 °C) in the shade. But the climate is not extremely unpleasant until August and September, when the humidity is relatively high. In January, the coldest month, temperatures average between 50 and 60 °F (10 and 16 °C). Besides desert scrub, Kuwait has little vegetation most of the year. Some grass grows from October to March, when an average of 2 to 6 inches (5 to 15 centimeters) of rain falls.

Government

Form of government: Constitutional monarchy.
Head of state: Emir.
Head of government: Prime minister appointed by the emir.
Legislature: National Assembly with 50 members elected to four-year terms.
Executive: Council of Ministers appointed by the prime minister and approved by the emir.
Judiciary: The highest court is the High Court of Appeal.
Political subdivisions: Five governorates.
Suffrage: Adult males who have been naturalized for 30 years or more or who have resided in Kuwait since before 1920 are allowed to vote, as are their male descendants when they reach the age of 21.
Armed forces: About 15,500 people serve in Kuwait's air force, navy, and land force.

People

Population: *Estimated 2002 population*—2,062,000. *1995 census*—1,575,983.
Population density: 300 per mi² (116 per km²).
Distribution: 100 percent urban.
Life expectancy: *Male*—72. *Female*—73.
Major ethnic groups: About 45 percent of the people are Kuwaiti Arabs, and about 35 percent are other Arabs. Other ethnic groups include Iranians and South Asians.
Major religions: About 45 percent of the people are Sunni Muslims, and about 40 percent are Shiite Muslims. Other religious groups in Kuwait include Christians and Hindus.
Literacy rate: About 79 percent of Kuwait's adult population can read and write.

Economy

Chief products: Petroleum, natural gas.
Money: *Basic unit*—dinar. One thousand fils equal one dinar.
International trade: *Major exports*—fertilizer, petroleum. *Major imports*—clothing, construction materials, food, transportation equipment. *Major trading partners*—Germany, Japan, Singapore, the United Kingdom, the United States, Vietnam.

Important dates in Kuwait

c. 1710 Some members of the Arab Anaza tribal confederation settled on the southern shore of Kuwait Bay.
c. 1760 The Al-Sabah family became the rulers of Kuwait.
1775 The British made Kuwait the starting point of their desert mail service to Aleppo, Syria.
1889 The United Kingdom became responsible for Kuwait's defense.
1936 Drilling for oil began.
1961 Kuwait became an independent nation.
1967 For about two months, Kuwait cut off shipments of oil to the United States and other Western countries during an Arab-Israeli war.
1973 In October, during another Arab-Israeli war, Kuwait stopped oil shipments to the United States and the Netherlands and reduced shipments to other countries that supported Israel.
1976 Kuwait's emir dissolved the National Assembly.
1981 A new National Assembly was elected.
1986 The emir dissolved the National Assembly and suspended the Constitution.
1990 Iraqi forces invaded and occupied Kuwait.
1991 In the Persian Gulf War, an allied coalition consisting of the United States and 38 other countries drove the Iraqis out of Kuwait.
1992 A new National Assembly was elected, and the Constitution was reinstated.

Lebanon in brief

General information

Capital: Beirut.

Official name: Al Jumhuriyah al Lubnaniyah (Lebanese Republic).

Official language: Arabic.

National anthem: "Kulluna Lil Watan Lil'ula Lil'alam" ("All of Us for Our Country, Flag, and Glory").

Largest city: Beirut (pop. 1,500,000).

Country flag: The flag has three horizontal stripes—red, white, and red. A cedar tree on the white stripe symbolizes holiness, eternity, and peace.

Land and climate

Land: Lebanon lies at the eastern end of the Mediterranean Sea. A narrow plain runs along the Lebanese coast. The Lebanon Mountains rise east of the plain, and the Anti-Lebanon Mountains run along the country's eastern border. A valley called the Bekaa lies between the two ranges.

Area: 4,015 mi² (10,400 km²). *Greatest distances*—north-south, 120 mi (193 km); east-west, 50 mi (80 km). *Coastline*—130 mi (210 km).

Elevation: *Highest*—Qurnat as Sawda, 10,115 ft (3,083 m) above sea level. *Lowest*—sea level.

WORLD BOOK map

Climate: Temperatures in the coastal area average about 55 °F (13 °C) in January and about 84 °F (29 °C) in June. Inland areas have generally lower average temperatures and less humidity than the coast. About 35 inches (89 centimeters) of rain falls annually along the coast. The mountains receive from 50 to 60 inches (130 to 150 centimeters) of rain yearly and much snow in the winter. The Bekaa receives less rain than the mountains.

Government

Form of government: Republic.

Head of state: President elected by the National Assembly. The president must be a Maronite Christian.

Head of government: Prime minister appointed by the president. The prime minister must be a Sunni Muslim.

Legislature: National Assembly with 128 members elected by the voters to four-year terms. The speaker of the National Assembly must be a Shiite Muslim.

Executive: President, prime minister, and Cabinet.

Judiciary: The highest court is the Court of Cassation.

Political subdivisions: Six provinces.

Suffrage: All Lebanese males 21 years of age or older are required to vote. Women 21 years of age or older who have received an elementary education are allowed to vote.

Armed forces: About 72,000 people serve in Lebanon's army, navy, and air force.

People

Population: *Estimated 2002 population*—3,373,000. *1970 census*—2,126,325.

Population density: 840 per mi² (324 per km²).

Distribution: 88 percent urban, 12 percent rural.

Life expectancy: *Male*—68. *Female*—73.

Major ethnic groups: About 95 percent of Lebanon's people are Arabs. Armenians are the largest minority group.

Major religions: About 70 percent of the Lebanese people are Muslims. Almost all the rest are Christians. The majority of Lebanese Christians belong to the Maronite Church.

Literacy rate: About 92 percent of Lebanon's adult population can read and write.

Economy

Chief products: *Agriculture*—apples, cherries, cucumbers, grapes, lemons, oranges, peaches, sugar beets, tomatoes. *Manufacturing*—cement, chemicals, electric appliances, furniture, processed foods, textiles.

Money: *Basic unit*—pound. One hundred piastres equal one pound.

International trade: *Major exports*—clothing, food products, gemstones, metal products. *Major imports*—chemicals, food products, machinery, textiles. *Major trading partners*—France, Italy, United Arab Emirates.

Important dates in Lebanon

c. 2000 B.C. Phoenicians moved into what is now Lebanon.

332 B.C. Alexander the Great conquered Lebanon.

64 B.C. The Roman Empire gained control of the area.

395 The region became part of the Byzantine Empire.

600's Muslim Arabs occupied Lebanon.

1516 Lebanon became part of the Ottoman Empire.

1922 France took over Lebanon's political affairs.

1943 Lebanon became completely independent.

1969 The Palestine Liberation Organization (PLO) began raiding targets in Israel from southern Lebanon.

1975 Civil war broke out in Lebanon.

1976 Syria sent thousands of troops into Lebanon to try to restore order.

1978 The United Nations (UN) sent a peacekeeping force to Lebanon, but some fighting continued to break out.

1982 Israeli forces invaded Lebanon and drove PLO forces out of the southern part of the country.

1983 On October 23, a suicide terrorist crashed a truck loaded with explosives into U.S. Marine headquarters at the Beirut airport, killing 241 U.S. marines.

1991 A peace plan ended most of the fighting in the civil war.

1998 Lebanon held its first presidential election since the end of its civil war.

Oman in brief

General information

Capital: Muscat.
Official name: Saltanat Uman (Sultanate of Oman).
Official language: Arabic.
National anthem: "Nashid as-Salaam as-Sultani" ("Sultan's National Anthem").
Largest city: Muscat (pop. 30,000).
Country flag: Oman's flag has a vertical red stripe and three horizontal stripes of white, red, and green.

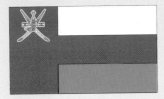

Land and climate

Land: Oman lies on the southeastern end of the Arabian Peninsula. Most of the country is dry and rocky. Al Batinah, a narrow coastal plain, lies along the Gulf of Oman. Mountains separate the Batinah from the interior. The interior is a vast, flat wasteland. The Rub al Khali (Empty Quarter), a desert, extends into western Oman from Saudi Arabia. Most of Oman's coast along the Arabian Sea is barren and rocky. But tropical vegetation grows along the coast in Dhofar, a region in the south. Dhofar is famous for its frankincense trees, the best of which grow on a plateau north of the Jabal al Qara, a mountain range.
Area: 82,030 mi² (212,457 km²). *Greatest distances*—north-south, 500 mi (805 km); east-west, 400 mi (644 km). *Coastline*—about 1,060 mi (1,700 km).
Elevation: *Highest*—Jabal Ash Sham, 9,957 ft (3,035 m) above sea level. *Lowest*—sea level.

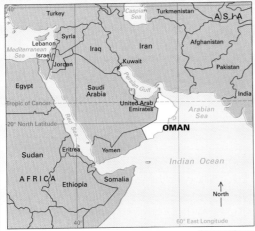

WORLD BOOK map

Climate: Temperatures in Oman may reach 130 °F (54.4 °C) during the summer. Most of Oman receives less than 6 inches (15 centimeters) of rain each year. However, annual rainfall in Dhofar reaches as high as 25 inches (63.5 centimeters).

Government

Form of government: Monarchy.
Head of state: Sultan.
Head of government: Sultan.
Legislature: Oman has two councils that advise the sultan—a 41-member Council of State and an 82-member Consultative Council. The sultan appoints members of the Council of State. He chooses the members of the Consultative Council from among candidates elected by voters in each of Oman's 59 *wilayats* (districts).
Executive: Cabinet appointed by the sultan.
Judiciary: The highest court is the Chief Court.
Political subdivisions: Six regions and two governorates.
Suffrage: Limited to voters chosen by the government.
Armed forces: About 40,000 people serve in Oman's armed forces.

People

Population: *Estimated 2002 population*—2,711,000. *1993 census*—2,018,074.
Population density: 33 per mi² (13 per km²).
Distribution: 72 percent urban, 28 percent rural.
Life expectancy: *Male*—69. *Female*—73.
Major ethnic groups: Most of the Omani population is Arab. The largest of the many non-Arab minorities that live in Oman are Baluchis—that is, people from the Arabian coast of Iran and Pakistan—and Asian Indians.
Major religions: About 75 percent of Oman's people belong to the Ibadi branch of the Kharijite division of Islam. Other religious groups include Sunni Muslims, Shiite Muslims, and Hindus.
Literacy rate: About 72 percent of Oman's adult population can read and write.

Economy

Chief products: *Agriculture*—alfalfa, bananas, coconuts, dates, limes, onions, pomegranates, tobacco, tomatoes, wheat. *Fishing industry*—sardines, cod, sharks. *Mining*—petroleum, natural gas, copper, chromite.
Money: *Basic unit*—Omani rial, or riyal. One thousand baizas equal one rial.
International trade: *Major exports*—petroleum and petroleum products. *Major imports*—electrical equipment, food products, machinery, metals, transportation equipment. *Major trading partners*—Japan, the United Arab Emirates, United Kingdom.

Important dates in Oman

600's Islam was introduced into Oman.
1500's Portuguese military forces built forts in Omani seaports, which had been used for trade since ancient times.
1650 Under the leadership of Sultan bin Saif al-Yaribi, Omani navy and tribal fighters forced the Portuguese from Oman.
1740's Ahmad bin Said, the first ruler of the Al Bu Said family, united the Omanis and took power.
1783 Ahmad died. Following Ahmad's death, Oman became increasingly divided.
1798 Sultan Said bin Ahmad signed the first of several treaties with the United Kingdom.
1955 Sultan Said bin Taimur reunited Oman.
1959 With British help, the sultan defeated rebellious Ibadi tribesmen of interior Oman.
1970 Qaboos bin Said overthrew his father and became sultan.
1970's Qaboos put down a rebellion in Dhofar.
1999 During the Persian Gulf War, Omani military forces took part in the allied ground campaign that liberated Kuwait from Iraqi control.

Pakistan in brief

General information

Capital: Islamabad.
Official name: The Islamic Republic of Pakistan.
Official language: Urdu.
Largest city: Karachi (pop. 5,208,170).
Country flag: Pakistan's flag has a star and crescent, tradi-
tional symbols of Islam. Green stands for the nation's Mus-
lim majority.

Land and climate

Land: Pakistan lies in southern Asia. Mountains cover much
of the northern and western parts of the country. The Pun-
jab and Sind plains occupy most of eastern Pakistan. The
Indus River flows to the Arabian Sea through both of the
plains. The dry and rocky Baluchistan Plateau is in southwestern Pakistan. The Thar Desert is located in southeastern Pakistan and extends into northwestern India. Much of
the desert is a sandy wasteland.
Area: 307,374 mi² (796,095 km²). *Greatest distances*—north-
south, 935 mi (1,505 km); east-west, 800 mi (1,287 km).
Coastline—506 mi (814 km).
Elevation: *Highest*—K2 (in Kashmir), 28,250 ft (8,611 m) above
sea level. *Lowest*—sea level.

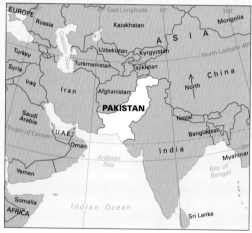

WORLD BOOK map

Climate: Most of Pakistan has a dry climate, with hot summers and cool winters. Pakistan averages only about 10
inches (25 centimeters) of rain a year. But the amount of
rainfall varies greatly from year to year. Long dry spells
may be broken by severe rainstorms that cause rivers to
overflow and flood the countryside. In general, most of
the rain falls from July to September, when the seasonal
wind called the *monsoon* blows across Pakistan.

Government

Form of government: Federal republic.
Head of state: President.
Head of government: Prime minister.
Legislature: Parliamentary elections were scheduled for Oc-
tober 2002. Parliament was to consist of the Senate (100
members) and the National Assembly (357 members).
Executive: The president and prime minister each have
some executive powers .
Judiciary: The highest court is the Supreme Court.
Political subdivisions: Four provinces and the Capital Terri-
tory of Islamabad.
Suffrage: All citizens 18 years of age or older may vote.
Armed forces: About 620,000 people serve in Pakistan's
army, navy, and air force.

People

Population: *Estimated 2002 population*—144,135,000. *1998
census*—130,579,571.
Population density: 469 per mi² (181 per km²).
Distribution: 67 percent rural, 33 percent urban.
Life expectancy: *Male*—58. *Female*—59.
Major ethnic groups: Punjabis make up the largest cultural
group. Other groups include the Muhajirs, the Sindhis,
the Pashtuns (also called Pakhtuns), and the Baluchi.
Major religions: About 77 percent of Pakistan's people are
Sunni Muslims, and about 20 percent are Shiite Muslims.
People of other religions in Pakistan include Christians,
Hindus, Buddhists, and Parsis.
Literacy rate: About 38 percent of Pakistan's adult popula-
tion can read and write.

Economy

Chief products: *Agriculture*—wheat, cotton, rice, sugar
cane, milk, chickpeas. *Manufacturing*—cotton textiles and
clothing, food products, fertilizer, steel, cement. *Mining*—
natural gas, petroleum.
Money: *Basic unit*—Pakistani rupee. One hundred paisas
equal one rupee.
International trade: *Major exports*—textiles, clothing, cotton, rice, leather goods, and carpets. *Major imports*—petroleum products, machinery, transportation equipment,
iron and steel, food products, electrical equipment, and
chemicals. *Major trading partners*—Germany, Japan, Saudi
Arabia, United Kingdom, United States.

Important dates in Pakistan

1947 Pakistan gained independence from the United Kingdom on August 14, the day before India became independent.
1947-1949 Pakistan and India fought over Kashmir.
1960's Military leaders controlled the Pakistani government.
1965 Pakistan and India fought another war over Kashmir.
1971 East Pakistan and West Pakistan fought a war against
each other. India sent troops in support of East Pakistan.
West Pakistan was defeated, and East Pakistan became the
independent nation of Bangladesh.
1973 Pakistan adopted a new constitution.
1977 General Zia-ul-Haq ousted Prime Minister Zulfikar Ali
Bhutto from office and declared martial law.
1988 Zia died in a plane crash.
1998 Pakistan responded to nuclear tests by India by conducting its own nuclear tests.
1999 General Pervez Musharraf led a military coup that overthrew the government of Prime Minister Nawaz Sharif.
2001 U.S. forces, with Musharraf's permission, began using
Pakistani military bases and flying over Pakistani territory
in a military campaign against terrorists in Afghanistan.

Qatar in brief

General information

Capital: Doha, also called Ad Dawhah.
Official name: Dawlat Qatar (State of Qatar).
Official language: Arabic.
Largest city: Doha (pop. 217,294).
Country flag: Qatar's flag was adopted in 1971. The left third of the nation's flag is white with a vertical series of points on the right side. The right two-thirds of the flag is maroon.

Land and climate

Land: Qatar lies in southwestern Asia. It occupies a peninsula that juts from eastern Arabia into the Persian Gulf. Most of Qatar's land is stony desert. Barren salt flats cover the southern part of the country.
Area: 4,247 mi² (11,000 km²). *Greatest distances*—north-south, 115 mi (185 km); east-west, 55 mi (89 km). *Coastline*—235 mi (378 km).
Elevation: *Highest*—Qurayn Abu al Bawl, 338 ft (103 m) above sea level. *Lowest*—sea level along the coast.

WORLD BOOK map

Climate: Summer temperatures sometimes rise above 120 °F (49 °C), but the winter is cooler. Qatar seldom gets more than 4 inches (10 centimeters) of rain a year.

Government

Form of government: Monarchy.
Head of state: Emir.
Head of government: Prime minister appointed by the emir.
Legislature: Council of Ministers with 18 members appointed by the emir and Advisory Council with 35 members appointed by the emir. Both bodies are advisory only. Neither has true legislative power.
Executive: Council of Ministers appointed by the emir.
Judiciary: The highest court is the Court of Appeal.
Political subdivisions: Nine municipalities.
Suffrage: Limited to municipal elections.
Armed forces: About 12,300 people serve in Qatar's army, navy, and air force.

People

Population: *Estimated 2002 population*—617,000. *1997 census*—520,500.
Population density: 145 per mi² (56 per km²).
Distribution: 91 percent urban, 8 percent rural.
Life expectancy: *Male*—70. *Female*—75.
Major ethnic groups: About 40 percent of Qatar's people are Arabs; about 18 percent are Pakistanis; about 18 percent are Indians; and about 10 percent are Iranians.
Major religions: About 95 percent of the people are Muslims.
Literacy rate: About 81 percent of Qatar's adult population can read and write.

Economy

Chief products: Petroleum and petroleum products.
Money: *Basic unit*—Qatar riyal. One hundred dirhams equal one riyal.
International trade: *Major exports*—petroleum and petroleum products. *Major imports*—chemicals, food, machinery and transportation equipment. *Major trading partners*—Italy, Japan, United Arab Emirates, United Kingdom, United States.

Important dates in Qatar

Late 1700's The Wahhabis, an Islamic sect from Saudi Arabia, took control of what is now Qatar.
Mid-1800's Sheiks of the al-Thani family became the leaders of Qatar's tribes.
Late 1800's The Ottomans added Qatar to their empire.
1916 Qatar became a British protectorate.
1939 Oil was found in western Qatar.
1971 Qatar became an independent nation.
1972 Khalifa bin Hamad al-Thani, the deputy ruler, became emir after peacefully overthrowing his cousin, Emir Ahmad bin Ali al-Thani.
Mid-1970's The government took ownership of Qatar's petroleum industry.
1991 Qatar took part in the bombing of Iraqi military targets and in the ground offensive to liberate Kuwait during the Persian Gulf War.
1995 Hamad bin Khalifa al-Thani peacefully overthrew his father, Khalifa bin Hamid al-Thani, to become emir.
1999 Municipal elections were held in which all men and women were allowed to vote. The emir formed a committee to draft a permanent constitution.

Saudi Arabia in brief

General information
Capital: Riyadh.
Official name: Al-Mamlaka Al-Arabiyya Al-Saudiyya (Kingdom of Saudi Arabia).
Official language: Arabic.
Largest city: Riyadh (pop. 2,776,096).
Country flag: The flag of Saudi Arabia was adopted in 1973. It includes a picture of a sword and the Muslim declaration of faith—"There is no God but Allah; Muhammad is the Messenger of Allah"—written in Arabic. Green is the traditional color of Islam.

Land and climate
Land: Saudi Arabia covers most of the Arabian Peninsula. The landscape is mainly barren. Coastal plains and mountains cover the western part of the country. Most of Saudi Arabia's central area is a high plateau. Deserts hem in the plateau to the north, south, and east.
Area: 830,000 mi² (2,149,690 km²). *Greatest distances*—north-south, 1,145 mi (1,843 km); east-west, 1,290 mi (2,076 km). *Coastline*—1,174 mi (1,889 km) on the Red Sea; 341 mi (549 km) on the Persian Gulf.
Elevation: *Highest*—10,279 ft (3,133 m) above sea level, in the Asir region in the southwest. *Lowest*—sea level.

WORLD BOOK map

Climate: Most of Saudi Arabia has a hot climate the year around. The coastal regions are hot and humid during the long summers, when the average daytime temperature is over 90 °F (32 °C). Summer temperatures in the central and desert regions may reach 120 °F (49 °C). But these areas have drier air and cool nights. Winter temperatures in parts of central, northern, and western Saudi Arabia occasionally dip below freezing.

Government
Form of government: Monarchy.
Head of state: King.
Head of government: King.
Legislature: Consultative Council with a chairman and 90 other members, all appointed by the king.
Executive: Council of Ministers appointed by the king.
Judiciary: The highest court is the Supreme Court of Justice.
Political subdivisions: 13 provinces.
Suffrage: None.
Armed forces: About 126,500 people serve in Saudi Arabia's army, navy, air force, and air defense forces.

People
Population: *Estimated 2002 population*—22,910,000. *1992 census*—16,929,294.
Population density: 28 per mi² (11 per km²).
Distribution: 83 percent urban, 17 percent rural.
Life expectancy: *Male*—68. *Female*—71.
Major ethnic groups: About 90 percent of the people are Arabs. Smaller groups include descendants of African, Indonesian, and Indian Muslims who originally came as pilgrims.
Major religions: All Saudis are Muslims. Most belong to the Sunni branch of Islam. The only non-Muslims in Saudi Arabia are foreigners.
Literacy rate: About 71 percent of Saudi Arabia's adult population can read and write.

Economy
Chief products: *Agriculture*—barley, dates, millet, sorghum, tomatoes, wheat. *Manufacturing*—cement, fertilizer, food products, petrochemicals, steel. *Mining*—petroleum.
Money: *Basic unit*—riyal. One hundred halalas equal one riyal.
International trade: *Major exports*—Petroleum, chemicals, plastics, processed foods. *Major imports*—automobiles, chemicals, electrical equipment and appliances, food products, machinery, military equipment, textiles. *Major trading partners*—Japan, United Kingdom, United States.

Important dates in Saudi Arabia

c. 570 Muhammad, prophet of Islam, was born in Mecca.
c. 1500 The Saud family established control over a small area around Dariyah, near present-day Riyadh.
1500's The Ottoman Empire gained control over the region of Hejaz in northwestern Saudi Arabia and parts of the region of Asir in the southwest.
Mid-1700's The Wahhabi movement, which urged strict observance of Islamic laws, spread across most of Arabia. The Saud family supported and helped spread the movement and took over a large part of the Arabian Peninsula.
1891 Tribal leaders and the Ottomans gained control of most of Arabia. Members of the Saud family fled in exile.
1902-1932 Abd al-Aziz ibn Saud, an exiled Saudi leader, conquered the Najd, Hasa, Asir, and Hejaz regions and formed the Kingdom of Saudi Arabia.
1933 The Saudi petroleum industry began.
1967 Saudi Arabia supported Egypt, Jordan, and Syria in the Six-Day War against Israel.
1973 Saudi Arabia stopped or reduced oil shipments to some Western nations after another Arab-Israeli war broke out.
1975 Faisal, king of Saudi Arabia since 1964, was assassinated. He was succeeded by his half brother Prince Khalid.
1982 Khalid died and was succeeded by his half brother Prince Fahd.
1991 Saudi Arabia and a coalition of other nations defeated Iraq in the Persian Gulf War.

Somalia in brief

General information

Capital: Mogadishu.
Official name: Somali Democratic Republic.
Official language: Somali.
Largest city: Mogadishu (pop. 750,000).
Country flag: Somalia has a light blue flag with a large white star in the center. The colors come from the United Nations flag.

Land and climate

Land: Somalia is the easternmost country on the mainland of Africa. Dry, grassy plains cover almost all of the country. A mountain ridge rises behind a narrow coastal plain in the north. Altitudes in some parts of northern Somalia reach over 7,000 feet (2,100 meters) above sea level. The central and southern areas of Somalia are flat and have an average altitude of less than 600 feet (180 meters) above sea level.
Area: 246,201 mi² (637,657 km²). *Greatest distances*—north-south, 950 mi (1,529 km); east-west, 730 mi (1,175 km). *Coastline*—1,800 mi (2,408 km).
Elevation: *Highest*—Mount Surud Ad, 7,900 ft (2,408 m) above sea level. *Lowest*—sea level along the coast.

WORLD BOOK map

Climate: The average temperature ranges from 85 F to 105 °F (29 to 41 °C) in the north, and from 65 to 105 °F (18 to 41 °C) in the south. Average annual rainfall is about 11 inches (28 centimeters). Total rainfall is rarely more than 20 inches (51 centimeters) a year, even in the south, which is the wettest region. Parts of northern Somalia receive only 2 to 3 inches (5 to 8 centimeters) of rain a year. In general, rain falls during two seasons—from March to May and from October to December. Droughts occur frequently.

Government

Form of government: Transitional.
Head of state: Interim president.
Head of government: Prime minister.
Legislature: Transitional National Assembly with 245 members.
Executive: Cabinet appointed by the prime minister.
Judiciary: Most regions have courts that follow the Shari`a—that is, Islamic law.
Political subdivisions: 18 regions.
Suffrage: All Somalis 18 years of age or older may vote.
Armed forces: The transitional government is creating a Somali National Army.

People

Population: *Estimated 2002 population*—10,837,000. *1986 census*—7,114,431.
Population density: 44 per mi² (17 per km²).
Distribution: 76 percent rural, 24 percent urban.
Life expectancy: *Male*—45. *Female*—48.
Major ethnic groups: About 95 percent of the people are ethnic Somalis who share the same language and culture. However, they are sharply divided according to traditional clan groupings.
Major religions: Almost all of Somalia's people are Sunni Muslims.
Literacy rate: About 24 percent of Somalia's adult population can read and write.

Economy

Chief products: *Agriculture*—bananas, grains, hides and skins, livestock, sugar cane. *Manufacturing*—processed foods, sugar.
Money: *Basic unit*—Somali shilling. One hundred cents equal one shilling.
International trade: *Major exports*—animal hides and skins, bananas, camels, goats, mangoes, papayas, sheep. *Major imports*—food, petroleum, textiles. *Major trading partners*—Brazil, Djibouti, Kenya.

Important dates in Somalia

Mid-1880's The British took over much of northern Somalia, which became British Somaliland.
1880's-1890's The Italians gained control of most of the Indian Ocean coast of Somalia. They eventually established the colony of Italian Somaliland.
Early 1900's Somali nationalists led by Sayyid Muhammad Abdille Hassan fought against British, Italian, and Ethiopian forces.
1936 Italian Somaliland became part of the Italian East African Empire.
1960 The United Kingdom and Italy granted their Somali territories independence. The two territories united to form the independent state of Somalia on July 1.
1969 Military officers led by Major General Mohamed Siad Barre seized control of the government.
1991 A rebel group called the United Somali Congress overthrew Somalia's military regime.
1992 The United Nations (UN) sent a coalition of military forces led by the United States to provide security for relief organizations that were trying to distribute food to drought-stricken areas of Somalia.
1993 Fighting broke out between UN troops, including U.S. forces, and the forces of Mohammed Farah Aidid, a powerful leader of one of Somalia's clans.
1994 U.S. forces withdrew from Somalia.
1995 The UN's remaining forces left Somalia.
2000 A Transitional National Assembly elected an interim government for Somalia.

Sudan in brief

General information

Capital: Khartoum.
Official name: Jumhuriyat as-Sudan (Republic of the Sudan).
Official language: Arabic.
National anthem: "Jundi al-Allah" ("Soldiers of God").
Largest city: Omdurman (pop. 526,827).
Country flag: Sudan's flag was adopted in 1970. It has three horizontal stripes of red, white, and black, with a green triangle symbolizing Islam.

Land and climate

Land: Sudan lies in northern Africa and covers a larger area than any other African country. Sudan's most important geographic feature is the Nile River. The river is called the Bahr al Jabal in southern Sudan. It floods the flatland of the south to form a vast swamp called the Sudd. North of the Sudd, the river is called the White Nile. It meets the Blue Nile at Khartoum. Together, the rivers form the main Nile River. North of Khartoum, Sudan is mainly desert.
Area: 967,500 mi² (2,505,813 km²). *Greatest distances*—north-south, 1,275 mi (2,050 km); east-west, 1,150 mi. (1,850 km). *Coastline*—400 mi (644 km).
Elevation: *Highest*—Mount Kinyeti, 10,456 ft (3,187 m) above sea level. *Lowest*—sea level.

WORLD BOOK map

Climate: Rainfall rarely amounts to more than 4 inches (10 centimeters) a year in the northern desert of Sudan. Average summer high temperatures reach 110 °F (43 °C), but the temperature can climb to more than 125 °F (52 °C). Average winter lows drop to about 60 °F (16 °C). Rainfall in southern Sudan varies from 4 to 32 inches (10 to 81 centimeters) per year. Average temperatures range from 74 °F (23 °C) in January to 89 °F (32 °C) in July.

Government

Form of government: Republic.
Head of state and head of government: President elected to a five-year term..
Legislature: National Assembly of 360 members elected to four-year terms.
Executive: Cabinet appointed by the president.
Judiciary: The highest court is the Supreme Court.
Political subdivisions: 26 states.
Suffrage: All Sudanese 17 years of age or older may vote.
Armed forces: About 117,000 people serve in Sudan's army, navy, and air force.

People

Population: *Estimated 2002 population*—30,742,000. *1993 census*—24,940,683.
Population density: 32 per mi² (12 per km²).
Distribution: 73 percent rural, 27 percent urban.
Life expectancy: *Male*—50. *Female*—52.
Major ethnic groups: About 50 percent of Sudan's people consider themselves Arabs. Most Arabs live in the northern two-thirds of the country. Various black African groups live in the southern third of Sudan. These groups include the Dinka, the largest black African group; the Nuer; the Shilluk; and the Azande.
Major religions: Nearly three-fourths of Sudan's people are Sunni Muslims. Most live in northern and central Sudan. Most people in the south of Sudan practice traditional African religions. About 5 percent of all Sudanese, nearly all southerners, are Christians.
Literacy rate: About 51 percent of Sudan's adult population can read and write.

Economy

Chief products: *Agriculture*—cotton, millet, peanuts, sesame, sorghum, sugar cane. *Forest industry*—gum arabic. *Manufacturing and processing*—cement, fertilizer, food products, shoes, textiles. *Mining*—chromium, gold, gypsum, petroleum.
Money: *Basic unit*—dinar and Sudanese pound.
International trade: *Major exports*—cotton, gum arabic, live animals, peanuts, sesame, sorghum. *Major imports*—petroleum, heavy machinery. *Major trading partners*—France, Germany, Japan, Saudi Arabia, United Kingdom.

Important dates in Sudan

c. 1000 B.C. A kingdom called Kush developed in what is now northern Sudan.
c. A.D. 350 Kush ceased to be an independent state.
600's-1500's Northern Sudan came under Muslim control.
1821 Egypt conquered the Funj, who ruled much of Sudan.
1881-1885 A Sudanese Muslim religious teacher named Muhammad Ahmed, who had proclaimed himself the *Mahdi* (divinely appointed guide), led a successful revolt against the Egyptians.
1898 British and Egyptian forces defeated the Sudanese at the Battle of Omdurman.
1956 Sudan became an independent nation.
1983 Gaafor Nimeiri, the head of the Sudanese government, established Islamic law throughout Sudan and ended a regional government in the south. Fighting broke out between government forces and southerners.
1989 Brigadier General Umar Hasan Ahmad al-Bashir took control of the government.
1996 Al-Bashir was elected president.
2000 Al-Bashir was reelected president..
2002 The southern rebels and the government agreed to a framework for talks to end the civil war.

Syria in brief

General information

Capital: Damascus.

Official name: Al-Jumhuria Al-Arabia Al-Suria (The Syrian Arab Republic).

Official language: Arabic.

National anthem: "Homat El Diyar" ("Guardians of the Homeland").

Largest city: Aleppo (1,583,000).

Country flag: Syria's flag, which was adopted in 1980, bears traditional Arab colors. Two green stars appear on the flag.

Land and climate

Land: Syria lies at the eastern end of the Mediterranean Sea. Its coast extends along the Mediterranean from Turkey to Lebanon. Most of the land along the coast is cultivated. The Jabal an Nusayriyah range stands east of the coast, and the Anti-Lebanon Mountains stretch along the border with Lebanon. Both ranges run from north to south. River valleys, plains, and deserts lie east of the mountains. Major waterways include the Orontes and Euphrates rivers.

Area: 71,498 mi² (185,180 km²). *Greatest distances*—east-west, 515 mi (829 km); north-south, 465 mi (748 km). *Coastline*—94 mi. (151 km).

Elevation: *Highest*—Mount Hermon, 9,232 ft (2,814 m) above sea level. *Lowest*—sea level along the coast.

WORLD BOOK map

Climate: Temperatures along the coast average about 48 °F (9 °C) in January and about 81 °F (27 °C) in July. About 40 inches (100 centimeters) of rain falls in the region yearly. The western slopes of the mountains receive up to 40 inches (100 centimeters) of rain yearly, but the land to the east remains dry. Temperatures average about 41 °F (5 °C) in January and about 72 °F (22 °C) in July. Little rain falls in valleys and plains region. Temperatures there average about 41 °F (5 °C) in January and about 88 °F (31 °C) in July.

Government

Form of government: Republic.

Head of state: President elected by the people to a seven-year term.

Head of government: Prime minister appointed by the president.

Legislature: Peoples Council with 250 members elected by the people to four-year terms.

Executive: Council of Ministers appointed by the president.

Judiciary: The highest court is the Court of Cassation.

Political subdivisions: 13 provinces and the city of Damascus.

Suffrage: All Syrians 18 years of age or older may vote.

Armed forces: About 420,000 people serve in Syria's army, navy, air force, and air defense command.

People

Population: *Estimated 2002 population*—16,928,000. *1994 census*—13,812,000.

Population density: 237 per mi² (91 per km²).

Distribution: 51 percent urban, 49 percent rural.

Life expectancy: *Male*—67. *Female*—68.

Major ethnic groups: About 90 percent of the people are Arabs. Smaller groups include Armenians and Kurds.

Major religions: About 74 percent of Syria's people are Sunni Muslims; about 16 percent are Alawite, Druse, and Shiite Muslims; about 10 percent are Christians. Syria also has a small number of Jews.

Literacy rate: About 80 percent of Syria's adult population can read and write.

Economy

Chief products: *Agriculture*—cotton, wheat, barley, milk, grapes, sugar beets. *Manufacturing*—textiles, fertilizer, petroleum products, cement, glass, processed foods. *Mining*—petroleum, phosphates.

Money: *Basic unit*—pound. One hundred piastres equal one pound.

International trade: *Major exports*—petroleum, raw cotton, woolens and other textiles. *Major imports*—fuels, grain, machinery, metals and metal products, motor vehicles. *Major trading partners*—France, Germany, Italy, Lebanon, Saudi Arabia, Turkey, United Kingdom, United States.

Important dates in Syria

331 B.C. Alexander the Great gained control of Syria.

64 B.C. Syria fell to the Romans.

A.D. 636 Muslim Arabs defeated Byzantine forces to gain control of Syria.

1516 The Ottomans added Syria to their empire.

1914-1918 Syrians and other Arabs revolted against Ottoman rule during World War I.

1920 France occupied Syria under a League of Nations mandate.

1946 Syria gained complete independence from France.

1948 Syrian and other Arab troops went to war with Israel. The United Nations (UN) eventually arranged a cease-fire.

1967 Israel defeated Syria, Egypt, and Jordan in a brief war, and Israel occupied Syria's Golan Heights.

1973 Syria and Egypt led an Arab war with Israel. Cease-fires ended the fighting.

1976 Syria sent troops into Lebanon in an effort to stop a civil war there.

1981 Israel claimed legal and political authority in the Golan Heights. Syria and many other nations denounced this action.

1991 Syrian troops helped end the Iraqi occupation of Kuwait.

Tajikistan in brief

General information

Capital: Dushanbe.
Official name: Jumhurii Tojikiston (Republic of Tajikistan).
Official language: Tajik.
Largest city: Dushanbe (pop. 595,000).
Country flag: The flag of Tajikistan has horizontal stripes of reddish-orange, white, and green. An emblem lies in the center of the middle white stripe. It consists of an arc of seven yellow, five-pointed stars over a yellow figure resembling a crown.

Land and climate

Land: Tajikistan lies in central Asia. Over 90 percent of Tajikistan is mountainous, and over half lies above 10,000 feet (3,050 meters). The Pamirs rise in the southeast. The Alay and Tian Shan mountain ranges stretch across much of the rest of the country. The Amu Darya, a major river of central Asia, flows along part of Tajikistan's southern border. Earthquakes often occur throughout the region.
Area: 55,251 mi² (143,100 km²). *Greatest distances*—north-south, 300 mi (485 km); east-west, 425 mi (685 km).
Elevation: *Highest*—Communism Peak, 24,590 ft (7,495 m) above sea level. *Lowest*—Syr Darya river at northwestern border, 980 ft (300 m) above sea level.

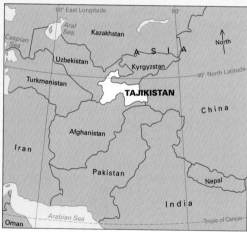

WORLD BOOK map

Climate: Summers in the valleys are typically long and hot. Winters in the highlands are long and cold. Valley temperatures average 36 °F (2 °C) in January and 86 °F (30 °C) in July. Highlands temperatures average -4 °F (-20 °C) in January and 72 °F (22 °C) in July. In parts of the eastern Pamirs, temperatures can drop to -58 °F (-50 °C). Tajikistan receives annual rainfall of less than 8 inches (20 centimeters).

Government

Form of government: Republic.
Head of state: President elected by the people to a seven-year term.
Head of government: Prime minister appointed by the president.
Legislature: Supreme Assembly consisting of two houses—Assembly of Representatives (63 members elected by the people to five-year terms) and National Assembly (25 members selected by local deputies and appointed by the president to five year terms).
Executive: Council of Ministers appointed by the president.
Judiciary: The highest court is the Supreme Court.
Political subdivisions: Two oblasts and one autonomous oblast.
Suffrage: All Tajikistanis 18 years of age or older may vote.
Armed forces: About 6,000 people serve in Tajikistan's army.

People

Population: *Estimated 2002 population*—6,347,000. *1989 census*—5,108,576.
Population density: 115 per mi² (44 per km²).
Distribution: 73 percent rural, 27 percent urban.
Life expectancy: *Male*—66. *Female*—71.
Major ethnic groups: About 62 percent of the people are ethnic Tajiks. Uzbeks make up about 24 percent of the population. Russians make up about 7 percent. Other ethnic groups include Tatars, Kyrgyz, Kazaks, and Turkmen.
Major religions: About 80 percent of the people are Sunni Muslims, and about 5 percent are Shiite Muslims.
Literacy rate: About 98 percent of Tajikistan's adult population can read and write.

Economy

Chief products: *Agriculture*—cotton, fruit, grain, livestock, vegetables. *Manufacturing*—food processing, textiles, wine. *Mining*—antimony, coal, fluorite, lead, molybdenum, natural gas, petroleum, salt, tungsten, uranium, zinc.
Money: *Basic unit*—somoni.
International trade: *Major exports*—aluminum, cotton, electric power. *Major imports*—aluminum oxide, electric power, food, petroleum products. *Major trading partners*—Iran, Kazakhstan, Russia, Ukraine, Uzbekistan.

Important dates in Tajikistan

331 B.C. Alexander the Great gained control of what is now Tajikistan.
A.D. 600's Arab armies swept into the region and introduced Islam.
1200's Mongols led by Genghis Khan conquered the region.
1500's-1800's Turkic tribes called Uzbeks ruled the region.
Late 1800's Russian forces conquered part of the region.
1924 The Tajik Autonomous Soviet Socialist Republic was formed within the Soviet Union's Uzbek Soviet Socialist Republic.
1929 The Tajik Autonomous Soviet Socialist Republic became the Tajik Soviet Socialist Republic.
1989 Tajik replaced Russian as the official language of the republic.
1990 Tajikistan declared that its laws overruled those of the Soviet central government.
1991 Tajikistan became independent.
1992 Civil war broke out in Tajikistan.
1994 Tajikistan adopted a new constitution.
1997 The government and opposition leaders signed a peace treaty to end the civil war.

Turkey in brief

General information

Capital: Ankara.
Official name: Turkiye Cumhuriyeti (Republic of Turkey).
Official language: Turkish.
National anthem: "Istiklal Marsi" ("Independence March").
Largest city: Istanbul (pop. 6,620,600).
Country flag: Turkey's flag was adopted in 1936. The crescent and five-pointed star are traditional symbols of the Islamic faith.

Land and climate

Land: Turkey lies in both Europe and Asia. Part of Turkey lies in Thrace, at the eastern edge of southern Europe. To the east, the rest of Turkey covers a large peninsula called Anatolia or Asia Minor. The Bosporus, the Sea of Marmara, and the Dardanelles separate Anatolia from Thrace. The Black Sea lies to the north of Turkey, the Aegean Sea to the west, and the Mediterranean Sea to the south. Much of the country is rocky, barren, and mountainous.
Area: 299,158 mi² (774,815 km²). *Greatest distances*—east-west, 1,015 mi (1,633 km); north-south, 465 mi (748 km). *Coastline*—2,211 mi (3,558 km).
Elevation: *Highest*—Mount Ararat, 16,849 ft (5,137 m) above sea level. *Lowest*—sea level along the coast.

WORLD BOOK map

Climate: The climate differs from one region of Turkey to another. The south and west coasts of Anatolia have mild, rainy winters and hot, dry summers. The Black Sea coast has cooler summers and receives more rainfall than the Aegean and Mediterranean coasts do. Northeastern Turkey has mild summers but bitterly cold winters. Southeastern Turkey and the interior of Anatolia have cold winters with heavy snowstorms. Summers are hot, windy, and extremely dry.

Government

Form of government: Republic.
Head of state: President elected by the Grand National Assembly to a seven-year term.
Head of government: Prime minister selected by the president.
Legislature: Grand National Assembly with 550 members elected by the voters to five-year terms.
Executive: Cabinet.
Judiciary: The highest courts are the Court of Cassation and the Constitutional Court.
Political subdivisions: 76 provinces.
Suffrage: All Turks 18 years of age or older may vote.
Armed forces: About 610,000 men serve in Turkey's army, navy, and air force.

People

Population: *Estimated 2002 population*—68,509,000. *1990 census*—56,473,035.
Population density: 229 per mi² (88 per km²).
Distribution: 66 percent urban, 34 percent rural.
Life expectancy: *Male*—67. *Female*—71.
Major ethnic groups: More than 80 percent of Turkey's people consider themselves descendants of a people called Turks. Kurds form Turkey's largest minority group.
Major religions: More than 98 percent of the Turkish people are Muslims. Some people are Armenian Apostolic and Eastern Orthodox Christians, Roman and Eastern Catholics, and Jews.
Literacy rate: About 82 percent of Turkey's adult population can read and write.

Economy

Chief products: *Agriculture*—barley, corn, cotton, fruits, potatoes, sugar beets, wheat. *Manufacturing*—iron and steel, machinery, motor vehicles, processed foods and beverages, pulp and paper products, textiles and clothing.
Money: *Basic unit*—lira. One hundred kurus equal one lira.
International trade: *Major exports*—clothing and textiles, iron and steel, other manufactured goods. *Major imports*—chemicals, machinery, iron and steel, motor vehicles, petroleum. *Major trading partners*—Germany, France, Italy, Russia, United Kingdom, United States.

Important dates in Turkey

1500 B.C. The Hittites ruled in Anatolia.
63 B.C. The Roman general Pompey conquered Anatolia.
A.D. 330 Constantine the Great moved the capital of the Roman Empire to Byzantium and renamed the town Constantinople (now Istanbul).
1071 The Seljuk Turks conquered most of Anatolia by defeating the Byzantine forces in the Battle of Manzikert.
1326 The Ottoman Turks captured Bursa, which marked the beginning of the Ottoman Empire.
1453 The Ottomans captured Constantinople, ending the Byzantine Empire.
1783-1914 The Ottoman Empire lost much of its territory.
1908 The Young Turks revolted against the government.
1914-1918 In World War I, the Ottoman Empire allied with Germany and lost much of its remaining territory.
1923 Mustafa Kemal (Atatürk) set up the Republic of Turkey and began a program to modernize the nation.
1960 Turkish army units overthrew the government and ruled until free elections were held in 1961.
1974 Turkish forces invaded Cyprus.
1980-1983 Army units again controlled the government.
1999 Turkish intelligence agents arrested Kurdish guerrilla leader Abdullah Ocalan. Kurdish guerrillas have battled the Turkish government since the mid-1980's.

Turkmenistan in brief

General information

Capital: Ashgabat.
Official name: Turkmenistan.
Official language: Turkmen.
Largest city: Ashgabat (pop. 407,000).
Country flag: The flag of Turkmenistan has three unequal vertical stripes of green, maroon, and green. On the maroon stripe are five traditional carpet patterns in black, white, maroon, and orange. To the upper right of the maroon stripe are five white stars and a white crescent.

Land and climate

Land: The Karakum desert covers more than 80 percent of Turkmenistan. The Kopet-Dag mountains stretch along the south and southwest of the country. The Amu Darya river flows through eastern Turkmenistan into Uzbekistan. The most heavily settled regions are the valleys of the Amu Darya, Murgab, and Tedzhen rivers, and the foothills of the Kopet-Dag mountains.
Area: 188,456 mi² (488,100 km²). *Greatest distances*—east-west, 750 mi (1,205 km); north-south, 525 mi (845 km).
Elevation: *Highest*—Kugitangtau (mountain range), 10,292 ft (3,137 m) above sea level. *Lowest*—Garabogazkol Gulf, 102 ft (31 m) below sea level.

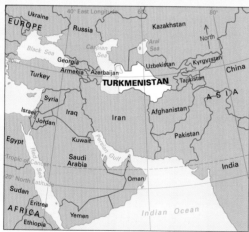

WORLD BOOK map

Climate: Summers in Turkmenistan are long, hot, and dry. Winters are cold. Desert temperatures range from about 95 to 122 °F (35 to 50 °C) in summer. Winter temperatures in the desert can drop below 32 °F (0 °C). Turkmenistan receives about 3 to 12 inches (8 to 30 centimeters) of rainfall annually.

Government

Form of government: Republic.
Head of state and head of government: President. According to the constitution, voters elect a president to a five-year term. However, the Turkmenistan legislature has granted the office for life to Saparmurad A. Niyazov.
Legislature: Majlis with 50 members elected by the voters to five-year terms.
Executive: Cabinet of Ministers appointed by the president.
Judiciary: The highest court is the Supreme Court.
Political subdivisions: Five regions.
Suffrage: All citizens 18 years of age or older may vote.
Armed forces: About 17,500 people serve in Turkmenistan's army and air force.

People

Population: *Estimated 2002 population*—4,605,000. *1995 census*—4,483,251.
Population density: 24 per mi² (9 per km²).
Distribution: 56 percent rural, 44 percent urban.
Life expectancy: *Male*—62. *Female*—69.
Major ethnic groups: About 70 percent of Turkmenistan's people are ethnic Turkmen, and about 10 percent are Russians. Other ethnic groups include Uzbeks, Kazakhs, Tatars, Ukrainians, and Armenians.
Major religions: Most Turkmen are Sunni Muslims. Other religious groups include Shiite Muslims and Russian Orthodox Christians. Although most Muslims worship in mosques, Turkmen follow a special Muslim practice of worshiping primarily at tombs of holy men.
Literacy rate: About 98 percent of Turkmenistan's adult population can read and write.

Economy

Chief products: *Agriculture*—camels, cotton, grains, grapes, horses, pigs, potatoes, sheep. *Manufacturing*—cement, chemicals, glass, textiles. *Mining*—bromine, copper, gold, iodine, lead, mercury, natural gas, petroleum, salt, sodium sulfate, zinc.
Money: *Basic unit*—manat. One hundred tenge equal one manat.
International trade: *Major exports*—cotton, natural gas, petroleum, textiles. *Major imports*—food products, machinery. *Major trading partners*—Germany, Russia, Turkey, Ukraine, United States.

Important dates in Turkmenistan

250 B.C.-A.D. 224 The kingdom of Parthia controlled the region.
c. 900's-early 1200's Turkic tribes ruled the region.
Early 1200's Mongols led by Genghis Khan invaded the region.
c. 1300's Islamic missionaries called *sufis* established Islam in the region.
Late 1300's Mongol conqueror Timur made the region part of his empire.
1400's-1600's The Safavids, a Persian dynasty, controlled the southern part of what is now Turkmenistan.
1600's Tribes from whom the Turkmen of today are descended began moving into the region.
1800's An alliance of Turkic tribes called the Tekke Confederation gained control of the area.
Late 1800's All Turkmen lands came under Russian control.
1924 Turkmenistan became a republic of the Soviet Union.
1990 Turkmenistan declared that its laws overruled those of the Soviet central government.
1991 Turkmenistan became independent.

United Arab Emirates in brief

General information

Capital: Abu Dhabi.
Official name: Al Imarat al Arabiyah al Muttahidah (United Arab Emirates).
Official language: Arabic.
Largest city: Dubayy, also spelled Dubai (pop. 669,181).
Country flag: The flag of the United Arab Emirates has a vertical reddish-orange stripe and horizontal stripes of green, white, and black. It was adopted in 1971.

Land and climate

Land: The United Arab Emirates (UAE) is a federation of seven Arab states in southwestern Asia. These states lie along the eastern coast of the Arabian Peninsula at the south end of the Persian Gulf. Swamps and salt marshes line much of the northern coast of the UAE. A desert occupies most of the inland area. Hills and mountains cover much of the eastern part of the UAE.
Area: 32,278 mi² (83,600 km²). *Greatest distances*—north-south, 250 mi (402 km); east-west, 350 mi (563 km). *Coast-line*—483 mi (777 km).
Elevation: *Highest*—Jabal Yibir, 5,010 ft (1,527 m) above sea level. *Lowest*—Salamiyah, a salt flat slightly below sea level.

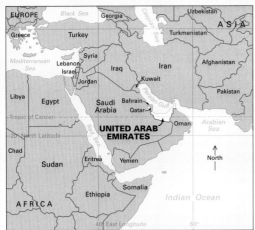

WORLD BOOK map

Climate: The United Arab Emirates has a hot climate. The humidity is often high along the coast, but the inland desert regions are dry. The mountainous areas are generally cooler. Summer temperatures in the UAE average over 90 °F (32 °C) and often reach 120 °F (49 °C). In winter, temperatures seldom drop below 60 °F (16 °C). The UAE receives an average of less than 5 inches (13 centimeters) of rain a year.

Government

Form of government: Federation of seven emirates.
Head of state: President appointed by the Supreme Council of the UAE. The Supreme Council consists of the seven emirs from the member states.
Head of government: Prime minister appointed by the Supreme Council.
Legislature: Federal National Council with 40 members appointed by the emirs to two-year terms.
Executive: Council of Ministers appointed by the president.
Judiciary: The highest court is the Union Supreme Court.
Political subdivisions: Seven emirates— Abu Dhabi, Ajman, Al Fujayrah, Ash Shariqah, Dubayy, Ras al Khaymah, Umm al Qaywayn.
Suffrage: None.
Armed forces: About 65,000 people serve in the army, navy, and air force.

People

Population: *Estimated 2002 population*—2,522,000. *1995 census*—2,377,453.
Population density: 78 per mi² (30 per km²).
Distribution: 84 percent urban, 16 percent rural.
Life expectancy: *Male*—73. *Female*—76.
Major ethnic groups: Emirati Arabs make up about 19 percent of the population; other Arabs and Iranians make up about 23 percent; South Asians, mainly immigrant workers, make up about 50 percent.
Major religions: About 96 percent of the people of the UAE are Muslims. Other religious groups include Christians and Hindus.
Literacy rate: About 76 percent of the UAE's adult population can read and write.

Economy

Chief products: *Agriculture*—dates, melons, tomatoes. *Fishing*—fish, shrimp. *Mining*—petroleum, natural gas.
Money: *Basic unit*—dirham. One hundred fils equal one dirham.
International trade: *Major exports*—dates, fish, natural gas, petroleum. *Major imports*—building supplies, clothing, food products, household goods, machinery. *Major trading partners*—China, India, Japan, United Kingdom, United States.

Important dates in the United Arab Emirates

600's Arab tribes in the region adopted Islam.
1500's Arab states that now make up the UAE began to develop. Ras Al Khaymah and Ash Shariqah became the strongest states.
Late 1700's-early1800's Ras al Khaymah and Ash Shariqah fought many wars with other Persian Gulf states.
1820 The British destroyed the city of Ras al Khaymah and forced all the states in the region to sign a truce forbidding warfare at sea. The region eventually became known as the Trucial States, and the United Kingdom took control of the states' foreign affairs.
Mid-1900's Foreign oil companies began to drill for oil in the region.
1958 Oil was discovered in Abu Dhabi.
1962 Abu Dhabi became the first of the Trucial States to export crude oil.
1971 The Trucial States gained full independence from the United Kingdom. On December 2, all the states except Ras al Khaymah joined together to form the UAE.
1972 Ras al Khaymah joined the UAE.
1991 During the Persian Gulf War, the UAE took part in the allied air and ground offensive that liberated Kuwait from Iraqi control.

Uzbekistan in brief

General information

Capital: Tashkent, also spelled Toshkent.
Official name: Uzbekiston Respublikasi (Republic of Uzbekistan).
Official language: Uzbek.
Largest city: Tashkent (pop. 1,986,000).
Country flag: The flag of Uzbekistan has three broad horizontal bands—light blue, white, and light green (top to bottom)—separated by thin red lines. The blue band shows a white crescent and 12 stars.

Land and climate

Land: Uzbekistan lies in central Asia. About 80 percent of the country's land consists of plains and deserts. The vast Kyzylkum desert lies in central Uzbekistan. Plains south and east of the desert are used mostly for growing cotton. Farmers raise livestock in the plains and in irrigated desert areas. Uzbekistan's most densely populated region is the Fergana Valley, in the east. The valley receives its water from mountains of the Tian Shan range that surround it. Central Asia's two most important rivers, the Syr Darya and the Amu Darya, flow through Uzbekistan.
Area: 172,742 mi² (447,400 km²). *Greatest distances*—north-south, 575 mi (925 km); east-west, 900 mi (1,450 km).
Elevation: *Highest*—peak in the Gissar mountain range, 15,233 ft (4,643 m). *Lowest*—Sarykamysh Lake (seasonal salt lake bed), 65 ft (20 m) below sea level.

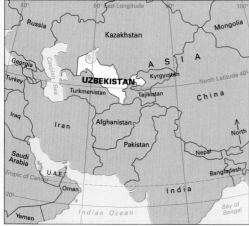

WORLD BOOK map

Climate: Summers in Uzbekistan are long, dry, and hot. Winters are cold. Summer temperatures in southern Uzbekistan may reach 113 °F (45 °C). In the north, winter temperatures may drop to –35 °F (–37 °C).

Government

Form of government: Republic.
Head of state: President elected by the people to a seven-year term.
Head of government: Prime minister appointed by the president.
Legislature: Supreme Assembly with 250 members elected by the voters to five-year terms.
Executive: Cabinet of Ministers appointed by the president.
Judiciary: The highest court is the Supreme Court.
Political subdivisions: 12 *wiloyatlar* (provinces), 1 autonomous republic, and 1 city (Tashkent).
Suffrage: All citizens 18 years of age or older may vote.
Armed forces: About 50,000 people serve in Uzbekistan's army and air force.

People

Population: *Estimated 2002 population*—25,355,000. *1989 census*—19,810,077.
Population density: 147 per mi² (57 per km²).
Distribution: 62 percent rural, 38 percent urban.
Life expectancy: *Male*—66. *Female*—72.
Major ethnic groups: About 80 percent of the people are ethnic Uzbeks. Smaller groups include Karakalpaks, Kazakhs, Russians, and Tajiks.
Major religions: About 88 percent of the people of Uzbekistan are Muslims. Most of the Muslims belong to the Sunni branch of Islam. About 9 percent of the people are Christians.
Literacy rate: About 99 percent of Uzbekistan's adult population can read and write.

Economy

Chief products: *Agriculture*—cotton, eggs, grapes, livestock, milk, potatoes, rice. *Manufacturing*—agricultural machinery, chemicals, food products, paper, textiles. *Mining*—coal, copper, gold, natural gas, petroleum.
Money: *Basic unit*—som. One hundred tijins equal one som.
International trade: *Major exports*—cotton, gold, natural gas, textiles. *Major imports*—chemicals, food products, machinery, metal and metal products. *Major trading partners*—Germany, Kazakhstan, Russia, South Korea, Switzerland.

Important dates in Uzbekistan

300's B.C. Alexander the Great conquered what is now Uzbekistan.
A.D. 600's Arabs invaded what is now Uzbekistan and introduced Islam to the region.
Early 1200's Mongols led by Genghis Khan conquered the region.
Late 1300's The Mongol conqueror Timur founded the capital of his vast Asian empire in Samarqand, now Uzbekistan's second largest city.
1500's A group of Turkic tribes known as the Uzbeks invaded what is now Uzbekistan.
1800's The khanates, the political states that had developed in the region, were conquered by Russia or came under Russian control.
1924 Uzbekistan became a republic of the Soviet Union, which had been formed under Russia's leadership in 1922.
1990 The Uzbek government declared its laws overruled those of the central Soviet government.
1991 Uzbekistan became independent. Islam A. Karimov became president.
1995 A referendum extended President Karimov's term to 2000.
2000 Karimov was reelected president.

Yemen in brief

General information

Capital: Sanaa.
Official name: Al-Jumhuriyah al Yamaniyah (the Republic of Yemen).
Official language: Arabic.
National anthem: "Al-Watani" ("Peace to the Land").
Largest city: Sanaa (pop. 427,185).
Country flag: The flag of Yemen has red, white, and black horizontal stripes. It was adopted in 1990.

Land and climate

Land: Yemen lies in the southern part of the Arabian Peninsula. The country has flat land along the west and south coasts. The coastal plain along the Red Sea is called the Tihamah. A few rocky hills border the Tihamah on the east. Then, cliffs rise steeply. East of the cliffs is an area called the High Yemen, where broad, high valleys and plateaus are surrounded by steep mountains. A dry, hilly plateau borders the Gulf of Aden coastal plain. The Rub al Khali (or Empty Quarter) lies north of the plateau.
Area: 203,850 mi² (527,968 km²). *Coastline*—about 1,020 mi (1,642 km).
Elevation: *Highest*—Jabal an Nabi Shu'ayb, 12,336 ft (3,760 m above sea level. *Lowest*—sea level.

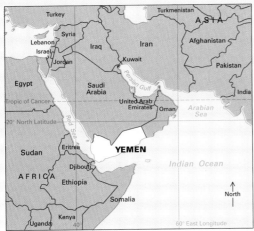

WORLD BOOK map

Climate: Temperatures in the Tihamah range from 68 to 130 °F (20 to 54 °C). The high altitude of the mountains of the High Yemen makes the region much cooler than the Tihamah. Rainfall averages 5 inches (13 centimeters) in Aden on the south coast. The High Yemen receives 10 to 15 inches (25 to 38 centimeters of rain a year. It is not uncommon for desert areas to receive no rain for five years or more.

Government

Form of government: Republic.
Head of state: President elected by the people to a seven-year term.
Head of government: Prime minister appointed by the president.
Legislature: Parliament consisting of two houses—House of Representatives (301 members elected to six-year terms) and Shura Council (111 members appointed by the president).
Executive: Council of Ministers appointed by the president.
Judiciary: The highest court is the Supreme Court.
Political subdivisions: 17 governorates.
Suffrage: All Yemenis 18 years of age or older may vote.
Armed forces: About 54,000 people serve in Yemen's army, navy, and air force.

People

Population: *Estimated 2002 population*—19,391,000. *1994 census*—14,587,807.
Population density: 95 per mi² (37 per km²).
Distribution: 74 percent rural, 26 percent urban.
Life expectancy: *Male*—58. *Female*—61.
Major ethnic groups: Most of Yemen's people are Arabs. The rest are Pakistanis, Eritreans, Somalis, or Indians.
Major religions: Most of Yemen's people are Muslims who belong to either the Zaydi sect of the Shiah branch of Islam or the Shafii sect of the Sunni branch of Islam.
Literacy rate: About 37 percent of Yemen's adult population can read and write.

Economy

Chief products: *Agriculture*—coffee, fruits, grains, khat, vegetables. *Manufacturing*—building materials, handicrafts. *Mining*—petroleum.
Money: *Basic unit*—rial.
International trade: *Major exports*—coffee, petroleum. *Major imports*—food products, grain, refined petroleum products, transportation equipment, machinery. *Major trading partners*—France, Malaysia, Saudi Arabia, United Arab Emirates, United Kingdom, United States.

Important dates in Yemen

900's B.C. The Queen of Sheba ruled Yemen.
A.D. 600's The Prophet Muhammad's son-in-law, Ali, introduced Islam to the people of Yemen.
1517 The Ottoman Empire took over Yemen.
1800's The United Kingdom seized most of Yemen, which became known as the Aden Protectorate.
1924 The Treaty of Lausanne ended Ottoman rule, which at that time was limited to northwestern Yemen.
1959 Six tribal states in the Aden Protectorate formed the Federation of the Arab Emirates of the South.
1962 The Federation of the Arab Emirates of the South changed its name to the Federation of South Arabia. Military officers supported by Egypt overthrew the government in what is now northwestern Yemen and set up a republic. The new country was named the Yemen Arab Republic, commonly called Yemen (Sanaa).
1967 A nationalist group called the National Liberation Front proclaimed the Federation of South Arabia an independent country with the name the People's Republic of South Yemen. The country was often called Yemen (Aden).
1972 Fighting began along the border between Yemen (Aden) and Yemen (Sanaa).
1990 Yemen (Aden) and Yemen (Sanaa) officially merged as the country of Yemen.
1994 A brief but bloody civil war was fought between northerners and southerners.

Gaza Strip and West Bank

Gaza Strip

The Gaza Strip is a piece of land that is administered by Palestinians. Israeli troops had occupied it from 1967 to 1994. It lies on the Mediterranean coast, where Egypt and Israel meet. The Gaza Strip covers 146 square miles (378 square kilometers) and has a population of about 1,215,000. Most of its land is sandy and flat. The vast majority of the people are Palestinian Arabs, including many who became refugees from Israel after the state of Israel was created in 1948. Israeli settlers make up a small percentage of the population. The economy is based on agriculture, including citrus fruit production. Some of the residents commute to jobs in Israel. Gaza, the major city, is overcrowded with refugees.

In ancient times, the Gaza Strip was ruled by the pharaohs of Egypt. Later, at various times, it was ruled by Philistines, Jews, Arabs, and Turks. From 1920 to 1948, it was part of the British-ruled Mandate of Palestine. Egypt gained control of the strip during the Arab-Israeli war of 1948. Israel took control of the strip after the 1967 Arab-Israeli War.

During the late 1980's, Palestinians in the Gaza Strip and West Bank staged widespread, often violent, demonstrations against Israel's occupation. Israeli forces clashed with protesters, killing many of them. In 1993, Israel and the Palestine Liberation Organization (PLO) signed agreements that led to the withdrawal of Israeli troops from most of the Gaza Strip in 1994. Palestinians then took control of the area. In 1996, Palestinians in the Gaza Strip and parts of the West Bank elected a legislature and a president to make laws and administer these areas. But there is still a large Israeli security presence.

In 1998, Israel and the PLO signed an agreement allowing a Palestinian airport to open in the Gaza Strip. In 2000, Israel and the Palestinians held peace talks but failed to resolve key remaining disagreements. Later that year, violence again broke out between Palestinians and Israeli forces in Jerusalem, the West Bank, and the Gaza Strip. In the following years, a series of Palestinian suicide bombings rocked Israel, and Israeli troops, tanks, and aircraft attacked suspected terrorist locations in Gaza City, Nablus, Ramallah, and other Palestinian-administered areas in the Gaza Strip and West Bank. By 2002, hundreds of people had been killed in the continuing violence.

West Bank

The West Bank is a territory in the Middle East that lies between Israel and Jordan. It covers about 2,270 square miles (5,880 square kilometers) with a population of more than 2 million. Most of the people are Palestinian Arabs.

East Jerusalem is the West Bank's largest city. But Israel, which includes West Jerusalem, does not consider East Jerusalem part of the West Bank. After the 1967 Arab-Israeli war, Israel made East Jerusalem a part of Israeli Jerusalem. But other countries do not recognize Israeli control.

People. Most West Bank Palestinians live in villages. About 12 percent of the Palestinians live in crowded refugee camps, where a United Nations (UN) agency provides schools and other services. Israelis make up about 15 percent of the West Bank's population. Many of the Israelis live in settlements built by the Israeli government. Many others live in East Jerusalem.

West Bank Palestinians speak Arabic. English is the most common second language. Most Palestinians are Sunni Muslims. About 8 percent of the people are Christians, chiefly members of the Eastern Orthodox or Eastern Catholic churches. The Israelis are Jewish and speak Hebrew.

Land and climate. The West Bank is hilly with generally thin, stony soil. The highlands that cover most of the West Bank have mild summers and occasional freezing temperatures and snow in winter. The Jordan River Valley, in the eastern part of the territory, has mild winters and hot summers. Much of the West Bank receives little rainfall.

The West Bank's main river is the Jordan. The Dead Sea is on the southeast border. Its shore, which lies about 1,310 feet (399 meters) below sea level, is the lowest place on the earth's surface.

Economy. Agriculture, which centers on the growing of citrus fruits and olives, is the most important economic activity in the West Bank. But water shortages limit expansion of agricultural production. The few industries are small. They include crafts, food processing, and textiles.

History and government. Historically part of Palestine, the West Bank was annexed by Jordan in 1950. In 1967, Israel defeated Jordan, Egypt, and Syria in a war and captured the West Bank. In 1974, King Hussein of Jordan gave up his government's responsibility for the West Bank to the Palestine Liberation Organization (PLO). In 1988, Jordan ended financial and administrative support it had continued to give the West Bank. Later that year, the PLO declared an independent Palestinian state in the West Bank and the Gaza Strip. However, Israel continued to occupy and, in effect, govern both territories. During the late 1980's, violence erupted between Israeli troops and Palestinians protesting Israeli occupation.

In 1972, Israel began allowing West Bank Palestinians to elect and operate municipal and village government councils. But the councils had little power. Beginning in 1993, however, Israel and the PLO signed several agreements that led to the withdrawal of Israeli troops from portions of the West Bank and from the Gaza Strip. As the Israelis withdrew, the areas came under Palestinian control. In January 1996, Palestinians in the Palestinian-controlled parts of the West Bank and in the Gaza Strip elected a legislature and a president for these areas.

By the end of the 1990's, Israel still occupied over half of the West Bank. In 2000, Israeli and Palestinian leaders failed to reach a final peace settlement. Later that year, violence erupted between Palestinians and Israeli forces in Jerusalem, the West Bank, and the Gaza Strip. In the following years, a series of Palestinian suicide bombings rocked Israel, and the Israeli military attacked suspected terrorist locations in Nablus, Ramallah, and other Palestinian-administered areas in the Gaza Strip and West Bank. By 2002, hundreds of people had been killed in the continuing violence.

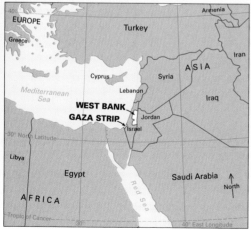

WORLD BOOK map

Arabs follow many ways of life. But they are united mainly by their history and their culture. Most Arabs are Muslims, like these men praying on a street in Amman, Jordan. Islam requires its followers to pray five times a day.

© Andy Hernandez, Sipa Press

Agricultural development in most parts of the Arab world is limited because of a scarcity of fresh water. The Egyptian potato farmers shown in this photograph live in one of the few fertile regions of the Arab world.

© Eddie Adams, Contact

Arabs

Arabs are a large group of people whose native language is Arabic and who share a common history and culture. A majority of Arabs live in the Middle East, which spreads across southwestern Asia and northern Africa. In addition, Arabs have migrated to such countries as Brazil, Britain, Canada, France, and the United States.

This article discusses the approximately 200 million Arabs who live in the *Arab world*. There are two chief definitions of the Arab world, a political definition and a *linguistic* (language-related) one.

Politically, the Arab world is usually said to include 18 countries—Algeria, Bahrain, Egypt, Iraq, Jordan, Kuwait, Lebanon, Libya, Mauritania, Morocco, Oman, Qatar, Saudi Arabia, Sudan, Syria, Tunisia, the United Arab Emirates, and Yemen. These are called Arab countries because a majority of their people are Arabs and their governments regard themselves as Arab. Two other countries—Djibouti and Somalia—have only small Arab populations, but they are sometimes included in this political definition because they belong to an organization of Arab states called the Arab League.

In a linguistic sense, the term *Arab world* refers to those areas where most people speak Arabic as their native language. This linguistic definition differs from the political one because some Arab countries include large areas populated by non-Arabs, and some non-Arab countries have significant Arab minorities. For example, the Kurds of Iraq and the Berbers of northern Africa are non-Arabs inhabiting Arab countries. At the same time, many Arabs live within the borders of such

non-Arab nations as Iran and Israel. In this article, the term *Arab world* chiefly refers to the 18 countries usually considered Arab in a political sense.

Originally, the word *Arab* was probably associated with the camel-herding nomadic tribes of the Arabian Peninsula and nearby parts of the Middle East. Later, it was applied to settled people who spoke the Arabic language. The number of Arabs who follow a nomadic way of life has gradually shrunk over the years. Today, almost all Arabs live in cities, towns, or villages.

Arabs today are united mainly by aspects of their culture—above all, by the Arabic language and Arabic literature and music. Religious and historical factors also bind the Arabs together. A majority of Arabs are Muslims, followers of a religion called Islam. The Arabs' rise to political and cultural importance during the Middle Ages was closely associated with the rise of Islam. For this reason, even non-Muslim Arabs hold Islam in special regard. The modern Arab identity emerged during the 1800's and 1900's, when most Arab lands were colonies of European powers. Thus, Arabs also share a sense of themselves as former subjects of European rule.

Despite this common heritage, deep differences exist among the Arab countries. For example, many Arab countries possess valuable petroleum deposits. The export of oil has made some of these countries, such as Kuwait and Qatar, extremely rich. But such countries as Sudan and Yemen remain poor. Some countries, including Jordan and Lebanon, have highly urban societies, where many people work in industry or commerce. Others, such as Mauritania and Yemen, have rural societies and rely on farming or herding. Some nations, such as Lebanon and Tunisia, have been heavily influenced by Western culture. Others, including Oman and Saudi Arabia, remain strongly traditional. These and other differences have caused conflicts, and even wars, within the Arab world.

Fred M. Donner, the contributor of this article, is Associate Professor of Islamic History at the University of Chicago.

The Arab world has both a political and a *linguistic* (language-related) definition. Politically, it includes 18 countries in the Middle East and across northern Africa. Western Sahara, also shown, is claimed by Morocco. In a linguistic sense, *Arab world* refers to those areas where most people speak Arabic as their native language.

────── Arab country boundary

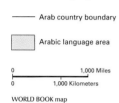　Arabic language area

```
0                    1,000 Miles
├──────────────────────┤
0                 1,000 Kilometers
```

WORLD BOOK map

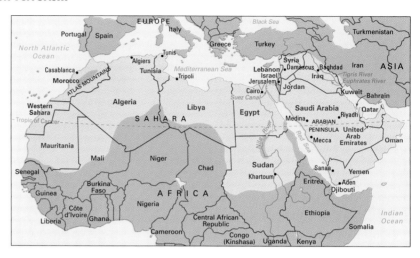

Land of the Arabs

The Arab world extends over about 5 million square miles (13 million square kilometers). It covers roughly three main regions: the Arabian Peninsula (sometimes called Arabia); northern Africa; and part of an area called the Fertile Crescent, which includes Iraq, Jordan, Lebanon, Syria, and the historical land of Palestine. Palestine today consists of the West Bank, the Gaza Strip, and the non-Arab state of Israel.

Despite the vast area of the Arab world, only a small percentage of it is suitable for human settlement. Much of the region is hot and dry, and it has large desert areas. These include the Sahara in northern Africa, the deserts of the Arabian Peninsula, and the Syrian Desert. At the other extreme are snow-capped mountains, such as those of the Grand Atlas range in Morocco and parts of the Lebanon Mountains. The vast majority of Arabs live in well-watered hilly regions, fertile river valleys, and humid coastal areas. The most densely settled area is the Nile Valley and Nile River Delta of Egypt. Virtually all the people of Egypt—about a fourth of all Arabs—live in this area. A large number of Iraq's people live in the fertile delta between the Tigris and Euphrates rivers. Other population centers include the coastal and hill zones of northwestern Africa and of Lebanon, Syria, and parts of Palestine.

Historically, the scarcity of water and the resulting limited farming capacity have hampered population growth and economic development in Arab lands. However, they may have encouraged the development of trade, especially before the 1800's.

Life in the Arab world

When people think of Arabs, they often picture nomadic herders, or Bedouins, living in tents and crossing the desert with their camels, sheep, goats, or cattle in search of water and grazing land. Today, less than 1 percent of Arabs are nomads. Livestock herding now resembles ranching rather than nomadic life, and animals—even camels—are usually transported by truck.

About half of all Arabs live in cities and large towns. Many of these people work in factories or in such fields as business, government, and health care. Most other Arabs live in villages or small towns and work as farmers or in local trades. In many Arab countries, the creation of modern road networks has enabled industries to spread to rural areas, and some villagers have jobs in nearby factories.

Language. Virtually all people who consider themselves Arabs speak Arabic as their native language. But the forms of spoken Arabic vary considerably from one region to another. Arabs who speak different dialects can communicate through a common form of Arabic, usually called Modern Standard Arabic (MSA)—*fusha* in Arabic. MSA is a simplified version of the Arabic of the Qur'ān, the sacred book of Islam. MSA serves as the chief form of written Arabic in all Arab lands. MSA is also the language used in most schools and in radio and TV news broadcasts throughout the Arab world.

Many other languages are used in various parts of the Arab world. For example, French is widely spoken in the former French colonies of Algeria, Morocco, and Tunisia, where the French language struck deep roots in cultural and political life.

Religion. About 90 percent of Arabs are Muslims. Most belong to the Sunni branch of Islam. However, significant Shiite Muslim communities exist in Iraq, the eastern Arabian Peninsula, and Lebanon. Some Shiites live in most other Arab countries. Small numbers of Arabs belong to other Muslim groups.

Druses, who follow a religion related to Islam, live mainly in Lebanon, Syria, and the historical region of Palestine. A majority of non-Muslim Arabs are Christians. The Copts of Egypt belong to one of the oldest Christian sects. Other Christian Arabs belong to Eastern Orthodox, Roman Catholic, or Protestant churches. They live mainly in Iraq, Jordan, Lebanon, Syria, and Palestine. Small communities of Jews live in some Arab countries.

Family life. Arabs strongly value family ties and hospitality. Traditionally, Arabs have placed great importance on belonging to family or kinship groups, includ-

Topic for study

Discuss the chief political and social influences of Islam on Arab society.

ing the *extended family, clan,* and *tribe.* An extended family includes members of two or more generations, many of them sharing one home. A clan consists of several related families. A tribe might include hundreds of families. In the past, most social and even a large number of business activities took place within these groups. Often, parents sought marriage partners for their children within the clan or tribe. The kinship system also stressed hospitality as a source of honor. A host who richly entertained a guest raised the standing of the entire tribe.

Today, some kinship ties have loosened, especially in the cities. The impact of Western values and the need for some people to move far from home to earn a living have tended to weaken family relationships. But for many Arabs, the family continues to be the main source of social and economic support. Many rural Arabs still live in extended families, and even most city dwellers live near relatives. Many Arab children are raised by grandparents, aunts, uncles, and other relatives in addition to their parents. It is still common for parents to arrange their children's marriages.

Traditionally, women formed the focus of family life. They supervised the raising of children, the preparation of meals, and the organizing of family celebrations. In some countries, economic pressures and educational opportunities have led a growing number of women to work outside the home.

Education. Until the 1900's, religious authorities operated most schools in the Arab world. Today, all Arab nations also have free, nonreligious primary and secondary schools. In most Arab countries, about 90 percent of all children receive at least an elementary education. Some Arabs consider education less important for girls than for boys. But all Arab nations provide public schooling at all levels for both sexes.

Some Arab institutions of higher education have existed for centuries. For example, al-Azhar University in Cairo, Egypt, was founded about 970. Today, there are approximately 85 universities in the Arab world.

Literature and the arts. Arabic literature began about 1,500 years ago. The first major Arabic work was the Qur'ān, the holy book of Islam, which dates to the 600's. The Qur'ān is still regarded as the greatest masterpiece of Arabic literary style.

Classical Arabic literature extends from the time of the Qur'ān to about the mid-1800's and includes a rich tradition in both poetry and prose. Prose literature covers a wide range of forms and styles, from the popular tales of the *Arabian Nights* to such scholarly works as the *Muqaddima* of Ibn Khaldun, a historian of the 1300's. The *Muqaddima* examines the rise and fall of civilizations. A highly developed poetic tradition flourished beginning in the 700's. Arabic poets produced verses of great lyric beauty as well as poetic works expressing deep philosophical or religious thought.

Today, poetry remains especially beloved by Arabs. Nearly all Arabs delight in reciting and listening to verses, and many compose their own poetry. In addition, stories, novels, and plays are published in great numbers.

Arabs took part in the flowering of art and architecture throughout the Muslim world from the mid-700's to about 1700. Such traditional crafts as glass blowing, met-alworking, and pottery making still flourish today. Since 1900, painting and sculpture have become popular in many Arab lands.

Traditional Arab music, with its strong rhythmic patterns, is closely linked with the poetic tradition. Today, many musicians experiment with new styles, mixing aspects of Arab and non-Arab music or combining styles from different parts of the Arab world.

Food and drink. Beans, chickpeas, lentils, and rice are basic foods in most Arab lands. They may be made into stews, or cooked with water, oil, vegetables, and seasonings to form various pastes. People eat the pastes by scooping up mouthfuls with thin Arab bread, called *pita* in the West. In northern Africa, *couscous* (steamed cracked wheat) replaces rice as a basic food to some extent. Arabs also enjoy meat, fish, and a wide variety of salads and cooked vegetables. Sesame seed paste or oil adds a special flavor to many dishes. Some form of yogurt often accompanies meals.

Fresh and dried fruits are the main desserts. But sweet pastries such as *baklava,* which is made with honey and chopped nuts, are served on special occasions. Coffee and tea are the most popular beverages.

Clothing. Because of the hot climate of most Arab lands, both men and women have traditionally worn loose-fitting garments that cover most of the body and head, shielding them from the sun. For women, such garments usually consist of a floor-length dress and a headscarf or hood. In areas where Islam is strong, women may wear a veil in public. Many women wear Western-style dresses or slacks. However, they rarely wear short or sleeveless dresses or let their hair hang free.

Traditional men's clothing might consist of a full-length robe, or a cloak over some combination of shirt, vest, skirt, and *loincloth* (a cloth wrapped around the hips and between the thighs). Some farmers wear baggy trousers. Many men also wear a turban, skullcap, or *kaffiyeh*—a loose, folded headscarf, often held in place by a decorative cord called an *agal,* also spelled *iqal.* Today, many men wear Western-style clothing, especially in the cities. Some men combine elements of Western and traditional dress. For example, they may wear a Western-style sports jacket over a robe.

Shelter. A majority of rural Arabs live in one- or two-story houses of brick, mud-brick, or stone. Mud-brick architecture, in particular, takes a wide variety of forms, from simple rectangular structures to the beehive-shaped houses of northern Syria. Mud-brick is cheap and easy to use, and it provides excellent insulation against heat and cold. However, concrete and cinder blocks are increasingly replacing mud-brick as building materials.

Western-style apartment buildings are common in large cities. But traditional Arab architecture can also be found in urban areas. The distinctive many-storied mud-brick or stone buildings of Yemen and southern Saudi Arabia rank among the world's first "skyscrapers." Privacy is an important factor in much Arab architecture, both urban and rural. Many homes or buildings open onto a private or semiprivate central courtyard, while blank walls face the street.

Economy. For centuries, the Arab world was a crossroads of international commerce. Arab and other mer-

© Richard Steedman, Corbis Stock Market

Traditional Arab architecture places great importance on privacy. Many houses are constructed around a central courtyard, like the homes in this neighborhood in Damascus, Syria.

chants carried such goods as spices, textiles, and glass between Asia, Africa, and Europe. Beginning in the 1700's, the expansion of European commerce and industry led to economic decline in the Arab world. Then, during the 1900's, petroleum became one of the world's most important economic resources. Together, the Arab lands hold about three-fifths of the world's reserves of oil. Petroleum has brought enormous prosperity to many Arab governments, permitting rapid improvement in education, health care, transportation, and other services. However, some Arab countries still face great poverty.

The countries most dependent on petroleum include Iraq, Kuwait, Libya, Oman, Qatar, Saudi Arabia, and the United Arab Emirates. But nearly all Arab states rely heavily on the export of petroleum, other raw materials, and agricultural products. Manufacturing is developing slowly in the Arab world. Only Jordan, Lebanon, Morocco, Tunisia, and, to a lesser extent, Egypt receive a significant amount of income from manufacturing.

A scarcity of fresh water limits agricultural development in most areas. Agriculture can be extended only through large-scale irrigation projects, which are expensive and unreliable. In addition, in many countries, a small number of wealthy landowners once controlled most of the farmland, which was worked by poverty-stricken peasants. Since the mid-1900's, Arab governments have put more land in the hands of the farmworkers. But most of them remain poor.

History

The Arabs before Islam. The word *Arab* first appears in documents about 850 B.C. The documents—written by the Assyrians, a people of what is now Iraq—suggest that the early Arabs were nomadic camel herders centered in what are now Jordan and Israel. The Arabs then spread north and east through present-day Syria and Iraq, and south into the Arabian Peninsula.

About the 400's B.C., Arab families or tribes began to

establish small states, often at centers for the overland caravan trade. Two important states were centered at Petra and Palmyra. Petra, in what is now Jordan, was the capital of Arabs known as Nabateans. It was conquered by the Romans in A.D. 106 but continued to flourish until the early A.D. 200's. Palmyra, in the Syrian Desert, fell under Roman domination by about A.D. 160. It reached its height in the mid-200's.

The rise and spread of Islam. Muslims believe that God revealed the teachings of Islam to the prophet Muhammad. Muhammad was born about A.D. 570 and grew up in Mecca, a town in western Arabia. He began to preach about 610. Muhammad founded the first community of Muslims in Medina, then called Yathrib, north of Mecca. This community rapidly grew into a state that controlled much of the peninsula.

After Muhammad's death in 632, leaders called *caliphs* headed the Islamic state. Armies under the caliphs soon seized the rest of Arabia and an area stretching from Egypt to Iran. The result was a vast new empire dominated by Arabian Muslims, with Islam as the official religion of the empire and Arabic as the official language.

For several hundred years, the political life of the empire was dominated by three families from Muhammad's tribe of Quraysh: the Umayyads, the Abbasids, and the Alids. The Umayyads ruled from 661 to 750. They extended the empire as far west as Spain and as far east as India. In 750, the Umayyads were overthrown by the Abbasids, though they retained control of Spain. After about 850, the Abbasids increasingly lost control of distant parts of the empire, which became independent under local Islamic *dynasties* (ruling families). The Alids, the main rivals of the Umayyads and Abbasids, made many unsuccessful attempts to overthrow them. The Alids finally established the Fatimid dynasty in northern Africa in 909. It ruled until 1171.

A sense of Arab identity seems to have emerged in connection with the spread of Islam. This sense of "Arabness" resulted partly from use of the Arabic language and partly from pride in the Islamic empire. It also stemmed from identification with the rich literary culture that developed under the Umayyads and Abbasids.

From the 1000's to the 1500's, parts of the eastern Arab lands were conquered by several waves of non-Arab invaders. Chief among these were the Seljuk Turks and the Mongols, who executed the last Abbasid caliph in 1258. Northern Africa remained in the hands of local groups, mainly Arabs and Berbers.

Ottoman and European rule. By the mid-1500's, nearly all the Arab lands had come under the control of the Ottoman Empire, centered in what is now Turkey. The Arab lands were an important part of the empire. Many high Ottoman officials were of Arab origin, and the Arabs regarded themselves as Ottomans and Muslims, not as Arabs.

Beginning in the mid-1700's, the rapid economic and military development of much of Europe gave European states an advantage over the Ottomans. In their efforts to modernize their economies, the Ottomans often developed large debts to European financiers. The financiers then sometimes persuaded their governments to seize economic or political control of Ottoman possessions to ensure repayment of the debts. In other cases, European nations simply invaded Ottoman territories. France began occupation of Algeria in 1830, and it controlled Tunisia and Morocco by the early 1900's. Beginning in the late 1800's, Britain took over Egypt and Sudan, and it controlled many coastal areas of Arabia. Italy gained control of Libya in 1912.

Arab nationalism arose against the background of both European colonial rule and increasing nationalist feeling among the Ottoman Empire's Turkish majority. It was part of a nationalist idea that spread through much of the world during the 1800's and 1900's. This idea stated that humanity was divided into distinct nations or peoples. The members of each nation shared a common history and language, and each nation had a historic claim to a particular national homeland.

Significant Arab nationalist movements did not develop until the early 1900's. These movements then took two forms. In some cases, nationalist feeling arose around particular areas. In others, it centered on the Arabic language as a source of unity. This form of nationalism later grew into the movement for Arab political unification called *Pan-Arabism*.

After the Ottoman Empire entered World War I (1914-1918) on the side of Germany in 1914, the United Kingdom helped stir up an Arab nationalist revolt against the Ottomans. The United Kingdom promised the leaders of the revolt that it would recognize an independent Arab government in former Ottoman territories after the war. However, the United Kingdom also made a secret agreement with France to divide these territories into British and French spheres of influence after the war. When World War I ended in 1918, the League of Nations—a forerunner of the United Nations—divided the Arab lands still held by the Ottomans between the United Kingdom and France. In turn, the United Kingdom and France were expected to supervise these lands—known as *mandated territories*—and help them attain self-government. The United Kingdom received mandates over Iraq and over Palestine, which then included present-day Jordan and Israel. France received what are now Syria and Lebanon.

Struggles for independence. By the early 1920's, the main centers of population in the Arab world had been split into more than 15 European colonies and *protectorates* (territories under partial control). These colonies had become divided politically, economically, and, increasingly, culturally. Because of these divisions, the goal of Pan-Arab unification became less important than that of independence within each colony.

Beginning in the 1920's, the Arab countries gradually gained independence. Some, such as Bahrain and Kuwait, made the change peacefully. In others, notably Algeria, violent struggles took place. The last colonies to become independent—British-ruled Bahrain, Qatar, and the states that now make up the United Arab Emirates—did so in 1971.

Since independence. Traditionally, political life in most Arab lands had been dominated either by a small number of wealthy individuals or by the army. The European powers took limited steps toward developing institutions of democratic government in their Arab colonies. But they kept such institutions from becoming strong enough to threaten colonial rule. They also failed

© Robert Harding Picture Library

Petroleum, the Arab world's most important resource, has brought great wealth to some Arab countries. Arab lands hold about three-fifths of the world's oil reserves.

to create economic or educational systems that would stimulate the growth of a middle class. As a result, the independent Arab states have continued to be ruled by traditional wealthy families or by the army.

The independent Arab nations have struggled with other issues as well. These include (1) the search for unity and (2) the Arab-Israeli conflict.

The search for unity. Several times, two or three Arab nations have attempted to unite into a single state. For example, Syria and Egypt joined to form the United Arab Republic in 1958. The union ended when Syria withdrew in 1961. Such efforts have stemmed partly from a belief in Pan-Arabism. But in many cases, they also represented attempts by a weak government to maintain its rule by uniting with a stronger neighbor.

In 1945, seven countries founded the Arab League. Today, 21 countries and the Palestine Liberation Organization (PLO) belong to the league. The organization works to promote closer political, economic, and social relations among its members.

Pan-Arab unity remains an ideal for some Arabs. However, the different economic needs and political goals of the Arab states have at times made them bitter rivals. The wealth of some Arab countries from petroleum exports has contributed greatly to tension. Petroleum-poor states resent the wealth of their richer neighbors and seek to share in the oil income. In addition, disagreements have occurred among petroleum exporters over pricing and production policies. Such disagreements helped set off the invasion of Kuwait by Iraq in 1990, which severely divided the Arab states. Several Arab countries, most notably Saudi Arabia and Egypt, took

Topic for study

In what ways has wealth from oil exports affected life in oil-producing Arab nations? Compare the way of life in one of these countries with that of an Arab nation that produces little or no oil.

part in the Persian Gulf War in 1991 helping expel Iraqi forces from Kuwait.

The Arab-Israeli conflict can best be understood as a struggle between two nationalist movements, both of which claim Palestine as their national homeland. The conflict dates to the early 1900's, after significant numbers of European Jewish immigrants began to enter Palestine. In 1917, the United Kingdom declared its support for the creation of a Jewish homeland in Palestine. But the United Kingdom had also promised support for an independent Arab state in former Ottoman Arab provinces, including Palestine. Tension between the Arabs and the Jewish settlers grew, accompanied increasingly by violence on both sides.

In 1947, the United Nations adopted a plan dividing Palestine into an Arab state and a Jewish one. The Arabs rejected this plan, and in 1948 several Arab nations invaded the newly formed state of Israel. During the war that followed, hundreds of thousands of Palestinian Arab refugees fled to neighboring Arab countries.

The war ended in 1949, but no peace treaty was signed. Since then, the Arab-Israeli conflict has been of major importance in the Arab world. Thousands of people died in wars fought in 1956, 1967, and 1973, and in an Israeli invasion of Lebanon in 1982. Thousands more have died in Palestinian guerrilla attacks and in two *intifadas* (uprisings) by Palestinians. The first intifada began in 1987 and lasted into the early 1990's. The second intifada began in 2000.

Egypt and Israel signed a peace treaty in 1979. In 1994, Jordan and Israel signed a declaration that formally ended the state of war between the two countries. But Israel has not made final peace agreements with Syria or with the Palestine Liberation Organization (PLO). The PLO is a group approved by Arab countries to represent the Palestinians. In 1993, Israel and the PLO agreed to a plan for Palestinian self-government in the Gaza Strip and the West Bank. Israel occupied those Arab lands in 1967. During the 1990's, Israel withdrew from most of the Gaza Strip and parts of the West Bank. But in 2000, peace talks between the two sides failed to resolve sev-

© Bill Lyons

Arab nations are working to develop a wider variety of economic activities. These computer operators, members of a growing middle class, work for a Jordanian papermaking firm.

Topic for study

What role did the Arabs play in transmitting much of ancient Greek culture to Western Europe?

eral remaining disagreements. Later that year, Palestinians began a violent intifada, and Israel responded with police crackdowns and military attacks.

The Arabs today continue to face major challenges. The problems of poverty, overpopulation, poor health care, and inadequate educational facilities are severe in some Arab states. In other countries—especially thinly populated ones—enormous oil wealth has provided high-quality medical care and education. But an effective way of bringing those benefits to poorer, more populated countries has yet to be found. In addition, the oil-rich states must plan carefully for the day when oil reserves run dry. Many of these countries are working to develop other economic activities that can help maintain their growth in the post-petroleum age.

Most Arab countries also must work to create strong institutions of multiparty, civilian government. Another challenge is to find ways to solve religious or ethnic conflicts, such as that between Arabs and Kurds in Iraq or among Sunni Muslims, Shiite Muslims, Christians, and Druses in Lebanon, as well as the Arab-Israeli dispute. Arabs also must deal with powerful conflicts between Islamic tradition and the influence of the West.

Fred M. Donner

Outline

I. **Land of the Arabs**
II. **Life in the Arab world**
   A. Language
   B. Religion
   C. Family life
   D. Education
   E. Literature and the arts
   F. Food and drink
   G. Clothing
   H. Shelter
   I. Economy
III. **History**

Questions

What percentage of Arabs today are nomads?
What is the most densely settled area in the Arab world?
When did a sense of "Arabness" first appear? Why?
What kind of literature is especially beloved by Arabs?
In what way is privacy important in much Arab architecture?
How did European nations gain control of many Arab lands in the 1800's and 1900's?
Where is French widely used in the Arab world?
When did significant Arab nationalist movements develop?
What is an extended family? A clan? A tribe?
What two groups have traditionally dominated political life in most Arab lands?

Additional resources

Fernea, Elizabeth W. and Robert A. *The Arab World: Forty Years of Change.* Rev. ed. Doubleday, 1997.
Morris, Benny. *Righteous Victims: A History of the Zionist-Arab Conflict, 1881-1999.* Knopf, 1999.

Web site

ArabNet
http://www.arab.net/
A comprehensive online resource on the Arab world, primarily dealing with countries in the Middle East and North Africa.

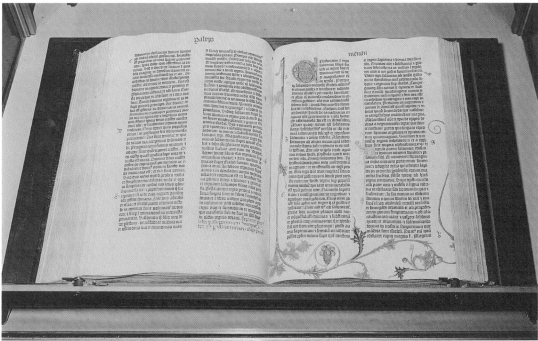

The Gutenberg Bible was the first Bible printed from movable type. It was produced in the workshop of Johannes Gutenberg in Mainz, Germany, during the mid-1400's. The Gutenberg Bible was an edition of the *Vulgate*, a Latin translation completed by Saint Jerome in A.D. 405.

Bible

Bible is the name given to several collections of writings held sacred by the Jewish and Christian religions. It is also known as the Holy Scriptures. Both religions regard the Bible as inspired by God. They base many of their beliefs and customs on the teachings found in the Bible. The Bible is the most widely distributed book in history. It has also been translated more times, and into more languages, than any other book.

The Jewish and Christian Bibles differ from each other in several ways. The Jewish Bible is commonly called the Hebrew Bible because most of it was written in Hebrew. It tells the story of Creation. It also contains information on pre-Israelite times and the history and religious life of ancient Israel from about 1300 B.C. to the 100's B.C. The Hebrew Bible, which Christians call the Old Testament, forms the first part of the Christian Bible. The second part of the Christian Bible, the New Testament, was written in Greek. It covers about 100 years, from the birth of Jesus Christ to about A.D. 125. Some Christian groups also include in the Old Testament additional originally Jewish writings that are not found in the Hebrew Bible. The individual writings collected in the Bible are known as *books*. The books that are officially accepted by any group as part of its Bible are called the *canon*.

Both the Jewish and the Christian Bibles view God as the supreme power behind the events they describe, though God's role may not always be apparent. The Bible does not define God or try to prove God's existence. Instead, it testifies to God's presence in history including, in the Christian Bible, the life of Jesus Christ and the development of the early church.

Scholars value the books of the Bible not only as important religious writings but also as great literary works. The Bible includes many forms of literature, such as letters, stories, history, laws, prophecies, prayers, songs, love poems, and epics. Its vivid, realistic tales of the struggles, failures, and triumphs of both great and ordinary people entertain as well as teach. Literary critics have praised its beautiful poetry and stirring calls to faith.

Readers have long differed over how to explain the meaning of the Bible. Some people believe that every event mentioned in the Bible actually happened exactly as the Bible says it did. Others feel that many events in the Bible must be read as symbols of religious belief. This article presents a broad survey of the Bible.

The Hebrew Bible

Almost all of the Hebrew Bible was written in Hebrew. A few parts, especially sections of the Book of Daniel and the Book of Ezra, were written in another ancient language called Aramaic.

Books of the Hebrew Bible. The Hebrew Bible consists of 24 books. The Christian Old Testament divides some of the books, increasing their number to 39. In addition, Roman Catholic Bibles add seven books to the Old Testament. These books first appeared in a Jewish translation of the Bible into Greek during the mid-200's B.C. The canon of the Greek Orthodox Church is the same as that of the Catholic Church, with five additional books. They are 1 and 2 Esdras, Prayer of Manasseh,

Psalm 151, and 3 Maccabees.

The books of the Hebrew Bible are organized into three sections—the Law (Pentateuch), the Prophets, and the Writings. The name by which Jews know the Hebrew Bible, *Tanakh,* is formed from the first letter of the Hebrew word for each section: *Torah, Nebiim,* and *Ketubim.* The Christian Old Testament is divided into four sections—Pentateuch, Historical Books, Wisdom Books, and Prophets. For a list of all the books found in the Hebrew Bible and the Roman Catholic and Protestant canons, see the table in this article. The following discussion describes the three sections of the Hebrew Bible.

The Law consists of five books. It is also called *Pentateuch,* from two Greek words meaning *five books,* and *Torah.* The Book of Genesis describes God's creation of the world, early human history, and the origin of the Israelites. The other books trace the early history of the Israelites, ancestors of the Jews. They begin with Exodus, containing the departure of the Israelites from Egypt under their leader Moses, and they end with the death of Moses at the entrance to Canaan (what is now Israel). These books also contain the Ten Commandments and many of the laws that serve as the basis of Judaism today.

The Law was the first part of the Bible to be accepted into the canon. A group of Jews called Samaritans still accept only this part of the Bible.

The Prophets were teachers and thinkers who played a major role in the political and religious life of the Israelites. This section of the Hebrew Bible was the second to be accepted into the canon. It is divided into the Former Prophets and the Latter Prophets. The division is based on the order of the books in the Bible and not on the order in which they were written.

The Former Prophets consist of four books—Joshua, Judges, Samuel, and Kings. These books continue the history of the Israelites from the settlement of Canaan to the capture of Jerusalem by the Babylonians in 587 or 586 B.C. The authors of the Former Prophets drew from historical sources for their discussions of prophets, judges, and kings. But their chief purpose was to demonstrate the power of God and the divine role in history.

The Latter Prophets also consist of four books. Three books relate teachings associated with prophets named Isaiah, Jeremiah, and Ezekiel. The fourth book gathers the teachings of 12 other prophets. The Book of Isaiah may include the teachings of more than one prophet. One prophet named Isaiah probably lived in the 700's B.C. Another prophet, also known as Isaiah, probably lived about 200 years later. In general, the earlier prophets, such as Jeremiah and the first Isaiah, called on the people to repent from their sins and renew their faith in God. The later prophets, including Ezekiel and the second Isaiah, taught after the exile of the Jews to Babylonia in 586 B.C. They spoke of their hope for God's forgiveness and a return to their land.

The Writings consist of 11 books of various kinds. The Book of Psalms is made up of religious poetry. The Books of Ruth, Esther, and Daniel are stories drawn from Jewish history. The Song of Songs (also called the Song of Solomon) is a collection of love poems. Lamentations consists of five poems that mourn the destruc-

tion of Jerusalem by the Babylonians. Other books include history (Ezra, Nehemiah, and Chronicles) and *wisdom literature,* or philosophical writings (Proverbs, Job, and Ecclesiastes). Of these books, Job concerns the unknowable nature of God. Ecclesiastes is a largely pessimistic discussion of the nature of life.

Development of the Hebrew Bible. Scholars have evidence of many similarities between ancient Hebrew literary and legal traditions and those of other Near Eastern cultures, including Mesopotamian law codes, Egyptian wisdom literature, and Canaanite poetry. But no written sources tell how the Hebrew Bible began to develop. Clues to its early development must be taken almost entirely from the Bible itself.

Jewish writers have discussed the origins of the Law since pre-Christian times. According to Jewish and Christian tradition, these books are "the books of Moses." But the books themselves do not say Moses was the author. Some scholars believe the Law began as oral literature and was written down following the reign of King David—that is, after about 1000 B.C.

In analyzing the books of the Law, Biblical scholars have noted differences in vocabulary, style, the names for God, and the idea of God. They have also noted duplications of stories. Many scholars believe this evidence shows that several persons or groups wrote the Law. They suggest that four documents originally existed. These documents were written over at least 500 years and were combined by a number of editors. The books of the Prophets may reflect the way the prophets' words were remembered and honored long after their deaths. The words of later generations are partly mixed with those of the prophets, either as an explanation or as actual changes in what the prophets said. Only by careful study can modern readers try to separate the original messages of the prophets from later revisions.

The authors of the Writings are unknown, though several are associated with various ancient leaders. Many of the Psalms begin with a one-line heading or introduction. The headings in about one-half of the Psalms contain David's name and some people take these references as indications of authorship. Other individuals are also mentioned in these headings, and may have been authors of some Psalms. The Book of Psalms, which actually consists of at least five ancient books, is best understood as a collection of anthologies of psalms written by many people. David's son Solomon is said to have written the Song of Songs. These traditions may have arisen because verses in the books can be understood as "Psalm of David" or "Song of Solomon." In fact, the Hebrew word used in these verses may mean *of, to,* or *for.*

Development of the Christian Old Testament. Jews living in Palestine used the Bible in its original Hebrew version. But many Jews living outside of Palestine spoke other languages. During the mid-200's B.C., Jewish scholars in Egypt translated the Bible into Greek. For more information on this translation, see the section on *The first translations* in this article.

Other books were added to the Hebrew Bible in its Greek translation. Some of these books were translations of Hebrew works. Others were original compositions in Greek. In addition, the Greek translation expanded the books of Esther and Daniel.

The books of the Bible

The tables below give the titles of the books of the Old Testament and the New Testament. The three lists of Old Testament books show the names and order of books as accepted by Jews, Protestants, and Roman Catholics. Protestants and Roman Catholics accept the same names and the same order of books in the New Testament.

The Hebrew Bible/Old Testament

Jewish version

The Law	Kings	Ruth
Genesis	Isaiah	Lamentations
Exodus	Jeremiah	Ecclesiastes
Leviticus	Ezekiel	Esther
Numbers	The Twelve*	Daniel
Deuteronomy	**The Writings**	Ezra-Nehemiah
The Prophets	Psalms	Chronicles
Joshua	Proverbs	
Judges	Job	
Samuel	Song of Songs	

Protestant version (King James Bible)

Pentateuch	2 Chronicles	Daniel
Genesis	Ezra	Hosea
Exodus	Nehemiah	Joel
Leviticus	Esther	Amos
Numbers	**Wisdom books**	Obadiah
Deuteronomy	Job	Jonah
Historical books	Psalms	Micah
Joshua	Proverbs	Nahum
Judges	Ecclesiastes	Habakkuk
Ruth	Song of Solomon	Zephaniah
1 Samuel	**Prophets**	Haggai
2 Samuel	Isaiah	Zechariah
1 Kings	Jeremiah	Malachi
2 Kings	Lamentations	
1 Chronicles	Ezekiel	

Roman Catholic version (New American Bible)

Pentateuch	Tobit	Baruch
Genesis	Judith	Ezekiel
Exodus	Esther	Daniel
Leviticus	1 Maccabees	Hosea
Numbers	2 Maccabees	Joel
Deuteronomy	**Wisdom books**	Amos
Historical books	Job	Obadiah
Joshua	Psalms	Jonah
Judges	Proverbs	Micah
Ruth	Ecclesiastes	Nahum
1 Samuel	Song of Songs	Habakkuk
2 Samuel	Wisdom	Zephaniah
1 Kings	Sirach	Haggai
2 Kings	(Ecclesiasticus)	Zechariah
1 Chronicles	**Prophets**	Malachi
2 Chronicles	Isaiah	
Ezra	Jeremiah	
Nehemiah	Lamentations	

The New Testament

Gospels	Galatians	Hebrews
Matthew	Ephesians	James
Mark	Philippians	1 Peter
Luke	Colossians	2 Peter
John	1 Thessalonians	1 John
Acts of the Apostles	2 Thessalonians	2 John
Letters	1 Timothy	3 John
Romans	2 Timothy	Jude
1 Corinthians	Titus	**Revelation**
2 Corinthians	Philemon	

*Hosea, Joel, Amos, Obadiah, Jonah, Micah, Nahum, Habakkuk, Zephaniah, Haggai, Zechariah, Malachi

When Christianity began to spread throughout the Greek-speaking world about the A.D. 50's, Christians used the Greek translation of the Bible. This translation became the Christian Old Testament.

During the A.D. 1500's, some Protestant scholars became concerned that the Old Testament contained books not found in the Hebrew Bible. The scholars removed these books from the Old Testament and called them *Apocrypha*. For this reason, the Protestant Old Testament includes only those writings that form the Hebrew Bible. Some Protestant editions of the Bible include the Apocrypha as a separate section. The word *apocrypha* comes from a Greek word meaning *hidden*. Scholars disagree on why the word was applied to these writings.

The list below gives the titles and order of the books in the Revised Standard Version of the Apocrypha.

1 Esdras	Baruch
2 Esdras	Letter of Jeremiah
Tobit	Prayer of Azariah and the
Judith	Song of the Three Young
Additions to the	Men
Book of Esther	Susanna (Additions to Daniel)
Wisdom of Solomon	
Ecclesiasticus, or the	Bel and the Dragon
Wisdom of Jesus the	Prayer of Manasseh
Son of Sirach	1 Maccabees
	2 Maccabees

The Roman Catholic Old Testament includes all of these books except 1 and 2 Esdras and the Prayer of

Fresco (about A.D. 300's) by an unknown artist in the Catacomb of San Callisto, Rome (Hirmer Verlag)

Scenes from Biblical stories decorate the walls of burial places used by early Christians in Rome. This painting shows Moses striking a rock to get water in the desert.

The Dead Sea Scrolls are the oldest known manuscripts of any books of the Bible. Some of the scrolls may be more than 2,000 years old. They were discovered in the mid-1900's in caves near the northwestern shore of the Dead Sea in Southwest Asia. The scroll at the left shows part of the Old Testament Book of Isaiah.

School of Theology at Claremont (John C. Trever)

Manasseh. The Letter of Jeremiah, Prayer of Azaria, and Bel and the Dragon occur as additions to Old Testament books. The Greek Orthodox Old Testament includes all of the books on this list.

The New Testament

The New Testament records the life of Jesus Christ. It also deals with the development of the early church and the meaning of faith in Jesus. The New Testament was written in Greek, which was widely spoken during the time of Jesus. Jesus and His disciples spoke Aramaic.

Books of the New Testament. The New Testament consists of 27 books organized into four sections—the Gospels, the Acts of the Apostles, the Letters, and Revelation. The number of books and their order are the same in the Roman Catholic and Protestant versions. For the complete canon, see the table in this article.

The Gospels consist of four books—Matthew, Mark, Luke, and John. They appear as the first books in the New Testament, though they are not the earliest works in the canon. The word *gospel* comes from the Old English word *godspell,* which means *good news.*

The Gospels themselves do not mention their authors' names. However, the early church attributed them to two of Christ's apostles, Matthew and John, and two companions of apostles, Mark and Luke. Today, many scholars doubt that these men were the actual authors of the gospels.

All four Gospels describe the life of Jesus. Matthew, Mark, and Luke have similarities of detail and arrangement. They are called the *Synoptic Gospels.* The word *synoptic* comes from a Greek word that means *see together.*

The Synoptic Gospels differ from the Gospel of John in several ways. In the Synoptic Gospels, for example, Jesus expresses His teachings chiefly in short sayings and in brief stories called *parables.* In John, He teaches through long statements.

Although the Synoptic Gospels generally deal with the same events, each of the four Gospels regards Jesus

differently. Matthew describes Him as the lawgiver who tells how Christians and their church should act. Mark shows Him as the Savior who triumphs through suffering. Luke presents Jesus as the Savior of all people. John concentrates on Jesus's divine nature.

Many scholars believe that Mark was the earliest Gospel. It was probably written just before or after the Roman army captured Jerusalem in A.D. 70. Matthew and Luke were written a little later. The contents of these two Gospels indicate that both authors knew Mark's Gospel but not each other's. John was written last, perhaps in the A.D. 90's. Each Gospel was probably first used in only one geographic area.

The Acts of the Apostles continues the story told in Luke and was written by the same author. Acts tells about the expansion of the early church. The story opens in Jerusalem, where the apostles gather after Jesus is raised from the dead. The book ends in Rome, where Saint Paul, the church's first great missionary, preaches to the Jews while a Roman prisoner.

The Letters make up 21 books. These books contain some of the earliest writings in the New Testament, though they appear in the canon after the Gospels and the Acts. The Letters are also known as *Epistles,* from a Greek word meaning *letter.* The first 13 letters are called the *Pauline letters.* They claim to be letters from Saint Paul mainly to Christian congregations he had founded. The last eight letters are called *General Letters.* Most of them claim to be letters from early church leaders.

Most scholars doubt that Paul actually wrote all 13 of the Pauline Letters. The letters he did write provide a record of Paul's preaching. The letters discuss problems of faith and conduct. Most of them were probably written in the A.D. 50's and early 60's.

The General Letters were written over a number of years to about A.D. 125. They deal with problems faced by second- and third-generation Christians. In form, the General Letters resemble the Pauline Letters.

Revelation is also called the *Apocalypse,* from a Greek word meaning *revelation.* A man named John wrote the book, but he is probably not the same person who wrote the Gospel of John.

Revelation begins as a letter "to the seven churches that are in Asia." It then gives a symbolic description of God's final triumph, through Christ, over evil and death. This description comes from a series of visions of the future sent by God to the author through an angel.

Development of the New Testament. The first generation of Christians preserved memories of Jesus Christ's teachings, deeds, and Crucifixion largely by word of mouth. The story of Jesus was not written down in the Gospels until the second generation of the church.

The authors of the New Testament did not deliberately try to create a Christian Bible. The early church had a Bible, the Hebrew Bible, especially in its Greek translation. But, differing views of Christian faith in the A.D. 100's led the church to form the New Testament canon. It needed the canon as authority against unacceptable religious views. The church also wanted to preserve the authentic story of Jesus's life and death in writing for future generations of Christians.

The church asked three main questions about the writings it considered for the canon. (1) Were the writings widely accepted and used in the church? (2) Did they follow the church's traditional teachings? (3) Were they thought to have been written or authorized by an apostle?

By about A.D. 200, the church canon included most of today's New Testament. In A.D. 367, the content of the New Testament was first listed exactly as we now know it. This canon was gradually adopted by all Christians.

The Bible as history

Historical study of the Bible has two main aspects. One aspect concerns the historical accuracy of events mentioned in the Bible. The second concerns how scholars can use the Bible to learn more about the history and people of the ancient Near East.

Historical accuracy of the Bible. Scholars have been able to confirm many of the statements of the Bible through archaeology and the study of documents written by other peoples of the ancient Near East. For ex-

The Ascension (about A.D. 586), a water color on parchment by Rabula, a Syrian priest; Laurentian Library, Florence, Italy (G. B. Pineider)

Illuminations were pictures and designs that decorated many hand-copied Bibles during the Middle Ages. This scene of Jesus Christ rising to heaven appears in a copy of the Gospels.

ample, scholars have discovered the decree of Cyrus, king of Persia, permitting the peoples exiled by his Babylonian predecessors to return to their ancestral lands and to reclaim their sacred shrines and holy objects. For this reason, the Biblical story of Cyrus's permitting the Jews to return to Israel with the utensils from the Jerusalem Temple and to rebuild the Temple may be taken as historically verified.

It is impossible to confirm the miraculous events described in the Bible. People may explain them in several

By permission of the John Rylands Library, Manchester, England

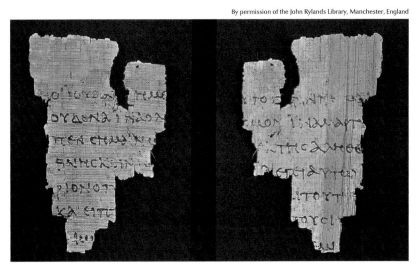

An ancient fragment of the Gospel of John dates from the early A.D. 100's, making it the oldest known example from any New Testament book. The two sides of the fragment, *left,* were part of a papyrus manuscript written in Greek.

The Masoretic text is the standard Jewish version of the Old Testament. It was prepared by Jewish scholars, called *Masoretes,* mainly from the A.D. 500's to the 900's. The Masoretes studied each letter, word, and phrase of the Old Testament in the original Hebrew language. They wrote marginal notes on the Biblical texts, commenting on proper grammar and spelling.

Ben Asher Codex (about A.D. 900); The British Library Board, London (John C. Trever)

ways. Some people regard miraculous occurrences, such as the appearance of angels, as dreams or prophetic visions. Others seek scientific explanations for Biblical miracles. They suggest that the story of Joshua's making the sun stand still in the sky represents a solar eclipse, or that Jesus and Elisha brought seemingly dead children back to life using mouth-to-mouth resuscitation. But such theories can never be proved, and they do not explain all Biblical miracles.

Many scholars and religious authorities believe that some Biblical stories originated in the desire of ancient Hebrew leaders to disprove certain ancient Near Eastern beliefs. Scholars have found such meanings in a number of Biblical stories, including the Creation, the Flood, and the Ten Plagues.

The Bible as a historical source. The authors of the Bible did not intend only to record the facts of history. They interpreted the facts and events to teach their philosophy of history and their beliefs about God and God's role in history. However, the Bible is the best source of information about many historical periods and events. In other cases, the Bible can add to what is already known from other sources. Whichever the case, it is the job of the historian to separate the facts of history from the Bible's interpretation of it. The historian must reconstruct this history using facts from the Bible and those obtained from non-Biblical sources.

An example of the Bible's treatment of history appears in the story of the Israelites' escape from Egypt and their journey to the land of Canaan. The Book of Exodus tells how God parted the waters of the Red Sea, leaving a dry path for the Israelites to walk across. God then closed the waters and drowned the pursuing Egyptians. The book goes on to describe the route the Israelites took in their journey to Canaan, and the battles and adventures they had along the way. Unfortunately, many of the locations mentioned are unknown today.

Some historians deny that the Israelites were ever in Egypt. Other historians argue that, because the Exodus is the most popular theme in the Hebrew Bible, it is impossible for it not to be true. There is a wide range of other opinion about the event. Some writers have sought scientific explanations for the crossing of the Red Sea, such as shifts in tides or storms. Others have

interpreted the story of the crossing as a myth.

Translations of the Bible

The first translations of the Bible were oral versions of the Hebrew Bible in Aramaic. An Aramaic translation is called a *Targum,* which comes from a Hebrew word meaning *translation.* Targums were made for ancient Jewish communities that spoke Aramaic rather than Hebrew. Jews who spoke only Aramaic could not understand the Bible when it was read aloud in Hebrew. In a synagogue, a translator would translate Hebrew passages into the local Aramaic language. Rabbinic tradition suggests that the practice of translating the Torah into Aramaic originated with the prophet Ezra when the Jews returned from Babylonia in the 400's B.C.

Jews who lived in Greek-speaking parts of the world also needed a translation of the Bible. In the mid-200's B.C., a group of scholars working in Alexandria, Egypt, translated the Law into Greek. According to tradition, Ptolemy, the Greek king of Egypt, called 70 or 72 Jewish scholars to Alexandria to translate the Law for his famous library. The story tells that the scholars, working separately, all arrived at the same translation. The translation is called the *Septuagint,* from a Latin word meaning *seventy.* Later Greek translations of the rest of the Bible came to be considered part of the Septuagint. Most of the first Christians spoke Greek, and so the early church used the Septuagint. But the need for more translations arose as Christianity spread to Syria and to Latin-speaking countries. Bibles translated into Syriac (an Aramaic dialect) and Latin appeared in the A.D. 100's.

About A.D. 383, Saint Jerome began a revision of the Latin Bible at the request of Pope Saint Damasus I. As his sources for the Old Testament, Jerome used Hebrew and Greek texts and Latin translations. For the New Testament, he used Greek texts and Latin translations. He completed the project in A.D. 405. His version became known as the *Vulgate,* from the Latin word meaning *popular.* For centuries, it was the only version of the Bible authorized by the Roman Catholic Church.

Early English translations. The first complete English translation of the Bible appeared in the 1380's. The translation was made by John Wycliffe, an English priest, and his followers.

The German Protestant reformer Martin Luther translated the New Testament into German in 1522. He and his colleagues finished translating the rest of the Bible in 1534. About the same time, William Tyndale, an Englishman, translated the Bible into English while living in Germany. Tyndale based some of his translation on Luther's German version. Publication of Tyndale's New Testament began in Cologne, Germany, in 1525. Portions of the Old Testament appeared in 1530 and 1531. The vigorous language of Tyndale's translation greatly influenced most later translations and revisions of the Bible in English.

Miles Coverdale, an English bishop, prepared the first complete English Bible to be printed. He used much of Tyndale's translation, portions of Luther's Bible, and the *Vulgate*. Coverdale's Bible was printed in Germany in 1535.

English refugees living in France made the first Roman Catholic translation of the Bible from Latin into English. The New Testament was published in Reims (also spelled *Rheims*), France, in 1582. The Old Testament was published in Douay, France, in 1609 and 1610. The translation became known as the *Douay-Rheims Bible* or the *Douay Bible*.

The King James Version. In 1604, King James I of England authorized a committee of about 50 scholars to prepare a revision of earlier English translations of the Bible. The new version appeared in 1611 and became known as the *King James,* or *Authorized, Version.* The

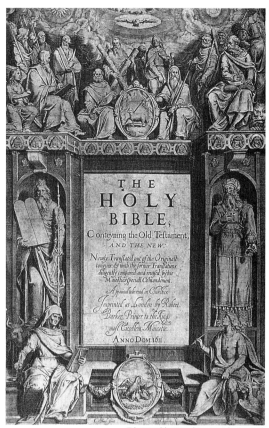

Title page of the 1611 edition; Beinecke Rare Book and Manuscript Library, Yale University

The King James Version of the Bible was printed in 1611. It served as the official translation for most English-speaking Protestants until the 1900's, when several new translations appeared.

beauty and grace of the translation established the King James Version as one of the great treasures of the English language. No important English translations of the Bible appeared for more than 200 years after the publication of the King James Version. During this time, the *King James Version* was the most widely used translation in the English-speaking world.

By the mid-1800's, scholars and religious leaders were calling for fresh translations of the Bible. Scholars had more accurate knowledge of the original Hebrew and Greek Biblical texts and so uncovered many errors in the texts used by the *King James* revisers. Scholars also gained more knowledge of other ancient Near Eastern languages, which added to their understanding of the Biblical languages. In addition, the English language itself had changed greatly over the years. A large number of words in the *King James Version* no longer had the same meaning or were even understood by readers of the Bible.

In 1870, the Church of England decided to revise the *King James Version.* The New Testament appeared in 1881, the Old Testament in 1885, and the Apocrypha in 1895. But the early popularity of the translation, called the *Revised Version,* did not last. Most individuals and churches still preferred the *King James Version.*

Saint Jerome, *right,* a great Biblical scholar of the early church, dictates to a scribe. Jerome's Vulgate was the only version of the Bible authorized by the Roman Catholic Church for centuries.

Modern English translations. Several modern English translations of the Bible have tried to replace the out-of-date language of older versions. They have attempted to reproduce the flavor of everyday speech. These translations also have made improvements in printing the text of the Bible. For example, paragraphs separate the text into logical divisions, dialogue is enclosed in quotation marks, and poetry is printed to show its verse form.

In the early 1900's, James Moffatt, a Scottish scholar, translated the Bible in a rather free style. His New Testament appeared in 1913, and his Old Testament in 1924. In the United States, Edgar Goodspeed published a translation of the New Testament in 1923, and four other scholars published a version of the Old Testament in 1927. Their translations appeared in 1931 under the title *The Bible: An American Translation.*

The National Council of Churches of Christ in the U.S.A. sponsored a translation called the *Revised Standard Version,* which became highly popular. The New Testament was published in 1946, the Old Testament in 1952, and the Apocrypha in 1957. Several British Protestant churches sponsored a translation called the *New English Bible* (New Testament,1961; Old Testament and the Apocrypha, 1970). American Protestant scholars prepared the *New American Standard Bible* (New Testament , 1963; both Testaments, 1971). The American Bible Society sponsored a version commonly known as the *Good News Bible* (New Testament, 1966; Old Testament, 1976). Kenneth N. Taylor, an American author, completed *The Living Bible Paraphrased* in 1971. Taylor based his version on the *American Standard Version*, a 1901 revision of the *King James Version.* The New York Bible Society sponsored the *New International Version* (New Testament, 1973; Old Testament, 1976). A revised and updated version of *The Living Bible* was published in 1996 as the *New Living Translation.*

Roman Catholic scholars in England produced the *Jerusalem Bible* in 1966. They based their translation on a French version published in 1956. The first completely American Roman Catholic translation of the Bible was published in 1970 as the *New American Bible.*

Before the mid-1800's, English-speaking Jews used either the original Hebrew text or the *King James Version* of the Old Testament. Then, during the last half of the 1800's, Jewish scholars in Britain made several translations of the Hebrew Bible into English. But their translations were largely revisions of the *King James Version.* In 1917, a new translation of the Hebrew Bible into English was published in the United States. The Jewish Publication Society of America and the Central Conference of American Rabbis sponsored the project. The Jewish Publication Society also sponsored a new translation of the Hebrew Bible. Publication began in 1962 and was completed in 1981. This translation is noteworthy for its commitment to following the Hebrew Bible.

In 1973, a new edition of the *Revised Standard Version* appeared as the *Common Bible.* This edition was the first English translation of the Bible to be approved by Protestant, Roman Catholic, and Greek Orthodox religious leaders. In 1990, leaders of the major Christian faiths endorsed another new edition called the *New Revised Standard Version.* This edition, sponsored by the National Council of Churches, replaced many masculine words with words applying to both sexes.

Terrance D. Callan and B. Barry Levy

Outline

I. **The Hebrew Bible**
  A. Books of the Hebrew Bible
  B. Development of the Hebrew Bible
  C. Development of the Christian Old Testament
II. **The New Testament**
  A. Books of the New Testament
  B. Development of the New Testament
III. **The Bible as history**
  A. Historical accuracy of the Bible
  B. The Bible as a historical source
IV. **Translations of the Bible**
  A. The first translations
  B. Early English translations
  C. The King James Version
  D. Modern English translations

Questions

Who produced the Vulgate translation of the Bible?

What was the original language of the Hebrew Bible? Of the New Testament?

How did the *Septuagint* get its name?

Why are the New Testament books of Matthew, Mark, and Luke called the *Synoptic Gospels?*

What is meant by the *canon?*

What were the three main questions the early church asked about the writings it considered for the canon?

How many books are in the Hebrew Bible? In the New Testament?

What is the purpose of a *Targum?*

What are the Dead Sea Scrolls?

What are *illuminations?*

Who translated the King James Version of the Bible?

In what way have readers long differed in how to explain the meaning of parts of the Bible?

Additional resources

Level I

Alexander, Pat, and others, eds. *The Lion Encyclopedia of the Bible.* 2nd ed. 1986. Reprint. B M H Bks., 1987.

Day, Malcolm. *The Ancient World of the Bible.* Viking, 1994.

Lucas, Daryl J. *The Baker Bible Dictionary for Kids.* Baker Bk. Hse., 1997.

Pipe, Rhona. *The Big Book of Bible Facts.* Thomas Nelson, 1993.

Schmidt, Gary D. *The Blessing of the Lord: Stories from the Old and New Testaments.* Eerdmans, 1997.

Level II

Achtemeier, Paul J., ed. *The HarperCollins Bible Dictionary.* Rev. ed. Harper San Francisco, 1996.

Freedman, David N., and others, eds. *The Anchor Bible Dictionary.* 6 vols. Doubleday, 1992.

Gordon, Cyrus H., and Rendsburg, Gary A. *The Bible and the Ancient Near East.* 4th ed. Norton, 1997.

Keck, Leander, and others, eds. *The New Interpreter's Bible.* Abingdon, 1994-. Multivolume work.

Web sites

Bible Browser
http://www.stg.brown.edu/webs/bible_browser/
An online tool for retrieving passages by their chapter and verse or by key words or phrases, created by the Scholarly Technology Group at Brown University.

West Semitic Research Project
http://www.usc.edu/dept/LAS/wsrp/
The official Web site of the West Semitic Research Project (WSRP) at the University of Southern California, which studies the Dead Sea Scrolls and other ancient texts and images relating to the Bible and the ancient Near East. Has an Educational Site section which includes interactive puzzles that help users understand how scholars decipher ancient writing.

Mosaic (500's) in the Church of Saint Cosmas and Saint Damian, Rome (SCALA/Art Resource)

Jesus Christ is the central figure of Christianity. This mosaic shows Saint Peter, in white on the left, and Saint Paul, in white on the right, presenting Saints Cosmas and Damian to Jesus. Saints Felix IV and Theodore stand at the far left and far right, respectively.

Christianity is the religion based on the life and teachings of Jesus Christ. Most followers of Christianity, called Christians, are members of one of three major groups—Roman Catholic, Protestant, or Eastern Orthodox. These groups have different beliefs about Jesus and His teachings. But all consider Jesus central to their religion. Most Christians believe God sent Jesus into the world as the Savior. Christianity teaches that humanity can achieve salvation through Jesus.

Jesus lived in Judea (later called Palestine), a Middle Eastern land ruled by the Romans. The Romans crucified Jesus about A.D. 30. Jesus's followers were convinced that He rose from the dead, and they soon spread Christianity to major cities throughout the Roman Empire. Today, Christians make up the largest religious group in the world. Christianity has almost 2 billion followers worldwide. It is the major religion in Europe, the Western Hemisphere, and Australia. Many Christians also live in Africa and Asia.

Christianity has had an enormous influence on Western civilization, especially on art, literature, and philosophy. The teachings of Christianity have had a lasting effect on the conduct of business, government, and social relations.

Beliefs

Christians believe that there is one God, and that He created the universe and continues to care for it. The belief in one God was first taught by the Jewish religion.

Christianity teaches that God sent His Son, Jesus, into the world as His chosen servant, called the *Messiah* (*Christos* in Greek), to help people fulfill their religious duties. Christianity also teaches that after Jesus's earthly

life, God's presence remained on earth in the form of the *Holy Spirit,* or *Holy Ghost.* The belief that in one God there are three Persons—the Father, the Son, and the Holy Spirit—is known as the *doctrine of the Trinity.* Roman Catholic and Eastern Orthodox Churches and many Protestant churches accept this doctrine as the central teaching of Christianity.

Some Christians regard Jesus as a great but human teacher. However, most Christians view Jesus as *God incarnate*—that is, a divine being who took on the human appearance and characteristics of a man. They believe that Jesus is the Savior who died to save humanity from sin. According to this view, Jesus's death made salvation and eternal life possible for others.

Christians gather in churches because they believe that God intended them to form special groups for worship. In addition, they meet in churches to encourage one another to lead upright lives according to God's moral law.

Two practices important to Christian worship usually take place in churches. These practices are (1) baptism and (2) the Eucharist, also called Holy Communion or the Lord's Supper. The ceremony of baptism celebrates an individual's entrance into Christianity. The Eucharist represents the Last Supper, the final meal that Jesus shared with His disciples. Worshipers share bread and wine in the Eucharist as a sign of their unity with each other and with Jesus.

Christians see Jesus as continuous with the God of Judaism. A collection of Christian writings was added to the Jewish scriptures known as the Old Testament, or Hebrew Bible. The Christian writings, called the New Testament, record the life and teachings of Jesus. They also describe the development of the early church and explain what faith in Jesus means. The Christian Bible includes both the Old and New Testaments. Some Christian groups also accept as part of the Bible a collection of writings called the Apocrypha.

The origin of Christianity

Jesus's ministry. Christianity originated in Jesus's ministry. During His lifetime, Jesus preached the gospel, meaning *good news,* that God was coming to earth to be among His people in a special way. Jesus called this special way the Kingdom of God. He warned His listeners to repent their sinful ways to be ready for the approaching Kingdom of God. In urging repentance for sin, Jesus gave His own interpretation of Jewish law to show how people could obey God and achieve righteousness.

For a time, Jesus's teaching brought Him great popularity. Reports spread that He performed such miracles as healing the sick and bringing the dead back to life. Jesus's popularity caused opposition from Jewish and Roman officials. The Romans charged Jesus with treason, and they crucified Him as a criminal.

Resurrection and Pentecost. The followers of Jesus did not accept His death as His end. Jesus's followers were certain that Jesus came back from the dead. They believed that He later rose to heaven. Many stories circulated about Jesus's appearance among His disciples after His death.

Reports of the Resurrection convinced many people that Jesus was the Son of God. Some followers began to call Jesus the Messiah, the Savior of the Jewish people promised in the Old Testament. Followers of Jesus came to believe that they, too, could receive eternal life because of Jesus's Resurrection.

Jesus had chosen 12 men, known as the *apostles,* to preach the gospel after His death. About 50 days after the Crucifixion, the apostles and other followers of Jesus claimed that the Holy Spirit had entered them and given them the ability to speak foreign languages. This ability enabled them to spread Jesus's teachings to all lands. Christians date the beginning of the church to this event, which they celebrate as Pentecost.

The first Christians were Jews. Soon, many *gentiles* (non-Jews) converted to the new faith. Peter and the other apostles urged people to accept Jesus as the divine Christ who had conquered sin and death. Peter founded churches in Palestine and, according to Christian tradition, headed the church in Rome.

Paul, an early convert to Christianity, preached mainly to gentiles outside Palestine. Paul believed that human nature is basically sinful. For that reason, he felt that people are unable to repent and live according to God's law. Yet Paul believed that human nature can be changed through faith in Jesus as the Son of God and belief in His power to forgive sin. According to Paul, people can share in Jesus's life through baptism and the Eucharist. Paul's version of Christianity has survived in his *epistles* (letters) to the young Christian churches. The epistles form part of the New Testament.

At first, there were many kinds of Christian leaders, both men and women. No central authority regulated their activities. But by A.D. 100, churches began to distinguish between religious leaders, called *clergy,* and the

general membership. The most important leader in every large church was a bishop who supervised other clergy. Christians relied on bishops to interpret Christian teachings and ensure correct belief.

The spread of Christianity

The early church. At first, the Roman government considered Christianity a legal Jewish sect. However, beginning in A.D. 64, and continuing for the next 250 years, various Roman emperors persecuted the followers of Christianity. Rather than weakening the young religion, persecution strengthened it. Persecution gave believers of Christianity an opportunity to prove their faith by dying for it.

The Roman Emperor Constantine the Great gave Christians freedom of worship in 313. He called the first *ecumenical* (general) church council in 325 to make doctrine uniform throughout the empire. The council adopted a statement known as the Nicene Creed, which said that Jesus Christ was of the same substance as God. The council condemned *Arianism,* a belief that Jesus was not completely divine.

By 392, Christianity had become the official religion of the Roman Empire. The church then grew more involved in worldly affairs. In protest, some believers adopted a way of life known as *monasticism.* They withdrew from everyday life to concentrate on prayer and meditation. During the 500's, Saint Benedict of Nursia established monasteries where monks and nuns lived in separate communities. He also set down rules for the monastic way of life. For 500 years, most monastics in Europe belonged to the Benedictine religious order. The Benedictines helped spread Christianity throughout western Europe.

Detail of a fresco (1290's) by Giotto in the Church of Saint Francis, Assisi, Italy (SCALA/Art Resource)

Saint Francis of Assisi established the influential Franciscan religious order during the Middle Ages. In this fresco, Francis and his followers kneel before Pope Innocent III.

In 395, the Roman Empire was split into the West and East Roman empires. In 476, the last West Roman emperor fell from power. German chieftains carved up the West Roman Empire. The East Roman Empire survived as the Byzantine Empire until 1453, when Turks captured its capital, Constantinople (now Istanbul).

Christianity also had a Western and an Eastern church. The center of the Western church was in Rome. The center of the Eastern church was in Constantinople. The most powerful church leaders were the bishop of Rome, called the *pope,* in the West and the patriarch of Constantinople in the East.

The Middle Ages began after the fall of the West Roman Empire and continued for about 1,000 years. During the Middle Ages, Christianity replaced the Roman Empire as the unifying force in western Europe.

After the fall of the West Roman Empire, the pope had more authority than any other person in Europe. The most influential early pope was Gregory the Great, whose reign began in 590. Gregory sent missionaries to convert the people of England. He also established rules of conduct for the clergy.

The pope exercised political as well as spiritual authority. In 800, Pope Leo III crowned the Frankish ruler Charlemagne emperor of the Romans. Charlemagne had united much of western Europe. He wanted to restore the stability of Roman rule in an empire built on the Christian faith. Charlemagne's empire declined after his death in 814. But Leo III had established the pope's right to make an emperor's authority lawful.

After Charlemagne, disputes arose over the distribution of power between the church and the state. A large number of kings and nobles insisted on the right to appoint church officials. The desire for an independent clergy led Pope Nicholas II to establish the Sacred College of Cardinals in 1059. The Sacred College of Cardinals assumed responsibility for electing a pope. In 1075, Pope Gregory VII announced that the pope would appoint clergy free from outside interference. He also outlawed *simony,* the practice of buying and selling church posts.

Medieval religious scholars called *scholastics* expanded Christian doctrine into a complete body of thought that included science and philosophy. The scholastics wished to reach a better understanding of Christian faith through reason. Saint Anselm, an early scholastic, attempted to prove God's existence through logic. In the 1200's, Saint Thomas Aquinas produced the most important scholastic work, the *Summa Theologica.* In it, he brought Christian doctrine into harmony with the teachings of the ancient Greek philosopher Aristotle.

Monasteries were centers of learning throughout the Middle Ages. In the 1200's, members of new religious orders, called *friars,* began to work among the people. Franciscan friars followed the selfless example of Saint Francis of Assisi, who founded their order in 1209. Franciscans were noted for their loving service to others. The Dominican order, founded in 1216 by Saint Dominic, became noted for its scholarship.

During the Middle Ages, Christian armies tried to recapture Palestine, which had been conquered by Muslim Turks. These military expeditions, known as *Crusades,* began just before 1100 and ended in the late 1200's. The crusaders failed to hold the Holy Land. But

their contact with the East greatly influenced European culture.

The division of the church

The split between East and West. The two centers of Christianity—Rome and Constantinople—drifted further apart during the early Middle Ages. Eastern Christians enjoyed political stability, and they tolerated a wide range of religious discussion. Western believers supported many different kingdoms, but they insisted on complete agreement over doctrine. Disagreements over the pope's authority in the East produced a *schism* (split) in 1054 between the Eastern Orthodox Churches and the Roman Catholic Church. The schism still exists today. However, some Eastern churches eventually reunited with the Roman Catholic Church, forming what are now called the Eastern Catholic Churches.

Decline of papal authority. In 1309, a French pope moved the *papacy* (office of the pope) from Rome to Avignon in what is now France. The papacy remained in Avignon until 1377. French kings and nobles exerted influence on the papacy and greatly reduced its prestige. This decline in the institution of the papacy made many members of the clergy impatient for reform.

In 1378, a disagreement among the cardinals resulted in the election of two rival popes. For a time, three men opposed one another as the rightful pope. Finally in 1417, the Council of Constance elected a pope who was accepted by all the rival groups.

The Reformation. The desire to reform Christianity grew stronger during the 1500's. In 1517, a movement called the Reformation began when Martin Luther, a German monk, criticized certain church practices. The Reformation divided Western Christianity into the Roman Catholic Church and Protestantism.

Luther disagreed with church teaching about the role of human effort in salvation. Appealing to the theology of Saint Paul, Luther emphasized solely God's role in salvation. Luther's position contrasted with Roman Catholic views that humanity must freely cooperate with God's grace. According to Luther, the Bible alone and not traditional church doctrine should guide Christians. The Lutheran movement based on his teachings spread rapidly through northern Germany and the Scandinavian countries during the 1520's.

The teachings of John Calvin, a French Protestant thinker, greatly influenced the Reformation in Switzerland, England, Scotland, France, and the Netherlands. Calvin agreed with Luther about salvation through faith. But Calvin was more interested in how Christianity could reform society. Calvin urged Christians to live in communities according to the divine law expressed in the Bible.

In England, King Henry VIII influenced Parliament to establish the Church of England after he had declared his independence from the pope in 1534. However, Calvinists in England wanted further reform. Their disputes with the Church of England led to the formation of the Presbyterian and Congregationalist churches in the 1600's.

Some smaller, more radical religious groups claimed that the Lutherans and Calvinists had not gone far enough in reforming Christianity. Some of these groups, including the Baptists, Quakers, and Mennonites, developed their own forms of worship.

The Counter Reformation. Some Christians wanted to reform the Roman Catholic Church without leaving it. To renew Catholic worship, the pope and other Catholic bishops called the Council of Trent, which met at various times from 1545 to 1563. A large number of decrees issued by the council deliberately opposed Protestant viewpoints. For this reason, the movement for reform within the church has been called the Counter Reformation. It is also known as the Catholic Reformation. The council emphasized church tradition as having equal authority with the Bible. In addition, the bishops at the council stressed the role of human effort in achieving salvation.

A leading force in the Counter Reformation was the Society of Jesus, or Jesuit order, founded by Saint Ignatius Loyola in 1534. The Jesuits quickly restored religious zeal among believers in southern Europe. Jesuit missionaries helped spread Roman Catholicism to many peoples throughout the world.

The 1700's and 1800's

The spread of Protestantism contributed to a series of religious wars between Catholics and Protestants that ended in 1648. Christianity faced many challenges in the periods that followed, even though conflicts among Christians lessened.

Rationalism and pietism were two viewpoints that reduced religious controversy during the 1700's. Rationalism was the belief in an orderly universe that could be explained by human reason, especially by scientific principles. Rationalist thinkers urged religious people of all beliefs to agree on certain basic ideas. These ideas included the existence of a purposeful God or maker of the world, the existence of the soul, and the certainty of rewards and punishment in a life after death. Rationalists thought that disputes over belief involved matters of opinion rather than reasoned truths. But they came into conflict with a large number of Christians because they rejected the Bible and church tradition as sources of truth.

Pietism avoided controversy in another way. Rather than appealing to reason, it emphasized the strong emotional power of personal religious experience. The pietists believed such experience was more important than intellectual formulas. The pietists considered a private relationship with God more important than doctrinal precision or correct forms of worship. The most important figure in the pietist movement was John Wesley, an English clergyman. Wesley's followers, called *Methodists,* separated from the Church of England in the late 1700's.

The rise of nationalism during the 1800's weakened the influence of Christianity, especially the Roman Catholic Church. After the French Revolution began in 1789, the forces of nationalism and democracy swept across Europe. New governments tended to separate the powers of church and state. Nationalist movements questioned the supreme authority of the pope.

In the mid-1800's, Pope Pius IX took steps to uphold the authority of the Roman Catholic Church. The *Syllabus of Errors,* issued by Pius in 1864, condemned republican government, rationalism, and other ideas that threatened the power and authority of the church. In 1869, Pius assembled Vatican Council I. It produced the most controversial act of his reign—the declaration of *papal infallibility.* According to this declaration, the pope cannot be in error when he speaks as head of the church on matters of faith or morals.

Science also challenged Christian belief. The evolutionary theory of biological development proposed by the British naturalist Charles Darwin conflicted with the Biblical version of creation.

Christianity today

Science and technology have changed the modern world and have created some new problems while solving old ones. A large number of people question whether religion can meet human needs in today's world of technology. In response, many Christians try to deal with basic issues of human welfare, and Christian leaders speak out on such issues as world peace and human rights. Some Christians seek a more emotional form of religious worship and turn to *charismatic Christianity* and other movements that stress a personal response to Jesus.

A search for unity, known as the *ecumenical movement,* became a major concern of Christians during the 1900's. Protestants began meeting to explore closer cooperation in 1910. Protestant leaders formed the World Council of Churches in 1948. This organization works to reduce differences on doctrine and to promote Christian unity. Today, the World Council of Churches also represents Eastern Orthodox Churches. The Roman Catholic Church expressed its support for the ecumenical movement at Vatican Council II, which met from 1962 to 1965.   Henry Warner Bowden

Additional resources

Chadwick, Henry, and Evans, G. R., eds. *Atlas of the Christian Church.* Facts on File, 1987.
Cooper, Jean C., ed. *Dictionary of Christianity.* Fitzroy Dearborn, 1996.
McManners, John, ed. *The Oxford Illustrated History of Christianity.* Oxford, 1990.
Mursell, Gordon, ed. *The Story of Christian Spirituality.* Fortress, 2001.
Olson, Roger E. *The Story of Christian Theology.* InterVarsity, 1999.
Penney, Sue. *Christianity.* Raintree Steck-Vaughn, 1997. Younger readers.

Web site

Christianity Resources
http://www.academicinfo.net/Christian.html
An annotated directory of online resources on Christianity.

Topics for study

The three major divisions of Christianity are the Protestant denominations, the Roman Catholic Church, and the Eastern Orthodox Churches. In what ways do these groups differ from one another?

The Roman Empire was renowned for its tolerance of diverse forms of religious expression. Why, then, did the empire strongly oppose Christianity during the church's first 300 years?

What are the goals of the Christian ecumenical movement? What do you think are the main problems in achieving these goals?

© Mehmet Biber, Photo Researchers

Muslim pilgrims pray at the Kaaba, the holiest shrine of Islam. The Kaaba is an empty cube-shaped building that stands in the center of the Great Mosque in the city of Mecca, Saudi Arabia. According to Islamic law, all adult Muslims must, if possible, make at least one pilgrimage to Mecca during their lifetime.

Islam, *ihs LAHM,* is the name given to the religion preached by the Prophet Muhammad in the A.D. 600's. Islam is an Arabic word that means *surrender* or *submission.* God is called *Allah* (in Arabic, pronounced *ah LAH),* which means *The God.* A person who submits to Allah and follows the teachings of Islam is called a *Muslim.* This article discusses the beliefs and practices of Islam.

Muhammad was born about A.D. 570 in the Arabian city of Mecca. Muslims believe that in about 610, he began to receive revelations from Allah that were transmitted by the angel Gabriel. These revelations took place in the cities of Mecca and Medina over about a 22-year period. They were assembled in a book called the Qur'ān *(ku RAHN),* sometimes spelled *Koran.* The Qur'ān is the holy book of the Muslims, who believe it contains God's actual words. The Qur'ān and the *Sunna (SOON uh),* the example of the words and practices of Muhammad, make up the foundation of Islamic law.

Islam is the world's second largest religion behind Christianity. Over 1.1 billion people follow Islam. Today, Muslims live in every country in the world. Although Islam began in Arabia, more than half of the world's Muslims live in South and Southeast Asia. The countries with the largest Muslim populations are Indonesia, India, Bangladesh, and Pakistan. About one-fourth of all Muslims live in the Middle East. They make up the majority of the population in the European country of Albania and nearly half the population in Bosnia-Herzegovina. Muslims rank as the second largest religious group in Belgium, France, and Germany. Several million Muslims live in the United States.

Teachings and practices

The central concept of Islam is *tawhid (taw HEED),* the oneness of God. For Muslims, there is one God who is the lord of the universe. People owe worship and obedience to God before any other thing. God is one, the creator, the all-knowing. In relations with humanity, God is the lawgiver, judge, and restorer of life after death.

Prophets. According to the Qur'ān, God has provided guidance for human beings in the teachings of

prophets, who have appeared in many nations throughout history. In Islam, prophets do not foretell the future. Instead, God selects the prophets to urge people to worship God alone and to teach them to live according to God's commandments. The Qur'ān mentions 25 prophets by name. According to tradition, God chose thousands of prophets beginning with Adam, the first prophet in Islam, and ending with Muhammad, the final prophet. The Qur'ān teaches that the Prophet Abraham was the first *monotheist* (believer in one God).

The most important type of prophet in Islam is the *rasul (rah SOOL),* which means *messenger.* A rasul is a person to whom God has revealed a book for the guidance of humanity. The messengers of God in Islam include Abraham, Moses, David, Jesus, and Muhammad.

Muslims believe children are born without sin and that all people can lead themselves to salvation once God has shown them the way. Believers in Islam achieve salvation by following the revealed books of God's messengers. Muslims believe in heaven and hell, where people go after death based on their actions during life.

The Sunna of Muhammad. In Islam, Muhammad is the final messenger of God, sent to confirm the authentic teachings of previous prophets. God also sent him to correct the alterations that followers of previous religions had introduced into God's original teachings. For Muslims, Muhammad's mission includes all humanity and is not limited to a specific region, group, or community. Therefore, his life serves as a model for all men and women. The example of Muhammad's sayings and acts, the Sunna, is presented in written collections

The symbol of Islam is a crescent and star. The symbol appears on the flags of several nations whose population has a Muslim majority, including Pakistan and Turkey.

called the *Hadith (hah DEETH).*

Muslims do not consider Islam to be a new religion. They believe its teachings contain the same message given to all prophets and messengers since the creation of Adam. Because Muslims confirm all of these teachings as a whole, they do not like to be called *Muhammadans.*

The Five Pillars of Islam. Every action performed in obedience to God is considered an act of worship in Islam. A majority of devout Muslims take care in their daily lives to respect their parents and elders, to be kind to animals and human beings, and to do their daily tasks to the best of their ability. The formal acts of worship called the Five Pillars of Islam provide the framework for all aspects of a Muslim's life. The pillars consist of (1) *shahada,* (2) prayer, (3) almsgiving, (4) fasting, and (5) pilgrimage.

Shahada is the first pillar and is considered the basis of all other pillars of the faith. *Shahada (shuh HAHD uh)* is an Arabic word that means *an act of bearing witness.* It consists of two statements: "I bear witness that there is no God but Allah," and "I bear witness that Muhammad is the Messenger of Allah." The first statement declares that there is only one God and that God alone is worthy of worship. The second statement says that Muhammad is God's messenger. For Muslims, the second statement also includes a declaration of belief in Muhammad's interpretation of Islam, as expressed in the Sunna.

Prayer. Muslims are required to pray five times a day—just before dawn, at midday, in midafternoon, just after sunset, and at night. Prayer, called *salat (suh LAHT),* is the most important demonstration of a Muslim's devotion to God. Muslims believe that prayer reinforces belief in Islam because it reduces the likelihood of disobeying God by committing sins. A prayer's timing is determined by the movement of the sun. A crier called a *muezzin (moo EHZ ihn)* makes the call to prayer. If the prayer is performed in a *mosque (masjid* in Arabic, meaning *house of worship),* the muezzin traditionally

calls worshipers from a tower called a *minaret.* Before making their prayers, Muslims must wash their hands, their face, parts of their arms and head, and their feet in a ritual manner.

The physical movements of the salat symbolize the believers' submission to God. When praying, Muslims stand facing the holy city of Mecca in Saudi Arabia. Raising their hands to their ears, they say in Arabic "God is greatest." They then recite the opening passage of the Qur'ān, known as the Fatiha *(FAH tee hah),* followed by another verse from the Qur'ān. After reciting these verses, they again say "God is greatest" and bow from the waist, praising God. After returning to an upright position, they say "God is greatest" a third time and fall to their knees, touching the floor with their foreheads. In this face-down position, they again praise God. After sitting back on their heels and asking God for forgiveness, worshipers kneel with their faces down one more time and then stand, saying "God is greatest" before each new position.

Each cycle of the prayer is called a *raka (RAHK uh),* which means *bowing* in Arabic. One cycle includes the first Qur'ān recitation, the bow, kneeling face down twice, sitting, and standing up. After the final cycle, worshipers offer a peace greeting. Depending on the time of day, the salat may have two to four cycles. On Fridays, Muslims gather at midday to pray as a group. Before the prayer, a religious leader called an *imam (ih MAHM)* recites two short sermons. Typically, men pray at the front of the group and women pray in a separate section behind or beside them.

Almsgiving is required as a way of assisting the poor. The Arabic term for almsgiving is *zakat,* which means *purification.* Muslims "purify" their wealth by giving a certain percentage of it to the needy and recognizing that all things ultimately belong to God. Zakat is paid once a year, in the form of a tax. Most zakat donations go to mosques, Islamic centers, or welfare organizations. Some Muslims supplement zakat with a voluntary

Muslims pray in a house of worship called a *mosque.* The worshipers face a decorative niche called a *mihrab* that points toward the holy city of Mecca, the direction Muslims must face while praying. Next to the mihrab is a pulpit called a *minbar.*

form of giving called *sadaqa (SAH dah kah),* which means *sincere gift* in Arabic.

Fasting. Every Muslim must fast in the month of Ramadan *(RAHM uh DAHN),* the ninth month of the Islamic calendar. The Islamic calendar is lunar, so each month follows the phases of the moon and lasts 29 or 30 days. As a result, Ramadan falls at different seasons of the year. Muslims believe that the first verses of the Qur'an were revealed to Muhammad during Ramadan about A.D. 610.

The Qur'an instructs Muslims to fast from dawn to sunset during Ramadan. While fasting, Muslims do not eat any food, drink any beverages, smoke, or engage in sexual relations during daylight hours. At night, they may eat, drink, and resume other normal activities. Muslims fast to practice spiritual reflection, self-restraint, concern for others, and obedience to God. Alms are normally given to the poor at the end of the fast. Because fasting can be physically demanding, some people are excused. Those excused include the sick, injured, elderly, and pregnant or nursing women. They are supposed to provide food for the poor, or if able, fast at a later time instead.

Pilgrimage. The Qur'an commands Muslims to make a *hajj* (pilgrimage) to Mecca at least once in their lifetime if they are physically and financially able to make the journey. The hajj takes place over the first several days of the 12th month of the Islamic calendar.

The rites of the hajj commemorate the trials and sacrifices of the Prophet Abraham, his wife Hagar, and their son the Prophet Ishmael. Muslims believe that Abraham and Ishmael built the Kaaba *(KAH bah)* as the first house of worship to God. The Kaaba is an empty cube-shaped building in the center of the Great Mosque in Mecca.

The first requirement of the hajj is that men wear two pieces of unsewn white cloth, called the *ihram,* which means *garment of consecration.* Women must wear a long white gown and headscarf. While wearing these garments, a pilgrim may not kill any animal or insect, remove any hair from his or her body, or engage in any sexual act. The second requirement is that pilgrims walk around the Kaaba seven times in a counterclockwise direction.

Most pilgrims perform three additional rites, though they are not official parts of the hajj. While walking, many pilgrims attempt to kiss or touch the Black Stone, which Abraham and Ishmael placed in one corner of the Kaaba. Pilgrims may also run seven times along a corridor of the Great Mosque to commemorate Hagar's search for water for her infant son, Ishmael. Finally, pilgrims may take water from a well called Zamzam on the grounds of the Great Mosque.

The third part of the hajj involves standing at Arafat, a plain outside Mecca, on the ninth day of the pilgrimage month. During the afternoon prayer, pilgrims listen to an imam deliver a sermon from the heights of Mount Arafat at the edge of the plain. This act commemorates the final pilgrimage of Muhammad, who delivered his farewell sermon from this site.

To finish the pilgrimage, Muslims next spend the night at Muzdalifah, an encampment near a place called Mina, on the way back to Mecca. The next day, they throw stones at the three pillars where, according to tradition, Ishmael drove away Satan's temptations. Many

Topic for study

How do Muslim women in various countries follow the teaching of the Qur'an regarding women's behavior? How has the influence of Western culture affected women in Islamic countries?

pilgrims also sacrifice an animal, usually a sheep or goat, at Mina. This action commemorates Abraham's vow to sacrifice his son. The hajj pilgrimage is completed after each pilgrim returns to Mecca and walks around the Kaaba seven more times.

Holidays and celebrations. All Muslims celebrate two major holidays, the Feast of Fast-Breaking and the Feast of Sacrifice. The first is held on the day following Ramadan and marks the end of the monthlong fast. The feast is a joyous occasion in which families gather for a rich meal and children receive sweets. The Feast of Sacrifice is held on the 10th day of Dhul-Hijja, the month of the hajj. On this day, many Muslims sacrifice an animal, such as a goat or sheep. A small portion of the meat is prepared for family and friends, and the rest is given to the poor.

In some countries, Muslims celebrate the birthday of Muhammad on the 12th day of the third Islamic month. Muslims spend the day praying, reading the Qur'an, and reciting poems and stories written in honor of the Prophet.

Muslims celebrate their New Year at the beginning of the first month of the Islamic calendar. On the 10th day of the month, members of the Shiite division hold a celebration called Ashura that marks the massacre in 680 of Husayn, a grandson of Muhammad. Muslims from Iran, Afghanistan, and central Asian countries follow an ancient solar calendar along with the Islamic lunar calendar. They often celebrate another New Year called Nawruz *(naw ROOZ)* on the first day of spring.

Islam's social structure

**The Shari`a.** Islam has two sources of authority. The first is the word of God given in the Qur'an. The second is the sunna, the body of traditions that preserves the words and conduct of Muhammad. Muslim scholars use these sources to understand the principles of the *Shari`a (shah REE ah),* also spelled *Shari`ah,* an Arabic word that means *the way that leads to God.* It refers to the divinely revealed and inspired Islamic law that plays a central role in the lives of Muslims. Scholars recognize four main sources for interpreting the Shari`a and applying it to daily life. The sources are (1) the Qur'an, (2) the sunna, (3) extending the reasoning of previous laws to new situations, and (4) the views of Muslim scholars and jurists.

In theory, all Islamic law is divine in origin. In practice, however, most sources of Muslim law are found in the sunna rather than the Qur'an, particularly in the part of the hadith that reflects Muhammad's interpretation of the rulings of the Qur'an. The practice of deriving present-day laws from the sources of the Shari`a is called *fiqh* (pronounced *fihk).* There are several schools of fiqh, each named after the founder of a method of interpretation. Although most Muslims agree about the major points of Islam, differences do exist, based on the opinions of the different schools of fiqh.

© Earl & Nazima Kowall, Corbis

Muslims celebrate their New Year at the beginning of Muharram, the first month of the Islamic calendar. In this picture, three Shiite Muslim men drink a special tea to mark the occasion.

Ethics and morals. Actions in Islamic law are judged on five values: (1) *obligatory* (required), (2) recommended, (3) neutral, (4) disapproved, and (5) forbidden. Most religious duties, such as the Five Pillars, are obligatory. Anyone who fails to perform them may be punished by God or the Islamic state. For example, in many Muslim countries, refusal to fast during Ramadan may result in fines or imprisonment. In some Muslim countries, special organizations ensure that people make their five daily prayers at the proper time and follow accepted standards of dress and behavior.

Most actions in Islamic law are not obligatory. People who fail to perform acts that are recommended or neutral are seldom punished. Most acts that are clearly forbidden are mentioned in the Qur'ān. These acts include adultery, gambling, cheating, consuming pork or alcoholic beverages, and lending money at interest. The Qur'ān details severe punishments for such crimes as murder, theft, and adultery. Crimes are punished harshly because they violate not only the rights of the victim, but also the commands of God. The Qur'ān seeks to lessen the severity of these punishments, however, by urging Muslims to practice mercy and not yield to revenge.

Islamic virtues. Islam teaches respect for parents, protection for orphans and widows, and charity to the poor. It also teaches the virtues of faith in God, kindness, honesty, hard work, honor, courage, cleanliness, and generosity. Heads of families must treat household members kindly and fairly. A wife has rights against her husband and may sue for divorce in cases of physical abuse, lack of financial support, or the inability to produce a child. Islam also teaches that a person must not refuse requests for help, even if they seem unnecessary.

Divisions of Islam. There are three historic divisions in Islam. The great majority of Muslims belong to the Sunni *(SOON ee)* division. Sunni Muslims call themselves by this name because they claim to follow the Sunna of Muhammad. They follow a traditional and widely held interpretation of Islam.

Topic for study

Compare the lives of Jesus, Buddha, and Muhammad. How were their teachings received by their contemporaries? How did they spread their teachings?

Most of the conservative Muslims whom Westerners call *fundamentalists* are Sunnis. Like fundamentalists of other religions, these Muslims follow a strict approach to religion. They reject modern and popular interpretations of Islamic law, which they view as too permissive. Fundamentalists insist instead on precise adherence to the Qur'ān and Hadith, as they interpret those writings. But many Muslims dislike the name *fundamentalists.*

The next largest division is the Shiah *(SHEE ah),* whose members are called Shiites. Shiite Muslims honor Ali, the cousin and son-in-law of Muhammad, and Ali's descendants, whom they believe should be the leaders of the Muslim community. Shiah comes from the Arabic phrase *shiat Ali,* meaning *supporters of Ali.*

The largest group of Shiites are the Imami *(ee MAHM ee)* Shiah. They are also known as the *Ithna Ashari,* or *Twelvers.* They see authority as residing in 12 imams, starting with Ali, who was born in about 600, and ending with Muhammad al-Mahdi, who was born in about 868. They believe this last imam is still alive, in a miraculous state of concealment from human view. He will return at the end of time to restore justice on earth. A small group of Shiites, known as the Ismaili *(ihs may EE lee)* Shiah, broke away from the Imamis in the 700's. One group of Ismailis, known as the Nizaris, still follow an imam called Aga Khan IV, who lives in France.

Today, the Kharijites make up the smallest division of Islam. Their name is based on an Arabic word that means *secessionists.* They received this name because they were former followers of Ali who broke away in 657. Kharijites are strict Muslims whose beliefs are based on precise adherence to the teachings of the Qur'ān and Sunna as their community interprets them. They are most noteworthy for their belief in equality under God. In the first centuries of their existence, they elected their leaders and proclaimed that the best Muslim should lead his fellow believers, even if he was a slave. In some Kharijite communities in Algeria, female scholars and religious leaders serve the needs of women while male scholars and religious leaders serve the needs of men.   Vincent J. Cornell

Additional resources

Ahmed, Akbar S. *Islam Today: A Short Introduction to the Muslim World.* I. B. Tauris, 1999.
Armstrong, Karen. *Islam: A Short History.* Modern Lib., 2000.
Esposito, John L. *Islam: The Straight Path.* 3rd ed. Oxford, 1998.
Esposito, John L., ed. *The Oxford Encyclopedia of the Modern Islamic World.* 4 vols. 1995. Reprint. Oxford, 2001. *The Oxford History of Islam.* 1999.
Morris, Neil. *Islam.* Bedrick, 2001. Younger readers.
Penney, Sue. *Islam.* Heinemann Lib., 2000. Younger readers.
Smith, Jane I. *Islam in America.* Columbia Univ. Pr., 1999.

Web site

Islamic Studies, Arabic, and Religion Web Page
http://www.arches.uga.edu/~godlas/#islam
Includes language aids, maps, art, music, history, texts, a glossary, and sections on the branches of Islam.

Jews from many nations come to Jerusalem to pray at the Western Wall, *above,* one of Israel's holiest shrines. The structure, also called the Wailing Wall, is all that remains of the Jews' holy Temple from Biblical times. It has long been a symbol of Jewish faith and unity.

Jews

Jews are the descendants of an ancient people called the Hebrews. During Biblical times, the Hebrews—who came to be called Israelites—lived in what is now Israel. But their country fell to a series of conquerors, and the Jews scattered throughout the world. By the A.D. 700's, they had established communities as far west as Spain and as far east as China.

The Jews have had great influence on history. They produced the Hebrew Bible, which, with its belief in one God and its moral teachings, became a cornerstone of two world religions, Christianity and Islam. But Jewish history has been full of tragedy. The Jews were a minority group almost everywhere they settled, and they often suffered persecution. During World War II (1939-1945), about 6 million Jews died in the Nazi campaign of mass murder known as the *Holocaust.*

Jews have always considered Israel their spiritual home. Beginning in the late 1800's, many Jews from Eastern Europe immigrated to Israel, then called Palestine. Many more Jews came to Palestine following the Holocaust. The state of Israel was founded in 1948.

Because of the long and varied history of the Jews, it is difficult to define a Jew. There is no such thing as a Jewish race. Jewish identity is a mixture of religious, historical, and ethnic factors. According to Jewish law, anyone born to a Jewish mother or converted to Judaism is considered a Jew. The branch of Judaism that is known

Elliot B. Lefkovitz, the contributor of this article, is Adjunct Professor of History at Loyola University and Spertus Institute of Jewish Studies.

as *Reform Judaism* also accepts as Jews children born to a non-Jewish mother and a Jewish father.

There are two broad groups of Jews. Most *Ashkenazim* are descendants of members of Jewish communities of central and Eastern Europe. The *Sephardim* are descendants of Jews from Spain, Portugal, or other Mediterranean countries and the Middle East. Other groups of Jews include those descended from Jewish communities of Ethiopia and India.

There are about 13 million Jews in the world. The largest Jewish population—about 6 million—lives in the United States. About $4\frac{3}{4}$ million Jews live in Israel. Other countries with large numbers of Jews include France, Russia, Britain, Canada, and Argentina. This article traces the history of the Jewish people throughout the world.

Early history of the Jewish people

Beginnings. The Jews trace their ancestry to a shepherd named Abraham, who lived sometime between 1800 and 1500 B.C. in southern Mesopotamia (now southeastern Iraq). According to the Bible, God told Abraham to leave Mesopotamia and settle in Canaan, the area that later became Israel. There, Abraham founded the people known as the Hebrews. Abraham, his son Isaac, and his grandson Jacob—also named Israel—are the *patriarchs* (fathers) of the Jewish people. The *matriarchs* (mothers) are Sarah (Abraham's wife), Rebecca (Isaac's wife), and Leah and Rachel (Jacob's wives). Jacob had 1 known daughter, Dinah, and 12 sons. By order of birth, they were Reuben, Simeon, Levi, Judah, Dan, Naphtali, Gad, Asher, Issachar, Zebulun, Joseph, and Benjamin. During the early centuries of their history, the

Hebrews were organized into groups that traced their descent to Jacob's sons. They called themselves the Twelve Tribes of Israel, or Israelites. The Bible describes how Jacob's son Joseph was sold into slavery in Egypt. Joseph's wisdom and honesty enabled him to become prime minister to the Egyptian pharaoh. Joseph invited the Israelites to Egypt after a famine struck Canaan. The Israelites lived peacefully in Egypt for many years until a new pharaoh enslaved them.

The Exodus. The Bible tells how a leader named Moses led the Israelites out of Egypt. According to the Bible, God helped the Israelites escape from slavery. The Jewish festival of Passover celebrates their deliverance, called the Exodus. Most scholars believe that the Exodus took place in the 1200's B.C.

According to tradition, God dictated His laws to Moses in a collection of teachings called the Torah after the Israelites left Egypt. Most scholars believe the Torah was written down much later. The Bible says that after receiving the Torah, the Israelites wandered in the wilderness for 40 years. Moses died before his people entered Canaan, but his successor, Joshua, led them into their old homeland. For about 200 years, the Israelites struggled to reestablish themselves in Canaan. They fought the Canaanites, the Philistines, and other peoples. This time is known as the period of the Judges. The Judges served as judicial and military leaders who united the Israelites in times of crisis. Deborah, Gideon, Samson, and Samuel were some famous Judges.

The kingdom of Israel. About 1029 B.C., the threat of warfare with the Philistines led the Israelites to choose a king, Saul, as their leader. Saul's successor, David, unified the people and founded the kingdom of Israel. Under David and his successor Solomon, the kingdom grew in size and power. David captured the city of Jerusalem from a people called the Jebusites and made it his capital. Solomon built a magnificent place of worship in Jerusalem. The Temple, known today as the First Temple, served as the center of religious life.

The divided kingdom. After Solomon died in about 928 B.C., the 10 northern tribes split away from the tribes of Benjamin and Judah in the south. The northern kingdom continued to be called Israel and had its capital in Samaria. The southern tribes kept Jerusalem as their capital and called their kingdom Judah. The word *Jew* comes from *Judah.* The kings of Judah came from the house of David. In the kingdom of Israel, there were struggles for power between various families.

During this period, religious teachers called *prophets* developed many of the principles of Judaism. The Bible contains the teachings of the major prophets, Isaiah, Jeremiah, and Ezekiel, and 12 minor prophets.

Foreign domination. In 722 or 721 B.C., the empire of Assyria conquered the northern kingdom. The people of Israel were exiled and scattered. They disappeared as a nation and became known as the *ten lost tribes.*

In 587 or 586 B.C., the Babylonians conquered Judah, destroyed the Temple, and took many Jews to Babylonia as prisoners. This period is called the *Babylonian Exile.* Unlike the ten lost tribes, the people of Judah did not lose their identity. Inspired by the prophet Ezekiel, they continued to practice their religion. The first *synagogues* (Jewish houses of worship) were probably developed by the Jews in Babylonia.

In 539 B.C., King Cyrus of Persia conquered Babylonia. The next year, Cyrus allowed the Jewish exiles to return to Judah. Many Jews returned and rebuilt the Temple, which became known as the Second Temple. However, some Jews remained in Babylonia. This was the first time since the Exodus that Jews had chosen to live outside Israel. Later, the communities of Jews scattered outside Israel became known as the Diaspora.

The Hellenistic period. Alexander the Great of Macedonia conquered the Persians in 331 B.C., and Judah came under his control. Alexander and his successors, the Ptolemies in Egypt and the Seleucids in Syria, brought *Hellenistic* (Greek) culture to the Jews. The Jews were allowed to follow their own religion. But in 168 or 167 B.C., King Antiochus IV of Syria tried to stop the practice of Judaism. The Jews, led by the warrior Judah Maccabee, revolted and overthrew the Syrians. The holiday of Hanukkah celebrates their victory. Judah Maccabee's family, the Hasmoneans, established an independent state that lasted about 80 years.

Under Hasmonean rule, different religious groups developed within Judaism. The groups disagreed over

The land of the early Jews

Abraham, the ancestor of the Jews, settled in Canaan (later called Palestine) between about 1800 and 1500 B.C. At first, the Jews were divided into tribes. About 1000 B.C., they united to form the kingdom of Israel, later called Judah or Judea. These maps show the changing boundaries of the area where the Jews lived during Biblical times.

_____ Boundary of present-day Israel

The kingdom of Israel was formed about 1000 B.C. and reached the height of its power during the 900's B.C.

The divided kingdom resulted from a split in the 900's B.C. between Israel in the north and Judah in the south.

An independent nation also called Judah existed in Palestine about 100 B.C. It was ruled by the Hasmoneans.

such matters as the *oral law*—the traditional interpretation of the Torah. The Pharisees believed God had revealed the oral law along with the Torah. Pharisees taught in synagogues and were supported by the common people. The Sadducees accepted only the Torah and found support among the rich and the temple priests. A third group, the Essenes, stressed personal holiness, through strict rules that included the sharing of property in communities apart from society.

Roman rule. In 63 B.C., the Romans conquered Judah, which they called Judea. Roman rule was generally harsh. The most famous ruler of Judea during this time, Herod the Great, is known for both his ruthlessness and his building activities.

Jesus was a Jew who was born in Judea. The Romans executed Jesus because they thought he was a threat to their rule. Jesus's followers, who came to be called Christians, believed that God sent Jesus to the world as the *Messiah* (Savior). Most Jews kept their traditional beliefs and did not accept Jesus as the Messiah.

The Jews revolted in A.D. 66 and drove out the Romans for a time. But in 70, the Roman general Titus conquered Jerusalem, destroyed the Temple, and took many Jewish captives to Rome. The Western, or Wailing, Wall in Jerusalem is all that remains of the Temple.

Some Jews, called Zealots, refused to surrender even after Jerusalem fell. Many Zealots retreated to a mountain fortress called Masada, where 960 men, women, and children held out for three years. As the Romans were about to conquer the fortress, the defenders supposedly committed suicide rather than surrender.

Under the spiritual leadership of the scholar Rabbi Akiva Baer ben Joseph, a warrior named Simeon Bar Kokhba led the Jews to rebel again in 132 and seize Jerusalem. In 135, the Romans crushed this final rebellion.

The Talmudic period and the Middle Ages

The Talmudic period. After the defeat of Bar Kokhba, the Romans prohibited Jews from living in Jerusalem. New centers of Jewish learning arose in Galilee, an area in northern Palestine; and in Babylonia. The Sanhedrin, the Jews' religious lawmaking body, met in Galilee. In about 200, the head of the Sanhedrin, Rabbi Judah ha-Nasi, wrote down the oral law in a book called the Mishnah. From about 200 to 500, other scholars collected interpretations of the Mishnah into a work called the Gemara. The Mishnah and the Gemara together form the Talmud. Two versions of the Talmud were created, one in Galilee (the Palestinian or Jerusalem Talmud) and the other in Babylonia (The Babylonian Talmud).

For many centuries, Jews throughout the world turned to the Babylonian Jewish community for religious and scholarly leadership. Jews sent questions of law and interpretation to scholars at Babylonian academies called *yeshivas*. The greatest such scholar, Saadia Gaon, lived in the late 800's and early 900's.

The Jews under Islam. In the mid-600's, Arabian Muslims founded an empire that soon included southwestern Asia, northern Africa, and Spain. The Muslims permitted Jews and Christians to practice their own religions. But both Jews and Christians had to pay a special tax and were not equal to Muslims under the law.

Large Jewish communities existed in such Muslim

Detail (about A.D. 239) from the west wall of the Second Synagogue, Dura Europas, Syria; National Museum of Damascus (Art Resource)

David ruled the kingdom of Israel about 1000 to 960 B.C. Under his rule, the kingdom grew in size and power. This wallpainting shows the prophet Samuel anointing David king.

lands as Babylonia, Egypt, Morocco, and Yemen. But the greatest center of Jewish culture arose in Muslim Spain. The period from the 900's to the 1100's in Spain is known as the Golden Age of Jewish history. Jews worked in crafts, in medicine and science, and in business and commerce. Some rose to high positions in government. Outstanding writers of the time included physician and philosopher Moses Maimonides, poet and philosopher Solomon ibn Gabirol, and poet Judah Halevi.

Jews in Christian Europe. After the fall of the Roman Empire, the Christian Church became the most powerful force in Europe. In the early Middle Ages, the Jews lived fairly peacefully with their Christian neighbors. Many Jews became merchants. Others practiced trades or owned land. Many Christians respected the Jews for their contributions to society. But some Christians blamed the Jews for the death of Jesus and mistrusted them because they would not accept Christianity. Such hatred of Jews later became known as *anti-Semitism*.

The situation of the Jews became worse beginning in 1096, when a series of military expeditions called the *Crusades* began. These campaigns to free the Holy Land from the Muslims stirred a wave of intense feeling against non-Christians. The Crusaders killed many Jews and sometimes massacred entire Jewish communities. The Crusades marked the beginning of a long period of Jewish *martyrdom* (death for a belief).

The Jews were seen by Christians more and more as outsiders. Some Christians accused Jews of bringing on the troubles of society. In the mid-1300's, a terrible plague, now known as the Black Death, swept Europe, eventually killing from a fourth to half of the population. Many Christians unfairly blamed the Jews for the Black Death, and mobs killed thousands of Jews. Christians commonly accused Jews of murdering Christian children as part of their religious rituals. This accusation, which became known as the *blood libel*, was used as an excuse to attack Jews.

Political and religious leaders required Jews in certain areas to wear badges or special clothes that identified them as Jews. In numerous cities, Jews were forced to live in separate communities that became known as

ghettos. Jews also lost the right to own land and to practice certain trades. To earn a living, many Jews became
peddlers or moneylenders.

Beginning in the late 1200's, the Jews were expelled
from England, France, and parts of central Europe. Many
settled in Eastern Europe, especially Poland.

To avoid persecution, some Jews in Spain and Portugal, which had become Christian countries, pretended
to convert to Christianity but continued to practice Judaism secretly. These Jews were known as *Marranos.*
Ferdinand and Isabella, the king and queen of Spain, established a special court called the *Inquisition* to punish
people suspected of not following Christian teachings.
The Inquisition used torture to force confessions from
its victims, many of whom were Marranos. In 1492, Jews
who had not converted to Christianity were expelled
from Spain. Soon after, Jews were forced to leave Portugal. Many Jews fled to what are now Italy and Turkey.
Some went to Palestine, where they studied the *Kabbal-
ah,* the Jewish mystical tradition.

In the 1500's, a movement called the *Reformation* led
to the development of Protestantism in Europe. It
seemed that the situation of the Jews might improve. But
when the Jews failed to convert to the new branch of
Christianity, persecution continued.

Eastern European religious movements. Jewish
life in Poland flourished in the 1500's. But in 1648 and
1649, the massacre of thousands of Jews in Ukraine—
then a part of Poland—began a time of crisis for Polish
Jews. Many hoped for someone to save them.

In 1665, a Jew named Shabbetai Zevi claimed to be
the Messiah. Hundreds of thousands of Jews in Europe
and the Middle East believed in Shabbetai. But Shabbetai converted to Islam, disappointing his followers.

Throughout Jewish history, learning and study had
formed the foundation of Jewish life and culture. In the
mid-1700's, a movement called *Hasidism* developed
among Jews of Eastern Europe. Hasidism, founded by a
Polish teacher known as Ba'al Shem Tov, stressed joyful
worship over the study of the Talmud. Most followers of
Hasidism, called *Hasidim,* were ordinary people. Opponents of Hasidism, called *Mitnaggedim,* considered Hasidism's noisy praying and dancing undignified. They
also looked down on the Hasidim as uneducated. Today,
some Jews in Europe, Israel, and the United States still
practice Hasidism.

The modern world

Emergence into freedom. At about the time that Hasidism developed in Eastern Europe, a movement called
the *Haskalah* (Enlightenment) arose in Western Europe.
The Haskalah, founded by German Jewish philosopher
Moses Mendelssohn, called on Jews to modernize their
religious thinking. The movement stressed the importance of nonreligious, as well as Jewish, education.

As the Haskalah modernized Jewish religious thinking, other forces were working to free the Jews from
discrimination. In France, the ideas of liberty and equality that took hold during the French Revolution (1789-
1799) led many Christians to demand equal rights for all.
French Jews were *emancipated* (given equal rights) in
1791. The French general and emperor Napoleon Bonaparte brought the idea of emancipation to countries outside France. By the end of the 1800's, most Western and

Central European Jews had been emancipated.

During the early and mid-1800's, two new branches of
Judaism developed. They were called *Reform* and *Conservative.*

Jews in America. The first Jews to arrive in the American colonies settled in what is now New York City in
1654. Jews also established sizable communities in
Charleston, South Carolina; Newport, Rhode Island;
Philadelphia; and Savannah, Georgia. During the Revolutionary War in America (1775-1783), many Jews fought in
the colonial army. A Jewish financier named Haym Sa-
lomon gave much of his fortune to help the newly established United States government. Jews gained full legal
equality in the new nation, and many Jews immigrated
to escape anti-Semitism in their native lands. By the
1920's, U.S. Jews were the largest and most secure Jewish community in the world, though they still suffered
discrimination.

The growth of anti-Semitism. During the late 1800's,
anti-Semitism became a powerful force in European politics, especially in Germany, Austria-Hungary, and
France. Many anti-Semitic writers tried to prove that
Jews were inferior to Germans and other peoples of
northern Europe, whom the writers called Aryans.

Jews also suffered from anti-Semitism in Eastern Europe. Unlike the Jews of Western Europe, those of the
east had never been emancipated. In Russia, Jews were
crowded in an area along the western border called the
Pale of Settlement. Beginning in 1881, many Jews were
killed in a series of massacres called *pogroms.* The
pogroms caused hundreds of thousands of Jews to flee
to the United States. Some fled to Palestine.

The Zionist movement. Many Jews saw an independent Jewish state in Palestine as the best escape
from anti-Semitism. They established a movement called
Zionism to establish such a state. In the late 1800's, Palestine was a poor, thinly populated region ruled by the
Muslim Ottoman Empire. Most of Palestine's people
were Muslim Arabs, though a small number of Jews

Central Zionist Archives, Jerusalem
The Zionist movement grew out of the Jews' longing for a national homeland. Theodor Herzl, a founder of Zionism, spoke to
the Second Zionist Congress in Basel, Switzerland, in 1898.

also lived there. The Zionists bought land in Palestine and established farming communities. The first all-Jewish city, Tel Aviv, was founded in 1909.

In 1894, the trial of Alfred Dreyfus, a French army officer and Jew who had been falsely accused of treason, helped convince Theodor Herzl, an Austrian Jewish journalist, that Jews could never be secure until they had a nation of their own. In 1897, at the First Zionist Congress, Herzl organized the Zionist movement on a worldwide scale.

During World War I (1914-1918), many Jews in Palestine fought with the British against the Ottomans. In 1917, the United Kingdom issued the Balfour Declaration, supporting the idea of a Jewish national home in Palestine. In addition, the United Kingdom promised Arab leaders support for an Arab state. The Arabs believed this state would include Palestine.

In 1918, the British captured Palestine from the Ottomans. The League of Nations—a forerunner of the United Nations—gave the British temporary control of Palestine in 1920. In the 1920's and 1930's, Jewish immigration to Palestine increased, despite Arab opposition.

Beginnings of Nazi persecution. Germany's defeat in World War I and a worldwide depression in the 1930's left the German economy in ruins and made many Germans angry and resentful. Adolf Hitler, leader of the Nazi Party, came to power in 1933. He blamed the Jews for Germany's troubles and began a vicious campaign against them. In 1935, the Nazis deprived German Jews of citizenship. They seized Jewish businesses and destroyed synagogues. Many Jews fled Germany. Others were trapped because no country would admit them. Most nations had restrictive immigration policies, and the Depression led workers to fear that Jewish refugees would take their jobs. Beginning in 1939, the United Kingdom bowed to Arab pressure and limited immigration to Palestine.

The Holocaust. World War II began in 1939. The Nazis soon conquered large parts of Europe, bringing

Israel Government Press Office

Israel's declaration of independence in 1948 led to the first Arab-Israeli war. Hours after Israeli leader David Ben-Gurion read the declaration, *shown here,* Arab forces invaded Israel.

most European Jews under their domination. The Nazis then began their campaign to exterminate all Jews. Firing squads shot more than 1 million Jews. About 4 million more were killed in concentration camps. Many others died from disease and starvation. By 1945, about 6 million Jews had been murdered—two of every three European Jews.

Several Jewish revolts against the Nazis took place in ghettos, slave labor camps, and death camps. The most famous revolt occurred in 1943, in the Warsaw ghetto. Although the Jews were surrounded and poorly armed, some held out for about four weeks. Many Jews who managed to escape the ghettos joined bands of fighters called *partisans* who performed acts of sabotage.

In most occupied countries, the local people were indifferent to the Holocaust. Some helped the Nazis. But some non-Jewish individuals risked their lives to save Jews. Swedish diplomat Raoul Wallenberg saved about 100,000 Hungarian Jews. The Danish underground saved 7,000 Jews, most of the Jews of Denmark.

The rebirth of Israel. The Holocaust left the Jewish people wounded in spirit and greatly reduced in numbers. But out of the tragedy came a new determination to establish a Jewish state in Palestine. The Arabs there continued to oppose this plan, and violence often broke out between Arabs and Jews. In 1947, the United Nations recommended that Palestine be divided into Arab and Jewish states. The Jewish state, which called itself Israel, declared its independence on May 14, 1948. The next day, neighboring Arab countries invaded Israel. Israel defeated the invaders, and hundreds of thousands of Jews flocked to the Jewish state.

The Arabs continued to oppose Israel, and full-scale wars broke out in 1956, 1967, and 1973. However, despite its constant struggle with its neighbors, Israel kept a democratic form of government and became one of the most prosperous countries in the Middle East.

The Jews today. Today, Jewish life continues to

AP/Wide World

The Holocaust was a vicious campaign against the Jews and others by the Nazis. This picture shows piles of bodies at the Dachau concentration camp after it was liberated in 1945.

thrive, both in Israel and in the Diaspora. But the Jews of each area face many challenges.

The Jews of Israel still face the threat of conflict with neighboring Arab states. They must also confront the social, military, and moral issues stemming from conflict with Palestinian Arabs living in lands occupied by Israel.

Israel still flourishes as a refuge for Jews. Among the most recent immigrants are hundreds of thousands of Jews from Russia, Ukraine, and other former republics of the Soviet Union. The large number of immigrants has led to overcrowding and unemployment.

In the Diaspora. For many years, the main centers of Jewish life in the Diaspora were the United States and the Soviet Union. In the Soviet Union, Jews suffered widespread discrimination. The government discouraged religious practice, and it restricted emigration to other countries. In the 1970's and 1980's, Soviet Jews attracted worldwide attention with demonstrations demanding the right to emigrate and to observe Jewish customs. In 1987, the government began to permit an increasing number of Jews to emigrate to Israel. After the Soviet Union was dissolved in 1991, Jews continued to move to Israel from the former Soviet republics.

In the United States, Jews have increasingly adopted the culture of the non-Jewish society in which they live. A growing number of American Jews do not practice Judaism, and many know little about Jewish traditions or history. Some Jews fear that this process, called *assimilation,* will cause Jews to lose their identity. A rising rate of intermarriage also contributes to the concern. But many other American Jews are experiencing a renewed interest in their heritage. A growing number worship in religious groups called *havurot.* Many send their children to Jewish day schools.   Elliot B. Lefkovitz

Outline

I. Early history of the Jewish people
  A. Beginnings
  B. The Exodus
  C. The kingdom of Israel
  D. The divided kingdom
  E. Foreign domination
  F. The Hellenistic period
  G. Roman rule
II. The Talmudic period and the Middle Ages
  A. The Talmudic period
  B. The Jews under Islam
  C. Jews in Christian Europe
  D. Eastern European religious movements
III. The modern world
  A. Emergence into freedom
  B. Jews in America
  C. The growth of anti-Semitism
  D. The Zionist movement
  E. Beginnings of Nazi persecution
  F. The Holocaust
  G. The rebirth of Israel
  H. The Jews today

Questions

Who was the founder of the kingdom of Israel?

What are the names of the two broad groups of Jews? How do they differ?

Why was the 1894 trial of Alfred Dreyfus important for the Zionist movement?

When did Israel declare its independence? What happened the day after this declaration?

What was the situation of Jews in Christian Europe during the Middle Ages?

When did the first Jews arrive in the American colonies? Where did they settle?

What was the Holocaust?

Additional resources

Level I

Scharfstein, Sol. *Understanding Jewish History.* Ktav, 1996.

Shamir, Ilana, and Shavit, Shlomo, eds. *The Young Reader's Encyclopedia of Jewish History.* Viking, 1987.

Westridge Young Writers Workshop. *Kids Explore America's Jewish Heritage.* John Muir, 1996.

Level II

Cohn-Sherbok, Dan. *Atlas of Jewish History.* Routledge, 1994.

De Lange, Nicholas, ed. *An Illustrated History of the Jewish People.* Harcourt, 1997.

Web site

HaReshima: The Jewish Internet Portal

http://www.hareshima.com/

A searchable directory of Jewish and Israeli Web sites, divided into such categories as Congregations, Holidays, and Kosher.

Jihad, *jih HAHD* or *jee HAH,* is an Arabic word that refers to an effort or struggle on behalf of the religion of Islam. Followers of Islam, called Muslims, view jihad in different ways. One meaning of jihad, called the *greater jihad,* is the internal effort of each person to overcome temptation and lead a moral life. Another meaning of jihad, called the *lesser jihad,* is an armed struggle against those perceived as enemies of Islam. Some writers have referred to jihad as the sixth *pillar* (formal spiritual duty) of Islam.

Muslims have engaged in armed jihad at various times since the early 600's, when Islam was first preached by the Prophet Muhammad. Muslims who have died in armed jihad have often been celebrated as *martyrs*—that is, people who sacrifice their lives for their beliefs. Today, most Muslims think of jihad only as a peaceful effort on behalf of their faith. But some radical Muslims call for armed jihad against countries or groups they consider to be threats to Islam.

The doctrine of lesser jihad developed in part from the example of Muhammad and his early followers. They launched a number of military campaigns to spread their faith. It also developed based on certain passages in the Qur'ān—the holy book of Islam. The doctrine is based on three related ideas. First, Islam is a universal community. Second, God and Muhammad have commanded all free and physically able male Muslims to spread their faith, even by waging war against non-Muslims when necessary. Finally, Muslims must spread their religion until all people have converted to Islam or agreed to live under an Islamic government.

In theory, armed jihad is the only type of warfare Islam allows, because Muslims are not permitted to take up arms against other Muslims. In practice, however, Muslims have sometimes declared war against other Muslims. Today, some radical Islamic groups call for armed jihad against the rulers of certain Islamic countries. These groups claim that the rulers of these countries have permitted Islam to become corrupt and that Islam must therefore be restored to a pure state.

In modern times, many Muslim thinkers have argued that it is acceptable for Islamic states to coexist with non-Islamic states peacefully. They have maintained that armed jihad should be allowed only for self-defense or for the defense of other Muslims.   Kate Lang

© Ted Spiegel, Black Star

© Ted Spiegel, Black Star

© Charles Harbutt, Magnum

Jewish religious life includes worship, special ceremonies, and joyous festivals. Jews gather in their synagogue to worship on the Sabbath, *left.* A ceremony called a *bar mitzvah* marks a Jewish boy's acceptance into the adult Jewish community, *upper right.* A Jewish family celebrates the harvest festival of Sukkot by eating in a *sukkah,* a hut built specially for the festival, *lower right.*

Judaism, *JOO dee ihz uhm,* is the religion of the world's approximately 15 million Jews. It is the oldest major religion and the first religion to teach the belief in one God.

Unlike the other major religions, Judaism is the religion of only one people—the Jews. Both Christianity and Islam developed from Judaism. These religions accept the Jewish belief in one God and the moral teachings of the Hebrew Bible. The Hebrew Bible is what Christians call the Old Testament. The basic laws and teachings of Judaism come from the *Torah,* the first five books of the Hebrew Bible.

This article discusses the principal teachings and sacred writings of Judaism. It also tells about the chief branches of Judaism and the structure of organized Judaism. Finally, it describes Jewish worship, holidays, and customs.

The teachings of Judaism

The most important teaching of Judaism is that there is one God, who wants people to do what is just and merciful. Judaism teaches that a person serves God by studying the scriptures and practicing what they teach. These teachings include both ritual practices and ethical laws. Judaism teaches that all people are created in the image of God and deserve to be treated with dignity

Lawrence H. Schiffman, the contributor of this article, is Edelman Professor of Hebrew and Judaic Studies at New York University.

and respect. Thus, moral and ethical teachings are as important in Judaism as teachings about God.

The covenant with God is a special agreement that Jews believe God made with Abraham, the ancestor of the Jewish people. According to the Bible, God promised to bless Abraham and his descendants if they worshiped and remained faithful to God. God renewed this covenant with Abraham's son Isaac and Isaac's son Jacob. Jacob was also called Israel, and so his descendants became known as the children of Israel or the Israelites. God later gave the Israelites the Ten Commandments and other laws through their leader, Moses. These laws explained how the Israelites should live their lives and build their community.

The Jews are sometimes called the *Chosen People,* meaning that they have special duties and responsibilities commanded by God. For example, the Jews must establish a just society and serve only God. Thus, the covenant assures the Jews of God's love and protection,

The Star of David is the symbol of Judaism and of Israel. It consists of two triangles that interlace and form a six-pointed star. In Hebrew, the symbol is called the *Magen David,* which means the *Shield of David.* The star appears on the flag of Israel.

but it also makes them accountable for their sins and shortcomings.

Unlike Christianity and many other religions throughout the world, Judaism does not actively try to convince others to adopt its beliefs and practices. However, under certain circumstances, it does accept people who choose to convert to Judaism.

The Messiah. Traditionally, Jews believed that God would send a Messiah to save them. The word *Messiah* comes from the Hebrew word *mashiah,* which means *the anointed one.* The Book of Isaiah describes the Messiah as a just ruler who will unite the Jewish people and lead them in God's way. The Messiah will correct wrongs and defeat the enemies of the people.

Many Jews still expect a Messiah to come. But others speak instead of a *Messianic age.* They believe a period of justice and peace will come through the cooperation of all people and the help of God.

The sacred writings of Judaism

Judaism has two major collections of sacred writings, the Bible and the Talmud. These works provide the basis for Judaism's beliefs and practices.

The Bible. The first five books of the Hebrew Bible make up the Torah, the most important of all Jewish scriptures. The Torah contains the basic laws of Judaism and describes the history of the Jews until the death of Moses in the 1200's B.C. According to Jewish tradition, Moses received and wrote down the word of God in the Torah, which is also called the *Five Books of Moses.* Today, however, many scholars believe that different parts of the Torah were passed down in several collections, which were later edited into the five books we have today. In addition to the Torah, the Hebrew Bible contains books of history and moral teachings called the *Prophets* and 11 other books called the *Writings.*

The Talmud is a collection of legal, ritual, and ethical writings, as well as Jewish history and folklore. It serves primarily as a guide to the civil and religious laws of Judaism. Orthodox Jews believe the laws in the Talmud were an "oral Torah," which God gave Moses as an explanation of the written Torah. About A.D. 200, scholars wrote down these oral laws in a work called the *Mishnah.* Later scholars interpreted the Mishnah. Their comments were recorded in the *Gemara,* which was written between 200 and 500. The Mishnah and Gemara together make up the Talmud.

The branches of Judaism

Modern culture has posed challenges to traditional Jewish observance and faith. Jews have made a variety of responses to these challenges that have resulted in the division into several branches of Judaism. In the United States and Canada, the three main branches are (1) Orthodox Judaism, (2) Reform Judaism, and (3) Conservative Judaism. Each represents a wide range of beliefs and practices.

Orthodox Judaism continues traditional Jewish beliefs and ways of life. Orthodox Jews believe that God revealed the laws of the Torah and the Talmud directly to Moses on Mount Sinai. They strictly observe all traditional Jewish laws, including the dietary rules and the laws for keeping the Sabbath. Orthodox Jews pray three times daily—in the morning, in late afternoon, and after sunset. The men wear hats or skullcaps *(yarmulkas* or *kipot)* at all times as a sign of respect to God.

A kind of Orthodox Judaism known as Modern Orthodoxy attempts to combine the traditional way of life with participation in the general culture. Hasidic Orthodox Jews, in contrast, wear traditional Eastern European Jewish clothing and stress the joy of worshiping God and performing His commandments.

Reform Judaism began during the early 1800's. At that time, some Jews started to question the traditional teachings of how the sacred writings of Judaism came into being. For example, they considered the oral law a human creation rather than the revelation of God, and so its authority was weakened for them. These people, who founded Reform Judaism, claimed that Judaism is defined principally by the Bible.

Today, Reform Jews believe that moral and ethical teachings form the most important part of Judaism. Many feel that Judaism's ritual practices have no significance for them. They have discarded many traditional customs and ceremonies. However, Reform Jews are increasingly returning to traditional practices.

Conservative Judaism developed during the mid-1800's. Conservative Jews consider the Talmud as much an authority as the Bible. However, they believe that Jewish practice may be changed to fit the times. They believe that in this way, Judaism can remain relevant for each generation. The Conservative movement requires observance of most traditional Jewish laws and customs. The Reconstructionist movement, a smaller group that developed from the Conservative movement, stresses the cultural and community aspects of Judaism.

The structure of Judaism

Judaism has no one person as its head and no international body with authority over religious practices. Each local congregation chooses its own rabbi and manages its own affairs.

The synagogue is the Jewish house of worship and the center of Jewish education and community activities. A synagogue has a sanctuary where religious services are held. In addition, it may include a school where children study Judaism, the Hebrew language, and Jewish history. Most synagogues have a social hall as well. Reform and Conservative synagogues are often called *temples.*

Most synagogues are constructed so that the worshipers face toward the holy city of Jerusalem during the service. At the front of the sanctuary stands the *ark,* a chest in which the scrolls of the Torah are kept. In front of the ark hangs the *eternal light,* an oil lamp whose constant flame symbolizes God's eternal presence.

The rabbi serves as spiritual leader, teacher, and interpreter of Jewish law. Traditionally, rabbis were chiefly teachers of the law. Today, rabbis also deliver sermons during worship services in the synagogue, give advice to people with problems, and perform other functions. A person who wants to become a rabbi must spend years studying Hebrew sacred writings and Jewish history, philosophy, and law. Most rabbinical students also study a wide range of nonreligious subjects. In the United States, Orthodox rabbis are trained at Yeshiva University and other rabbinical seminaries, Reform rabbis at the Hebrew Union College, and Conservative rabbis at the Jewish Theological Seminary of America.

The cantor chants the prayers during worship in the synagogue. The cantor is often a professional who has a trained voice and special knowledge of Hebrew and the traditions of chanting. The cantor may also direct a choir and conduct religious education.

Worship in Judaism takes place in the home and the synagogue. Important parts of home worship include daily prayers, the lighting of the Sabbath candles, and the blessing of the wine and bread at the Sabbath meal. Jews also observe many holiday rituals at home.

Worship practices in the synagogue differ among the branches of Judaism and even within these groups. Orthodox and Conservative synagogues conduct services daily, but most Reform synagogues have services only on the Sabbath and holidays. In all Orthodox and some Conservative synagogues, at least 10 men must be present for a service to take place. This minimum number of participants is called a *minyan.* Any male who is at least 13 years old may lead the service. In most Conservative and Reform congregations, women may lead the service and be part of the minyan.

Synagogue worship consists mainly of readings from the Torah and the chanting of prayers from a prayer book called the *siddur.* A different portion of the Torah is read each week, so the entire Torah is completed in a year. In Orthodox synagogues, men and women sit separately and chant almost all the prayers in Hebrew. In Conservative and Reform congregations, men and women sit together, and much of the service is in the language of the country. Most Sabbath and holiday services include a sermon.

Holy days and festivals

The Sabbath in Judaism is the seventh day of the week, Saturday, which is a holy day of rest. The Sabbath begins at sundown on Friday and ends at nightfall Saturday, at the time when it is calculated that three stars can be seen in the evening sky. On the Sabbath, Jews attend worship services in the synagogue and have special meals at home. Orthodox Jews do not work, travel, or

Topic for study

Explain the differences among Judaism's three main branches: Conservative Judaism, Orthodox Judaism, and Reform Judaism.

carry money on the Sabbath.

The High Holidays, called *Rosh Ha-Shanah* and *Yom Kippur,* are the most sacred days of the Jewish year. Like all Jewish holidays, they occur on different dates each year because they are based on the Hebrew calendar. The High Holidays come during *Tishri,* the first month of the Hebrew calendar, which usually falls in September or October.

Rosh Ha-Shanah, the Jewish New Year, begins on the first day of Tishri and lasts two days. It celebrates the creation of the world and God's rule over it. According to Jewish tradition, people are judged on Rosh Ha-Shanah for their deeds of the past year. The chief symbol is the *shofar,* a ram's horn that is sounded during the holiday worship.

Rosh Ha-Shanah begins the Ten Days of Penitence, which end on Yom Kippur, the Day of Atonement. On Yom Kippur, Jews fast and express their regret for bad deeds during the past year and their hope to perform good deeds in the coming year. The day is observed mainly through synagogue worship.

The pilgrimage festivals. In ancient times, Jews were expected to make a pilgrimage to Jerusalem during three major festivals—*Passover, Shavuot,* and *Sukkot.* Each festival is associated with the Jews' escape from Egypt and their journey to Canaan (now Israel).

Passover, or Pesah, comes in March or April and celebrates the exodus of the Jews from Egypt. Jews observe Passover at home at a ceremonial feast called the *Seder.* During the week of Passover, Jews eat an unleavened bread called *matzah.* Shavuot, or Pentecost, comes 50 days after the beginning of Passover and commemorates the giving of the Torah to the Jewish people on Mount Sinai. Many Reform congregations celebrate Shavuot by holding confirmation ceremonies as well.

© Shelley Gazin, Corbis

Passover is a Jewish festival that honors the flight of the Israelites from Egyptian slavery, probably in the 1200's B.C. This picture shows a family sharing a traditional Passover meal called the *Seder.*

Miniature (about 1320) from *Golden Haggadah* of Barcelona, Spain; British Library, London

Moses was an Israelite leader. This painting shows events from his life. At the upper right, an angel in a burning bush appears to Moses. At the upper left, Moses and his wife return to Egypt from Midian and meet his brother Aaron. At the lower right, the brothers perform a miracle for the elders of Israel. At the lower left, Moses and Aaron appear before the pharaoh.

Topic for study

Describe a Jewish religious ceremony or festival, such as a bar mitzvah or a bat mitzvah or the Passover Seder. Explain the significance of the prayers and rituals involved.

Sukkot is a harvest festival that begins five days after Yom Kippur. Jews build small huts for Sukkot as a reminder of the huts the Israelites lived in during their wandering in the wilderness. On the last day of this festival, called *Simhat Torah,* Jews celebrate the completion of the yearly reading of the Torah.

Other holidays commemorate major events in the history of the Jewish people. *Hanukkah,* or the Feast of Lights, is a celebration of God's deliverance of the Jews in 165 B.C. That year, the Jews won their first struggle for religious freedom by defeating the Syrians, who wanted them to give up Judaism. Hanukkah usually comes in December and is celebrated by the lighting of candles in a special Hanukkah branched candlestick called a *menorah.*

Purim is a festive holiday in February or March that commemorates the rescue of the Jews of Persia (now Iran) from a plot to kill them. On Purim, Jews read the Book of Esther, which tells the story of this rescue. Judaism also has several fast days. The most important of these, *Tishah be-av* (the Ninth of Av), commemorates the destruction of the Temple in Jerusalem by the Babylonians in 586 B.C. and the Romans in A.D. 70.

Customs and ceremonies

Dietary laws. The Bible, chiefly in the books of Leviticus and Deuteronomy, commands that Jews follow certain dietary rules. Jews who observe these rules do not eat pork or shellfish, such as shrimp or oysters. They also store meat and milk products separately and do not serve them at the same meal. The dietary laws allow only meat that comes from a healthy animal killed by ritual slaughter called *shehitah.* This method of slaughter is designed to kill animals quickly and with as little pain as possible. The ritual must be performed by a specially trained slaughterer, who says a special blessing before killing the animal.

Food prepared in accordance with Jewish dietary laws is called *kosher,* which means *ritually correct.* Orthodox Jews consider these laws divine commandments and observe them strictly. Many other Jews observe the rules as a sign of their faith or simply as a means of maintaining their Jewish identity.

Special occasions. When a Jewish boy is 8 days old, he is circumcised as a symbol of the covenant God made with Abraham. At the age of 13, a boy becomes a full member of the Jewish community. This event is celebrated in the synagogue with a ceremony called a *bar mitzvah.* Some Reform and Conservative synagogues have a similar ceremony for girls called a *bat mitzvah* or *bas mitzvah.* The young person reads from the Torah during the ceremony, which is followed by a social celebration.

A traditional Jewish marriage ceremony takes place under a *huppa,* a canopy that symbolizes the union of the bride and groom. If a marriage breaks up, the husband must give the wife a writ of divorce called a *get.*

Jews observe special rituals in connection with death. Burial takes place as soon as possible, in most cases within a day after a death. After the funeral, the family enters a seven-day period of deep mourning called *Shiva.* The mourners recite the *Kaddish,* a prayer that praises God but does not mention death. On each anniversary of the death, the relatives observe a memorial called a *yahrzeit,* reciting the Kaddish and lighting a candle in memory of the person.   Lawrence H. Schiffman

Additional resources

Abramowitz, Yosef I., and Silverman, Susan. *Jewish Family and Life: Traditions, Holidays, and Values for Today's Parents and Children.* Golden Bks., 1997.
Goldman, Ari L. *Being Jewish: The Spiritual and Cultural Practice of Judaism Today.* Simon & Schuster, 2000.
Penney, Sue. *Judaism.* Raintree Steck-Vaughn, 1997. Younger readers.
Robinson, George. *Essential Judaism: A Complete Guide to Beliefs, Customs, and Rituals.* Pocket Bks., 2000.
Werblowsky, R. J. Zwi, and Wigoder, Geoffrey, eds. *The Oxford Dictionary of the Jewish Religion.* Oxford, 1997.

Web sites

Shamash Home Page
http://www.shamash.org/
Resources for study of Israel and Judaism, provided by the Shamash Project.

The Jewish Student Online Research Center: Judaism
http://www.us-israel.org/jsource/judaism.html
Information about the Jewish faith from The American-Israeli Cooperative Enterprise.

Muslims, *MUHZ luhmz,* sometimes spelled *Moslems,* are people who practice the religion of Islam. The Prophet Muhammad first preached the religion in the A.D. 600's. Islam originated with the Arabs in the Middle East. By the mid-700's, Muslims had built an empire that stretched from the Atlantic Ocean to the borders of China. This article traces the history of the Muslim people throughout the world.

Before Muhammad

Abraham and Ishmael. According to Muslim tradition, the history of the Muslims begins with the story of Abraham and Ishmael. Both Jews and Arabs regard Abraham, who may have lived between about 1800 and 1500 B.C., as the father of their people. Abraham's wife Sarah was past childbearing age, so she gave her handmaiden Hagar to her husband as a second wife. Hagar bore a son, the prophet Ishmael. Later, Sarah and Abraham also had a son, the prophet Isaac. After Isaac's birth, Sarah pressured Abraham into expelling Hagar and Ishmael from his house.

Muslim tradition teaches that Hagar and Ishmael traveled to a valley in western Arabia called Bakka, which is now the city of Mecca. There they found a sacred well, called Zamzam, that sustained Hagar and Ishmael with its water. When Ishmael reached adulthood, Abraham visited him. Near the well of Zamzam, the two prophets built the Kaaba as a temple to God (Allah). In the eastern corner of the Kaaba, they placed the Black Stone, which Muslims believe was brought to them by an angel. The Kaaba became the holiest shrine of Islam. Muslims who perform the pilgrimage to Mecca walk around the Kaaba seven times. Many of them will try to kiss or touch the Black Stone.

The Arabs before Islam included nomads, traders, farmers, and town-dwellers. They belonged to many tribes and had many religions. Most Arabs worshiped multiple gods. Arab deities included the goddesses al-Lat, al-Uzza, and Manat, who were important in the Mecca region. The supreme deity of the Arabs was a remote heavenly god, whom they called Allah, which means "the god." The Arabs believed he was the creator of the universe, the bringer of life and rain. He was the god on whom people called in times of great danger or distress.

Muhammad

The Prophet Muhammad was born in Mecca in about A.D. 570. At that time, Mecca was a major commercial center controlled by an Arab tribe called the Quraysh (pronounced *koo RAYSH),* who had abandoned the traditional Arab nomadic way of life and become merchants. The Quraysh were divided into clans, including the Banu Umayya *(BA noo oo MAY ah)* and the Banu Hashim *(BA noo HA shihm).* The Banu Umayya were the wealthiest and most powerful clan in Mecca. The Banu Hashim, into which Muhammad was born, were responsible for supplying food and drink for pilgrims who came to Mecca to visit the Kaaba.

In about A.D. 610, Muhammad began to receive revelations from Allah. For Muslims, the greatest miracle of Muhammad's prophethood was the Qur'ān *(ku RAHN),* sometimes spelled Koran, the holy book of Allah's revelations. The revelation of the Qur'ān to Muhammad took place over a period of about 22 years. Muhammad dictated the verses to his followers, who wrote them down. Several of these "Scribes of Revelation," such as Ali, Uthman *(ooth MAN),* and Muawiya *(moo AH wih yah),* became important Muslim leaders.

Several years after Muhammad's death, when Uthman was *caliph* (leader) of the Muslims, he formed a committee to collect these revelations into a single volume. Their work produced a master copy of the Qur'ān that became the model for the book used by Muslims today.

The people of Mecca persecuted the early Muslims because Muhammad had rejected their gods and because he condemned wealthy Meccans for not helping those in need, such as widows, orphans, and the poor. Eventually, Muhammad and his followers were forced to abandon Mecca.

In 622, a delegation from Medina, a town then called Yathrib which is north of Mecca, invited him to act as *arbitrator* (judge) between its feuding tribes. Muhammad's

Vincent J. Cornell is Associate Professor of Religion at Duke University.

Where Muslims live

This map shows the distribution of Muslims throughout the world. Colors on the map indicate the percentage of Muslims in the total population of each country.

Percent of Muslim population by country

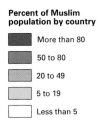

More than 80

50 to 80

20 to 49

5 to 19

Less than 5

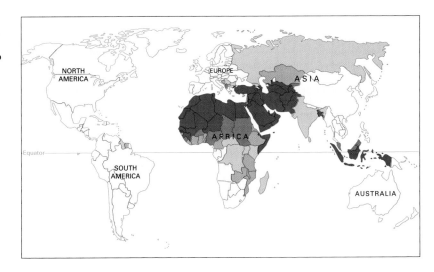

WORLD BOOK map

journey from Mecca to Medina is called the *Hijra,* also spelled *Hegira.* Muslims consider it so important that the Islamic calendar begins with the year of the Hijra. In Medina, Muhammad and his companions laid the foundations of Islamic society, which was based on the *Sunna* and the *Shari`a,* also spelled *Shari`ah.* The Sunna was the example of the Prophet's sayings and behavior. The Shari`a was the code of Islamic law.

To defend Islam from its enemies, Muhammad launched several military campaigns against Mecca and other parts of the Arabian Peninsula. Mecca surrendered to him in 630. In 631, delegations from many tribes and clans in Arabia swore to give up the worship of multiple gods and submit to Muhammad's authority. In 632, Muhammad died in Medina.

The early caliphs

After the Prophet died, a dispute arose over his successor. On one side were members of the tribes of Medina, who wanted one of their own leaders to rule the town again. Another side included Muhammad's friend Abu Bakr, along with Umar, one of the most powerful of the early Muslims. After the death of his first wife, Muhammad had married both Abu Bakr's daughter Aisha *(ah YEE shah)* and Umar's daughter Hafsa. They were the most influential of the Prophet's wives. In addition, some Muslims thought Muhammad's cousin and son-in-law, Ali, who had adopted Islam as a child and was like a son to the Prophet, should succeed him as leader. On the day of Muhammad's death, Umar acknowledged Abu Bakr as *caliph* (successor) to the Prophet, and soon others followed his example. Umar said he took the action to prevent divisions in the Muslim community.

Abu Bakr ruled as caliph in Medina for two years. He took political charge of the Muslim community and led prayers in the Prophet's place, but he refused to assume Muhammad's role as the interpreter of Islamic doctrine. He left interpretation to the collective judgment of the Prophet's companions. Abu Bakr's example in referring religious decisions to community leaders eventually formed the basis of the Sunni *(SOON ee)* division in Islam. The followers of Sunni Islam are called Sunnites.

Abu Bakr faced revolts by Arabian tribes against the authority of the Islamic state. Some tribes even put forth their own prophets. But within about a year, Abu Bakr put down these revolts, and the tribes accepted Islam.

Umar. In 634, Abu Bakr died, naming Umar to succeed him as caliph. Umar's 10-year rule became a great period of Islamic expansion. First, he sent Qur'ān reciters to the tribes of Arabia to teach them Islam. Next, he embarked on the full-scale conquest of the Middle East. During this period, Islam was largely a religion of the Arabs, and Umar concentrated on spreading Islam among the tribes of Syria and Iraq. Most Arabs converted to Islam at this time.

By the end of Umar's caliphate in 644, the Muslims had conquered Syria, Palestine, Egypt, and most of Iraq. Because of the great increase in the number of people under their rule, the Muslims set up an administration to govern the new territories. They sent Muslim soldiers and their families to settle in strategically located towns, which rapidly grew into major cities. Each town centered on a main *mosque* (Muslim place of worship) and was ruled by the provincial governor. Soldiers and other Muslims each received a payment from a share of the booty taken during conquests and taxes from conquered lands. The payments varied depending on how long each person had been a Muslim. Thus, the earliest converts had great political power and often made fortunes.

Uthman. Just before Umar died, he appointed a committee to choose his successor. When the committee asked Ali to be caliph and follow the rulings of his predecessors, he refused. He claimed that he knew more than the previous caliphs about Muhammad's original views and intentions. Uthman, another son-in-law of the Prophet, agreed to the request and became caliph.

Under Uthman, the Muslims completed the conquest of Iran and began to spread across North Africa from Egypt. But political conflicts broke out and marked the

© Superstock

The Dome of the Rock in Jerusalem is one of the holiest places in Islam. The dome encloses a rock, shown in the foreground, from which the Prophet Muhammad is believed to have ascended to heaven. The dome was built between 688 and 691, during the rule of the Umayyad caliph Abd al-Malik.

end of Muslim political and religious unity. Despite Uthman's piety, his enemies accused him of favoritism and a love of wealth and luxury. Political corruption and stricter economic policies in the provinces caused the Muslims of Egypt to revolt against their governor, Uthman's foster brother. Uthman's half-brother, who was the governor of Kufa in southern Iraq, disgraced himself by appearing drunk in public.

In 656, delegations from Egypt and Iraq arrived in Medina to protest Uthman's policies. Many of Medina's citizens also opposed Uthman, including Muhammad's widow Aisha and his son-in-law Ali. But Ali had no desire to start a rebellion. When Uthman appealed to him to help settle the dispute, he did so, but he asked the caliph to change his policies. Ali's attempt at a settlement failed, and protesters killed Uthman. Immediately afterward, a delegation went to Ali and proclaimed him caliph. At first, he refused because Uthman had been murdered. But he consented after other delegations from Medina and the provinces urged him to accept.

Ali. The caliphate of Ali marks the beginning of the Shiite division of Islam. As the closest living relative of Muhammad, Ali claimed a unique understanding of the Prophet's teachings. Ali's followers, the Shiah *(SHEE ah)*, considered him the only true *Imam* (Muslim leader). After Ali's death, his sons and descendants led the Shiah as Imams. Although the Shiites agreed with most Muslims on matters of doctrine, they felt their Imams should have priority in the interpretation of Islamic doctrine.

When Ali accepted the caliphate, several Muslim leaders opposed him, including Muhammad's widow Aisha and Muawiya, the governor of Syria and Uthman's cousin. From this point, Medina no longer served as the capital of the Islamic state. Ali moved to Kufa (now Al Kufah, Iraq), where most of his supporters lived. Aisha and her allies moved to Basra (now Al Basrah, Iraq). In 656, Ali and Aisha fought the Battle of the Camel, the first conflict of Muslim against Muslim. Ali won the battle, named for the camel that carried Aisha.

Ali next turned against Muawiya, who demanded that Ali produce Uthman's assassins or be considered an accomplice in the murder. In 657, the armies of Ali and Muawiya fought at Siffin, on the Euphrates River in northern Syria. During the battle, soldiers in Muawiya's army raised pages of the Qur'an on their spears and called for arbitrators to settle the conflict peacefully. Ali agreed, so the battle ended indecisively. Many of Ali's followers, however, opposed arbitration and turned against him. These followers, called Kharijites, which means *secessionists*, make up the third major division in Islam, along with the Sunnites and the Shiites.

The Kharijites rejected both Muawiya and Ali. They felt the best Muslim should be caliph, even if that person were a slave. In 658, Ali fought the Kharijites at Nahrawan in central Iraq. He won the battle, but many faithful Muslims were killed in the fighting, causing even more people to turn against him. In 660, Muawiya was proclaimed caliph in Jerusalem. In 661, Ali, who refused to step down as caliph, was murdered by a Kharijite assassin seeking revenge for Nahrawan.

The Muslim empire

The Umayyads. After the death of Ali, Muawiya founded the Umayyad *(oo MY ad)* caliphate and made

British Library, London/Art Resource

The Prophet Muhammad, according to Islam, ascended to heaven on the back of a creature called Buraq. Muhammad's face is veiled because of a Muslim prohibition on showing the Prophet's face.

Damascus his capital in 661. Under the Umayyads, the Islamic state became an imperial power, much like its rival, the Byzantine Empire. When choosing ruling officials, the Umayyads preferred Arabs over their non-Arab subjects. Under the Umayyads, the Muslims extended their conquests into Afghanistan and central Asia in the east and across North Africa and into Spain in the west. Their main source of power was an Arab army based in Syria. This army swore personal loyalty to the caliph and acted as his bodyguard. Administratively, the Umayyads adopted many of the customs and institutions of the Byzantine Empire and of the Sassanian Empire, which had ruled Persia until the Muslim conquest.

In 680, Muawiya died and was succeeded by his son Yazid, who became notorious for corruption and misrule. The inhabitants of Medina refused to recognize Yazid. Ali's son Husayn also rose against him. Husayn set off toward Kufa to gather support, but the Kufans refused to help him. The Umayyads massacred Husayn and his small band of followers at Karbala in southern Iraq. This violence against the Prophet's family shocked the Muslim world.

In 684, Yazid's cousin Marwan, a former aide of Uthman, succeeded to power in Syria. Abd al-Malik, Marwan's son, was proclaimed caliph in 685, and began the second phase of Umayyad rule. The later Umayyads faced a long series of revolts. Kharijites, Shiites, and other rebels agitated against them in the name of Islam, advocating a return to the religion as it was practiced by Muhammad and his companions.

The Abbasids. By the mid-700's, important changes had occurred in Muslim society. An increasing rate of conversion to Islam, combined with intermarriage between Arabs and non-Arabs, had transformed the makeup of the Muslim population. For the first time, non-Arab Muslims outnumbered Arab Muslims in many regions. Many of the Kharijite and Shiite rebels against the Umayyads came from non-Arab converts. In North Africa, the Kharijites were mainly Berbers. In eastern Iran, many Kharijites and Shiites were Persian. Such new Muslims demanded equality with Arabs. The new Muslims called for a society in which each Muslim would have the same privileges and be subject to the same taxes, regardless of ethnic background. Religious scholars, who sought a return to a higher standard of piety, supported them.

The Abbasids *(uh BAS ihdz)* took up the cause of the new Muslims. The Abbasids descended from Muhammad's uncle Abbas. At first they joined forces with the

Gouache manuscript painting (1588); Giraudon/Art Resource

The Ottoman Empire under Sultan Süleyman I dominated much of Europe and North Africa. Süleyman led Muslim armies as far west as the walls of Vienna, *shown here,* in 1529.

Shiites, claiming that the most qualified member of the Prophet's family should be caliph. The Abbasids eventually dominated the anti-Umayyad movement. The Abbasids called for revenge against the Umayyads for their treatment of Muhammad's family. They conquered the Umayyads in 750, after a struggle lasting only three years. When some descendants of Ali claimed that one of them should hold the office of caliph, the Abbasids suppressed them and their supporters.

From 750 to the mid-800's, the Abbasids transformed the Islamic state into an empire that blended many cultures and was ruled by an absolute monarch. The caliph continued to uphold the sunna of the Prophet and the Islamic Sharī`a. The Abbasid caliph was a magnificent ruler, living in splendid isolation and surrounded by thousands of officials and slaves. Only the most privileged were allowed to speak with him.

The capital of the Abbasids was Baghdad in central Iraq, established in 762 by the caliph Abu Jafar al-Mansur. At the heart of Baghdad was a huge administrative complex called the City of Peace. Beyond its walls stretched Baghdad and its suburbs, with more than a million inhabitants.

The Abbasid Empire was a highly centralized monarchy, the greatest since the Roman Empire. It drew support from one of the largest and most integrated economic systems known until modern times. Through the Persian Gulf flowed the products of east Africa, Arabia, India, southeast Asia, and China. Across the desert from Syria and down the Euphrates River came goods from North Africa, Egypt, and the Mediterranean. To Muslim scholars and historians of this period, Baghdad was the center of the world.

During the Abbasid period, the Islamic arts and sciences flourished. Several schools of Islamic law formed during this period. Study of the Qur'ān and of Arabic grammar developed. In about 830, the caliph al-Mamun created a research library called the House of Wisdom. A staff translated the works of Plato, Aristotle, and other Greek philosophers into Arabic. These translations stimulated the development of an Islamic philosophical tradition that played a major role in reintroducing many important works and ideas from Greek philosophy into western Europe.

The Abbasid period also witnessed the emergence of Sufism, which is Islamic mysticism. The Sufis do not make up a separate division, like the Shiites and Kharijites. Most Sufis are Sunni Muslims and see Sufism as a school of thought within mainstream Islam. Most Sufis follow the Sharī`a closely and differ from other Muslims only in their desire to create a closer personal relationship with Allah.

The fall of the Abbasids. As a highly centralized monarchy, the Abbasid Empire lasted little more than 100 years. Its authority never became fully established in the Islamic west. In 756, Abd al-Rahman, an Umayyad prince who had escaped to Spain, founded a second Umayyad line of rulers that lasted until 1031. In the 780's, Idris ibn Abdallah, a descendant of Ali's son Hasan, fled from Abbasid persecution and created an independent kingdom in Morocco. In the 800's, the Abbasid governors of Tunisia and Egypt broke away from Baghdad and formed their own states.

From 929 to 1031, there were three competing

Gouache and gold painting on paper (1590); Victoria & Albert Museum, London/Art Resource

Babur founded the Mughal Empire in India in 1526. Babur was a cultured ruler who encouraged religious tolerance. This painting shows him supervising the laying out of a garden in Afghanistan.

caliphates at one time—the Abbasids in Iraq, an Umayyad caliphate in Spain, and the Fatimids in North Africa and, from 969, in Egypt. By this time, the Abbasids ruled over the Muslim world in name only. From the mid-900's until the Mongols captured Baghdad in 1258, most of the caliphs were puppet rulers, serving at the whim of military dictators. The blending of many cultures within Islam had led to the development of multiple centers of power and culture in the Muslim world. The diversity of the Muslim world continues to this day.

The spread of Islam

The Mongols killed the last Abbasid caliph in 1258 and captured Baghdad, but the vitality of the Muslims did not diminish. Socially and culturally, the Muslim world became more diverse than ever. In west Africa and what are now Malaysia and Indonesia, Muslim merchants and scholars introduced Islam and converted kings, who made Islam the state religion. In China, the Muslim population also grew from communities of merchants. In Africa south of the Sahara, large-scale conversions began in the 1400's. Most of these conversions resulted from trade and personal contact rather than conquest.

Muslim power reached a new height in the 1500's. By that century, the Muslims had established three power-

ful empires: (1) the Ottoman Empire, which began in what is now Turkey; (2) the Safavid dynasty in Iran; and (3) the Mughal Empire in India.

The Ottoman Empire lasted from about 1300 to 1922. The Ottomans were named after Osman I, a Turkish chieftain who founded a state in Anatolia, now Turkey, in the late 1200's. The Ottomans claimed to be the champions of Sunni Islam. In 1453, Sultan Mehmet II conquered Constantinople, the capital of the Byzantine Empire. The city, now called Istanbul, became the capital of the Ottoman Empire.

By 1600, the Ottoman Empire formed a crescent around the Mediterranean extending from Hungary in eastern Europe through Palestine and Egypt to Algeria in North Africa. Under the reign of Sultan Süleyman I in the 1500's, the Muslim world achieved its greatest level of unity since the time of the Abbasids. Under the Ottomans, many cultures maintained their identities within Muslim society. The Ottoman sultans were Turkish, but the generals, admirals, and administrators of the Ottoman Empire came from throughout the Mediterranean world. Many Ottoman aristocrats were skilled in the arts, languages, and literature, and they set the standard for culture in the Muslim world.

Many Ottoman officials came from Christian families. Each year, recruiting teams collected boys from eastern Europe. The youths were taken to Istanbul, converted to Islam, and educated. Legally, they became slaves of the sultan and were supposed to be loyal only to him. The most physically active boys became "Men of the Sword" and served in the Janissary Corps, a special division of infantry that formed the core of the Ottoman army. The more scholarly students became "Men of the Pen" and served in administrative posts, from which they could rise to the rank of grand vizier, the highest Ottoman official after the sultan.

The Safavid dynasty. The main rivals of the Ottomans were the Safavids in Iran. The Safavids, originally Sufis from northwestern Iran, rose to power as the leaders of Shiite Turks. Under Shah Ismail I in the early 1500's, Iran, formerly a Sunni country, converted to Shiism. Through the middle of the 1600's, the Ottomans and Safavids fought each other in a series of devastating wars. The wars ended in a costly stalemate that drained the resources of both empires. Safavid kings ruled Iran until 1722.

The Mughal Empire of India was founded by Babur, a central Asian prince, in 1526. Using firearms, Babur's small invasion force easily defeated much larger Indian armies. The Mughal Empire reached its peak under Akbar, who reigned from 1556 to 1605. His empire covered two-thirds of South Asia, including most of present-day Afghanistan, Pakistan, north and central India, and Bangladesh. Mughal society under Akbar tolerated many different religious beliefs. Akbar's son Jahangir was a Muslim, but he had a Hindu mother. The empire officially was Sunni, but many Shiites held high offices. The empire grew less tolerant and declined in the 1700's. It ended in 1858.

Colonialism

Domination by the West. In 1798, the French general Napoleon invaded and conquered Egypt. The conquest shocked the Muslim world. Since the time of the

A religious procession in Karachi, Pakistan, honors the birthday of the Prophet Muhammad. Pakistan is one of the largest Muslim nations in the world. Although Islam originated in the Middle East, the majority of Muslims today live in other parts of the world, especially south Asia.

© Anis Hamdani, Getty Images

Abbasids, Muslims had viewed Europe as a barbaric land, where culture and morality remained at a low level. With Egypt's defeat, Muslims faced a Europe that had superior military strength and openly challenged their social values. Muslims were impressed by Western military technology and influenced by their contacts with European scientists and historians. Muslim delegations began to travel to Europe to study the latest trends in science and philosophy.

Although the French left Egypt in 1801, they returned to the Muslim world, invading Algeria in 1830. During the last half of the 1800's and the early 1900's, Europe either directly or indirectly controlled every Muslim country except Arabia, Turkey, and Iran. Most states of north and west Africa became French colonies. British political influence and territorial control in India grew in the 1700's and 1800's. Egypt was under British control from 1882. Indonesia began to fall under the rule of the Netherlands as early as the 1600's.

Colonialism caused drastic changes within all Muslim societies. Colonial governments brought administrative changes and built roads, railroads, and bridges. But colonial authorities also deprived Islam of its former role in the organization of social and economic life. They reorganized the Islamic Shari`a and supplemented it with a European system of laws. To the present day, most Muslim countries have a dual legal system. Laws governing marriage, family, inheritance, and other personal matters are usually based on the Shari`a, while most criminal and commercial laws are based on European models.

Reform and renewal. The most influential Muslim movement of the colonial period was the Salafiyyah (Way of the Ancestors). It was founded by Jamal al-Din al-Afghani, an Iranian politician and philosopher, and Muhammad Abduh, an Egyptian theologian and expert on Islamic law. The Salafiyyah attempted to reform Islam using modern Western concepts of reason and science. Afghani also helped found Pan-Islamism, a movement that called for the unity of all Muslims. He feared that nationalism would divide the Muslim world and believed that Muslim unity was more important than ethnic identity. Muhammad Abduh's main concerns were the reform of Islamic law and theology. He rejected the blind acceptance of the past.

The most important successors of the Salafiyyah movement were the Muslim Brotherhood, the Jamaat-i-Islami, and the Muhammadiyah. Hasan al-Banna, an Egyptian teacher, founded the Muslim Brotherhood in 1928. The organization inspired Islamic reform movements in other Arab countries, including Jordan, Sudan, and Syria. The Muslim Brotherhood started as a religious and philanthropic society that promoted morality and good works. It eventually moved into politics and supported the replacement of nonreligious governments with governments based on Islamic principles. Today, the Muslim Brotherhood is one of the most influential movements in the Muslim world. It is affiliated with Islamic reform movements in non-Arab countries, such as Pakistan, Bangladesh, and Malaysia. In addition, the Muslim Brotherhood influences Islamic centers in the United States.

The Jamaat-i-Islami was founded in 1941 in what is now Pakistan by Abu al-Ala Maududi, who was dedicated to reviving Islam in India. After British rule ended in India in 1947, he supported the creation of an Islamic republic in Pakistan. Throughout its history, the Jamaat-i-Islami has supported conservative Muslim politics. The leaders have called for curtailing the influence of minority Islamic sects in Pakistan and have stirred up opposition to nonreligious governments. Although its political influence declined after the death of its founder, the Jamaat-i-Islami continues to attract a following among university students and the lower middle class. It also has considerable influence among Pakistani immigrants in Europe and the United States.

The Muhammadiyah is the largest Muslim reform organization in Southeast Asia. It was founded on the Indonesian island of Java in 1912 and was heavily influenced by the views of Muhammad Abduh. The Muhammadiyah supports a form of Islam based on reason. It has called for the social liberation of Muslim women. Aishiya, the Muhammadiyah's women's organization, was named after the Prophet's wife. It ranks as one of the most dynamic women's organizations in the Muslim world.

The Muslim world today

A goal held by many Muslims is the formation of a unified community of believers. But the great diversity of the modern Muslim world acts against this goal. Although a majority of Muslims believe that "Islam is one," there remain important differences of doctrine and practice within the Muslim world. The practice of Islam in Morocco, for example, differs in many ways from the practice of Islam in Iran or Oman. Only about 15 percent of Muslims are Arabs. The largest group of Muslims live in south Asia in Bangladesh, India, and Pakistan and speak languages, such as Bengali and Urdu, which are much different from Arabic. The single nation with the largest Muslim population is Indonesia in Southeast Asia. And as Islam becomes more prominent in Europe and North America, new cultural forms will add to this diversity.

Cultural differences lie behind many social controversies in Islam, especially regarding the role of women. The treatment of women varies widely throughout the Muslim world. Women in such countries as Afghanistan and Saudi Arabia live largely in seclusion and have little social or economic independence. In other countries, however, including Bangladesh, Malaysia, Pakistan, Turkey, and Tunisia, women are elected to parliament, serve as government officials, and may even become prime minister.

In the late 1900's and early 2000's, some Islamic fundamentalist groups strongly opposed countries with governments that did not follow their interpretation of Islam. Some declared that the United States was an enemy of Islam. They especially objected to U.S. support of Israel and the presence of American troops in Saudi Arabia. Some Islamic extremists called for a "holy war" against the United States and launched terrorist attacks against American citizens and property.

Vincent J. Cornell

Questions

What are the three major divisions in Islam?
Who built the Kaaba?
Where was the Mughal Empire founded?
What was the *Hijra* or *Hegira?*
Who founded the Umayyad caliphate?
What is the goal of the Muslim Brotherhood?
What was the Salafiyyah movement?
Who was the first caliph?
What is *Sufism?*
Who were the Safavids?

Additional resources

Ahmed, Akbar S. *Islam Today.* I. B. Tauris, 1999.
Esposito, John L., ed. *The Oxford History of Islam.* Oxford, 1999.
Jenkins, Everett, Jr. *The Muslim Diaspora.* McFarland, 1999-. Multivolume work.
Nanji, Azim A., Ed. *The Muslim Almanac.* Gale Research, 1996.

Web site

Understanding Islam and Muslims
http://www.ummah.org.uk/learning/islam&muslims/allpages.html
Provides answers to some basic questions about Islam and Muslims in a question-and-answer format.

Palestinians are an ethnic and national group native to the historic region of Palestine that now consists of Israel, the West Bank, and the Gaza Strip. Today, there are about 8 million Palestinians. Nearly half now live outside what was Palestine—in nearby Arab countries and elsewhere. Most of these Palestinians are refugees or the descendants of the more than 700,000 refugees who fled or were driven out of Israel when it was created in 1948. Some are people who were forced to leave the Gaza Strip and the West Bank, which were occupied by Israel in 1967. Today, though some Palestinians still live in refugee camps, most have integrated socially and economically within the host countries.

Modern Palestinians claim to be descendants of the *Philistines,* an ancient people who settled the region near the end of the 1200's B.C., and other groups who arrived later. Arab culture became a dominant influence beginning about A.D. 638, when Muslim Arabs conquered much of the region. Palestinians today speak Arabic with regional accents that distinguish them from other Arab groups. Nearly all Palestinians are Muslims, with a large Christian minority.

The Palestinian people began to develop a modern national identity around 1900. Palestinian national identity has a number of sources. It comes in part from the religious attachment of Muslims and Christians to Palestine as a holy land. Palestinian nationalism and the desire for self-determination also developed as a response to *Zionism,* a movement that began in the 1800's and called for a Jewish national state in Palestine. In 1947, the United Nations voted to partition Palestine into a Jewish state and an Arab state. Jerusalem was put under international control. The Jews in Palestine accepted this plan, but the Arabs rejected it. Israel came into existence in 1948. War quickly broke out between Israel and the surrounding Arab countries. By 1949, Israel had won the war and taken control of about half the land planned for the new Arab state. Egypt and Jordan held the rest of Palestine. These areas came under Israeli control in 1967.

Today, Palestinians hold a variety of professional positions and are an important part of the economies of several Middle Eastern countries. About 2 million Palestinians are citizens of Jordan. Many other Palestinians carry passports from the Palestinian Authority, which is the political body that administers Palestinian-controlled portions of the Gaza Strip and West Bank. About 1 million Palestinians are citizens of Israel, where they are subject to discrimination and many legal restrictions. A large number of Palestinians in Lebanon, Syria, and Egypt remain stateless refugees with no citizenship.

Rashid I. Khalidi

Pashtuns, *pash TOONZ,* are one of the largest ethnic groups in Afghanistan and Pakistan. They make up about half the population of Afghanistan and about one-fifth of the people of Pakistan. Most Pashtuns live near the border between Afghanistan and Pakistan.

Other names for the Pashtuns include *Pathans, Pakhtuns, Pukhtuns,* and *Pushtuns.* They speak Pashto, also called Pushtu or Pukhtu, a language related to Persian. Almost all Pashtuns are Muslims.

The Pashtuns consist of about 40 tribes divided into groups of related families. Democratic councils called *jirgah* govern tribal affairs. Although the tribes unite to fight invaders, they often feud with one another. Some of the feuds have raged for centuries.

Many Pashtuns work as farmers, raising wheat and other grains, fruits, nuts, and sugar cane. Others are nomads who breed horses and herd sheep, goats, cattle, and camels. Many farmers live in homes made of mudbrick. A majority of nomads live in tents made of goat hair. Some Pashtuns combine farming with nomadic herding.

Ancestors of the Pashtuns lived in what is now Afghanistan by about 4000 B.C. In the A.D. 1500's, some Pashtuns moved to present-day Pakistan. In the 1800's and early 1900's, Pashtun warriors became the dominant group among Afghans who fought and won a series of wars against the British. The United Kingdom was seeking control of Afghanistan's foreign policy as part of its competition with Russia for influence in the region.

In late 1979 and early 1980, the Soviet Union invaded Afghanistan. Pashtuns formed guerrilla bands to help repel the invasion. The Soviets withdrew from Afghanistan in 1988 and 1989. By the late 1990's, a Pashtun-dominated group known as the Taliban had taken control of most of Afghanistan. Afghan rebels, aided by the United States and its allies, forced the Taliban from power in 2001.   Thomas E. Gouttierre

Web site

Pashtuns of Afghanistan
http://www.afghan-network.net/Ethnic-Groups/pashtuns.html
Information on the dominant ethnic and linguistic group in Afghanistan.

Qur'ān, *ku RAHN* or *ku RAN,* is the sacred book of the Muslims. It is also spelled Koran. The name *Qur'ān* means *a recitation* or *something to be recited,* presumably in worship.

Muslims believe the angel Gabriel revealed the Qur'ān to the Prophet Muhammad a little at a time. The revelations began about A.D. 610 and continued until Muhammad's death in 632. Muhammad's followers, who wrote down the revelations, collected them into the book that is now known as the Qur'ān. The standard text of the Qur'ān was formed during the reign of Caliph Uthman, who ruled from 644 to 656. Muslims consider the Qur'ān to be the words of God Himself, and in no sense the composition of Muhammad. They believe that the earthly book, bound between covers, is a copy of an eternal book that is kept in heaven.

The Qur'ān consists of verses grouped into 114 chapters. The chapters vary in length from a few lines to over 200 verses. Much of the Qur'ān is written in rhymed Arabic prose. Muslims believe that the rich, forceful language of the text is humanly unmatchable, and a miracle that confirms Muhammad's prophethood.

Teachings. The central teaching of the Qur'ān is that there is only one God. The word for God in Arabic is *Allah.* Allah is the creator of the universe and requires *Islam* (submission) to Himself. Allah, in His mercy, sent the Qur'ān as a guide for humanity. Another important teaching concerns the prophets who have been God's messengers to different peoples. The Qur'ān mentions the prophets Abraham, Moses, Jesus, and many others. The Qur'ān describes Muhammad as the last of the prophets.

The Qur'ān speaks of a day of judgment when people shall stand before God to account for their lives. It contains a large number of teachings to regulate Muslim daily life. The Qur'ān requires daily prayers, and stresses charity and brotherly love among Muslims. The Qur'ān teaches that one should be humble, temperate, brave, and just.

Influence. The Qur'ān is one of the most widely read books in the world. Its teachings formed the basis of the great Islamic civilization of the past, and it guides and in-spires millions of Muslims. The Qur'ān is the final authority in matters of faith and practice for all Muslims. It is the highest authority for Islamic law.

The Qur'ān has been taught orally and is memorized, at least in part, by virtually all Muslims. Thus, even illiterate Muslims possess and prize the text. The reverence for the holy book is so great that many Muslims learn the entire work by heart. The art of properly reciting the Qur'ān has been preserved and passed on through the centuries, and has been enhanced by the modern technology of audio cassette recording.

For hundreds of years, Muslims refused to translate the Qur'ān into other languages. They thought they should preserve the words of God in their original form. But in the early 1900's, Muslims began to translate the Qur'ān into Eastern and Western languages.
          Richard C. Martin

Additional resources

Abdel Haleem, Muhammad. *Understanding the Qur'an.* I. B. Tauris, 1999.
Cragg, Kenneth, ed. *Readings on the Qur'an.* 1988. Reprint. International Specialized Bk., 1999.
Khan, Muhammad Z. *The Qur'an.* Interlink Pub. Group, 1997.

Web site

Quran Browser
http://www.stg.brown.edu/webs/quran_browser/
An online tool for exploring the Qur'ān in English created by the Scholarly Technology Group at Brown University.

Sharī'a, *shuh REE uh,* is the legal and moral code of Islam. Muslims believe that the Sharī'a, also spelled Sharī'ah, is divinely inspired. It is the law of the land in the Islamic countries of Saudi Arabia and Iran, and it exerts great influence in other Islamic countries and cultures. *Sharī'a* is an Arabic word that originally meant *a path to a source of water,* which suggests purity and nourishment. It has come to be understood as *The way that leads to God.*

The Sharī'a is a system of morals, religious observance, ethics, and politics. It covers religious and nonreligious aspects of life. For example, the Sharī'a includes guidelines on how Muslims wash, eat, pray, maintain friendships, conduct business, and govern. In religious matters, the interpretation of the Sharī'a has remained largely unchanged over the years. But in social, political, and cultural affairs, it has undergone considerable interpretation by generations of Islamic scholars.

The Sharī'a is based on several sources. The most important are the Islamic holy book called the Qur'ān and the *Sunna,* which is the example demonstrated by the sayings and acts of the prophet Muhammad. The Sunna is preserved in written collections called the *Hadith.* For the majority of Muslims, the nature of the Sharī'a is determined by *ijma,* which is a general agreement of views among religious scholars. However, among followers of the Shi'ah division of Islam, the guidance and example of certain leaders called Imams was considered more important.

The formal method for determining points of practice and procedure according to the Sharī'a is the discipline of *fiqh* (law). This discipline and the basic interpretations of the Sharī'a developed during the second and third centuries of Islamic history. That period corresponds to the A.D. 700's and 800's.   Hugh Talat Halman

Abdullah, *ahb DUL lah*, (1924-   ), is crown prince and first deputy prime minister of Saudi Arabia. He was named to these positions in 1982, when his half brother Fahd became king and prime minister of Saudi Arabia. In the mid-1990's, Fahd suffered a stroke, and his health began to decline. As first deputy prime minister, Abdullah became increasingly responsible for governing the country.

Abdullah supports moderate reforms within Saudi Arabia. He also has become a spokesman for the Arab people and has played a leadership role in trying to end the Israeli-Palestinian conflict.

Abdullah was born in Riyadh, Saudi Arabia. His full name is Abdullah ibn Abd al-Aziz Al Saud. He spent part of his youth living with Bedouin tribes in the deserts of Saudi Arabia. In 1962, Abdullah was appointed commander of the country's National Guard. He still holds that position.

© Corbis/AFP

Jordan's King Abdullah II and Saudi Crown Prince Abdullah are important Arab leaders. Abdullah II, *left,* became king of Jordan in 1999. Crown Prince Abdullah, *right,* has taken on increasing responsibility for governing Saudi Arabia from his ailing half brother King Fahd since the mid-1990's.

Abdullah II, *ab DUHL uh* or *ab dool LAH* (1962-   ), became king of Jordan in 1999, following the death of his father, Hussein. He is the oldest son of Hussein and his second wife, Princess Muna al-Hussein. Before taking the throne, Abdullah was a career military officer.

Abdullah was born in Amman, the capital of Jordan, and attended high school at Deerfield Academy in the United States. In the 1980's, he studied international relations at Oxford University in the United Kingdom and Georgetown University in the United States. He also had military training at schools in both countries.

In 1981, Abdullah joined the Jordanian army as a second lieutenant. He was promoted to colonel in 1993 and became commander of Jordan's special forces in 1994. While in the military, Abdullah represented his father on diplomatic missions to the Middle East, Europe, and the United States.   Peter Gubser

Arafat, *AHR uh FAT,* **Yasir** (1929-   ), has been chairman of the Palestine Liberation Organization (PLO) since 1969 and president of the Palestinian Authority since 1996. The PLO is an alliance of Palestinian Arab groups that work to establish an Arab state in what was once Palestine. The area that made up Palestine now consists mainly of Israel, the Gaza Strip, and the West Bank. The

Palestinian Authority was created in 1994 to govern Palestinian-controlled parts of the West Bank and Gaza Strip.

Arafat was born in 1929, probably on August 24. He claims he was born in Jerusalem, in what was then the British mandate of Palestine, but many sources say he was born in Cairo, Egypt. His full name is Mohammed Ab-

©Barthelemy, Sipa Press
Yasir Arafat

del-Raouf Arafat al-Qudwa al-Husseini. He acquired the nickname Yasir, which means *easygoing,* as a teen-ager. He earned a degree in civil engineering at Cairo University. In the 1950's, he helped organize Arab guerrilla groups, including *Al Fatah,* now part of the PLO. Beginning in the 1960's, he helped plan many Al Fatah raids against Israel. Israel then attacked PLO bases. Arafat addressed the United Nations (UN) General Assembly in 1974, and the UN then recognized the PLO as the representative of Palestinian Arabs.

In 1983, fighting broke out between PLO supporters of Arafat and those who opposed him. The rebels forced Arafat and his supporters to leave their bases in northern Lebanon. But Arafat remained as PLO chairman.

The PLO did not recognize Israel's right to exist. But in 1988, Arafat persuaded the PLO to accept Israel's right to exist alongside a Palestinian state in the Gaza Strip and West Bank. Israel had occupied them after the 1967 Arab-Israeli war. The PLO declared the existence of the state and elected Arafat its president. But Israel continued to occupy and, in effect, govern the areas.

In 1993, the PLO—under Arafat's leadership—and Israel gave recognition to each other. In 1993 and 1995, they signed agreements that led to the withdrawal of Israeli troops from the Gaza Strip and most West Bank towns by early 1996. As the Israelis withdrew, the Palestinian Authority took control of these areas. In 1994, Arafat and the Israeli leaders Yitzhak Rabin and Shimon Peres shared the Nobel Peace Prize for their peace efforts. In January 1996, Arafat was elected president of the Palestinian Authority.   Michael C. Hudson

Assad, *ah SAHD,* **Bashar al-,** *bah SHAHR uhl* (1965-   ), became president of Syria in July 2000. His name is also spelled Bashar al-Asad. He took over the presidency following the death of his father, Hafez al-Assad (also spelled Hafiz al-Asad), Syria's leader since 1970. Hafez al-Assad began preparing Bashar to be his successor after the death in 1994 of Bashar's older brother, Basil. Basil had been expected to assume the presidency.

Bashar al-Assad was born in Damascus. Assad received a medical degree from the University of

AP/Wide World
Bashar al-Assad

Damascus in 1988. He trained in *ophthalmology* (the study of diseases of the eye) at the Tishrin military hospital in Damascus from 1988 until 1992. He moved to England in 1992 to complete a medical residency program.

In 1994, Bashar's brother Basil was killed in a car accident. Bashar was called back to Syria to train to take over the presidency. He attended the military academy at Homs, north of Damascus, earning the rank of colonel. After his father's death, Assad was promoted to lieutenant general and made commander in chief of the armed forces. He also became head of the ruling Baath Party.   As'ad AbuKhalil

Fahd (1923-   ) became king and prime minister of Saudi Arabia in 1982. He came to power following the death of his half brother King Khalid. When Khalid became king in 1975, Fahd was named crown prince and first deputy prime minister of Saudi Arabia. Fahd ran the day-to-day affairs of the government because Khalid was not in good health and he lacked Fahd's detailed knowledge of government functions. Fahd tried to maintain Saudi Arabia's traditional Islamic values while continuing the modernization made possible by the country's great oil wealth.

Saudi Arabian Information Service, Washington, D.C.

Fahd

In August 1990, Iraqi forces invaded and occupied oil-rich Kuwait. Many people feared Iraq would next invade Saudi Arabia. Fahd invited foreign troops, including those from the United States, to come to Saudi Arabia to defend that country. The Saudis and foreign nations formed an alliance. In February 1991, under U.S. military leadership, these allies drove the Iraqis out of Kuwait.

In 1993, Fahd appointed a 60-member Consultative Council to advise him on government matters. The council has no legislative powers, but it provides Saudi citizens with a voice in the government.

In the mid-1990's, King Fahd's health began to decline. His half brother Crown Prince Abdullah became increasingly responsible for running the Saudi government.

Fahd was born in Riyadh. His full name is Fahd ibn Abd al-Aziz Al Saud.   Malcolm C. Peck

Hussein, *hoo SAYN,* **Saddam,** *sah DAHM* (1937-   ), has been president of Iraq since 1979. He is chairman of the Revolutionary Command Council of the Baath Party, which sets government policies. Using Iraq's huge petroleum resources, Hussein supervised a successful development program in the 1970's. This was halted by a war between Iraq and Iran from 1980 until 1988, when a cease-fire was declared. Hussein became known for his ruthless actions. For example, in the 1980's, he used chemical weapons against Kurdish people of Iraq, who were seeking self-government.

In August 1990, Hussein ordered Iraqi forces to occupy Kuwait. He accused Kuwait of violating oil production limits set by the Organization of the Petroleum Exporting Countries (OPEC), thus lowering the price of oil. Hussein announced that his country had annexed Kuwait.

Many countries, including the United States, Canada,

and several Arab and Western European nations, opposed the invasion and sent forces to the region. These nations formed an allied military coalition. The United Nations Security Council approved the use of military force to remove the Iraqi troops from Kuwait if they did not leave Kuwait. But Hussein refused to withdraw his troops, and war broke out on January 16 U.S. time, which was January 17 in Iraq. The allies launched fighter-bombers against military targets in Iraq and Kuwait, and Iraq launched missiles against Saudi Arabia and Israel. In February, allied land forces moved into Kuwait. They quickly defeated the occupying Iraqi forces. Hussein's government failed to fulfill the terms of a United Nations cease-fire agreement. The United Nations maintained a trade embargo on Iraq, harming the country's economy.

© Corbis/Bettmann

Saddam Hussein

Hussein was born in Tikrit. He became active in the Baath Party in 1956. In 1959, Hussein left Iraq after he took part in an attempt to kill Iraqi dictator Abdul Karim Kassem. He was imprisoned in 1964, after he returned to Iraq. He had been elected to the Regional Command of the Baath in 1963. In 1965, while in prison, he was elected to the National Command. Hussein escaped from jail in 1966. The Baath took control of Iraq in 1968. During his rise to power, Hussein held important party and government posts.   Michel Le Gall

Karzai, *KAHR zy,* **Hamid,** *HAH mihd,* (1957-   ), is the president of Afghanistan. He is also head of the Popalzai (also spelled Popolzai or Populzai), an important clan of the country's dominant Pashtun ethnic group. As Afghanistan's leader, Karzai has worked to establish a new national government and to control the country's warring regional leaders. He also has sought international aid to help rebuild Afghanistan after many years of war.

Karzai became the leader of a temporary government of Afghanistan after he was chosen for the post by a United Nations-sponsored conference of Afghan delegates in late 2001. In June 2002, a traditional Afghan council called a *loya jirga* elected Karzai to serve as president of a transitional government that would hold office for up to two years.

Before Karzai became leader of the Afghan government, a coalition of countries led by the United States had attacked Afghanistan's ruling Taliban, an extremist Islamic group that controlled much of the country. The coalition and its Afghan allies drove the Taliban from power. The coalition believed that the Taliban was protecting Osama bin Laden, a Saudi-born millionaire and terrorist. Bin

AP/Wide World

Hamid Karzai

Laden was considered to have been behind the Sept. 11, 2001, terrorist attacks on the World Trade Center in New York City and the Pentagon Building near Washington, D.C.

To help the coalition, Karzai rallied tribes in southern Afghanistan to fight against the Taliban. At one point, Karzai was nearly captured by the Taliban, but he managed to escape. Karzai also played an important role in the coalition's victory in Kandahar, the Afghan city that was the spiritual center of Taliban activities.

During the 1980's, Karzai was active in the war against the Soviet Union, which had invaded Afghanistan in 1979 and 1980. He spent much of his time in Pakistan, where he helped fund and arm anti-Soviet Afghan fighters. The Soviet Union withdrew its troops from Afghanistan in 1988 and 1989. After a period of fighting among various groups, a new government came to power in Afghanistan in 1992, with Karzai as deputy foreign minister. When the Taliban began operating in Afghanistan in 1994, Karzai initially supported the group. However, he withdrew his support over concerns about the influence of Arab and Pakistani extremists within the Taliban.

Karzai was born on Dec. 24, 1957, in Kandahar. His grandfather, Abdul Ahad Karzai, once served as president of Afghanistan's national council. His father, also named Abdul Ahad Karzai, once served as speaker of the Afghan parliament. Like his son Hamid, Abdul Ahad Karzai opposed the Taliban. He was assassinated in 1999, reportedly by the Taliban.

Khamenei, *kah MAY nee* or *hah MEE nee,* **Ali,** *ah LEE* (1939-   ), is the supreme leader of the Islamic Republic of Iran. Members of Iran's government selected him to succeed Ayatollah Ruhollah Khomeini in this position, called the *faqih,* following Khomeini's death in 1989. Khamenei had served as president from 1981 to 1989. He is considered a rigid political and religious leader who is unwilling to compromise on improving relations with Western countries.

Khamenei was born on July 15, 1939, in Meshed in northeastern Iran. He studied Islam under Khomeini and later taught theology. Khamenei earned the religious title of *ayatollah,* the highest that can be held by a Shiite Muslim. During the 1960's and 1970's, Khamenei became a prominent opponent of the *secular* (nonreligious) government of Shah Mohammad Reza Pahlavi. In 1979, revolutionaries overthrew the shah's government and replaced it with an Islamic republic. Khamenei was named to the Revolutionary Council, which governed Iran after the revolution. He also held several other positions in

AP/Wide World
Ali Khamenei

the new government. As a result, he had much influence in the shaping of the Islamic state.   Rudi Matthee

Khatami, *kah TAH mee,* **Mohammad,** *moh HAM mad* (1943-   ), was elected president of Iran in 1997 and won reelection in 2001. He is known for his moder-

ate views. For example, Khatami supports individual rights and a more open society in Iran, including a free press. He has also called for closer economic ties between Iran and Western nations. His ability to bring about real change is limited, however. As president, Khatami has less power than the nation's supreme leader, Ayatollah Ali Khamenei, who is known as the *faqih.* Khatami's views have frequently brought him into conflict with Khamenei and other conservative members of Iran's ruling Islamic clergy.

Khatami was born in Ardakan, near Yazd, in central Iran. He studied education, philosophy, and theology at schools in Isfahan, Qom, and Tehran and became an Islamic clergyman. From 1978 to 1980, Khatami headed the Islamic Center in Hamburg, West Germany (now Germany). In 1980 and 1981, he served in the Iranian parliament and as a newspaper editor. He was minister of Culture and Islamic Guidance from 1982 to 1992, when his tolerant position on freedom of the media led to his dis-

AP/Wide World
Mohammad Khatami

missal. He was then appointed to the less important position of head of the National Library.   Rudi Matthee

Mubarak, *muh BAHR ak,* **Hosni,** *HAHS nee* (1928-   ), became president of Egypt in October 1981. He succeeded Anwar el-Sadat, who was assassinated by Islamic fundamentalist extremists. As president, Mubarak continued Sadat's policies, including the fulfillment of the 1979 peace agreement between Egypt and Israel. Mubarak faces strong opposition from Islamic extremists in Egypt, who also challenged Sadat's policies and Egypt's negotiations with Israel.

In August 1990, Iraq invaded and occupied Kuwait. Mubarak played a leading role in organizing Arab opposition to Iraq. Egypt and other Arab nations and the United States and other Western nations formed a military coalition against Iraq. In February 1991, the coalition drove the Iraqis out of Kuwait.

Violence by Islamic extremists increased greatly in the early 1990's in Egypt. These people attacked Egyptian Christians, foreign tourists, and other foreigners. In 1992, Mubarak's government began raiding extremist strongholds and making arrests.

Mubarak was born on May 4, 1928, in Kafr-El-Meselha, a village about 80 miles (130 kilometers) north of Cairo. He graduated from Egypt's Military Academy in 1949 and its Air Force Academy in 1950. He then served as a fighter pilot and a bomber squadron commander in the Egyptian Air Force. Mubarak commanded the

AP/Wide World
Hosni Mubarak

air force from 1972 to 1975, when Sadat appointed him vice president.   <small>Malcolm C. Peck</small>

Musharraf, *moo SHAHR rahf,* **Pervez,** *PEHR vehz,* (1943-   ), has ruled Pakistan since coming to power in a military coup in 1999. Following the coup, Musharraf suspended the country's democratic bodies and claimed all power for himself.

In 2001, Musharraf became a key ally of the United States and other countries in their efforts to fight terrorists in Afghanistan, Pakistan's neighbor to the north. On Sept. 11, 2001, terrorists had attacked the World Trade Center in New York City and the Pentagon Building near Washington, D.C. United States officials blamed the attacks on exiled Saudi millionaire Osama bin Laden and his al-Qa`ida terrorist organization. Bin Laden was hiding out in Afghanistan, where he was protected by the Taliban regime. The Taliban, a conservative Islamic group, had taken control of Afghanistan in the mid-1990's. In October 2001, the United States began military action in Afghanistan in support of Afghan rebels who opposed the Taliban and al-Qa`ida. Musharraf cooperated with the United States in this operation. He agreed to share intelligence with the United States and allowed the United States to use some Pakistani air bases. Musharraf's cooperation with the United States displeased some Pakistanis,

AP/Wide World
Pervez Musharraf

particularly supporters of the Taliban, and led to sometimes violent protests. The Afghan rebels drove the Taliban from power in late 2001.

Musharraf was born in Delhi, India, on Aug. 11, 1943. When Pakistan and India gained independence as separate countries in 1947, his family moved to Pakistan.

Musharraf graduated from the Pakistan Military Academy in 1964 and joined an artillery regiment. He later attended other military schools, including the Royal College of Defence Studies in the United Kingdom. Musharraf fought in several conflicts and rose through the ranks of Pakistan's military. He was promoted to major general in 1991 and to lieutenant general in 1995. In 1998, Musharraf was promoted to the rank of general and appointed army chief of staff.

In 1999, Musharraf led a military take-over of Pakistan's government. He arrested the democratically elected prime minister, Nawaz Sharif, and later forced him into exile. Musharraf named himself chief executive and suspended Pakistan's national parliament and state legislatures. In 2001, Musharraf appointed himself president and head of state and formally dissolved the country's legislative bodies. Pakistan's Supreme Court ordered that civilian government be restored by October 2002, and Musharraf agreed to follow the order.

In 2002, Musharraf called for a referendum to extend his term as president for five years. The referendum was held in April of that year. In the referendum, voters approved the extension of Musharraf's term, though some people questioned whether the vote violated Pakistan's

constitution. Parliamentary elections were scheduled for October 2002.

Sharon, *shah ROHN,* **Ariel,** *ah ree EHL,* (1928-   ), the leader of the conservative Likud party, became prime minister of Israel in 2001. He has been known as an outspoken opponent of peace agreements between Israel and the Palestinians. Sharon also has strongly supported Jewish settlements in the West Bank and Gaza Strip, territories that Israel occupied in 1967. Israel withdrew from most of the Gaza Strip in 1994 and from part of the West Bank in the late 1990's.

AP/Wide World
Ariel Sharon

Sharon was born in 1928, probably on February 27, in Kfar Malal, a Jewish cooperative farming settlement near Tel Aviv in what was then Palestine. As a teen-ager, he joined an underground Jewish defense force that had been set up to protect Jewish settlers from Arab raiding parties. From 1948 to 1973, he served in the Israel Defense Forces. He eventually became a major general in 1967. He fought in the Israeli war of independence in 1948, the Sinai campaign of 1956, the Six-Day War of 1967, and the Yom Kippur War of 1973. Among some people, he gained a reputation for bravery. Others, particularly Palestinians, considered him ruthless.

In 1973, Sharon resigned from the military and entered politics. He was first elected to the Knesset (Israeli Parliament) that same year. He held a number of Cabinet posts, including minister of agriculture in charge of settlements from 1977 to 1981 and minister of defense from 1981 to 1983. As defense minister, he directed the Israeli invasion of Lebanon in June 1982 in retaliation for terrorist attacks on northern Israel by members of the Palestine Liberation Organization (PLO). The invasion was intended to eliminate the military threat to Israel's northern border. Sharon was criticized for failing to try to prevent a massacre of hundreds of Palestinian civilians in September 1982 by members of the Lebanese Christian militia in the Israeli-occupied part of Beirut. He was forced to resign as defense minister in February 1983 after an Israeli commission that investigated the massacre declared him indirectly responsible for the incident. Sharon went on to serve in other Cabinet roles.

In 1999, Sharon was elected head of the Likud party. In September 2000, he made a controversial visit to the Temple Mount in Jerusalem. The Temple Mount, known to Muslims as Haram al-Sharif, is a holy site for both Jews and Muslims. Disagreement over who would govern the site, as well as other parts of Jerusalem, was a major stumbling block in peace talks between Israel and the Palestinians. Sharon's visit angered Palestinians. Violent clashes broke out between Palestinian protesters and Israeli troops in Palestinian areas of the West Bank and Gaza Strip after Sharon's visit. The continuing violence led Israeli Prime Minister Ehud Barak to call for an election for prime minister to be held in February 2001. In the election, Sharon defeated Barak.   <small>Bernard Reich</small>

Focus on
TERRORISM

Conflicts Within Islam: Moderates vs. Extremists

The September 11 terrorists and other Islamist extremists represent a minority of the more than 1 billion Muslim believers around the world. In fact, most Muslims condemned the attacks as a crime that could not be tolerated by their religion. This section explores the cultural and political context of the attacks by examining the history of the debate between moderate and extremist followers of Islam.

Traditional Islamic training often takes place at religious schools called *madrasahs*. In this photo, a *mullah* (Islamic religious leader) instructs students at a madrasah in Peshawar, Pakistan. Some madrasahs have fostered religious extremism.

© Robert Nickelsberg, Getty Images

Muslim women attend a memorial service in New York City for the people killed in the Sept. 11, 2001, terrorist attacks. Moderate Muslims throughout the world condemned the attacks as a crime that violated the beliefs and principles of Islam.

AP/Wide World

Conflicts Within Islam: Moderates vs. Extremists

In 1998, the Saudi-born terrorist leader Osama bin Laden wrote that Muslims had "the personal duty to kill Americans and their allies, whether civilians or military personnel, in every country where this is possible." In August 1998, members of bin Laden's al-Qa`ida terrorist organization acted on his decree and destroyed the U.S. embassies in Nairobi, Kenya, and Dar es-Salaam, Tanzania. The attacks left hundreds dead and wounded. In November 2000, al-Qa`ida attacked the U.S.S. *Cole* in Aden, Yemen, killing 17 U.S. sailors. On September 11, 2001, al-Qa`ida terrorists, using hijacked commercial airliners, deliberately crashed into the World Trade Center in New York City and the Pentagon Building near Washington, D.C. About 3,000 people were killed in these attacks.

In attempting to justify his attacks against United States citizens, bin Laden claimed to be fighting a holy struggle for the religion of Islam. He cited the Qur`ān, the sacred book of Islam; the sayings and deeds of the Prophet Muhammad; and the teachings of influential

Muslim scholars throughout history. He reportedly calculated that the September 11 attacks, and any U.S. military response, would unite the Islamic world in a common struggle against the United States and its allies.

However, the great majority of the Islamic world did not rally behind bin Laden. Instead, most Muslims condemned the attacks as the killing of innocents. And even though many Muslims strongly disagree with U.S. policy in the Middle East, particularly the U.S. embargo against Iraq and U.S. support for Israel, they believed the killing of innocent people was a crime that could not be tolerated by Islam.

In the days following September 11, a number of highly respected Muslim scholars signed a decree stating that the terrorist attacks, from the perspective of Islamic law, constituted the crime of warfare against society. Zaki Badawi, the principal of the Muslim College in London, wrote that "neither the law of Islam nor its ethical system justify such a crime." According to King Abdullah II of Jordan, "what these people [the terrorists] stand for is completely against all the principles that Arab Muslims believe in." Statements from these and other prominent Muslims illustrate the conflicts between moderate and extremist followers of Islam. In the

John C. M. Calvert, the contributor of this article, is Assistant Professor of History at Creighton University.

eyes of many, extremists such as bin Laden and his supporters do not represent the Islam that is shared by more than a billion Muslim believers worldwide.

The teachings of Islam

Islam is the world's second largest religion behind Christianity. Muslims live in every country of the world. They are especially numerous in the Middle East, Africa, and southern Asia.

Central teachings. *Islam* is an Arabic word that means *surrender* or *submission*. In the Muslim perspective, submission to God—*Allah,* in Arabic—is necessary because men and women are in need of divine guidance, without which they will harm themselves and society. God, Muslims believe, has communicated His will to humankind through prophets and messengers. These prophets include the biblical leaders Abraham, David, and Moses. Muslims also revere Jesus Christ as a prophet, but unlike Christians, they do not consider Him to be the Son of God. In addition, Muslims honor an Arabian line of prophets, including such figures as Hud and Salih.

For Muslims, the last, and most significant, of God's messengers was the Prophet Muhammad. Muhammad was born about A.D. 570 in the city of Mecca, located in what is now Saudi Arabia. Around 610, while meditating in a cave outside Mecca, Muhammad received a vision. Muslims believe the vision was of the angel Gabriel, revealing God's message and calling on Muhammad to serve as a prophet. Muhammad continued to receive revelations until his death in 632.

The revelations made to Muhammad are collected in the Qur'ān (also spelled Koran), the holy book of Islam. Muslims believe that the Qur'ān is the literal word of God. The other main text of Islam is the Hadith. The Hadith is a written collection that presents the Sunna—that is, examples of the words and deeds of Muhammad. In the Muslim view, Muhammad's life serves as a model for all men and women.

The Five Pillars of Islam provide the framework for a Muslim's life. The pillars consist of (1) *shahada,* the declaration of belief in God and in Muhammad as God's messenger; (2) prayer, which should take place five times a day; (3) almsgiving, or assisting the poor; (4) fasting during the month of Ramadan; and (5) the *hajj,* a pilgrimage to Mecca, required of all who are financially and physically able.

**The Sharī`a** is the Islamic law that outlines an individual's responsibility to God and to others in society. The Qur'ān is the most important source of the Sharī`a. If the Qur'ān is silent on an issue, the Sharī`a is supplemented by the Hadith. The Sharī`a requires Muslims to practice the virtues of mercy and forgiveness. It regulates marriage, divorce, and inheritance, and it forbids false testimony, the drinking of alcohol, and other activities considered harmful to individual and public welfare. The Qur'ān requires that Muslims uphold the moral order of the Sharī`a.

In the first centuries of Islam, the Sharī`a remained reasonably flexible in response to changing circumstances. By the 900's, however, the content of the Sharī`a was considered fixed, as Muslim *jurists* (law experts) concluded that the essentials of God's law had been adequately explained. As a result, new religious practices and interpretations of scripture were condemned. Beginning in the 1800's, however, a number of Islamic scholars attempted to reform the Sharī`a in order to make it relevant to the modern age.

The rise of Islamic radicalism

Following World War II (1939-1945), many governments in Muslim countries of Asia and the Middle East increasingly adopted Western ideologies. Many began using European law codes in the place of the Sharī`a. In making these changes, the governments hoped to build strong, prosperous states and societies. However, by the 1960's, many people in Muslim countries remained poor and, in some cases, were politically oppressed by their governments. Many felt alienated from the Western culture favored by their governments. In addition, many Muslims resented the presence of the Jewish nation of Israel, created in 1948, in the Middle East.

Islamism. The political and cultural developments in the Middle East led many Muslims to turn to a different interpretation of Islam known in the West as *Islamism* or *Islamic fundamentalism.* Basically, Islamism is the belief in creating a modern Islamic society to resist the cultural influence of the West. In the Islamist view, such a society would represent a culturally authentic alternative to Westernized societies. Islamists believe that using the whole Sharī`a, and only the Sharī`a, as the law is the key to a just Muslim society. Such a society would be free of government corruption and immorality, both of which Islamists believe have a Western source. According to Islamists, once Qur'ānic principles have been put into practice, Muslim societies will find their potential and take their place among the developed nations.

Islamists do not define Islam as a religion of private devotion. Instead, they see Islam more broadly as a way of life that is concerned with all aspects of social, political, and cultural existence. Islamists seek to combine the spiritual values of Islam with the technological and organizational benefits of modern times.

Islamists have used two basic strategies to try to bring about their vision for society. The most widespread strategy is the effort of moderate Islamists to build an Islamic society by working within the current political and social systems. In Egypt and Pakistan, for example, moderate Islamists have won the support of large numbers of people by establishing Islamic schools and hospitals and by providing services that the governments are unable or unwilling to provide. Islamists who represent this moderate approach are widespread in Asia and the Middle East.

The second, and more radical, Islamist strategy, adopted by a smaller number of people, aims to impose an Islamic state upon society through the use of force. Such Islamist extremism has a number of sources. For example, some radicals have been inspired by Saudi Arabian Wahhabism. Wahhabism, also called Salafism, is a conservative and strict form of Islam that spread throughout the Arabian Peninsula in the early 1900's. Unlike most Muslims, Wahhabis do not support religious tolerance. Instead, they make a distinction between those whom they consider to uphold "true" Islam and "unrighteous" others, including Sufis (Islamic mystics), Christians, and Jews.

Many Islamist extremists, including bin Laden, have

also been influenced by the works of the Islamist thinker Sayyid Qutb of Egypt. In the mid-1900's, Qutb wrote that the *secular* (nonreligious) governments of the Muslim world threatened God's sovereignty on the earth. Qutb claimed that the creation of a true Islamic society depended on the formation of a small group of devoted Muslims who would strive to bring about the Islamic view of life. Qutb's followers believed this striving required violent confrontation with the secular state. In the late 1900's, the Islamic Jihad and other underground groups waged a deadly campaign of terror and assassination against the regimes of the Egyptian presidents Anwar el-Sadat and Hosni Mubarak.

The Iranian Revolution. In 1979, Islamist revolutionaries succeeded in taking control of the government of Iran through the use of force. Following the revolution, the religious leader Ayatollah Ruhollah Khomeini declared Iran an Islamic republic. Hundreds of officials of the former government were tried in revolutionary courts and put to death.

The mujahideen. In 1979 and 1980, the Soviet Union invaded Afghanistan to battle the *mujahideen,* a Muslim resistance movement that was fighting against the Soviet-backed government of Afghanistan. Soon, Arabs from various nations came to Afghanistan to join the mujahideen. The conflict provided opportunities for Wahhabi fighters from Saudi Arabia to link up with warriors from Egypt, Algeria, the Palestinian territories, and elsewhere. For the Arab fighters, the war was a source of heroism, solidarity, and total devotion to Islam. Many fighters found the struggle against the Soviet Union to be a school in which to learn the violent techniques needed to topple their governments at home.

Bin Laden joined the mujahideen in the early 1980's. In the late 1980's, he founded his al-Qaʾida network to wage a worldwide campaign against governments he felt violated strict Islamic law. Since then, many extremist members of the mujahideen have become associated with al-Qaʾida.

Disagreements between moderates and extremists

The majority of Muslims, including members of moderate Islamist organizations, have severely criticized the ideologies and tactics of extremist groups. In the view of most Muslim *ulama* (scholars), whose opinions represent conservative public opinion, the extremists threaten the very fabric of Islamic civilization.

Extremism and society. According to Yusuf al-Qaradawi, a leading Egyptian scholar based in Qatar, radical groups such as Egypt's Islamic Jihad create divisions within Islamic society by condemning those they believe are not true Muslims. Muslims, in al-Qaradawi's view, must be tolerant of other opinions and work toward reconciliation in society.

Al-Qaradawi also questions the ability of radical Muslims to guide others in religious affairs. In the view of al-Qaradawi, the definition of Islam should be left to the scholars who possess the necessary education to make judgments bearing on public welfare. Unqualified individuals, he writes, are likely to cloud their judgments with emotion or tailor their interpretations of the Qur'ān to fit a particular agenda.

Al-Qaradawi and other scholars are sympathetic to the issues raised by the militants, including what they regard as the authoritarian nature of many political regimes and the growing materialism of society. Yet any response to these problems, the scholars argue, must be disciplined by a sound understanding of the Qur'ān and the example of Muhammad's life.

Jihad. One difference between extremists and moderates concerns the the term *jihad,* which means *to strive.* According to Muslim jurists, jihad is any endeavor to further the cause of God. Traditionally, jurists have distinguished between the *greater jihad,* which is the individual struggle of a person to become a better Muslim, and the *lesser jihad,* which is the effort to spread Islam in the world and to defend it from its enemies.

Muslim jurists' regulations covering the lesser jihad are strict. These regulations state that Muslim armies may not kill women, children, the elderly, or peasants, except in self-defense. In addition, prisoners should not be harmed. The extremists, on the other hand, largely ignore the consensus of Muslim jurists and claim that jihad justifies acts of terrorism. Many militants, including bin Laden, regard violent jihad against "unbelievers" as a religious obligation for all Muslims.

The role of women. Moderates and extremists also disagree about the roles of women in society. Most Muslims agree that men and women are equal before God but have different roles in society. The primary roles of women, traditional Muslims believe, are those of wife and mother. Men are traditionally considered the heads of Muslim households.

Many conservative and radical Islamist Muslims have more extreme beliefs regarding gender roles. They point to verses in the Qur'ān that allow men to marry up to four women; grant only husbands, and not wives, the right to divorce; and provide men with greater rights of inheritance and testimonial power in court. Other verses, supplemented by the Hadith, discuss the need for strict gender segregation and the veiling of women. Still other passages claim that women are unfit for leadership roles in the state and society. As a result, many strict regulations concerning women exist in Iran, Sudan, and the Wahhabi-oriented societies of the Arabian Peninsula and South Asia.

More moderate Muslims, on the other hand, argue that the extreme ideas concerning gender roles entered into Islam from non-Islamic sources or have been rendered irrelevant by modern conditions. Regarding dress, for example, most moderates believe that it is sufficient for women, like men, to dress modestly. Moderate Muslims also support higher education for women and their right to enter into all types of employment.

Islamism and democracy

In addition to the violent tactics and theological rigidity of radical Islamist movements, the authoritarian character of Islamist extremists has been a cause for concern to many people. However, many contemporary Islamist thinkers have demonstrated a desire to promote the values of political participation, which they believe have an Islamic basis. Building upon the Qur'ānic principle of *shura* (consultation), they state that it is necessary for rulers to consult with representatives of the people on points of Sharʿia legislation. Such thinkers represent a trend in the Middle East and elsewhere that may point to an Islamic path to democracy.   John C. M. Calvert

Focus on
TERRORISM

Terrorism: Methods and Weapons

Terrorists create fear and alarm through the use of violence. This section includes a collection of 16 *World Book* articles on various weapons and methods that terrorists have used in the past and continue to use today, such as assassination, guerrilla warfare, hijacking, and sabotage, and that they may use in the future, such as nuclear weapons. The section begins with the expanded *World Book* article titled Terrorism.

The worst terrorist attack in United States history destroyed the towers of the World Trade Center in New York City on Sept. 11, 2001. Terrorists crashed hijacked planes into the buildings.

Terrorism is the use or threat of violence to create fear and alarm, usually for political purposes. Terrorists murder and kidnap people, set off bombs, hijack airplanes, set fires, release harmful substances, and commit other serious crimes. Terrorists may act individually, in small groups, through organized networks, or from within a government. Some governments secretly support certain terrorist groups by providing weapons, training, and money for attacks in other countries.

Terrorist acts are committed for various reasons. Some individuals and groups that use terrorism support particular political philosophies or religious beliefs. Others represent groups seeking a change in government or liberation from a governing power. Most terrorist groups believe the threat or use of violence to create fear is the best way to gain publicity and support for their causes. Some governments use *state-conducted* or *state-sponsored terrorism* to frighten the civilian population or to eliminate their opponents. During armed conflicts, governments may use torture or other acts of violence to break the will of enemies. Governments may also use terrorist methods to destroy resistance within a population.

Generally, terrorists attack people who oppose their cause or objects that symbolize such opposition. Common victims of kidnappings and assassinations include business executives, diplomats, judges, police, and political leaders. Terrorists also attack churches, mosques, and synagogues, as well as oil refineries and government offices. At other times, terrorists choose any target

certain to attract media coverage. Many terrorists, unlike other criminals, publicly claim responsibility for their acts. All terrorist acts are crimes under international law.

Most terrorist groups fail to achieve their long-range political goals. Governments fight terrorism by refusing to accept terrorist demands, by increasing security at airports and other likely targets, and by carefully monitoring suspected terrorist individuals and groups. Some countries train special military units to confront terrorist situations. Efforts to prevent or fight terrorism are called *counterterrorism*.

Features of terrorism

Terrorist acts, by definition, share several characteristics. They typically involve violence or the threat of violence, carry political motivations, and are designed to inflict psychological effects on a target audience. Many terrorists hope that widespread fear will cause people to lose their sense of security and their confidence in the existing government. Terrorists attempt to create instability and alarm through a number of methods.

Types of terrorism. Traditional methods of terrorism include bombings, hijackings, kidnappings, and shootings. Newer threats include biological, chemical, and nuclear attacks, as well as computer-based terrorism.

Bombings make up about half of all terrorist acts. Bombs may be hidden in automobiles, backpacks, garbage cans, suitcases, or elsewhere. Terrorists may try to smuggle bombs onto airplanes or into crowded events. In some cases, a bomber intentionally takes his or her own life while blowing up a target. Such bombings are called *suicide bombings*.

Hijackings. Some terrorists hijack airplanes, buses, trucks, or other vehicles. Hijackers may threaten to kill hostages if demands are not met. In other cases, they may threaten to blow up an airplane or intentionally crash a plane into an intended target. Terrorists may also attempt to hijack trucks that are transporting dangerous materials. Hijackers typically use weapons or bomb threats to gain control of a vehicle.

Chemical attacks involve the intentional public release of toxic chemicals. Harmful chemical *agents* (substances) may affect the nervous system, breathing centers, skin, eyes, nose, or throat. They include gases, liquids, sprays, and powders. Potentially lethal agents include mustard gas, hydrogen cyanide, and Sarin. Terrorists may attempt to purchase, steal, or make these agents and disperse them in target areas.

Biological attacks, sometimes called *bioterrorism,* involve the intentional spreading of harmful bacteria, viruses, and *toxins* (poisons). The use of biological agents to inflict harm is sometimes called *germ warfare.* Possible bioterrorist activities include the intentional spreading of dangerous diseases such as anthrax or smallpox. Bioterrorists may seek to contaminate food or water supplies. They may also send contaminated items through the mail.

Nuclear attacks. Terrorists who possess nuclear materials may use them to make bombs or to release harmful radioactive substances. Dangerous nuclear materials include plutonium and uranium. Radiological agents give off invisible radiation that can damage a person's internal organs and cause death. Terrorists may seek to acquire or build their own nuclear weapons, or they may seek to cause explosions at existing nuclear facilities.

Computer-based terrorism, also called *cyberterrorism,* involves the use of computer technology to sabotage information systems. Computer *viruses* can spread through networks and disrupt computer operations and destroy data. Computer terrorists may seek to steal or alter sensitive information, or to attack systems that provide important services.

Other forms of terrorism. Terrorists may use kidnappings, assassinations, and mass shootings to create panic. In addition, certain government policies may be considered terrorist in nature. International crimes such as genocide, crimes against humanity, war crimes, and torture are strategies of terror designed to create fear within a population.

Types of terrorists. Terrorists may act individually or in groups. They may operate with or without the support of a government, and their actions may be local, regional, or global in scope. In some cases, government leaders may engage in terrorist acts against their own citizens.

Individual terrorists carry out terrorist activities by themselves. These activities commonly involve bombings, computer viruses, and other attacks that involve little or no coordination with others. Individual terrorists are most often young males from a middle class family background.

Terrorist groups. Most terrorist attacks are carried out by members of terrorist groups. These groups vary greatly in terms of size, structure, and organization. Most groups are small and focus on activities within their own nation. Other groups, however, have international networks that carry out attacks in countries throughout the world. Some groups run terrorist training camps and actively recruit new members.

Most terrorist organizations have a leader or group of leaders who develop strategies and plan operations. Active terrorists within the organization—often divided into small groups called *cells*—then carry out the plans. Terrorist cells typically have about five people and focus on an assigned task. Other group members may provide housing, money, supplies, transportation, and weapons. Further assistance may come from government sponsors and outside donors. Terrorist groups make great efforts to hide the identities of group members, the locations of bases, and the sources of funding.

Fighting terrorism

Effective counterterrorism efforts involve several elements. Governments work to gather information about terrorist individuals and groups, and to identify potential terrorist threats. They develop advanced security systems and prepare emergency procedures. Nations also use international cooperation, economic pressure, and military force to help reduce terrorist threats. Many governments refuse to negotiate with terrorists or with nations that support terrorists. In the United States, government agencies such as the Federal Bureau of Investigation (FBI), the Central Intelligence Agency (CIA), and the Office of Homeland Security lead advanced counterterrorism efforts.

Intelligence efforts involve the gathering and evaluation of information. Intelligence agencies are able to prevent many terrorist attacks by identifying terrorists

and by detecting terrorist plots early.

Intelligence agencies obtain information from a variety of sources. They can monitor suspected terrorists and intercept telephone calls or electronic communication. Aircraft and artificial satellites can produce detailed images of terrorist camps. Intelligence agencies can recruit agents from foreign countries and send undercover agents to obtain information from within terrorist groups. They can also examine financial records and trace the funding of terrorist groups.

Security procedures. Potential terrorist targets—such as airports and airplanes, crowded sporting events, political gatherings, and famous buildings and monuments—require careful security checks and trained security personnel. People who travel on airplanes must pass through multiple airport security checkpoints. Checked baggage and carry-on items may be scanned or searched, and passengers may be frisked before boarding the plane. Other security measures take place inside airplanes. These include the use of reinforced cockpit doors and armed *air marshals* on certain flights.

Many skyscrapers, government buildings, and office buildings also require visitors to pass through metal detectors or other security checkpoints. The use of surveillance cameras is common. At some crowded events, cameras scan people's faces and attempt to match them with the photos of suspected terrorists in a computer database. As technology improves, new security procedures will continue to emerge.

Diplomatic, economic, and military pressure from the international community may also help stop terrorism. The United Nations and other international bodies have developed numerous treaties to prevent and control terrorist activity. However, many countries do not agree on the definition of terrorism and on the proper ways to address it.

Governments may impose *economic sanctions* on nations that support terrorism. In other words, they may limit or end economic relations with a country in order to persuade that country to change its policies toward terrorism. Governments may order banks to *freeze* (make unusable) the assets of individuals or groups believed to be funding terrorist activities.

Countries may also launch military strikes against terrorist bases and camps or against countries that sponsor terrorism.

History of terrorism

Throughout history, governments, opposition forces, and other individuals and groups have used violence to terrorize or eliminate enemies. Many early governments used assassinations, massacres, and other forms of cruelty to increase power or to gain territory. Warring armies often set fires and murdered the inhabitants of captured cities.

In the 1100's, a band of Muslims called *assassins* or *hashshashin* (hemp-eaters) carried out violent campaigns in Persia and Asia Minor. They smoked a drug called *hashish,* made from the hemp plant, and killed their enemies while under its influence. Starting in the late 1200's, Japanese ninja created terror using advanced combat techniques, disguises, bombs, and poisons.

The word *terrorism* first appeared during the French

Revolution (1789-1799). Some of the revolutionaries who seized power in France adopted a policy of violence against their enemies. The period of their rule became known as the Reign of Terror.

Terrorism in the 1900's. An American group, the Ku Klux Klan, used violence to terrorize blacks and their sympathizers in the late 1800's and the 1900's. In the 1930's, the dictators Adolf Hitler of Germany, Benito Mussolini of Italy, and Joseph Stalin of the Soviet Union used terrorism to discourage opposition to their governments.

In Northern Ireland, Roman Catholic and Protestant extremists have used violence to push for, respectively, the end and the continuation of British rule. In Spain's Basque provinces, some people have used terrorism to call for the establishment of a independent Basque government.

Some terrorist groups in the 1960's sought the destruction of the political and economic systems in their home countries and the development of new systems. These groups included the Red Brigades in Italy and the Red Army Faction in West Germany.

Before the independence of Israel in 1948, a Jewish group used terror to speed the end of British rule in Palestine and create a Jewish homeland. Since 1960, Palestinian groups, including Hamas and Hezbollah, have carried out campaigns of terrorism aimed at establishing an independent Palestinian state.

In 1995, members of a Japanese religious cult released Sarin, a nerve agent, into the Tokyo subway system. The chemical attack killed 12 people and injured thousands. The leader of the cult was later arrested.

Several terrorist attacks during the 1990's targeted the United States. In 1993, a bomb exploded in the parking garage of the World Trade Center in New York City. A federal court convicted four men, including two Palestinians, of planning the bombing. Another major terrorist bombing occurred in Oklahoma City in 1995. Two Americans, Timothy McVeigh and Terry Nichols, were convicted for their role in the attack. From 1975 to 1995, an American terrorist known as the Unabomber sent bombs through the mail. He targeted the computer and

Homeland Security Advisory System

In March 2002, the U.S. government announced the formation of a Homeland Security Advisory System designed to measure and evaluate terrorist threats and communicate them to the public. The system included five threat conditions or alert levels:

Low (green)—Low risk of terrorist attacks.
Guarded (blue)—General risk of terrorist attacks.
Elevated (yellow)—Significant risk of terrorist attacks.
High (orange)—High risk of terrorist attacks.
Severe (red)—Severe risk of terrorist attacks.

The U.S. attorney general has the responsibility for assigning a threat condition. A condition can apply to the country as a whole or to only portions of it. At the time the advisory system was announced, the United States was at the yellow condition.

high-technology industries. The Unabomber, identified as Theodore Kaczynski, was convicted in 1998.

In 1998, terrorists bombed U.S. embassies in Nairobi, Kenya, and Tanzania. American officials linked the bombings to Osama bin Laden, a Saudi-born millionaire and radical Muslim leader. Bin Laden's group, called al-Qa'ida, was also suspected in the 2000 bombing of a U.S. Navy warship at a port in Yemen.

The war against terrorism. On Sept. 11, 2001, thousands of people died as a result of the worst terrorist attack in U.S. history. Terrorists in two hijacked commercial airplanes deliberately crashed into the two 110-story towers of the World Trade Center. Less than an hour later, another hijacked plane crashed into the Pentagon Building just outside Washington, D.C. Shortly after that, a fourth hijacked plane crashed into a rural area in Somerset County, Pennsylvania. The U.S. government named bin Laden as the prime suspect behind the attack.

In response to the attack, U.S. President George W. Bush called for a worldwide campaign against international terrorist networks. He announced that the effort would involve tightened security, widespread intelligence efforts, economic restrictions, and military action. He targeted terrorist organizations and any governments that supported them. Bin Laden and his organization were being protected by Afghanistan's ruling party, the Taliban. In November 2001, U.S. military strikes caused the Taliban to fall from power in Afghanistan.

Also in 2001, authorities found that several offices in the United States and other countries had been mailed envelopes containing traces of anthrax bacteria. Several people died from the disease. The U.S. government declared the mailings acts of terrorism.   M. Cherif Bassiouni

Additional resources

Anderson, Sean, and Sloan, Stephen. *Historical Dictionary of Terrorism.* Scarecrow, 1995.
Seymour-Jones, Carole. *Terrorism.* New Discovery Bks., 1992. Younger readers.

Web sites

Counterterrorism Office
http://www.state.gov/s/ct/
This U.S. State Department site includes an overview of efforts to combat terrorism, annual reports on global terrorism patterns, and travel alerts.

Most Wanted Terrorists
http://www.fbi.gov/mostwant/terrorists/fugitives.htm
This Federal Bureau of Investigation (FBI) site includes pictures and descriptions of the agency's most wanted terrorists.

AP/Wide World
Airport security procedures aim to prevent terrorist attacks involving airplanes. Trained security personnel check passengers and baggage for dangerous items and materials.

A giant passenger jet can bring all parts of the world within easy reach of one another by flying passengers long distances. The Boeing 747 jumbo jet is the world's largest commercial airliner.

Airplane is an engine-driven machine that can fly through the air supported by the flow of air around its wings. Most large transport planes routinely fly 500 to 600 miles per hour (mph), or 800 to 970 kilometers per hour (kph). The fastest airplanes are supersonic, which means they can fly faster than sound travels. At sea level, sound has a speed of 760 mph (1,225 kph). Some supersonic military jets can reach speeds of more than 2,000 mph (3,200 kph).

Airplanes range in size from training planes, which have only two seats, to jumbo jets, which can carry hundreds of passengers. In the United States, about 90 percent of all airplanes have one or two engines and carry only a few passengers at a time.

Hundreds of thousands of airplanes are used throughout the world. Millions of people depend on aircraft for swift transportation. Businesses rely on quick airmail and air express service, and many industries ship their products by air. Airplanes have many other uses, from helping fight forest fires to carrying emergency aid.

In addition, airplanes have become the targets of hijackers. Hijacking that involves airplanes is often called *skyjacking.* Airplanes are also a major weapon of war.

An airplane is a *heavier-than-air* aircraft, meaning it is heavier than the air it displaces. An airplane achieves flight in a different way than an *airship,* also called a *blimp,* which is a *lighter-than-air* aircraft. A typical airship rises and floats in the air because it is filled with a gas that is lighter than the surrounding air.

During the late 1700's, people made their first flights into the air using balloons, which were an early form of airship. After the first balloon flights, inventors tried to develop a heavier-than-air flying machine. Some inventors experimented with gliders (engineless planes). They studied birds' wings and discovered that the wings are curved. By building gliders with curved wings instead of flat ones, they could make the vehicles fly hundreds of feet or meters. But long-distance flight in a heavier-than-air machine did not become possible until the invention of an engine light enough but powerful enough to keep a plane in flight. The first such engines were four-stroke gasoline engines, developed during the 1880's and initially used to power bicycles, boats, and carriages.

In 1903, the brothers Orville and Wilbur Wright—two American bicycle makers—made the first successful powered airplane flights in history near Kitty Hawk, North Carolina. After the Wright brothers' success, pilots and inventors worked continually to improve airplane design. By the late 1950's, passenger planes with jet engines had brought all countries within easy reach of one another, and the world seemed much smaller than it had just a few years before.

Skyjackings and airport security. Skyjackings in the United States began in 1961. Since the late 1960's, skyjackers have seized several hundred planes around the world. On Sept. 11, 2001, about 3,000 people died as a result of the worst skyjacking incident in U.S. history. Terrorists in hijacked commercial airplanes deliberately crashed into the two towers of the World Trade Center in New York City and into the Pentagon Building outside Washington, D.C. Later that day, another hijacked plane crashed in Somerset County, Pennsylvania.

In 1973, the U.S. government, in response to skyjackings, had begun to require inspection of all passengers and other security action to prevent armed people from boarding planes. Today, personnel from the Transportation Security Administration, a U.S. government agency established after the September 11 attacks, search airplanes for hidden weapons and explosives at all airports that serve commercial airlines. They also inspect passengers' baggage before it goes onto the plane. Passengers must pass through electronic scanners that detect guns, knives, and other metal objects.

The federal government has established security regulations for all airports in the United States that serve commercial airlines. The regulations include rules on inspection of planes, baggage, and passengers. The airports are required to have law enforcement personnel on the premises as part of their security programs. Federal legislation passed after terrorist attacks in the United States in September 2001 set deadlines for increased security measures at airports. These measures include screening all checked baggage for explosives. The new law also transferred responsibility for passenger and baggage screening from personnel employed by private security firms to federal employees.

The war in Afghanistan. The United States and its allies used airplanes heavily in the war in Afghanistan that followed the September 11 terrorist attacks. The U.S. government blamed the attacks on al-Qa'ida, a worldwide terrorist group headed by Osama bin Laden, a

Saudi-born millionaire. Bin Laden was hiding in Afghanistan, where he was protected by the Taliban regime. The Taliban, an extremely conservative Islamic group, had taken control of Afghanistan in the mid-1990's.

In October 2001, the United States began military action in Afghanistan in support of Afghan rebels who opposed the Taliban and al-Qa'ida. Throughout October, November, and early December, U.S. bombers and fighter jets attacked the barracks and encampments of Taliban troops across Afghanistan. Among the airplanes used by U.S. military forces were B-52 Stratofortress bombers, F-15 Eagle fighters, C-130 Hercules transports, and E-3B Sentry surveillance planes. By the end of 2001, the Taliban had been driven from power, and according to U.S. Secretary of State Colin Powell, al-Qa'ida had been destroyed in Afghanistan.

Web site

FAA
http://www.faa.gov/
Official Web site of the U.S. Federal Aviation Administration.

Anthrax is a serious infectious disease that chiefly affects animals but can also occur in people. It is caused by the bacterium *Bacillus anthracis*. Anthrax usually affects plant-eating animals infected by eating anthrax *spores* (inactive bacteria) from the soil. Anthrax spores can survive harsh conditions and occur in soil throughout the world, including the United States. People can get anthrax through contact with infected animals or contaminated animal products. But, naturally occurring anthrax is rare in human beings today.

In people, anthrax infection can occur in three main forms: *inhalational,* caused by breathing in spores; *cutaneous,* caused by spores infecting skin sores; and *gastrointestinal,* caused by swallowing spores. Inhalational anthrax causes a severe illness that begins in the chest and rapidly spreads through the body. Cutaneous anthrax, the most common form, can cause a severe skin infection. Gastrointestinal anthrax results from eating undercooked, contaminated meat.

Symptoms include fever, vomiting, abdominal pain, and bloody diarrhea. Anthrax can be cured with antibiotics if patients receive treatment early. However, inhalational and gastrointestinal anthrax are often fatal if not rapidly treated.

Some nations and international terrorist groups are known to have developed or suspected of having developed anthrax as a biological weapon. In 1979, the accidental release of anthrax spores from a military facility in the Soviet Union caused 68 deaths. In the 1990's, Russia—which had been the largest part of the Soviet Union—announced it had ended all biological weapons programs. Many nations are now working to end the development and use of biological weapons, including anthrax.

In 2001, anthrax spores were used as a weapon when they were sent through the United States mail to several business and government offices. As a result, a number of office buildings and post office facilities were contaminated. Some people became ill with inhalational anthrax, and several of them died. Other people contracted cutaneous anthrax. Investigators began trying to determine who was responsible for the attack.

Thomas V. Inglesby

Web sites

Anthrax-General Information
http://www.cdc.gov/ncidod/dbmd/diseaseinfo/anthrax_g.htm
Centers for Disease Control and Prevention overview of the disease.

Communicable Disease Fact Sheet: Anthrax
http://www.health.state.ny.us/nysdoh/consumer/anthrax.htm
Information from the New York State Department of Health.

Assassination is the murder of a person who holds a position of public importance. Ordinarily, assassinations are committed for one or more of three reasons: to gain revenge, to earn a reward, or to remove a political enemy from office. The assassination of a ruler has often been applauded. Brutus, one of the assassins of Julius Caesar, was considered a hero by many Romans.

The assassination of Archduke Ferdinand of Austria, in 1914, was one cause of World War I. The series of assassinations committed by the Black Dragon Society in Japan in the 1930's threw control of the government into the hands of the Japanese Army. Four presidents of the United States have been assassinated: Abraham Lincoln in 1865, James A. Garfield in 1881, William McKinley in 1901, and John F. Kennedy in 1963.

The word *assassination* comes from *assassins* or *hashshashin* (hemp-eaters), a band of Muslims in Persia and Asia Minor in the 1100's. They smoked a drug called *hashish,* which is made from the hemp plant, and killed their enemies while under its influence.   Stephen Goode

Chemical-biological-radiological warfare (CBR) is war waged with chemicals, biological agents, or radioactive materials. CBR includes both the use of CBR weapons and the application of defenses against such weapons. CBR weapons can be designed to kill large numbers of people, temporarily disable them, or destroy their food supplies. The weapons are usually effective without destroying property.

Chemical agents affect the nervous system, breathing centers, skin, eyes, nose, or throat. They include gases, liquids, sprays, and powders. They can be sprayed from airplanes, dropped as bombs, fired by artillery in explosive shells, or dispersed by land mines.

Some chemical agents, called *nerve agents* or *poison gas,* can cause death. They may be colorless, odorless, and tasteless. They can cause death rapidly if the victim inhales them or if they are splashed on bare skin. Chemical agents have not been widely used in warfare since World War I ended in 1918. Other chemical agents are not fatal, but they make their victims unable to fight. Blister agents cause huge blisters on the skin. A blister agent called *mustard gas* caused many casualties during World War I. Other chemical agents can cause temporary blindness or confusion. Gas masks, other protective coverings, and injections of antidotes are used as defenses against chemical agents.

Chemical agents also have nonmilitary uses. Some agents, including *tear gas,* may be used to control rioting crowds. These agents affect the eyes, nose, and throat. They cause blinding tears and often violent coughing. But these effects disappear soon after the victim reaches fresh air. Other chemicals are used to kill harmful insects or to strip leaves from trees.

Biological warfare is the military use of harmful microorganisms, or the *toxins* (poisons) they produce, as weapons against people, animals, or crops. It is sometimes called *germ warfare.* A small number of these microorganisms could kill millions of people if effectively distributed. Biological agents could also be used to make enemy soldiers too sick to fight, or to ruin an enemy's food supply. A biological agent that seriously damaged the enemy country's crops might be a decisive factor in a war. Biological weapons have not played a part in modern warfare. But military strategists must assume that the enemy has such weapons. Thus, much research is devoted to defenses against biological weapons.

In 1969, President Richard M. Nixon stated that the United States would not conduct biological warfare against another nation even if that nation used such warfare against the United States. Nixon ordered U.S. stocks of biological weapons destroyed.

An international treaty banning biological weapons went into effect in 1975. It bars the production, possession, and use of such weapons. More than 140 nations have ratified the treaty.

Radiological agents give off invisible radiation that can damage a person's internal organs and even cause death. Radiation from nuclear *fallout* could be a major factor in any war involving nuclear weapons. Radiological warfare is dangerous for all sides in a war. A nuclear weapon used against an enemy would create fallout that might be carried by winds back to the country or troops that used the weapon. Radioactivity might also make an area temporarily unfit for human life.

History. Radiological warfare became possible with the development of atomic weapons during the 1940's. However, chemical and biological warfare have long histories. The Spartans used pitch and sulfur in a form of chemical warfare during the Peloponnesian War in the 400's B.C. During ancient and medieval times, soldiers sometimes threw bodies of people who died from plague over the walls of besieged cities, or into water wells. During the French and Indian wars (1689-1763), blankets used by smallpox victims were purposefully given to Indians in the hope that the blankets would infect them.

Germany introduced the use of gas in war during World War I. In 1915, the Germans used gas against Allied forces at Ypres, Belgium. Before the end of the war, gases of many types were used by all armies. Gas caused nearly 30 percent of all United States casualties in the war.

Gas warfare proved so destructive that most nations have agreed to avoid the use of poison gas and other chemical weapons. But Iraq used chemical weapons against Iranian troops during the war between Iran and Iraq (1980-1988). This use may have begun in 1983. In 1988, Iraq was also accused of using chemical weapons against its Kurdish citizens, who were seeking independence from Iraq.   Frances M. Lussier

Web site

Arms Control and Non-Proliferation
http://usinfo.state.gov/topical/pol/arms/
Background on arms control and U.S. policy on the issue provided by the U.S. Department of State.

Conspiracy, *kuhn SPIHR uh see,* is an agreement between two or more people to do something that is against the law. One person cannot conspire with himself or herself. It is usually not necessary that the planned act actually be committed or that any person be defrauded or injured. The act of conspiring constitutes a crime. Each person involved in the conspiracy is criminally responsible for everything that results, whether it was intended or not. Conspiracy is punishable by fines or imprisonment. If loss of human life results from a conspiracy, murder may be charged.   George T. Felkenes

Explosive is a material that produces a rapid, violent reaction when acted upon by heat or a strong blow. During this reaction, explosives give off large amounts of gases at high pressure. The enormous power released during an explosion gives explosives many commercial and military uses. Explosives enable construction workers to clear land of tree stumps and boulders to begin building roads or structures. They are used in *excavating* (digging) mines and to loosen the flow of oil deep beneath rock in oil wells. They blast tunnels through mountains. In war, explosives are used to damage cities, destroy ships and airplanes, and kill enemy troops.

Explosives may be solids, liquids, or gases. However, all explosives consist of a fuel and an *oxidizer*—a substance that supplies the oxygen needed to make the fuel burn. When the most powerful explosives *detonate* (explode), a chemical reaction takes place in less than a millionth of a second. Liquids and solids change to hot gases that expand with a great blast of heat and pressure. The higher the pressure, the more powerful the explosion will be.

Certain types of explosives detonate in a nuclear reaction rather than a chemical reaction. This article discusses four chief types of chemical explosives—primary explosives, high explosives, blasting agents, and low explosives.

Primary explosives must be handled in small quantities. They are extremely sensitive to heat, and even a spark of static electricity can cause them to explode. Common primary explosives include lead azide, lead styphnate, and mercury fulminate. They are chiefly used in devices called *detonators* to set off other explosives.

High explosives detonate with greater power than primary explosives but are less sensitive. Common types of high explosives include nitroglycerin; RDX; TNT; PETN; and *pentolite,* a combination of TNT and PETN. Most high explosives are used commercially for blasting and excavating, but they also are used by the military in bombs, artillery shells, and grenades.

High explosives are sometimes mixed with substances called *plasticizers* to produce *plastic explosives.* Plasticizers, such as oil and wax, make it easy to mold the explosives into various shapes. Plastic explosives have been used by terrorists in bombs and by armed forces in land mines.

Blasting agents are the safest and least expensive explosives used in industry. They are often used to shatter and heave rock in mining and excavating operations. Common blasting agents include dynamite and mixtures of ammonium nitrate and fuel oil.

Low explosives *deflagrate* (burn rapidly) rather than detonate. The most common type of low explosive is gunpowder. It serves as a *propellant* to shoot ammunition from guns and other weapons. Fireworks are also low explosives.   James E. Kennedy

In guerrilla warfare, bands of fighters often take advantage of hills and other natural features in staging surprise attacks against enemy armies. Afghan guerrillas, like the one shown here, fought Soviet soldiers after the Soviet invasion of Afghanistan in late 1979 and early 1980.

P. Manoukian, Sygma

Guerrilla warfare, *guh RIHL uh,* is warfare by roving bands of fighters who torment the enemy with ambushes, sudden raids, and other small-scale attacks. Guerrillas may be organized, but they usually fight in small bands. They most often operate behind enemy lines and use hit-and-run tactics and sabotage to surprise and torment the enemy. They take advantage of natural features of the terrain—such as forests, hills, lakes, and rivers—to conceal and launch attacks. When waged in cities, such operations are usually called "urban terrorism." They feature bombings, kidnappings, and other violent actions. Guerrillas are sometimes called *underground* or *resistance fighters,* or *partisans.* Guerrilla tactics are usually used by groups with limited resources against an enemy with vastly superior power and strength. The word *guerrilla* means *little war* in Spanish and was first used during the Napoleonic Peninsular War (1808-1814).

Since ancient times, people have waged guerrilla warfare against invading armies. Guerrilla tactics deprived the enemy of food and shelter, destroyed lines of communication and supply, and helped organize resistance among the people.

In modern times, many peoples have used guerrilla warfare to fight and try to overthrow an existing government. Guerrilla warfare against a government occurs most frequently in rural areas of chiefly agricultural nations. The people of such nations often feel that the government does not act in their best interest. In turn, the people have little loyalty to, or contact with, the government. In outlying areas, the people may even have a different culture and speak a different language than the nation's rulers. They do not cooperate with the government and generally oppose it. Their guerrilla activities may range from ordinary banditry and theft to raids by disciplined, well-trained forces. Members of many guerrilla bands are civilians, such as farmers or laborers, who act secretly as guerrillas. After making an attack, they disappear into the civilian population.

Because of the importance of guerrilla warfare, the United States Army has formed units of specially trained troops who are experts in guerrilla tactics. These Special Forces soldiers are often called *Green Berets* because of the caps they wear.

Modern guerrilla techniques were perfected by

Mao Zedong, leader of the Chinese Communists, during his long—and finally successful—fight against the Chinese Nationalists from 1927 to 1949. In modern guerrilla warfare, small groups of revolutionaries try to gain the sympathy and support of—and control over—the people of the countryside. They gain recruits and build up supplies of food and other necessities. Guerrillas may take years to gain popular support.

The guerrillas use ambush, sabotage, assassination, and other terrorist attacks to torment government forces. They design these tactics to weaken the people's confidence in the government and to persuade them to believe that the government cannot defend either itself or the people. At this stage, guerrillas deliberately avoid combat except under conditions and against targets that they select. A guerrilla band could easily be wiped out in open battle by a superior government force using infantry, artillery, and warplanes. The guerrillas sometimes become strong enough to "liberate" some areas of the country, provoke a civil war, and overcome the government troops in battle.

The guerrillas' strength comes mainly from their ability to control the people. Guerrillas use many methods to appeal to the people and gain their sympathy and support. They provoke political, racial, and social troubles so that the government acts against the people. The guerrillas hope that such action will set more and more people against the government.

Most guerrilla propaganda includes promises to take land from the rich and give it to the poor. Such promises help stir up a nation's peasants against the ruling class. Peasant support is sometimes sought by appeals to nationalism, especially in countries where a foreign nation has much influence. Guerrillas also try to take advantage of the hopes and ambitions of the peasants for improving their way of life. If all peaceful methods fail, guerrillas use threats and force to gain support.

To defeat guerrillas, a government must win back the people's support. For example, the people may be pacified with political and social reform. They may be given such necessities as food, clothing, shelter, and medicine. The people must also be protected from the guerrillas and trained to defend themselves.

History. Guerrilla tactics against enemy armies date

back to ancient times. Fierce Scottish Highland tribes launched guerrilla attacks against the Roman armies that occupied Great Britain during the first century after Christ. During the Thirty Years' War (1618-1648), bands of armed peasants in some European countries attacked soldiers who had wandered from their camps. American Indians used guerrilla tactics against enemy tribes and, later, against the white settlers. During the Revolutionary War in America (1775-1783), General Francis Marion used guerrilla tactics against the British. In the American Civil War (1861-1865), Confederate guerrillas made cavalry raids on Union forces.

During World War I (1914-1918), guerrilla warfare did not occur in Europe mainly because armies fought from trenches along fixed battlefronts. But in the Middle East, Arabs used guerrilla tactics when they revolted and won independence from the Ottoman Empire.

During World War II (1939-1945), citizens of several European countries, including France and Yugoslavia, formed underground guerrilla groups that fought the Nazi invaders. In Burma (now Myanmar) and the Philippines, guerrillas operated against the invading Japanese.

After World War II, people of many countries waged guerrilla warfare against their governments. Some fought the colonial governments of European powers. In China, Mao Zedong led the Communists to victory over the Nationalists in 1949 after a 22-year struggle. In 1954, France lost its Indochinese colonies to Communist forces following eight years of fighting against guerrillas. France lost Algeria in 1962 after guerrillas in Algeria revolted and gained independence.

In the Western Hemisphere, the Cuban leader Fidel Castro began an attempt in 1953 to overthrow the country's government. Castro's small force of revolutionaries was almost wiped out at first. But Castro used guerrilla methods skillfully and he gradually gained recruits from the population. Using strong appeals and propaganda, Castro also encouraged soldiers to desert from the Cuban Army. By 1959, the guerrillas had become strong enough to defeat the army and Castro took over as dictator. Several years after the Cuban revolution, one of Castro's top aides, Ché Guevara, went to South America to head a similar revolt. Guevara was killed in 1967 while leading a force against Bolivian government troops.

Many other guerrilla revolts have failed. In the Philippines, the Communist Huks turned against their government after the Japanese occupation ended in 1945. To overcome them, the government undertook a campaign that included land reform, rewards for Huks who surrendered, and attacks on guerrilla hideouts. By 1954, the Huks had been defeated.

The British conducted a successful antiguerrilla campaign in Malaya after Communist revolutionaries tried to take over that nation in 1948. British troops attacked the guerrillas, and the government improved economic, political, and social conditions. The revolutionaries had used these conditions to gain the people's support. By 1957, when Malaya became an independent nation, the guerrillas had been defeated.

After 1960, guerrilla fighters battled government troops in many parts of the world. In Northern Ireland, the Irish Republican Army (IRA) used guerrilla tactics against British government forces and installations. Arab guerrillas raided Israel from neighboring Egypt, Jordan,

and Syria. Communist guerrillas in the Philippines battled government troops there. In Southeast Asia, the Viet Cong used guerrilla tactics in the Vietnam War (1957-1975).

During the 1960's and 1970's, various urban guerrilla bands in the United States, Latin America, and Western Europe staged kidnappings, bombings of public buildings, assassinations, and other terrorist acts. But none of these groups seized power.

In Rhodesia, now called Zimbabwe, black guerrillas fought government troops during most of the 1970's in an attempt to overthrow the white-ruled government. In 1979, blacks gained control of the government. That same year, Afghan guerrillas began fighting both the government of Afghanistan and Soviet troops supporting the government. The Soviet troops withdrew in 1988 and 1989. The guerrillas overthrew the Afghan government in 1992, but continued to fight among themselves afterward.   Stephen Goode

Additional resources

Beckett, Ian F. W. *Encyclopedia of Guerrilla Warfare.* ABC-CLIO, 1999.
Joes, Anthony J. *America and Guerrilla Warfare.* Univ. Pr. of Ky., 2000. *Guerrilla Warfare: A Historical, Biographical, and Bibliographical Sourcebook.* Greenwood, 1996.

Hijacking is the seizure of a commercial vehicle by force or the threat of force. For years, trucks have been hijacked and their cargo stolen. Today, hijacking involves chiefly airplanes and is also called *skyjacking* or *air piracy.* Since the late 1960's, skyjackers have seized several hundred planes. In most of these incidents, no one was killed. But several skyjackings resulted in deaths and the destruction of aircraft. A number of governments impose severe penalties for skyjacking.

Plane hijackers may threaten to destroy an aircraft, kill the people aboard, or crash the aircraft into a heavily populated area. Some hijackers make political demands, such as certain policy changes by a nation's government or the release of imprisoned associates. Others demand a large sum of money in exchange for the safe return of the plane and the people aboard. Still other hijackers want to flee a country in order to escape punishment for a crime.

Gangsters frequently hijacked truckloads of liquor from one another in the 1920's and early 1930's, when alcoholic beverages were prohibited in the United States. One of the first skyjackings took place in 1930 in Peru. Skyjackings in the United States began in 1961, and a record total of 40 attempts occurred in 1969. In 1970, the airlines began a voluntary program of skyjack prevention. In 1973, the U.S. government began to require inspection of all passengers and other security action to prevent armed people from boarding planes.

On Sept. 11, 2001, skyjackers staged the worst terrorist attack in U.S. history. Terrorists hijacked four commercial airplanes. They crashed two planes into the two 110-story towers of the World Trade Center in New York City, and another into the Pentagon Building, just outside Washington, D.C. The other hijacked jet crashed in a field in Somerset County, Pennsylvania. The two towers collapsed to the ground, and part of the Pentagon was destroyed. About 3,000 people were killed.

The domestic law of most nations considers the hijacking of a transnational airliner to be a crime. The

Hague Convention of 1970 is a treaty providing international law for the trial and punishment of skyjackers. About 130 nations, including the United States and Canada, have agreed to support the treaty.   Edwin B. Firmage

Hostage is a person held prisoner to force fulfillment of a demand. If the demand is not met, the hostage may be killed. The taking of hostages is illegal under both international law and the laws of individual nations. The physical mistreatment of hostages is also illegal but is considered a separate crime.

Most hostage taking occurs in connection with other crimes or as a result of political struggles. A bank robber, for example, may seize hostages and threaten to kill them unless the police allow him or her to escape. Hijackers of a ship or airplane may hold passengers and crew hostage to obtain such goals as a ransom payment or transportation to a safe destination. Kidnappers, too, sometimes hold their victims for ransom.

Hijackers and other terrorists often take hostages to demand a certain action by a government. In 1979, Iranian revolutionaries seized the U.S. Embassy in Tehran, Iran, and held a group of Americans hostage. The revolutionaries demanded that the deposed shah of Iran be returned to the country for trial in exchange for the hostages. The shah died in 1980, but the Americans were not released until 1981.

During times of war, countries have sometimes taken civilians as hostages. During World War II (1939-1945), for example, Germany sought to control underground resistance forces by taking hostages in France, Poland, and other occupied countries. Such hostage taking is illegal under international law. It is distinguished from the lawful action of taking enemy soldiers as prisoners of war.

In ancient and medieval times, nations often exchanged hostages to guarantee that both sides would carry out the terms of a treaty. The hostages, who were nobles or other notable people, were treated as honored guests. But they could be executed if the treaty was broken.   M. Cherif Bassiouni

Kidnapping is the act of seizing and holding a person against his or her will. The word *kidnap* comes from the two slang words *kid*, or *child*, and *nab*, which means *to steal*. At one time, kidnapping referred especially to stealing children. But the word *kidnapping* has come to be used also in cases where adults are seized and held.

Slaves were often kidnapped and sold in the slave market. Sailors were *shanghaied*, or kidnapped, and forced to work on ships. During the early 1800's, ships were occasionally stopped and entire crews *impressed*, or forced to work on other ships. An illegal arrest is actually a form of kidnapping. Fleeing criminals often kidnap one or more people and hold them as *hostages* to reduce the chance of being captured.

Kidnapping for *ransom*, or reward, became common in the United States during the 1920's and 1930's. After Charles A. Lindbergh's son was kidnapped and killed in 1932, Congress passed the "Lindbergh law." This law makes kidnapping a federal crime if the victim is taken out of the state. In 1956, Congress changed the law to allow the Federal Bureau of Investigation to work on any kidnap case after 24 hours. Under federal law, the maximum punishment for kidnapping is life imprisonment.

George T. Felkenes

Additional resources

Auerbach, Ann H. *Ransom*. Henry Holt, 1998.
Fass, Paula S. *Kidnapped*. 1997. Reprint. Harvard Univ. Pr., 1999.
Greif, Geoffrey L., and Hegar, R. L. *When Parents Kidnap*. Free Pr., 1992.
Steele, Philip. *Kidnapping*. Heinemann Educational, 1992.

Web site

Child Abduction
http://www.fbi.gov/kids/crimepre/abduct/abduct.htm
The FBI presents a guide to how agents work in kidnap cases, a list of safety rules, and real life stories.

Murder. When one person intentionally kills another without legal justification or excuse, the crime is called *murder*. The clearest example of this is a case where one person deliberately kills another because of hatred, envy, or greed. But there are also situations where a killing is considered murder even when no specific intent to kill exists. For example, a person who accidentally kills someone while committing a robbery is guilty of murder. The fact that the person is committing a serious crime indicates that he or she has a reckless disregard for human life and safety. This takes the place of intent to kill. The penalty for murder is a long prison sentence or death. However, a large number of national, state, and provincial governments have done away with the death penalty.

A killing that has legal justification is called *justifiable homicide*. For example, a killing in self-defense would be a justifiable homicide. The law regards a purely accidental killing as an *excusable homicide*. For example, if a pedestrian steps in front of a carefully driven automobile and is killed, the accident would be considered an excusable homicide. When a person in a fit of anger intentionally kills another person after the victim has provoked the attack, the killing is called *voluntary manslaughter*. When a person's death results from reckless driving or other extreme negligence on the part of the killer, the offense is called *involuntary manslaughter*. The penalties in most cases of manslaughter are less severe than those for murder.   Charles F. Wellford

Web site

Homicide trends in the United States
http://www.ojp.usdoj.gov/bjs/homicide/homtrnd.htm
Information from the U.S. Department of Justice, Bureau of Justice Statistics.

Nuclear weapon is any weapon that gets its destructive power from the transformation of matter in atoms into energy. All nuclear weapons are explosive devices. They are carried in missiles, bombs, artillery shells, mines, or torpedoes. The most powerful nuclear weapons are far more destructive than any *conventional* (nonnuclear) weapon.

Nuclear weapons can be *fission weapons*, also called *atomic bombs* or *atomic weapons*, or they can be *thermonuclear weapons*, also known as *hydrogen bombs*, *hydrogen weapons*, or *fusion weapons*. In fission weapons, matter converts to energy when the *nuclei* (cores) of certain kinds of uranium or plutonium atoms are split. Thermonuclear weapons convert matter to energy by combining pairs of certain kinds of hydrogen nuclei to form single nuclei. Thermonuclear weapons are generally far more powerful than fission weapons. Most nuclear weapons are thermonuclear.

© Photri USA

© Photri USA

U.S. Army

Nuclear weapons include missiles and artillery shells. The top photograph at the left shows the launching of two long-range nuclear missiles. Such missiles carry extremely powerful thermonuclear devices. The explosion of such a device creates a huge mushroom-shaped cloud like the one shown at the right. A self-propelled howitzer, *bottom left,* can fire nuclear artillery shells.

The first nuclear weapons were two fission bombs dropped by the United States on the Japanese cities of Hiroshima and Nagasaki during World War II (1939-1945). The bombs killed from 110,000 to 140,000 people and destroyed large areas of both cities. The terrible destruction caused by the bombs became a major factor in Japan's decision to surrender to the United States and its Allies. Japan's surrender ended the war. The bombs exploded at Hiroshima and Nagasaki are the only two nuclear weapons that have ever been used.

Most experts believe that the threat of nuclear war probably helped keep the peace during the Cold War, a period of intense hostility between Communist and non-Communist nations, and their respective allies, following World War II. To avoid the terrible damage that nuclear weapons could cause, many nations have long sought ways to control such weapons and reduce the risk of nuclear war.

The United States and Russia have most of the world's nuclear weapons. The United Kingdom and France also developed small, potent *arsenals* (supplies) of nuclear weapons during the Cold War. Other countries that possess nuclear arms include China, India, Pakistan, and South Africa. Several other nations may have the ability to build nuclear weapons.

The growing number of nuclear powers increases the danger that regional tensions could possibly lead to use of nuclear weapons. An example of such tensions was a crisis between India and Pakistan in the disputed region of Kashmir in 2002. Troops on both sides exchanged artillery fire, and the two countries, both with nuclear weapons, seemed on the brink of war. Tensions also run high in the Middle East. Many experts believe the Mid-

dle Eastern nations of Israel, Iraq, and Iran either possess or are close to building nuclear weapons. Other threats may involve terrorist groups without governmental ties that could acquire and use nuclear devices.

How nuclear weapons work

Fission weapons generate their destructive power through the *fission* (splitting) of atomic nuclei. The only three materials known to be fissionable in weapons are two isotopes of uranium (U), U-235 and U-238, and one isotope of plutonium (Pu), Pu-239. Isotopes are different kinds of atoms of the same element. Each kind has a different *mass* (total amount of matter).

Nuclear fission occurs when a *neutron*—a subatomic particle with no electric charge—strikes the nucleus of a uranium or plutonium atom. Splitting the nucleus transforms a small amount of its matter into a large amount of energy. In addition, two or three additional neutrons are released. These neutrons may then split other nuclei. If this process continues, a self-sustaining *chain reaction* begins in which many nuclei split rapidly, and their combined energies produce a fission explosion.

Generating a self-sustaining chain reaction requires a minimum amount of fissionable material known as the *critical mass.* A mass too small to support a self-sustaining chain reaction is called a *subcritical mass.*

A fission weapon uses one of two methods to create a critical mass: (1) the *gun-type method* or (2) the *implosion method.* In the gun-type method, two subcritical pieces of material are placed in a device similar to the barrel of a gun. One piece rests at one end of the barrel. The other is some distance from the first piece, with a powerful conventional explosive behind it. The barrel is sealed at both ends. When the weapon's fuse is triggered, the conventional explosive propels the second subcritical mass at high speed into the first. The resulting combined mass immediately becomes *supercritical* (greater than critical), causing a rapid, self-sustaining chain reaction, and thus a nuclear explosion. The United States used a gun-type fission bomb at Hiroshima.

In the implosion method, a subcritical mass is made supercritical by compressing it into a smaller volume. The subcritical mass is in the center of the weapon, surrounded by conventional explosives. When the fuse is triggered, all the conventional explosives go off at the same time. The explosions compress the mass into a high-density supercritical mass. A self-sustaining chain reaction occurs, causing the explosion. The United States used an implosion-type fission bomb at Nagasaki.

Thermonuclear weapons get their power from the *fusion* (combining) of atomic nuclei under intense heat. The nuclei fused in thermonuclear weapons are of the hydrogen isotopes deuterium (H-2) and tritium (H-3).

Fusion reactions require temperatures equal to, or greater than, those found in the sun's core—about 27,000,000 °F (15,000,000 °C). The only practical way to achieve such temperatures is by a fission explosion. Thus, an implosion-type fission device triggers thermonuclear explosions. When the fission device explodes, it also releases neutrons that bombard a compound inside the weapon. This compound, called *lithium 6 deuteride,* consists of deuterium and lithium 6 (Li-6), an isotope of the element lithium. When struck by the released neutrons, the Li-6 forms helium and tritium. Then, pairs of tritium nuclei, pairs of deuterium nuclei, and pairs of one tritium nucleus and one deuterium nucleus each fuse to form helium nuclei. A small amount of matter from each deuterium and tritium nucleus converts to a large amount of energy, and a thermonuclear explosion occurs. The *yield* (explosive power) of a thermonuclear weapon can be increased by blanketing the lithium 6 deuteride with the uranium isotope U-238. The U-238 fissions during the hydrogen explosion.

Gun-type fission bomb

Radar antenna

Gun barrel

Nonnuclear explosive

2 ft. 4 in. (71 cm)

Uranium target

Uranium wedge

10 ft. (3 m)

Implosion-type fission bomb

Beryllium-polonium core   Radar antenna   Nonnuclear explosive

5 ft. (1.5 m)

Plutonium sphere

10 ft. 8 in. (3.3 m)

WORLD BOOK illustrations by J. Harlan Hunt (adapted from artwork by Van Dyke, Dec. 19, 1960, *Newsweek*)

© Corbis/Bettmann

Hiroshima, Japan, was largely destroyed by a gun-type fission bomb called the Little Boy bomb, *top,* on Aug. 6, 1945. The bomb was dropped from a B-29 bomber. When the bomb reached 1,850 feet (564 meters), a radar echo set off an explosive inside. This explosive drove a wedge of U-235 into a larger piece of U-235, setting off the nuclear blast. This photograph shows Hiroshima after the explosion.

Atomic Energy Commission

Nagasaki, Japan, was struck by an implosion-type fission bomb called the Fat Man bomb, *top,* on Aug. 9, 1945. In this bomb, an explosive crushed a hollow sphere of plutonium into a core made up of the chemical elements beryllium and polonium. This core then released neutrons, which triggered a fission chain reaction in the plutonium. This photograph shows Nagasaki after the nuclear blast.

Effects of nuclear weapons

Nuclear explosive devices have different yields. Some older bombs had yields of about 20 *megatons,* equivalent to the yield of about 1,540 Hiroshima bombs. A megaton is the amount of energy released by 1 million tons (907,000 metric tons) of TNT. Today, most nuclear devices have yields of less than 1 megaton. Most large thermonuclear weapons are about 8 to 40 times as powerful as the Hiroshima bomb.

The effects of a nuclear explosion can vary greatly, depending on a number of factors. These factors include weather, terrain, the point of explosion in relation to Earth's surface, and the weapon's yield. This section describes the possible effects of a large nuclear weapon. The weapon's explosion would produce four basic effects: (1) a blast wave, (2) thermal radiation, (3) initial nuclear radiation, and (4) residual nuclear radiation.

Blast wave. The explosion begins with the formation of a *fireball,* a cloud of dust and extremely hot gases under high pressure. A fraction of a second after the explosion, the gases begin to expand and form a blast wave, also called a *shock wave.* This wave is like a wall of highly compressed air moving rapidly away from the fireball. The blast wave created by a 1-megaton explosion could travel about 12 miles (19 kilometers) from *ground zero* in just 50 seconds. Ground zero is the point on the ground directly below the explosion.

The blast wave causes most of the explosion's damage. As the wave moves forward, it creates *overpressure,* atmospheric pressure above the normal level. A 1-megaton explosion can produce enough overpressure to destroy most buildings within 1 mile (1.6 kilometers) of ground zero. This overpressure can also cause moderate to severe damage within 6 miles (9.6 kilometers) of ground zero. Strong winds accompany the blast wave. These winds may reach speeds of 400 miles (640 kilometers) per hour at 2 miles (3.2 kilometers) from ground zero. The blast wave and wind probably would kill the majority of people within 3 miles (4.8 kilometers) of ground zero and some people between 3 and 6 miles (4.8 and 9.6 kilometers) from ground zero. Many other people within 6 miles of ground zero would be injured.

Thermal radiation consists of ultraviolet, visible, and infrared radiation given off by the fireball. Particles in the air rapidly absorb the ultraviolet radiation, and so it does little harm. However, the visible and infrared radiation can cause eye injuries as well as skin burns called *flash burns.* Flash burns caused from 20 to 30 percent of the deaths at Hiroshima and Nagasaki.

Thermal radiation also can ignite flammable materials, such as newspapers and dry leaves, causing large fires. Some scientists theorize that, in a nuclear war, the smoke from such fires would absorb enough sunlight to lower the temperature for several months or years. These scientists speculate that the lowered temperatures would result in widespread crop failure and famine. This possible effect of nuclear war is called *nuclear winter.* However, the effects of thermal radiation can vary considerably, depending on a number of conditions at the time of the explosion. In a light atmospheric haze, for example, the effects could be only one-hundredth as strong as they would be in clear air.

A person can be shielded from the direct effects of thermal radiation by solid, nontransparent objects, such as walls, buildings, trees, and rocks. In addition, light-colored clothing reflects heat, and so can help protect a person from flash burns. However, thermal radiation from a 1-megaton explosion can produce *second-degree burns* (blistering) of exposed human skin up to 11 miles (18 kilometers) from ground zero. The thermal radiation would last only about 10 seconds. Thus it would char, but not completely burn, heavy fabrics and thick pieces of wood or plastic.

Initial nuclear radiation occurs within the first minute beginning at the instant of the explosion. It consists of neutrons and *gamma rays,* a form of radiation similar to X rays. The fireball emits neutrons and some of the gamma rays almost instantaneously. The rest of the gamma rays are given off by a huge mushroom-shaped cloud of radioactive material formed by the explosion. Nuclear radiation can destroy living cells and prevent normal cell replacement. Large doses can cause death.

The amount of harm to a person from initial nuclear radiation depends in part on the person's location in relation to ground zero. Initial radiation decreases rapidly in strength as it moves away from ground zero. In all nuclear explosions, for example, initial radiation at about $\frac{1}{3}$ to $\frac{2}{3}$ mile (0.5 to 1 kilometer) from ground zero is only about one-tenth to one-hundredth as strong as radiation at ground zero.

Residual nuclear radiation is given off later than one minute after the explosion. Residual radiation created by fission consists of gamma rays and *beta particles* (electrons). Residual radiation produced by fusion is made up primarily of neutrons. It strikes particles of rock, soil, water, and other materials that make up the mushroom-shaped cloud. As a result, these particles become radioactive. They fall back to earth and are known as *fallout.* The closer an explosion occurs to Earth's surface, the more fallout it produces.

Early fallout reaches the ground within 24 hours of the explosion. Its heavier particles are highly radioactive, and most fall downwind from ground zero. Early fallout kills or severely injures living things.

Delayed fallout reaches the ground from 24 hours to a number of years after the explosion. It consists of tiny, often invisible, particles that may fall in small amounts over large areas. Such fallout causes long-term radiation damage to living things. George W. S. Kuhn

Plastic explosive is a puttylike explosive that can be molded into any shape. Plastic explosive is made of a *plasticizer* (a substance that makes the explosive flexible) and either a mixture of two explosive substances called *RDX* and *PETN* or RDX alone. Only a powerful *detonator* (a capsule containing an easily explodable charge) can set off a plastic explosive.

The United States Army developed plastic explosives during World War II (1939-1945). The explosives became famous in the early 1960's when a French terrorist group, the Secret Army Organization (OAS), used them to try to prevent Algeria from becoming independent. Plastic explosives have remained a popular weapon among terrorists because they are powerful, easily hidden, and difficult to detect. Frances M. Lussier

Propaganda is one-sided communication designed to influence people's thinking and actions. A television commercial or a poster urging people to vote for a po-

Two propaganda versions of Adolf Hitler show the German dictator from opposite viewpoints. A pro-Hitler poster, *left,* portrays him as a heroic warrior crowned with a halo of light. An anti-Hitler cartoon, *right,* pictures him as a ridiculous, loudmouthed tyrant.

litical candidate might be propaganda, depending on its method of persuasion.

Propaganda differs from education in democratic societies. But education in a dictatorship can involve teaching children and youth by techniques that could be classified as propaganda. Educators in democratic societies teach people how to think, but propagandists tell them what to think. Most educators are willing to change their opinions on the basis of new evidence, but propagandists ignore evidence that contradicts them. Educators present all sides of an issue and encourage debate. Propagandists build the strongest possible case for their views and discourage discussion.

The intention of the communicator to influence or deceive is an important issue in identifying propaganda. But experts disagree about what is propaganda and what is not, and whether propaganda differs from other forms of persuasion, such as advertising and political campaigning. Some look upon all slanted communication as propaganda. Others believe that the method of persuasion determines whether a message is propaganda. For example, the majority of advertisers and political campaigners function openly and state their purposes truthfully. Others present any combination of truths, half-truths, lies, and distortions that they think will most effectively influence their audience. Some experts say all these people are propagandists. Others regard only the second group as propagandists.

Some people consider propaganda neither good nor bad. For example, many favor the use of propaganda to raise money for charity. Other individuals argue that the public needs reliable information to make wise decisions, and that propaganda blocks the spreading of such information. They also fear that propaganda deadens people's power of reasoning. The results of some propaganda may be short term and relatively insignificant, such as the purchase of a product. Other types of propaganda can have more serious results.

The greatest use of propaganda occurs during wartime. At such times, government propaganda campaigns urge people to save resources, volunteer for military service, support the war effort, and make sacrifices

necessary for victory. *Psychological warfare* is a type of propaganda that aims to weaken the enemy's will to fight or belief in their government. A related technique, called *brainwashing,* is used against prisoners. It combines political propaganda with harsh treatment to reduce a prisoner's resistance.

Much wartime propaganda is called *covert* (secret) *propaganda* because it comes from hidden sources. For example, a propagandist might try to discourage enemy troops by sending them counterfeit newspapers reporting huge losses among their forces. Some covert propaganda is spread by people in a country who secretly support its enemies. A group of such people is called a *fifth column.* The opposite of covert propaganda is called *overt* (open) *propaganda,* which comes from known sources.

How propaganda works

Propaganda appeals to its audience in three ways. (1) It calls for an action or opinion that it makes seem wise and reasonable. (2) It suggests that the action or opinion is moral and right. (3) It provides a pleasant feeling, such as a sense of importance or of belonging.

Many propaganda methods are common-sense techniques that resemble those of persuasive speaking. These techniques include gaining people's trust, simplicity and repetition, and the use of symbols. However, propagandists often use such underhanded methods as distortion, concealment, and lying. In nations ruled by dictators, governments increase the effectiveness of their propaganda by using censorship.

Gaining people's trust. Above all, propagandists must be believable, and their audience must consider them reliable authorities. One way to gain an audience's trust is to report unfavorable news that the audience knows or will discover. During World War II (1939-1945), the British Broadcasting Corporation (BBC) made propaganda broadcasts to Europe. The BBC began many newscasts with a report of British defeats and losses. This practice helped give the BBC a worldwide reputation for truthfulness.

Another way to gain people's trust is to agree with

their existing opinions. Scientists have found that people place most trust in speakers and writers whose ideas are similar to their own. As a result, propaganda is most successful if much of it agrees with what people already believe and if only a little of it is new.

Simplicity and repetition. Propaganda must be easy to understand and to remember. As far as possible, propagandists make their appeals in simple, catchy slogans that they repeat over and over. The Nazi dictator Adolf Hitler wrote: "The intelligence of the masses is small. Their forgetfulness is great. They must be told the same thing a thousand times."

The use of symbols involves words and illustrations that bring strong responses from people. Individuals react not only to the actual meaning of words and the actual content of pictures but also to the feelings aroused by such symbols. For example, nearly all cultures have favorable reactions to a picture of a mother and baby or to such words as *homeland* and *justice.* Propagandists try to create an association in people's minds between such symbols and the messages they are trying to spread. Powerful negative images are frequently used to increase prejudice, hostility, and hatred toward the desired targets of propaganda.

Distortion and concealment. Propagandists deliberately exaggerate the importance of some facts and twist the meaning of others. They try to conceal facts that might prevent the response they seek from people. In addition, propagandists try to shift attention away from embarrassing facts that cannot be hidden.

Lying. Deliberate lying is relatively rare as a propaganda technique because propagandists fear their lies might be discovered and they might lose their audience's trust. Propaganda usually includes some accurate information. But some propagandists readily lie if they think they can deceive their audience. Propagandists may believe in their causes, but their chief goal is to shape and control the public's beliefs and actions.

Censorship is most common where the government controls the newspapers, television, and other means of communication. It increases the effectiveness of propaganda because the government can silence people who contradict its official views.

Who uses propaganda?

Propaganda comes from many sources. Three of the most important ones are (1) governments, (2) organizations, and (3) businesses.

Governments. Nearly all governments, including democratic ones, use propaganda to win support from other nations. Governments also sponsor propaganda and information programs to promote desired behavior among their own citizens. For example, government propaganda might urge people to support certain policies or to oppose foreign political systems.

Organizations represent members of various professions, religions, and many other fields. During election campaigns, many organizations distribute propaganda that supports candidates who agree with their views. Between elections, organizations may also use propaganda to influence public opinion. Many groups employ people called *lobbyists,* who work to persuade legislators to support their programs. A group that tries to further its own interests by exerting pressure on legislators

or other officials is often called a *pressure group.* Group members outline their goals on such controversial topics as abortion, busing, civil rights, the environment, foreign policy issues, gun control, and nuclear energy.

Businesses often use propaganda in their advertising. For example, a mouthwash commercial on television might be aimed at people's desire to be attractive and popular. Advertising agencies employ psychologists and other social scientists to study why people buy certain products. They try to determine what slogans will lead to purchases. Many large businesses also have public relations departments that use propaganda to spread favorable opinions of company policies.

History

Today, the word *propaganda* suggests shady or underhanded activity, but that was not its original meaning. The term came from the Latin name of a group of Roman Catholic cardinals, the *Congregatio de Propaganda Fide* (Congregation for the Propagation of the Faith). Pope Gregory XV established the committee—called the *propaganda* for short—in 1622 to supervise missionaries. Gradually, the word came to mean any effort to spread a belief. It acquired its present meaning after World War I (1914-1918), when writers exposed the dishonest but effective techniques that propagandists had used during the war.

American Cancer Society

Propaganda uses emotions rather than logic to persuade its audience. This antismoking poster tries to create an association in people's minds between smoking and unattractiveness.

© Dennis E. Cox, Getty Images

Governments use propaganda to promote desired behavior among their citizens. This Chinese poster encourages people to adopt modern attitudes in industry and in education.

Propaganda as it is used today began in the early 1900's. V. I. Lenin, who led the revolution that established Communist control of Russia, emphasized the importance of propaganda. He distinguished between two types of persuasion—propaganda and agitation. Lenin regarded propaganda as the use of historical and scientific arguments to convince the well-educated minority. He defined agitation as the use of half-truths and slogans to arouse the masses, whom he considered incapable of understanding complicated ideas. Traditionally, each Communist Party has included a unit that specializes in *agitprop*—agitation and propaganda.

During World War I, the Allies—including France, Russia, the United Kingdom, and the United States—fought the Central Powers, led by Germany. The warring nations conducted widespread propaganda operations. The major U.S. propaganda effort was handled by an agency called the Committee on Public Information. The committee distributed over 100 million posters and publications designed to increase support for the war.

Between the wars, several famous dictators used propaganda to help them achieve power. In 1922, Benito Mussolini established a Fascist dictatorship in Italy. Fascist propaganda promised to restore Italy to the glory of ancient Rome. Joseph Stalin, who became dictator of the Soviet Union by the late 1920's, used propaganda and terrorism to crush all opposition. The Soviet Union had been formed under Russia's leadership in 1922. In 1933, Adolf Hitler set up his Nazi dictatorship in Germany. The Nazis' effective use of education, motion pictures, press, and radio to shape opinion and behavior remains one of the most famous examples of propaganda.

During World War II, Germany, Italy, and Japan fought the Soviet Union, the United Kingdom, the United States, and the other Allies. All of the major powers spread far-reaching propaganda. The United States had two primary propaganda agencies. The Office of War Information handled overt propaganda, and the Office of Strategic Services (OSS) carried on covert operations.

After World War II ended in 1945, the Cold War began. The Communist nations, led by the Soviet Union, and the non-Communist nations, led by the United States, used a variety of propaganda techniques to influence world opinion, as well as their own citizens.

In 1953, the U.S. government created the U.S. Information Agency (USIA) to create support of its foreign policy. The Voice of America, the radio division of the USIA, broadcast entertainment, news, and propaganda throughout the world. The government used the Central Intelligence Agency (CIA) to spread covert propaganda against governments unfriendly to the United States. These governments included those of the Soviet Union and the Communist countries of Eastern Europe. The CIA also provided funds to establish radio networks called Radio Free Europe and Radio Liberty, which broadcast to Communist countries.

Since 1960. In the early 1960's, China began to challenge the Soviet Union for leadership of the Communist world, and a bitter propaganda struggle developed between them. Each accused the other of betraying Communism. After 1970, several Communist and non-Communist nations at times enjoyed friendlier relations and altered their propaganda operations against one another. The United States and the Soviet Union enjoyed such relations in the early 1970's and beginning again in the late 1980's. In 1989 and the early 1990's, Communists lost control of the governments of many Eastern European countries and the Soviet Union, and in 1991 the Soviet Union broke up into a number of independent states. However, Radio Free Europe continued to broadcast to Eastern Europe, and Radio Liberty kept transmitting to former Soviet areas. In addition, Voice of America continued to broadcast throughout the world. Radio Free Asia, another U.S. service, began broadcasting in 1996. Its programs are transmitted to China, North Korea, and Southeast Asia. Propaganda is still used today in many nations.   Taylor Stults

Web site

Propaganda Analysis: Home Page
http://carmen.artsci.washington.edu/propaganda/home.htm
A critical look at propaganda from the Institute for Propaganda Analysis.

Sabotage, *SAB uh tahzh,* is any means of deliberately wasting or damaging the tools, machinery, or production of an employer or government. The word originated in the 1800's when French workers would throw their *sabots* (wooden shoes) into machines to halt production. In Spain, France, and Italy, sabotage was used by the *syndicalists,* members of anarchist trade unions.

In wartime, sabotage by trained agents called *saboteurs* is a means of damaging war production and communications in enemy countries. Since World War II ended in 1945, a number of countries have used sabotage in *covert* (secret) wars to intimidate or overthrow other governments.   Edwin B. Firmage

Focus on
TERRORISM

Section Five

Homeland Security: Fighting Terrorism at Home

A number of agencies and departments have the responsibility of protecting the United States from terrorist attacks. They include the Central Intelligence Agency (CIA), the Federal Bureau of Investigation (FBI), the Office of Homeland Security, and the Coast Guard. This section brings together 20 *World Book* articles that focus on these agencies and departments and the techniques they use in protecting the homeland and fighting the war on terrorism.

Border Patrol, United States, is an enforcement agency within the Immigration and Naturalization Service. It operates along United States land borders and in coastal areas of Florida and the Gulf of Mexico. Its main purpose is to prevent the unlawful entry of *aliens* (noncitizens) into the United States. It also works to intercept illegal drugs being smuggled into the country. Border Patrol officers are trained at the Border Patrol Academy in Glynco, Georgia. They learn immigration laws and related subjects, methods of operation, the Spanish language, and law enforcement.

Critically reviewed by the Immigration and Naturalization Service

Web site

Border Patrol
http://www.ins.usdoj.gov/graphics/lawenfor/bpatrol/
Home page of the United States Border Patrol.

Centers for Disease Control and Prevention, often referred to as the CDC, is an agency of the Public Health Service and part of the United States Department of Health and Human Services. It works to protect public health by administering national programs for the prevention and control of disease and disability.

The agency provides health information and statistics and conducts research to track down the sources of epidemics. It works with state and local agencies and private organizations to develop immunization services and other programs to eliminate or prevent causes of disease. It also has established programs to ensure a rapid response by federal, state, and local agencies to attacks that involve biological warfare or biological terrorism.

The National Institute for Occupational Safety and Health, a unit of the CDC, develops standards for safe and healthful working conditions. The CDC cooperates with foreign governments and international agencies in a worldwide effort to prevent disease and improve health. The CDC was established in 1946. Its headquarters and many of its laboratories are in Atlanta, Georgia.

Critically reviewed by the Centers for Disease Control and Prevention

Web site

Centers for Disease Control and Prevention Home Page
http://www.cdc.gov/
Information about the CDC, which works to prevent and control disease, injury, and disability.

Central Intelligence Agency (CIA) is a major United States government agency that gathers information about foreign governments and certain nongovernmental groups, including those that engage in terrorism or organized crime. The information collected by the CIA is political, economic, and military in nature, and much of it is secret. The CIA analyzes the information, which is called *intelligence,* for the president, Congress, and other federal agencies. The CIA also engages in *counterintelligence,* which consists of attempts to identify, neutralize, and manipulate the intelligence activities of other countries. Another important CIA function is *covert action*—that is, secret efforts to influence events abroad.

The CIA collects intelligence about the intentions and capabilities of countries that threaten the security of the United States or its citizens. Much of the information is *classified* (secret). Sources include reports from spies, documents obtained illegally, recordings from secret listening devices, and pictures taken from spy satellites in space. News organizations may report what foreign officials say at press conferences, but the CIA also tries to determine what the officials say in private meetings.

CIA analysts try to make world events understandable for U.S. leaders. They analyze information gathered by the CIA and other U.S. government agencies—including the Departments of Defense, State, and the Treasury—to tell policymakers who is doing what, when they are doing it, and why. Analysts also identify opportunities for the United States to influence world events.

Counterintelligence protects U.S. secrets from foreign spies. Such secrets include information about U.S. armed forces and military plans. CIA counterintelligence units also try to learn whether a foreign government is giving American spies *disinformation* (false information) intended to deceive the U.S. government.

The CIA's covert actions include propaganda, unofficial military operations, and secret aid to foreign political and military groups that support U.S. interests. During the Cold War, the CIA used propaganda and secret transfers of money and information to limit the Soviet Union's own covert actions in Western Europe. The Cold War was a period of intense U.S.-Soviet rivalry that began after World War II (1939-1945) and lasted until the early 1990's. The U.S. government does not publicly acknowledge its role in covert actions.

The CIA's headquarters are in Langley, Virginia, but many of its officers and agents are stationed in other countries. Sometimes, CIA employees claim to work for other parts of the U.S. government. Some operate under *nonofficial cover,* meaning they pose as private citizens of the United States or of a foreign country.

The CIA is an executive branch agency responsible to the president. The National Security Council, whose members include the president, the vice president, and the secretaries of state and defense, oversees the CIA. The director of the CIA also guides other U.S. foreign intelligence agencies. They include the Defense Intelligence Agency, which gives intelligence to the armed forces, and the National Security Agency, which specializes in communication and *cryptography* (using and deciphering secret communication).

Congress and President Harry S. Truman created the CIA early in the Cold War by approving the National Security Act of 1947. After the Cold War, the CIA's focus shifted toward such problems as terrorism, organized crime, and the spread of weapons of mass destruction.

CIA operations have sometimes created controversy. In the mid-1970's, the CIA was the focus of congressional and other federal investigations of charges that it had abused its powers. The investigators concluded that some of the charges were false, but found others to be true. For example, a commission headed by Vice President Nelson A. Rockefeller reported that the CIA had spied on some Americans who opposed U.S. involvement in the Vietnam War. To guard against future abuses, a number of reforms were adopted to make the CIA and other U.S. intelligence agencies more accountable to Congress. Today, the CIA must report major activities to two congressional committees that specialize in intelligence matters.

On Sept. 11, 2001, terrorists crashed hijacked jetliners into the World Trade Center in New York City and the

Pentagon Building near Washington, D.C. About 3,000 people were killed. Following the attacks, the CIA and other government agencies received criticism for failing to detect the terrorists' activity before the attacks.

Roy Godson

Additional resources

Doyle, David W. *True Men & Traitors.* Wiley, 2001. Memoir of a former CIA agent.
Kessler, Ronald. *Inside the CIA.* 1992. Reprint. Pocket Bks., 1994.

Web site

Central Intelligence Agency Home Page
http://www.cia.gov
Information about the Central Intelligence Agency, whose role is to support the president, the National Security Council, and all officials who make and execute United States national security policy.

Coast Guard, United States, is a branch of the armed services. The Coast Guard works to protect the public, the environment, U.S. economic interests, and national security in maritime regions. The regions where the Coast Guard operates include U.S. coasts, ports, and inland waters; and international waters. Its many duties give special meaning to its motto, *Semper Paratus,* which means *always ready.*

The Coast Guard is the nation's oldest continuous seagoing force. Since 1790, it has grown from a fleet of 10 small vessels to a force of modern ships and aircraft. Its members have fought in every major war of the United States. They have rescued hundreds of thousands of people from disasters and have saved billions of dollars worth of property from shipwrecks and floods.

The Coast Guard maintains an active-duty force of about 35,000 men and women. It has 14,000 reserve members; a 34,000-member, all-volunteer Coast Guard Auxiliary; and a civilian work force of more than 5,000.

The Coast Guard emblem was adopted in 1927. "Semper Paratus" is the Coast Guard's famous marching song.

Coast Guard activities

The Coast Guard enforces all federal laws and treaties on the high seas and on the navigable waters of the United States. These include criminal laws, inspection laws, pollution laws, revenue and navigation laws, and nautical rules of the road. Coast Guard activities are directed toward five main purposes: (1) safety, (2) national defense, (3) maritime security, (4) mobility, and (5) protection of the environment.

Safety. The Coast Guard works worldwide to limit deaths, injuries, and property damage associated with maritime transportation, fishing, and recreational boating. It enforces and helps establish safety regulations governing the construction and operation of merchant ships and passenger ships. It establishes safety rules for passengers, and tests and licenses crew members. In addition, the Coast Guard establishes safety standards for yachts, motorboats, and other noncommercial vessels.

Coast Guard ships, which are called *cutters,* patrol oceans and inland waterways. The Coast Guard operates search-and-rescue stations along the coasts of the United States and its territories, and in the Great Lakes. When accidents occur, rescue boats and aircraft go into action immediately. They rescue people who have been involved in boating accidents, shipwrecks, airplane crashes, and hurricanes. They also tow damaged vessels to shore. The Coast Guard helps rescue any person or ship, regardless of nationality. It provides emergency medical aid to crews of all vessels at sea and takes injured or critically ill crew members to shore bases for treatment.

Ships at sea depend on Coast Guard aids to navigation. Such guides as beacons, buoys, fog signals, lighthouses, and radio stations reduce the dangers of navigation. The Coast Guard uses loran radio navigation and the Global Positioning System to help ships determine their exact positions at sea. Coast Guard units report weather information to the U.S. National Weather Service, which uses the data for forecasting. The International Ice Patrol, operated by the Coast Guard, locates and tracks icebergs in shipping lanes in the North Atlantic and warns ships about them.

The Coast Guard Auxiliary, a voluntary association of yacht and motorboat sailors and owners and aircraft owners, also promotes safety. It checks boats for safety

U.S. Coast Guard

The United States Coast Guard patrols the oceans in such vessels as the high-endurance cutter *Mellon, shown here.* The Coast Guard also protects United States ports and ships and enforces maritime laws.

equipment, helps with rescues, and conducts classes on boating safety.

National defense. The Coast Guard defends the United States as one of the five armed services. In both peacetime and wartime, the Coast Guard and the United States Navy work together. The Coast Guard participates in military exercises with the Navy and with forces of countries that are members of the North Atlantic Treaty Organization (NATO). In wartime, the Coast Guard serves as part of the Navy. It provides escorts for merchant ships, helps guard ports and shipping lanes for the United States and its allies, and provides air-sea rescue services.

Maritime security. The Coast Guard helps other federal agencies enforce their laws concerning customs, immigration, and quarantines. Patrols along U.S. coasts serve to prevent the transport of illegal drugs, immigrants, and contraband into the United States through sea routes. The Navy aids the Coast Guard in preventing the smuggling of illegal drugs. The Coast Guard also prevents illegal fishing. Its port security program helps keep waterfronts safe by controlling traffic and regulating shipment of dangerous cargoes.

Mobility. The Coast Guard works to ease maritime commerce by eliminating interruptions and obstacles to the efficient and economical movement of goods and people. Special Coast Guard cutters called *icebreakers* clear icebound harbors on the North Atlantic coast, on the Great Lakes, and on inland rivers. The Coast Guard works to provide the greatest possible access to water for recreation.

Protection of the environment. The Coast Guard works to eliminate damage to natural resources and the environment associated with maritime transportation, fishing, and recreational boating. Its work in preventing illegal fishing helps to preserve valuable fish stocks. The port security program monitors pollution on waterfronts. Coast Guard icebreakers support research scientists in the Arctic and Antarctic.

Ships, aircraft, and weapons of the Coast Guard

Ships and stations. The Coast Guard maintains a fleet of several hundred ships and boats that can perform various assignments. These vessels include buoy tenders, cutters, icebreakers, lifeboats, surfboats, and tugboats. The service operates about 70 offices devoted to marine safety, port security, and shipping-inspection duties. The Coast Guard also maintains light towers, navigational aids, and about 190 law enforcement and search-and-rescue stations.

Aircraft play a major part in Coast Guard operations. The Coast Guard uses cargo planes, jets, and helicopters for patrol, law enforcement, and search-and-rescue missions. Helicopters are particularly important to the Coast Guard in air-sea rescues, in bringing help to flood victims, and in rescuing disaster victims in inland areas that could not otherwise be reached. During World War II (1939-1945), Coast Guard aircraft bombed enemy submarines. Aircraft of the Coast Guard also rescued many survivors of torpedoed ships.

Weapons. All Coast Guard vessels are armed with at least small arms. Weapons used by the Coast Guard range from 9-millimeter pistols, M-16 rifles, and machine guns on small patrol vessels to 76-millimeter cannons on large cutters. The crews of larger Coast Guard vessels periodically train with the Navy.

Organization of the Coast Guard

Coast Guard headquarters are in Washington, D.C. The commandant of the Coast Guard—an admiral— heads the service, assisted by a vice commandant, a planning and control staff, and various Coast Guard departments. The United States and its possessions are divided into nine Coast Guard districts. Each district is headed by a district commander.

Active-duty and reserves. The *active-duty Coast Guard* makes up the core of the service. It consists of officers and enlisted men and women who have chosen the Coast Guard as a full-time career. The Coast Guard Reserve is a group whose members may be called to active duty in time of emergency. Their training is similar to that of the regulars and includes port security and other wartime missions.

Women in the Coast Guard can serve in any occupational specialty. Women first entered the Coast Guard in 1942 as a reserve group called the SPARS. The name SPAR comes from the first letters of the Coast Guard motto, *Semper Paratus*, and its English translation, *Always Ready*. The SPARS filled administrative jobs to free Coast Guard men for sea duty during World War II. When the war ended in 1945, the SPARS had 10,000 enlisted women and 1,000 officers. All of them were discharged or placed on inactive duty by June 1946, and the group was dissolved. In November 1949, shortly before the Korean War, the SPARS was reactivated. It was disbanded again in 1974, when women became a part of the regular Coast Guard.

Critically reviewed by the United States Coast Guard

Important dates in Coast Guard history

1790	The U.S. Congress authorized the construction of 10 cutters for a Revenue Cutter Service.
1819	Congress authorized revenue cutters to protect United States merchant vessels against piracy.
1861	The cutter *Harriet Lane* fired the first shot from any vessel in the Civil War.
1898	The cutter *McCulloch* sent the first news of the victory over the Spanish fleet at Manila Bay.
1915	The Revenue Cutter Service and the Life-Saving Service combined to form the U.S. Coast Guard.
1917	During World War I, the Coast Guard served as part of the Navy.
1939	The Lighthouse Service of the Department of Commerce was transferred to the Coast Guard.
1945	The icebreaker *Mackinaw* made the first winter trip through the Soo locks on Lake Superior.
1957	The cutters *Storis, Bramble,* and *Spar* became the first U.S. ships to sail through the Northwest Passage.
1967	The Coast Guard was transferred from the Treasury Department to the Department of Transportation.
1976	The Coast Guard Academy admitted women students for the first time.
1979	Two Coast Guard women officers became the first women to command U.S. warships.
1989	The Coast Guard supervised the cleanup of a huge oil spill off the coast of Alaska after the tanker *Exxon Valdez* ran aground in Prince William Sound.

Web site

United States Coast Guard
http://www.uscg.mil/
Official Web site of the U.S. Coast Guard. Includes information about the Coast Guard's history, organization, and services.

Customs Service, United States, is an agency of the United States government that helps protect the nation and collects taxes on imported merchandise. These taxes, called *tariffs,* include customs duties, excise taxes, and penalties. The agency collects about $20 billion a year, more than any other federal agency except the Internal Revenue Service, which collects income taxes.

The Customs Service processes goods, people, and vehicles entering or leaving the United States. The agency works to prevent smuggling and to enforce many other federal laws, including those governing environmental protection and motor vehicle safety. It also works to protect U.S. business and labor by enforcing copyright, patent, and trademark regulations.

The service administers seven customs regions in the United States, Puerto Rico, and the Virgin Islands. These regions are divided into 44 districts with about 300 *ports of entry.* Ports of entry are cities with customs facilities where goods may enter the country legally. The commissioner of customs directs the agency.

The First Congress established the service in 1789. The service's headquarters are in Washington, D.C.

Critically reviewed by the United States Customs Service

Web site

United States Customs Service
http://www.customs.ustreas.gov
Home page of the United States Customs Service.

Defense, Department of, is an executive department of the United States government. The Department of Defense directs the operations of the nation's armed forces, including the Army, Navy, and Air Force.

The department's leaders also advise the president on military matters. The department headquarters are in the Pentagon Building, which is in Arlington, Virginia, near Washington, D.C.

Organization. The Department of Defense is headed by the secretary of defense. The department also includes (1) the Joint Chiefs of Staff, (2) the military departments, and (3) the unified combatant commands.

The secretary of defense is a member of the president's Cabinet. The secretary is a civilian and is appointed by the president with approval of the U.S. Senate. The secretary's assistants deal with such matters as acquiring and building weapons, developing and protecting military communications systems, gathering intelligence, planning strategy, and preventing the spread of nuclear weapons. The secretary of defense and the assistants of the secretary are supported in their work by a number of agencies of the Department of Defense.

The secretary is a member of the National Security Council and the North Atlantic Council. The National Security Council, part of the Executive Office of the President of the United States, advises the president on a range of security issues. The North Atlantic Council directs the North Atlantic Treaty Organization (NATO), a defense alliance to which the United States belongs. The secretary of defense maintains close contact with top officials in other parts of the United States government, especially the Department of State.

The Joint Chiefs of Staff (JCS) consists of a chairman, a vice chairman, the chiefs of staff of the Army and Air Force, the Navy's chief of naval operations, and the commandant of the Marine Corps. The JCS is the top military staff of the secretary of defense. Members of the JCS serve as military advisers to the president, the National Security Council, and the secretary of defense.

The military departments are the departments of the Army, Navy, and Air Force. The Marine Corps is included in the Department of the Navy. Each military department is headed by a

The seal of the Department of Defense

civilian secretary who administers the department under the authority, direction, and control of the secretary of defense. The military departments organize, train, equip, and maintain the readiness of their forces.

The unified combatant commands carry out military missions. They consist of large forces from more than one branch of the U.S. military.

History. In 1789, Congress established the Department of War to administer and conduct military affairs. In 1798, Congress separated the naval forces from the land forces, creating the Department of the Navy. The secretaries of both the Department of War and the Department of the Navy were Cabinet members who reported directly to the president.

During World War II (1939-1945), President Franklin D. Roosevelt directed U.S. combat forces through a Joint Chiefs of Staff, which functioned without a formal charter. The United States armed services cooperated with one another through unified commands that operated overseas. But at home, the Army and Navy competed for scarce personnel and materials. The Army Air Forces also pressed for equal status with the Army and Navy.

The National Security Act of 1947 created the National Military Establishment. The Department of War became the Department of the Army. The Army Air Forces became a separate service under a new Department of the Air Force. The Navy and Marine Corps continued under the Department of the Navy.

The secretary of defense became a member of the Cabinet and formulated general policies and programs for the National Military Establishment. The heads of the military departments also served on the Cabinet. In 1947, Congress formally chartered the Joint Chiefs of Staff.

In 1949, Congress set up the Department of Defense to replace the National Military Establishment. Congress removed the heads of the military departments from the Cabinet and provided that the military departments be administered separately and directed by the secretary of defense.   Critically reviewed by the Department of Defense

Web site

Office of the Secretary of Defense
http://www.defenselink.mil/pubs/almanac/osd.html
The official Web site of the United States secretary of defense.

Espionage, *EHS pee uh NAHZH,* or *EHS pee uh NIHJ,* is the act of spying on a country, organization, movement, or person. It involves a system of spies that governments and other groups send into an enemy area or a possible enemy area to gather information. The spies seek valuable military, political, scientific, and production facts and secrets. People spy for money, adventure, and love as well as for their country or to help a cause. Some are forced to spy against their will. They usually work as members of an organization through which they get instructions and send back information.

Espionage is one of the main information-gathering methods used in intelligence organizations. The agency evaluates and interprets information from its agents, researchers, and such mechanical devices as electronic eavesdropping equipment. Some governments also use spy planes and space-based satellites. This process produces knowledge that is useful to political and military leaders in their foreign and defense policies.

Counterespionage is set up to protect a country and its intelligence services against spying by hostile forces. A counterespionage agency seeks to prevent the theft of secret information and to detect the presence of spies within organizations. Such an agency works to discover and arrest hostile spies. It also may place its own spies in an opposing organization. An agency may try to get hostile spies to give it information about the enemy's system. Such spies are called *double agents.* All countries have counterespionage agencies.

History. Espionage is older than war. The first spies were probably prehistoric people who were curious about their neighbors' hunting techniques. The Bible tells of Moses's sending spies into Canaan. In modern times, Frederick the Great of Prussia is credited with originating systematically organized espionage.

George Washington's network of spies obtained intelligence and information for the Continental Army during the Revolutionary War in America (1775-1783). Allan Pinkerton directed espionage and counterespionage for the Union Army during the early days of the Civil War (1861-1865). Later, a Bureau of Information carried on this work. During World War II (1939-1945), the Office of Strategic Services (OSS) conducted government overseas espionage and intelligence operations. In 1947, Congress established the U.S. Central Intelligence Agency (CIA) to coordinate government intelligence activities and to carry on its own operations. In 1954, Congress passed a law making peacetime espionage against the United States punishable by death. The death penalty for espionage had been imposed previously only during wartime.   Douglas L. Wheeler

Federal Bureau of Investigation (FBI) is the primary investigating branch of the United States Department of Justice. The FBI investigates a wide variety of crimes that deal with the safety and security of the United States and its citizens. The FBI also collects evidence in lawsuits that involve the federal government. In addition, the bureau gathers *intelligence* (information) about individuals or groups that it considers dangerous to national security. FBI investigators are called *special agents.*

Laws passed by the U.S. Congress provide the basic framework for many of the FBI's powers and procedures. A director, appointed by the president with the approval of the Senate, supervises the FBI from headquarters in Washington, D.C. The FBI has about 60 offices in the United States and Puerto Rico and more than 40 posts in other countries.

FBI operations

Criminal investigation. The FBI investigates such federal crimes as assault on the president, bank robbery, bombing, hijacking, and kidnapping. It handles cases involving stolen money, property, or vehicles that have been taken from one state to another. The bureau fights organized crime groups and investigates financial crimes such as counterfeiting and check fraud. The FBI investigates computer-related crimes involving criminal acts and national security issues.

At the request of state or local authorities, the FBI helps capture fleeing criminals. The FBI also examines violations of civil rights laws and violations of laws concerning toxic wastes. In addition, it works with the federal Drug Enforcement Administration to investigate violations of criminal drug laws.

The FBI has several programs that specialize in handling investigations of specific crimes. Some of these programs include the Domestic Terrorism Program, the Organized Crime/ Drug Program, and the Violent Crimes and Major Offenders Program. In all criminal investigations, the FBI presents its findings to the Department of Justice, which determines whether to prosecute.

Intelligence operations of the FBI consist of gathering information about individuals or organizations engaged in activities that may be dangerous to national security. These operations include the investigation of terrorist groups, riots, spy activities, treason, and threats to overthrow the government. The FBI is responsible for detecting and counteracting the actions of foreign intelligence operations that seek to gather sensitive information about the United States. The FBI reports to the president, Congress, or the Justice Department for action.

Other services. The FBI provides various services to law enforcement agencies throughout the United States and in other countries. Such agencies may request help from the FBI Identification Division, the FBI Laboratory,

Federal Bureau of Investigation

The FBI Academy in Quantico, Virginia, trains future agents in the use of firearms and other crime-fighting methods.

and the National Crime Information Center (NCIC). The bureau also trains selected police officials.

The Identification Division has the world's largest fingerprint collections. The division's files contain prints of both criminals and civilians. The FBI Laboratory is widely regarded as one of the world's finest crime laboratories. FBI scientists examine pieces of evidence there and often testify in court. The NCIC is a computerized system that stores records on criminal suspects and stolen property.

The FBI issues an annual publication called *Uniform Crime Reports for the United States,* which includes a record of rates and trends in major crimes. The bureau also distributes descriptions of its *Ten Most Wanted Fugitives.* The FBI Academy in Quantico, Virginia, provides training in advanced methods of fighting crime.

FBI agents

Men and women who wish to be special agents must be U.S. citizens between 23 and 37 years old and in excellent physical condition. They must also have a college degree. Future agents go through a 15-week training program at the FBI National Academy. They study crime detection, evidence, constitutional and criminal law, and methods of investigation. They also learn self-defense and how to use firearms. Agents later receive periodic refresher training to keep them up to date.

History

In 1908, Attorney General Charles J. Bonaparte organized a group of special investigators in the Justice Department. This group, called the Bureau of Investigation, investigated such offenses as illegal business practices and land sales. Its first director was Stanley W. Finch, an attorney. J. Edgar Hoover, a Justice Department lawyer, became director of the bureau in 1924 and headed it until his death in 1972. Congress gave the bureau its present name in 1935.

A wave of bank robberies, kidnappings, and other violent crimes broke out in the United States during the 1930's. Congress passed laws giving the FBI increased authority to combat this lawlessness. FBI agents, who were nicknamed *G-Men,* or *Government Men,* became admired for tracking down such gangsters as John Dillinger and George "Machine Gun" Kelly.

During World War II (1939-1945), the FBI broke up enemy spy rings in the United States. In the 1950's and 1960's, special agents arrested Communist spies who had stolen secret atomic and military information. The bureau also investigated protest organizations in the 1960's and early 1970's. Clarence M. Kelley, a former special agent, became director of the FBI in 1973.

In 1975, a Senate committee reported that the FBI had acted illegally or improperly in a number of cases. The committee revealed that FBI agents had committed burglaries and spied illegally on U.S. citizens during some domestic security investigations. The Senate investigators also charged that Hoover had given certain presidents damaging personal information about some of their political opponents. The Justice Department set up guidelines to prevent further abuses.

In 1976, Congress limited the term of the FBI director to 10 years. William H. Webster, a federal judge, became director of the bureau in 1978. In 1987, William S. Sessions, also a federal judge, became head of the FBI. In 1993, the Justice Department accused Sessions of taking personal trips at government expense and of other unethical conduct. That year, President Bill Clinton dismissed him, and Louis J. Freeh, a federal judge and former FBI agent, became the agency's director.

In 2001, the FBI arrested one of its own agents for providing classified information to Russia. He confessed and was convicted. Later that year, the FBI revealed that agents had mishandled documents relating to the 1995 terrorist bombing of a federal building in Oklahoma City. Freeh stepped down as director in 2001, and Robert S. Mueller III, a Justice Department lawyer, succeeded him.

On Sept. 11, 2001, terrorists crashed hijacked commercial airplanes into the two 110-story towers of the World Trade Center in New York City and into the Pentagon Building near Washington, D.C. A fourth hijacked plane crashed in Pennsylvania. Following the attacks, the FBI launched a widespread campaign to identify members of terrorist groups and to prevent future terrorist acts. The antiterrorist effort is believed to be the largest investigation in the FBI's history.   Robert W. Taylor

Web site

FBI Home Page
http://www.fbi.gov/
Information about the Federal Bureau of Investigation.

Homeland Security, Office of, is a United States government agency that aims to protect the nation against terrorism. The office coordinates efforts to detect, prepare for, prevent, respond to, and recover from terrorist attacks. It works with numerous federal, state, and local agencies in designing and implementing national strategies. The president appoints the head of the office, who is known as the assistant to the president for homeland security. The office is part of the Executive Office of the President.

The duties of the Office of Homeland Security include assisting intelligence-gathering efforts and distributing information to appropriate departments. The office reviews, evaluates, and maintains federal security procedures and emergency response plans. It helps plan protection for important structures and facilities within the United States. The assistant to the president for homeland security determines the agenda for the Homeland Security Council. This council, which includes the heads of a number of executive departments and agencies, advises and assists the president in matters of security in the United States.

President George W. Bush established the Office of Homeland Security in October 2001. This move followed attacks on the World Trade Center in New York City and the Pentagon Building near Washington, D.C., the previous month.

In 2002, Bush proposed that the Office of Homeland Security be expanded into a new executive department called the Department of Homeland Security. The new department, according to Bush's proposal, would then take over a number of government agencies and responsibilities related to the prevention of terrorism. These agencies could include the Federal Emergency Management Agency, the Immigration and Naturalization Service, the Transportation Security Administration, the U.S. Coast Guard, the U.S. Customs Service, and the U.S. Secret Service.　　M. Cherif Bassiouni

Web site

Homeland Security
http://www.whitehouse.gov/homeland/
Home page of the United States Office of Homeland Security.

Immigration and Naturalization Service (INS) is a United States government agency that administers and enforces U.S. immigration laws. The agency chiefly regulates the entrance of *aliens* (noncitizens) into the United States and their presence there. A commissioner appointed by the president supervises the agency.

The United States Border Patrol, a part of the INS, helps prevent the illegal entry of aliens. The INS also works to investigate and remove aliens who entered the United States illegally or whose legal stay has ended. In addition, the INS takes part in programs to prevent people from bringing illegal drugs into the United States.

The INS also provides various immigration benefits. It processes visa claims for temporary and permanent workers, and for their immediate family members. The agency also determines the eligibility of aliens who wish to become U.S. citizens and presents those who are eligible to a federal or state court for naturalization.

Congress created the INS in 1891 as part of the Department of Labor. The agency was transferred to the Department of Justice in 1940. The INS grew significantly in the 1990's, when Congress increased funding for border enforcement and personnel.

Many critics of the INS claim that the agency fails to enforce security, maintain accurate records, and process immigration benefits in a timely manner. Calls for reform received much attention following the Sept. 11, 2001, terrorist attacks in New York City and on the Pentagon Building. Several of the terrorists responsible for the attacks were in the United States illegally or had broken the terms of their admittance. In 2002, President George W. Bush proposed moving the INS from the Department of Justice to a newly created Department of Homeland Security.　　B. Lindsay Lowell

Web site

INS Online
http://www.ins.usdoj.gov/graphics/index.htm
Home page of the U.S. Immigration and Naturalization Service (INS).

Intelligence service is an agency that chiefly gathers and evaluates information for a country's political and military leaders. These leaders use the evaluated information, called *intelligence,* to shape military policy, fight wars, and conduct foreign relations.

There are generally two kinds of intelligence services. One kind is a *foreign intelligence service,* which gathers information about foreign countries and institutions, analyzes such information, or both. Such a service may also engage in *covert operations,* in which it secretly tries to influence events in foreign countries. The other type of intelligence service is an *internal security service.* It seeks to neutralize hostile intelligence services operating within the country and detect and stop the activities of terrorist groups.

Intelligence services get information from a variety of sources. Aircraft and artificial satellites produce detailed images. Space, air, and ground systems can monitor electronic signals. Intelligence services also recruit agents in foreign governments and other institutions. In addition, they rely on such "open sources" as books, magazines, newspapers, and TV broadcasts.

In nondemocratic countries, the internal security service often works with the police and other institutions to eliminate dissent and to imprison or kill dissenters. The agency may be part of a larger service that also conducts foreign intelligence operations.

The major United States foreign intelligence services are the Central Intelligence Agency, the Defense Intelligence Agency, the National Imagery and Mapping Agency, the National Reconnaissance Office, and the National Security Agency/Central Security Service. The nation's internal security service is the Federal Bureau of Investigation. In addition, each of the U.S. military services and some government departments operate one or more intelligence organizations.　　Jeffrey T. Richelson

Web sites

Australian Secret Intelligence Service (ASIS)
http://www.asis.gov.au/
Home page of ASIS, Australia's overseas intelligence collection agency.

Britain's Security Services
http://www.five.org.uk/security/security.htm
Information on the United Kingdom's Security Service (MI5), which is responsible for internal security, and the Secret Intelligence Service (MI6), which gathers intelligence overseas.

CSIS
http://www.csis-scrs.gc.ca/
Internet site of the Canadian Security Intelligence Service (CSIS), a government agency dedicated to protecting the national security interests of Canada and safeguarding its citizens.

Justice, Department of, is an executive department of the United States government. It enforces federal laws and provides legal advice for the president and the heads of the government's other executive departments. The attorney general, a member of the president's Cabinet, heads the department and ranks as the government's chief legal officer. The president appoints the attorney general with U.S. Senate approval.

In 2002, President George W. Bush proposed a reorganization of the federal government with an emphasis on protection against terrorism. Under Bush's plan, some of the agencies of the Department of Justice would be transferred to a newly created Department of Homeland Security.

Functions. The Department of Justice investigates and prosecutes violations of federal laws. These laws include antitrust, criminal, environmental, and civil rights laws. The department also administers federal prisons. In addition, it represents the federal government in the U.S. Supreme Court and in other federal courts. A Justice Department official known as the solicitor general supervises this representation in Supreme Court cases.

The seal of the Department of Justice

Important agencies of the Justice Department include the Federal Bureau of Prisons, the Drug Enforcement Administration, the Federal Bureau of Investigation (FBI), and the Immigration and Naturalization Service. The Bureau of Prisons oversees federal prisons and supervises the custody of all federal prisoners. The Drug Enforcement Administration enforces federal laws and regulations that apply to narcotics and other dangerous drugs. The FBI investigates federal crimes and collects evidence in lawsuits that involve the federal government. It also gathers information about individuals and groups that it believes are dangerous to national security. The Immigration and Naturalization Service administers and enforces U.S. immigration laws.

The Department of Justice also includes the Bureau of Justice Statistics and the National Institute of Justice. These agencies support police programs that are designed to prevent and control crime in the United States. The agencies provide this support mainly by researching and analyzing various aspects of crime and the U.S. criminal justice system.

History. Congress set up the office of the Attorney General in 1789. The attorney general served in the Cabinet but did not head an executive department. The attorney general advised the president and represented the federal government in cases before the Supreme Court. Almost every federal department had some part in enforcing national laws. In 1870, Congress set up a new Department of Justice under the attorney general. The new department took over most law-enforcement duties from the other departments.

Critically reviewed by the Department of Justice

Web site

United States Department of Justice Home Page
http://www.usdoj.gov/
Information about the Department of Justice.

National Guard is one of the organizations of the United States Army and Air Force. An outgrowth of the volunteer militia that was first authorized in 1792, the National Guard is a reserve group. Other civilian reserves, such as the Army, Air Force, and naval reserves, have no connection with the National Guard.

Each state, each territory, and the District of Columbia has its own National Guard. The National Guard Bureau of the Department of the Army directs Army units. The Department of the Air Force supervises Air National Guard units. About 350,000 men and women serve in Army units of the National Guard. About 110,000 serve in the Air National Guard.

Members of the National Guard enlist voluntarily and are formed into distinctive units. The Army and Air Force supervise the training of the National Guard. State funds provide armories and other storage facilities. Federal funds provide clothing, weapons, and equipment.

During peacetime, National Guard personnel attend one weekend of training each month. They also receive two weeks of field training every year. The federal government pays them for the time they spend training. About 80,000 members serve full-time to help organize, administer, recruit, and train the National Guard.

Guard members have a *dual status* because they take an oath of allegiance to their state and to the federal government. Until 1903, the state controlled the militia

units. The president had to call units into federal service through the governors of the states. The National Defense Acts of 1920 and 1933 extended federal authority. Since that time, the president may order units to active duty for up to two years upon declaring a national emergency, or for up to six months without declaring a national emergency. State governors may order units to active duty during emergencies, such as strikes, riots, and disasters.   Joel Slackman

Web site

The National Guard
http://www.ngb.dtic.mil/
Official Web site of the United States National Guard.

National Security Agency/Central Security Service is an agency of the United States Department of Defense. The agency has two primary missions: (1) ensuring the security of United States information systems and (2) gathering secret information transmitted by other countries. The agency is responsible for providing centralized coordination, direction, and performance of United States government activities related to these missions. The National Security Agency was established in 1952. The Central Security Service was created in 1972.

Critically reviewed by the National Security Agency/Central Security Service

Web site

National Security Agency
http://www.nsa.gov/
Home page for the National Security Agency/Central Security Service.

National Security Council (NSC) is a part of the Executive Office of the President of the United States. The council serves as an interdepartmental cabinet on defense, foreign policy, and intelligence matters. Members include the president, the vice president, and the secretaries of state and defense.

The NSC advises the president on many security problems. It brings together the departments and agencies most concerned with foreign policy and military matters. The council supervises the Central Intelligence Agency. The president calls meetings of the NSC. If a crisis develops, the president may call the group into immediate session.

The NSC is assisted by a staff headed by the assistant to the president for national security affairs. The staff works with the member departments and agencies to prepare studies and policy papers for the council's action. Congress created the council in 1947.

In 1986, the NSC was criticized for exceeding its authority as an advisory agency. This criticism arose when it was revealed that the NSC staff carried out secret arms sales to Iran and provided the profits to U.S.-supported rebels in Nicaragua. Some legal experts argued that both activities violated federal government policies at the time. In 1987, President Ronald Reagan responded to the criticism by adding a special legal adviser to the staff of the NSC.   Harvey Glickman

Web site

National Security Council
http://www.whitehouse.gov/nsc/index.html
Information on the National Security Council.

Audio Visual Unit, Philadelphia Police Department

Officers on foot patrol

WORLD BOOK photo by Ralph Brunke

Police department communications center

© Bart Bartholomew, Black Star

Patrol officer in squad car

Police

Police are government officers who enforce the law and maintain order. They work to prevent crime and to protect the lives and property of the people of a community. Policemen and policewomen serve their communities in many ways. They patrol streets to guard against crime and to assist people with various problems. Police officers direct traffic to keep it running smoothly and safely. The police are often called to settle quarrels, find lost people, and aid accident victims. During floods, fires, terrorist attacks, and other emergencies, they help provide assistance, transportation, and protection for victims.

The police form part of a nation's *criminal justice system,* which also includes courts and prisons. Police officers enforce *criminal law,* which covers murder, robbery, terrorism, and other crimes that threaten society.

George T. Felkenes, the contributor of this article, is Professor Emeritus of Criminal Justice at Claremont Graduate University and author of The Criminal Justice System.

Police officers investigate such crimes and arrest suspected lawbreakers. They also testify in court trials.

Every nation in the world has a police system. In the United States, there are about 40,000 separate police agencies that operate under city, county, state, or federal governments. In many countries, the national government directs all police operations.

Police officers in the United States are often called *cops.* During the late 1800's, they were called *constables.* The word cop may have come from the initials *c. o. p.,* which stood for *constable on patrol.* Some experts believe *cop* is short for *copper,* a word that referred to the copper badges worn by police officers.

Police activities

Patrol operations are the foundation of police work. Patrol officers are assigned *beats* (areas or routes) to cover on foot, in squad cars, or on motorcycles. In some cities, they patrol parks on horseback.

Patrol officers survey their beats repeatedly. Foot patrol officers carry two-way pocket radios, and patrol cars are equipped with larger two-way radios. Officers may receive assignments over their radios to handle an auto accident, investigate a reported crime, or settle a family

Bomb squad technician

© Andy Levin

Audio Visual Unit, Philadelphia Police Department

Special weapons unit

argument. If necessary, they may call the police station for assistance in handling an assignment. Patrol officers are often assigned to control crowds at parades, fairs, and other public events.

Police officers may arrest a person they see committing a crime. They also may arrest a person if they have reasonable cause to suspect that the person is committing a crime or is about to commit one. But in some cases, police officers are required to get a court order called a *warrant* before making an arrest.

Traffic operations. Traffic officers promote public safety on streets and highways. They direct traffic; protect pedestrians; aid motorists; and enforce parking, speed, and other traffic laws. Traffic officers also investigate traffic accidents and enforce safety and license regulations for motor vehicles. Some police departments use helicopters to survey traffic.

Investigations of crimes are conducted by detectives, who are sometimes called *plainclothes officers* because they do not wear uniforms. In some police departments, the term *plainclothes officers* refers to members of the *vice squad*. The vice squad investigates cases that involve gambling, prostitution, or other illegal activities considered to be immoral.

Detectives work in various specialized fields that deal with such crimes as murder, robbery, or the illegal sale of drugs. In a murder case, detectives may start their investigation by searching for bloodstains, fingerprints, and weapons. They question any witnesses, suspects, or others who may have information about the crime.

Various technical units in a police department assist the detectives in an investigation. The *photography unit* takes pictures of the crime scene and the evidence. The *crime laboratory* collects and examines bloodstains, bullets, hair samples, fingerprints, weapons, and other evidence. Experts in the laboratory may perform chemical tests to identify any unknown substance connected with the crime. The detectives in charge of an investigation supervise the technical units involved. Later, the reports of the detectives and the technical units are used in court.

Criminal intelligence. Some police officers are assigned to gather *intelligence* (information) about the activities of suspected criminals. The women and men who work in the criminal intelligence division of a police department are sometimes called *undercover agents.* They gather information on such criminal operations as large-scale gambling, the illegal sale of drugs, and terrorist activity. The reports of intelligence officers are used in planning ways to fight criminal activities.

Juvenile work. Officers in the juvenile division of a police department handle cases involving youths accused of breaking the law. In most states of the United States, anyone under the age of 18 is considered a juvenile. Juvenile officers often refer young people to social agencies rather than bring criminal charges against them in a court. These officers try to help the young people and their parents with personal problems. They also investigate crimes that involve the neglect or abuse of young children. The officers may testify in court to protect the rights of the youngsters. In addition, juvenile officers often work with young people in community programs.

Records and communications. The records bureau of a police department keeps files on all reported crimes, investigations, and arrests, and on various police activities. Many police departments use computers to process and store these records.

The communications center is another important unit of a police department. Its *central dispatch office* receives calls for help or reports of crimes and sends officers to the scene. Many larger police agencies use computers in this operation. When a report of a crime or a call for help comes into the central dispatch office, the information is typed on the *terminal* of a computer. A terminal is an electronic keyboard that can both receive and send information. A dispatch officer reviews the problem and sends the information to one or more available patrol cars. The patrol officers receive the assignment over terminals in their cars.

Other activities. Large police agencies have various specialized units, including *search-and-rescue teams, hostage negotiating teams, bomb squads, special weapons units,* and *computer crime specialists.* Most members of such units work at other assignments until their special skills are needed. Some medium-sized and large police departments also have data processing and research offices.

Search-and-rescue teams try to find persons lost in forests, mountains, caves, or other out-of-the-way places. Members of these teams are trained in rock climbing, mountain survival, and other skills. They often use helicopters and airplanes in rescue missions.

Hostage-negotiating teams handle cases in which criminals hold people captive. During some crimes, including bank robberies and airplane hijackings, the criminals may take innocent people as hostages. They threaten to injure or kill the hostages if certain demands are not met. Members of the hostage-negotiating team try to persuade the criminals to release the hostages without harm. Team members are skilled in psychology and personal relations.

Bomb squads respond to reports of bomb threats. They search the building or other place where a bomb supposedly has been planted. If they find a bomb, they try to prevent it from exploding or move it to a place where it cannot damage property or injure people.

Special weapons units handle dangerous situations involving armed criminals. Members of these units are skilled in the use of high-powered rifles and other weapons. They know how to surround and capture criminals with the least possible danger to others. Special weapons units are often called *S.W.A.T.* teams. Those letters stand for *S*pecial *W*eapons and *T*actics or *S*pecial *W*eapons *A*ttack *T*eam.

Data processing and research offices perform a variety of services. These offices may be staffed by police officers or by private citizens. Staff members compile crime statistics to help identify high-crime areas. They also prepare reports on personnel needs. In addition, they research new investigation techniques.

Computer crime specialists fight crimes that are committed with computers. Such crimes include embezzlement by bank employees and others who have access to their employers' computer systems. Computer crime experts also may work to prevent fraud and other criminal activities on the global computer network known as the Internet.

Police in the United States

In the United States, police agencies operate under the city, county, state, and federal governments. Each agency is responsible only to its own division of government. Private police agencies are licensed by the states to provide certain types of police services.

City police. The size of a city police force depends on the size and needs of the community. New York City has the largest city police department in the United States—about 29,000 police officers. A small town may have a police force of only one or two officers.

City police are mainly responsible for enforcing the law in their own city. In some states, city police may exercise police powers in other communities only under special circumstances. In other states, city police may exercise police powers throughout the state. A few communities have combined their city and county police forces into a single *metropolitan police* force.

Some city police departments have specialized forces with certain limited powers. These specialized forces include airport police, housing police, park police, and transit police.

In most cities, the mayor appoints the head of the police department. This official may have the title of *chief, commissioner, director,* or *superintendent.* Other ranking police officers include *inspectors, lieutenant colonels, majors, captains, lieutenants,* and *sergeants.*

County police. The powers of a county police force extend throughout the county. In some states, however, these powers are restricted in towns and cities that have their own force. A *sheriff,* elected by the people, is the chief law enforcement officer in most counties. In some states, the sheriff's department provides police services on a contract basis to cities and towns that lie within the county.

The duties and powers of the sheriff's department vary from county to county. In some counties, the sheriff takes charge of prisoners in the county jails, attends sessions of the county court, and carries out court rulings in matters of *civil law.* Civil law covers such matters as business disputes and the transfer of property. In other counties, the sheriff's department may also conduct full-scale police operations and provide training and technical services to city police.

State police. Every state except Hawaii has either a state police force or a state highway patrol force. The powers of these forces vary from state to state. Both types of agencies are headed by a commissioner or superintendent appointed by the governor. Hawaii has only county police forces.

State police enforce state laws. They also may coordinate police activities within the state and provide technical services and training programs to city and county police departments. State police officers are sometimes called *troopers* because they were originally organized along military lines and often rode horses. Most state highway patrol forces have the primary duty of enforcing highway and motor vehicle regulations. Some also conduct full-scale police operations.

Federal law enforcement agencies include the Federal Bureau of Investigation (FBI). The FBI is the chief investigating branch of the United States Department of Justice. It investigates federal crimes and handles cases involving stolen money or property that has been taken from one state to another. The FBI also operates the National Crime Information Center (NCIC) in Washington, D.C. The NCIC is a computerized information system that stores records on wanted persons and stolen property. Police departments in every state are linked with the NCIC through local terminals and may obtain information at any time.

Nine other major federal law enforcement agencies also have full police powers. They are the Bureau of Alcohol, Tobacco, and Firearms; the Drug Enforcement Administration; the Immigration and Naturalization Service; the Internal Revenue Service; the Postal Inspection Service; the United States Coast Guard; the United States Customs Service; the United States Marshals Service; and the United States Secret Service.

The Department of Justice also includes the Bureau of Justice Statistics and the National Institute of Justice. These offices do not enforce laws, but they support police programs aimed at preventing and controlling crime. They do this mainly through research and analysis of various aspects of crime and the criminal justice system.

Private police agencies are licensed by the states to

Police around the world

© Art Brown

China

© Owen Franken, Stock Boston

France

© Marc & Evelyne Bernheim,
Woodfin Camp, Inc.

Ghana

© Odyssey Productions

Mexico

perform limited types of police work. *Industrial security police* guard factories and warehouses. *Campus police* protect the people and property of colleges and universities. *Private investigative agencies* provide detective services to individuals and businesses.

Police around the world

In many countries, the national government directs the police system and maintains a national police force.

In Canada. Canada has national, provincial, and city police forces. The Royal Canadian Mounted Police (RCMP) enforces federal laws throughout Canada. It serves as a provincial police force in all provinces except Ontario and Quebec, which have their own forces. The RCMP is the only police force in the Yukon Territory, the Northwest Territories, and Nunavut. The RCMP

Royal Canadian Mounted Police
The Royal Canadian Mounted Police enforces federal laws throughout Canada. This officer is checking the driver's license of a motorist she has stopped for a traffic violation.

provides police services on a contract basis to about 175 cities.

Members of the RCMP are traditionally called "mounties," though they now ride horses only in special ceremonies. For their daily assignments, they travel in cars, snowmobiles, helicopters, and other vehicles.

In other countries. In the United Kingdom, the police system is organized into about 50 large forces that are connected with local governments. These forces operate under the direction of the national government. The London Metropolitan Police serve Greater London except for an area that is called the City of London, which has its own force. The headquarters of the Metropolitan Police is called New Scotland Yard. The name *Scotland Yard* is often used to refer to the Criminal Investigation Department of the Metropolitan Police.

In Australia, each of the six states and two mainland territories has a police force. Australia also has a national police force, the Commonwealth Police Force.

In France, the national law enforcement agency is the Sûreté Nationale. The Sûreté Nationale forms part of the Ministry of the Interior. Police officers called *gendarmes* serve as military police and provide police services in rural areas.

In Germany, the police are organized under the individual states. The states also maintain stand-by police who assist the state police when necessary.

In Russia, the Ministry of Internal Affairs (MVD) is in charge of providing general police services. It also provides border guards and investigates activities considered a threat to the security of the national government.

In China, a national police force called the People's Police is directed locally by provincial public security bureaus. These bureaus function under the Ministry of Public Security, an agency of the national government.

Interpol is an international organization of police forces from almost all countries. Its official name is the *Inte*rnational Criminal *Pol*ice Organization. Members of Interpol exchange information about international crimi-

© Photoworld, Getty Images

Bobbies stand guard outside a royal wedding in London in 1923. British police were nicknamed *bobbies* after Sir Robert Peel, who founded the first modern type of police force in 1829.

nals and cooperate in fighting such international crimes as counterfeiting, smuggling, and illegal buying and selling of weapons. The headquarters of Interpol are in the city of Lyon in France.

History

In a large number of ancient societies, the military forces served as police. In ancient Rome, for example, the military legions of the rulers enforced the law. Augustus, who became emperor in 27 B.C., formed a non-military police force called the *vigiles*. The vigiles were responsible for keeping the peace and fighting fires in Rome.

Early law enforcement in England. During the A.D. 800's, England developed a system of law enforcement based on citizen responsibility. The people of a community were divided into *tithings* (groups of 10 families), and each tithing was responsible for the conduct of its members. Males more than 16 years old stood watch duty. When a serious crime occurred, all able-bodied men joined in a *hue and cry* (chase of the suspect). Each *shire* (county) was headed by a *reeve* (chief). The word *sheriff* is a shortened form of *shire reeve.*

In 1750, Henry Fielding, a London *magistrate* (judge) and author, organized a group of law enforcement officers called the Bow Street Runners. These officers ran to the scene of a crime to capture the criminal and begin an investigation.

Sir Robert Peel, a British statesman, founded the London Metropolitan Police in 1829. The force was established along military lines, and its officers were carefully selected and trained. The public called the officers *bobbies,* after Sir Robert, and they still have that nickname.

Peel is regarded as the father of modern police organizations.

Law and order in America. The American colonists established the English watch system in the towns and villages of New England. In many colonial areas, sheriffs and constables were responsible for keeping the peace.

Later, on the Western frontier, sheriffs and marshals enforced the law. But citizens sometimes formed groups of self-appointed law officers called *vigilantes* to capture and punish outlaws. The Texas Rangers, a band of mounted riflemen organized in the early 1800's, were the first form of state police. They fought Indians, patrolled the Mexican border, and tracked down cattle rustlers and other outlaws. In 1905, Pennsylvania established the first state police force.

In 1845, New York City combined its separate day and night watches into a single city police force modeled after the London Metropolitan Police. Other U.S. cities formed similar police forces during the following years.

Many early city police departments were poorly organized. Officers were underpaid and got little training. In many communities, city leaders gained control of the police. They used the police in conducting their political campaigns and for other personal purposes.

During the early 1900's, August Vollmer, the police chief of Berkeley, California, gained fame as a police reformer. Vollmer brought about many changes in the police system. He urged reorganization of police departments, college education for police officers, and the use of scientific methods in police work.

Today, most medium-sized and large police departments hire officers through the civil service process. In this way, officers are not subject to political influence.

In the United States since the mid-1900's, riots have broken out from time to time in a number of cities. In some of these uprisings, especially in the 1960's and 1970's, African Americans rioted in anger at their poor living conditions and few job opportunities. In other cases, the rioters were college students who opposed various policies of the government or of their schools. In trying to control the rioters, the police were sometimes charged with using unnecessary force. In later years, a number of riots were triggered by incidents in which the police were believed to have used excessive force in dealing with individual members of minority groups. As a result of these events, hostility toward police officers sometimes has became widespread, especially among minorities. These groups have accused the police of treating them unfairly and giving them poor protection in their neighborhoods.

In an effort to improve their relations with citizens and to reduce crime, some police departments have developed or expanded community relations and crime prevention programs. Police officers meet with neighborhood residents and civic organizations to discuss problems and explain police services. Neighborhood police teams have been established to bring the police into closer contact with neighborhood residents. These teams of police officers patrol specific neighborhoods and investigate all crimes there. In some areas, special juvenile gang units focus on preventing gang membership, identifying gang members, and stopping illegal gang activities.

The police also encourage citizens to help fight crime.

In some communities, citizen volunteers organize patrols to guard housing projects and homes. Other communities organize Neighborhood Watch programs in which residents report any suspicious activities in their neighborhood to the police. Many police departments have employed more nonpolice personnel to handle such police duties as traffic control and dispatching. The use of these employees has enabled the departments to assign more police officers to the fight against crime.

Since 1970, the number of women entering police work has increased substantially. Also, police departments now assign female officers to patrol duty and crime investigation. Formerly, female police officers served chiefly as office workers, as juvenile officers, and as guards in women's prisons. Police agencies also have made more of an effort to hire more members of minority groups as police officers.

Investigations of several city police departments since 1970 have revealed cases of police corruption. Some officers have been found guilty of taking bribes and committing other crimes. As a result of these investigations, police leaders have stressed the need to maintain high standards in hiring recruits, to provide the best possible training for officers, and to promote professional integrity throughout the police department.

Careers

Police work offers many opportunities to help people and to serve a community. However, it can be dangerous and sometimes requires working irregular hours.

The requirements for applicants for positions with police agencies vary among the cities and states. The minimum age requirement for police work varies from 18 to 21. Some police agencies have a maximum entry-level age of 35. Candidates must pass a thorough physical examination, be honest and even-tempered, and have good judgment and a sense of responsibility. Most police agencies require that candidates obtain a high school education, and many require some college training. Applicants must pass a written examination. Some police agencies require officers to live and work in the same community.

Recruits attend police academies connected with the city, county, or state police agencies. Training periods vary from 6 weeks to a year. Recruits study such subjects as law, psychology, sociology, traffic control, weapons, and rules of evidence. Many police agencies also require recruits to spend a period with a field training officer in a squad car before going on duty alone.

Numerous police agencies have continuing education programs to keep officers informed of changes in the law and new techniques in police work. Some agencies offer the benefit of paying the cost of a college education for officers who wish to acquire this schooling.

George T. Felkenes

Outline

I. **Police activities**
   A. Patrol operations
   B. Traffic operations
   C. Investigations of crimes
   D. Criminal intelligence
   E. Juvenile work
   F. Records and communications
   G. Other activities

AP/Wide World

Security checkpoints were set up in New York City's financial district after the September 11 terrorist attacks. A member of the National Guard and a police officer check identifications, *above.*

II. **Police in the United States**
   A. City police
   B. County police
   C. State police
   D. Federal law enforcement
   E. Private police agencies
III. **Police around the world**
   A. In Canada
   B. In other countries
   C. Interpol
IV. **History**
V. **Careers**

Questions

How is the police system in the United States organized?
What are the duties of patrol officers? Traffic officers?
How do citizen volunteers help the police prevent crime?
What does the Royal Canadian Mounted Police do?
How do photography units, ballistics squads, and crime laboratories assist detectives?
What is Interpol?
Why are London Metropolitan Police officers called *bobbies?*
What is the National Crime Information Center?
Who was August Vollmer? How did he help reform police departments in the United States?
What are S.W.A.T. teams?

Additional resources

Level I
Kronenwetter, Michael. *The FBI and Law Enforcement Agencies of the United States.* Enslow, 1997.
Miller, Maryann. *Everything You Need to Know About Dealing with the Police.* Rosen Pub. Group, 1995.
Roden, Katie. *Solving International Crime.* Copper Beech, 1996.
Wirths, Claudine G. *Choosing a Career in Law Enforcement.* Rosen Pub. Group, 1997.

Level II
Bayley, David H. *Police for the Future.* Oxford, 1994.
Cohen, Paul and Shari. *Careers in Law Enforcement and Security.* Rev. ed. Rosen Pub. Group, 1995.
Das, Dilip K., ed. *Police Practices: An International Review.* Scarecrow, 1994.

Reiner, Robert, ed. *Policing.* 2 vols. Dartmouth Pub., 1996.

Web site

NYPD
http://www.ci.nyc.ny.us/html/nypd/home.html
Official New York City Police Department Web site.

Secret Service, United States, is a bureau of the U.S. Department of the Treasury. Its primary job is to protect the president, the president's immediate family, and certain other government officials. The Secret Service also investigates the counterfeiting of certain U.S. government identification documents and U.S. and foreign currency, securities, and stamps; fraudulent use of false identification documents; the theft or forgery of U.S. government checks and bonds; and major fraud cases involving computers, automatic teller machines, telecommunications, electronic fund transfers, credit cards, or *debit cards.* Debit cards are used to charge purchases directly to a bank account.

Congress created the Secret Service in 1865 to fight the counterfeiting of U.S. currency. The service began protecting the president in 1901, after the assassination of President William McKinley.

Critically reviewed by the United States Secret Service

Spy is a person who tries to get secret information, especially about the enemy in time of war. A spy usually does so by operating in the enemy's territory in disguise. Spies seek valuable military, political, scientific, and economic facts and secrets. They sometimes operate under legal cover as diplomats, commercial representatives, or journalists. Countries use *counterspies* to prevent theft of information. Counterspies called *double agents* pretend to spy for an organization but actually spy against it. The punishment for wartime spying usually is death. The United States and many other nations have laws making peacetime spying punishable by death as well. In the United States, the first law to establish specific punishments for spying was the Defense Secrets Act of 1911.   Douglas L. Wheeler

Transportation Security Administration is a United States government agency responsible for protecting the nation's transportation systems. It aims to ensure the continued freedom of movement for people and commerce in the United States. The agency, sometimes called the TSA, works to prevent criminal acts involving aircraft, airports, bridges, highways, pipelines, ports, and railways. The TSA is part of the U.S. Department of Transportation.

On Sept. 11, 2001, terrorists hijacked four commercial airplanes and deliberately crashed two into the World Trade Center in New York City and one into the Pentagon Building near Washington, D.C. The fourth hijacked plane crashed in a field in Pennsylvania. About 3,000 people died in the attacks. In November 2001, Congress passed the Aviation and Transportation Security Act (ATSA). The act established the TSA and introduced new security measures to prevent future attacks against the nation's transportation system.

Critically reviewed by the Transportation Security Administration.

Wiretapping usually means the interception of telephone conversations by a listening device connected to the telephone wire or placed nearby. The message may be heard live, or it may be recorded or transmitted to another location.

Wiretapping is sometimes used in an investigative procedure called *audio surveillance.* The term *wiretapping* sometimes refers to the use of any electrical or electronic device to eavesdrop on private conversations. But the interception of nontelephone conversations is usually called *bugging* or *electronic eavesdropping.*

Sophisticated methods and devices allow eavesdropping in nearly any situation. Some types of microphones may be attached to a wall or door so that conversations can be overheard through the partition. Directional microphones may be beamed or focused to pick up conversations from long distances. Even greater distances can be overcome by concealed miniature microphones and transmitters that send messages to a radio receiver.

In most countries, the right of people to speak freely in their homes and businesses and in public places—without fear of eavesdroppers—is considered extremely important. Many nations, states, and provinces have passed laws restricting or prohibiting various types of electronic surveillance. But much illegal eavesdropping continues, both by individuals and by governments.

In the United States, the problem of wiretapping and electronic eavesdropping has become a confusing and controversial legal issue. There is much disagreement about (1) the constitutionality of electronic surveillance by law enforcement agencies and (2) methods of controlling government eavesdropping if it is permitted. However, many Americans oppose wiretapping and bugging by either governments or private individuals.

The wiretapping controversy began in 1928, when the Supreme Court of the United States ruled that wiretapping did not violate the Fourth Amendment to the Constitution. This amendment sets forth restrictions on search and seizure. In 1934, Congress passed the Federal Communications Act, which prohibits the interception and public disclosure of any wire or radio communication. On the basis of this law, the Supreme Court ruled in 1937 that evidence obtained by wiretapping cannot be used in a federal court. Following this ruling, federal officials argued that the 1934 law did not prohibit wiretapping by the government so long as the evidence was not used in court. Since 1940, U.S. presidents have claimed constitutional power to order wiretaps in matters of national security.

In 1968, Congress passed a law permitting federal, state, and local government agencies to use wiretapping and bugging devices in certain crime investigations. Before undertaking such surveillance, an agency would have to obtain a court order. The law stated that nothing in it was intended to limit the president's constitutional authority to order wiretapping without court warrants in national security cases.

In the late 1960's and early 1970's, the executive branch broadly interpreted the national security provisions of the 1968 law. It conducted electronic surveillance without court approval on a number of domestic radicals it considered subversive. In 1972, the Supreme Court ruled that such surveillance without a court warrant was unconstitutional. Also in 1972, wiretapping of the Democratic Party's national headquarters became a main issue in the Watergate Scandal. Members of a committee working for the reelection of President Richard M. Nixon, a Republican, were involved in this wiretapping.   George T. Felkenes

Focus on
TERRORISM

Section Six

Terrorism and a Free Society

The attacks of September 11 raised a number of questions about the relationship between security and civil rights in a free society. The first part of this section provides a look at the tension between the need for security and the exercise of civil rights throughout U.S. history, especially in the aftermath of September 11. The second part of this section (beginning on p. 140) consists of a collection of *World Book* articles that deal with civil rights.

AP/Wide World

Inland detention camps held thousands of U.S. residents of Japanese descent during World War II (1939-1945). The establishment of the camps followed the Japanese attack on Pearl Harbor.

AP/Wide World

Camp X-Ray, a U.S. prison camp at Guantánamo Bay, Cuba, began holding Taliban and al-Qa'ida detainees from the war in Afghanistan that followed the terrorist attacks of Sept. 11, 2001.

A Delicate Balance:
Security and Civil Rights in Times of Crisis

Following the terrorist attacks of September 11, 2001, on the World Trade Center in New York City and the Pentagon Building near Washington, D.C., President George W. Bush addressed Congress and a grieving nation. He described the challenges facing the United States: "Tonight we are a country awakened to danger and called to defend freedom. Our grief has turned to anger, and anger to resolution. ... I know there are struggles ahead and dangers to face. But this country will define our times, not be defined by them."

The challenges of the war against terrorism are many. One of the most significant is the need to provide effective national security while respecting the rights of citizens of and visitors to the United States. The government's ability to prevent terrorist attacks depends largely on its ability to intercept communication to and from terrorist suspects, to search individuals for weapons and dangerous materials, and to investigate and detain suspected terrorists. However, many of these steps require the people in the United States to sacrifice a certain degree of freedom and privacy.

William H. Rehnquist, chief justice of the Supreme Court of the United States, once wrote, "Generally, chief executives in wartime are not very sympathetic to the protection of civil liberties." At various points throughout history, the same has been said of both the United States Congress and the Supreme Court. Although temporary sacrifices of certain liberties may be necessary to maintain the nation's security, a word of caution comes to us from one of America's founders. Benjamin

Bruce Allen Murphy, the contributor of this article, is Fred Morgan Kirby Professor of Civil Rights at Lafayette College.

Franklin, in 1759, wrote that "they that can give up essential liberty to purchase a little temporary safety, deserve neither liberty nor safety."

This article explores past and present attempts to find a proper balance between civil rights and national security during times of crisis.

Examples throughout history

In the more than two centuries since the framing of the U.S. Constitution, the U.S. government has at times operated under the Roman rule of *Inter arma silent leges,* which means, *In time of war, the laws are silent.* In other words, in times of crisis, government policies have often emphasized security at the expense of liberty. But in most cases, such policies have been scaled back or ended once the crisis has passed.

The Alien and Sedition Acts. In 1798, as the United States prepared for an expected war with France, Congress passed a series of laws known as the Alien and Sedition Acts. One of the laws, the Alien Enemies Act, authorized the president to imprison or deport citizens of enemy nations. The Alien Friends Act permitted citizens of friendly nations to be deported if the president considered them dangerous. The Sedition Act was used to fine or imprison people who encouraged resistance to federal laws or who criticized the government. By passing the acts, the Federalist Party, which controlled Congress at the time, hoped to silence their political opponents. But many people objected to the acts, and after the Democratic-Republican Party beat the Federalists in the election of 1800, the laws were no longer enforced. Still, the precedent for limiting rights during times of crisis had been established.

During the American Civil War (1861-1865), President Abraham Lincoln authorized the establishment of *martial law*—that is, a temporary, emergency form of government under military rule—in parts of the North. He also suspended the right known as *habeas corpus* in many cases involving Southern sympathizers. Habeas corpus guarantees a person under arrest a chance to be heard in court. The Supreme Court later ruled that the suspension of habeas corpus was unconstitutional.

Also during the Civil War, the Union Army used military commissions to try people accused of creating civil disorder that aided the Confederacy. The government also used a military commission to try several people believed to have been involved in Lincoln's assassination. One year after the Civil War ended, the Supreme Court ruled that trials of civilians by military courts were not constitutional if civilian courts were open and operating at the time.

During World War I (1914-1918), President Woodrow Wilson's administration prosecuted people who spoke out against the draft and the war. The Espionage Act of 1917 and the Sedition Act of 1918 forbade speech and publications that interfered with the war effort. The prosecutions led to a series of court rulings that limited First Amendment protections during wartime. In the landmark Supreme Court ruling of *Schenck v. United States* (1919), Justice Oliver Wendell Holmes created the "clear and present danger" test. Under the test, speech could be restricted in cases where there was a "clear and present danger" that it would bring about "substantive evils that Congress has a right to prevent."

In the years following World War I, U.S. Attorney General A. Mitchell Palmer led an extensive surveillance effort against radical groups in the United States. In the Palmer Raids of 1920, thousands of suspected anarchists and Communists were jailed with little regard for their constitutional rights.

During World War II (1939-1945), following the Japanese attack on Pearl Harbor on Dec. 7, 1941, the U.S. government became increasingly concerned about suspected traitors, spies, and terrorists within the United States. In 1942, the government moved about 110,000 West Coast residents of Japanese descent to inland detention camps. The Supreme Court, after initially upholding the program, eventually ruled that the government must release internees who could prove that they were loyal to the country.

Also during World War II, a military commission investigated and sentenced to death eight German marines who had landed on U.S. shores from submarines. The Supreme Court upheld the use of military trials in this case.

The Smith Act, also called the Alien Registration Act of 1940, made it a crime to advocate the violent overthrow of the U.S. government or to belong knowingly to a group advocating such action. By the 1950's, the Smith Act was used to prosecute Communists, even if they had not personally advocated the overthrow of the U.S. government. Although the Supreme Court originally upheld the law, it later ruled that accused Communists must be shown to advocate "concrete action" instead of just "abstract doctrine." In 1969, the court reinterpreted the "clear and present danger" test so that the state must show that the accused's speech was "directed to inciting

or producing imminent lawless action" and was "likely to incite or produce such action."

During the Vietnam War (1957-1975), protests against the war and of the military draft were frequent, passionate, and sometimes violent. The government responded by using law enforcement and national guard troops to contain the protests. In addition, government agencies, including the Federal Bureau of Investigation (FBI), began keeping track of protest organizers and attendees. In some cases, the government tapped people's telephones, sometimes without a warrant. Despite these abuses, a growing number of Americans exercised their right to protest. The protests eventually influenced government policy and helped lead to the U.S. withdrawal from the conflict.

Security efforts in the war against terrorism

Since the events of September 11, the Bush administration has taken a number of steps aimed at bringing terrorists to justice and at preventing future acts of terrorism. But, as in past cases, many of the government's policies have required significant limitations of civil rights and have led to heated criticism from civil rights activists.

The U.S.A. Patriot Act, also called the Uniting and Strengthening America by Providing Appropriate Tools Required to Intercept and Obstruct Terrorism Act, was passed in October 2001. The act broadens the definition of terrorists to include anyone who has supported a terrorist group, even if the aid had nothing to do with terrorism. The act also gives law enforcement the power to detain for seven days—or, in some cases, indefinitely—any noncitizen suspected of being a risk to national security. One of the act's most controversial provisions grants authorities greater freedom to conduct searches, in some cases without giving notice to the subject of the search. Other provisions allow authorities to share secret grand jury information and to obtain information from wiretaps.

AP/Wide World

Demonstrations against the Vietnam War were widespread, and they significantly influenced U.S. government policy. This picture shows protesters marching in New York City in 1969.

Detentions and military trials. The terrorists who carried out the September 11 attacks were all Arabs with ties to al-Qa'ida, a terrorist organization headed by the Saudi-born millionaire Osama bin Laden. Al-Qa'ida had a number of training camps in Afghanistan, and bin Laden himself lived there, supported by Afghanistan's Islamic extremist Taliban regime.

Following the attacks of September 11, the U.S. government detained more than 1,000 individuals indefinitely. The government refused to disclose the identities of those being held in custody.

As part of its investigations, the U.S. government also asked several thousand foreign visitors of Arab descent to appear for interviews with the Justice Department and immigration officials. The purpose of the interview process was to find evidence and information that could be used in the war against terrorism.

In October 2001, a coalition of military forces led by the United States began bombing Afghanistan in an attempt to drive the Taliban from power and to destroy al-Qa'ida operations there. In November 2001, President Bush issued an executive order establishing a system of military tribunals to try noncitizens suspected of terrorism. By using military trials, with military judges and fewer defendants' rights, the president hoped that justice could be made swifter and more secure. In January 2002, the first Taliban and al-Qa'ida detainees from the war in Afghanistan arrived at Camp X-Ray, a prison camp at the U.S. naval base at Guantánamo Bay, Cuba. The detainees were to be subject to questioning and possible trial by military tribunals.

Criticisms. A number of people have questioned some of the steps taken in the war on terrorism. For example, many people have charged that the U.S.A. Patriot Act threatens individuals' privacy and civil rights. The detention of noncitizens for an indefinite period and without releasing their names has led some to raise questions of whether the detainees were being denied "due process of law," as guaranteed by the Fifth Amendment to the U.S. Constitution. Because the requests to foreign visitors in the United States to report for interviews with the Justice Department and immigration officials were directed to people of Arab descent, many groups accused the government of *racial profiling.* Racial profiling involves targeting people for investigation primarily because of racial or ethnic characteristics rather than because there is *probable cause* (good reason for assuming) that the people committed a crime. Many people also criticized the decision to create military tribunals, again partly because of the possible denial of due process, including the right of appeal.

In December 2001, Attorney General John D. Ashcroft responded to critics of administration policies. He stated: "To those … who scare peace-loving people with phantoms of lost liberty, my message is this: Your tactics only aid terrorists, for they erode our national unity and diminish our resolve." Ashcroft's statement drew harsh criticism from many free-speech advocates.

Determining the proper balance

As the United States faces the challenge of rooting out, combating, and bringing to justice the perpetrators of terrorist violence, the government hopes to make use of sweeping new powers of law enforcement. But as the campaign against terrorism plays out, the Bush administration will need to address a number of important questions: What happens when there is no formal declaration of war? For how long will the American public continue to accept the personal sacrifices required by government investigations and security procedures? At what point will the crisis be declared over, and for how long will antiterrorist security measures remain in effect? The government's policies during this time will likely become the benchmark by which future administrations will measure their own policies.

Bruce Allen Murphy

Bill of rights is a document that describes the fundamental liberties of the people. It also forbids the government to violate these rights. The constitutions of many democratic countries have bills of rights that guarantee everyone the freedoms of speech, of religion, and of the press, and the right of assembly.

Individuals are considered to be born with certain *inalienable rights*—that is, rights that governments may not take away from them. These rights are considered part of a "higher law," a body of universal principles of right and justice that is superior to laws created by governments. Some of these rights, such as the freedoms of speech and of the press, support democracy. Others, such as the right to trial by jury, are essential to justice.

Many of these ideas were developed in ancient Greek and Roman civilizations. In modern history, such individuals as the philosophers John Locke and John Stuart Mill, the writers John Milton and Thomas Paine, and the statesmen Thomas Jefferson and James Madison fought for the acceptance of these views.

The United States Constitution, adopted in 1788, contained few personal guarantees. James Madison led in the adoption of 10 amendments that became known as the *Bill of Rights.* The bill came into effect on Dec. 15, 1791. This day is celebrated as Bill of Rights Day.

The first 8 amendments contain the fundamental rights and freedoms of every citizen. The 9th Amendment forbids the government to limit freedoms and rights that are not listed in the Constitution. The 10th Amendment limits the powers of the federal government to those that are granted to it in the Constitution.

The U.S. Supreme Court decides if a law restricts any liberties listed in, or implied by, the Bill of Rights. However, it has not stated exactly which rights are implied. The Supreme Court has held that under the 14th Amendment most of the Bill of Rights also applies to state governments.

The freedoms and rights of individuals, however, are not without limits. For example, freedom of speech does not protect a person who shouts "Fire" in a crowded theater when there is no fire. The Supreme Court has held that freedom of speech may be limited only when its exercise creates a "clear and present danger" to society.

State constitutions. Each state constitution contains a bill of rights or declaration of rights. Some state bills of rights are more extensive than the federal bill of rights. Virginia adopted the first state bill of rights in 1776.

Canada's constitution includes a bill of rights called the *Canadian Charter of Rights and Freedoms.* The charter took effect on April 17, 1982. Previously, Canada had a bill of rights that applied only to areas under federal jurisdiction and did not bind provincial governments.

United States Bill of Rights

Amendment 1

Congress shall make no law respecting an establishment of religion, or prohibiting the free exercise thereof; or abridging the freedom of speech, or of the press; or the right of the people peaceably to assemble, and to petition the government for a redress of grievances.

Amendment 2

A well-regulated militia, being necessary to the security of a free state, the right of the people to keep and bear arms shall not be infringed.

Amendment 3

No soldier shall, in time of peace, be quartered in any house without the consent of the owner; nor in time of war but in a manner to be prescribed by law.

Amendment 4

The right of the people to be secure in their persons, houses, papers and effects, against unreasonable searches and seizures, shall not be violated, and no warrants shall issue but upon probable cause, supported by oath or affirmation, and particularly describing the place to be searched, and the persons or things to be seized.

Amendment 5

No person shall be held to answer for a capital or otherwise infamous crime, unless on a presentment or indictment of a grand jury, except in cases arising in the land or naval forces, or in the militia, when in actual service in time of war or public danger; nor shall any person be subject for the same offense to be twice put in jeopardy of life or limb; nor shall be compelled in any criminal case to be a witness against himself, nor be de-

prived of life, liberty, or property, without due process of law; nor shall private property be taken for public use, without just compensation.

Amendment 6

In all criminal prosecutions the accused shall enjoy the right to a speedy and public trial, by an impartial jury of the state and district wherein the crime shall have been committed, which district shall have been previously ascertained by law, and to be informed of the nature and cause of the accusation; to be confronted with the witnesses against him; to have compulsory process for obtaining witnesses in his favor, and to have the assistance of counsel for his defense.

Amendment 7

In suits at common law, where the value in controversy shall exceed twenty dollars, the right of trial by jury shall be preserved, and no fact tried by a jury shall be otherwise reexamined in any court of the United States than according to the rules of the common law.

Amendment 8

Excessive bail shall not be required, nor excessive fines imposed, nor cruel and unusual punishments inflicted.

Amendment 9

The enumeration in the Constitution of certain rights shall not be construed to deny or disparage others retained by the people.

Amendment 10

The powers not delegated to the United States by the Constitution, nor prohibited by it to the states, are reserved to the states respectively, or to the people.

The charter guarantees freedom of speech, religion, assembly, and other basic rights. It also guarantees democratic government and bans discrimination based on race, ethnic or national background, color, religion, age, sex, or mental or physical disability.

The charter establishes the right of every Canadian citizen to move freely from one province to another and guarantees other mobility rights. It declares that English and French are the official languages of Canada and have equal status in Parliament, the courts, and the government of Canada. All of the rights in the Canadian Charter of Rights and Freedoms are guaranteed equally to men and women.

A key provision of the charter centers on minority language educational rights. Under this provision, English- and French-speaking parents can have their children educated, "where numbers warrant," in their own language. Officials of the province of Quebec oppose the minority language provision. They argue that it restricts the province's power over education and its ability to preserve the French culture. The majority of Quebec's people by far are of French descent, and they prefer that

most children there be educated in French.

The charter's protections extend to citizens in all of Canada's provinces and territories. A clause in the charter allows Parliament and the provincial legislatures to pass laws overriding certain rights that are guaranteed. However, such laws must be renewed every five years.

English Bill of Rights. In 1689, Parliament presented to King William III and Queen Mary a declaration that became known as the *Bill of Rights*. It stands with Magna Carta and the Petition of Right as the legal guarantees of English liberty. The Bill of Rights listed certain rights that were the "true, ancient, and indubitable rights and liberties of the people" of the English kingdom. It settled the succession to the throne, and limited the powers of the king in such matters as taxation and keeping up a standing army.

In 2000, the United Kingdom (U.K.) began enforcing the Human Rights Act of 1998. This act incorporates into U.K. law most of the European Convention for the Protection of Human Rights and Fundamental Freedoms. The European Convention is an international agreement on human rights that was signed by members of the Council of Europe in 1950. By including provisions of the convention in a law of its own, the United Kingdom provided U.K. citizens with a specific list of freedoms similar to those in the United States Bill of Rights.

French bill of rights. The French adopted the Declaration of the Rights of Man and of the Citizen in 1789. This document attempted to define the revolutionary

Topic for study

Following the attacks of September 2001, the U.S. Congress passed the USA Patriot Act. Discuss the main provisions of the act and any controversies surrounding them.

war cry of "Liberty, Equality, Fraternity." It guarantees religious freedom, freedom of speech and of the press, and personal security. This bill of rights has been added to the French Constitution.

The United Nations General Assembly adopted the Universal Declaration of Human Rights on Dec. 10, 1948. The declaration asserts that all persons are equal in dignity and rights, and have the right to life, liberty, and security. It also lists certain social and cultural rights.

Barry Cooper and Peter Woll

Web sites

Bill of Rights
http://www.nara.gov/exhall/charters/billrights/billmain.html
An online exhibition from the U.S. National Archives and
    Records Administration.

Canadian Charter of Rights and Freedoms
http://lois.justice.gc.ca/en/charter/
Text of the Canadian bill of rights.

Censorship is the control of what people may say or hear, write or read, or see or do. In most cases, this kind of control comes from a government or from various types of private groups. Censorship can affect books, newspapers, magazines, motion pictures, radio and television programs, and speeches. It also may influence music, painting, sculpture, and other arts.

Whenever a government or a private group feels endangered by free expression, it may turn to censorship to protect its basic beliefs. Every society, including democratic ones, has had some kind of censorship when its rulers have felt it would benefit the nation—or themselves. But the strictest control of expression and information occurs in dictatorships and during wartime. The difference between censorship in democracies and in dictatorships is that democracies have ways to limit such action. In the United States, for example, the Bill of Rights and the Supreme Court serve as checks on unlimited censorship.

There are four major types of censorship: (1) moral, (2) military, (3) political, and (4) religious.

Moral censorship is the most common kind of censorship today. Many governments or groups try to preserve their standards of morality by preventing people from learning about or following other standards. Moral censorship may result when some people believe they have the right to force their values on others. It also may result if most of the people of a country believe that their government should promote certain moral codes.

Many countries, including the United States, have obscenity laws. Since the 1960's, however, the definition of obscenity in the United States has narrowed considerably.

Military censorship. During a war, battle plans, troop movement schedules, weapons data, and other information could help the enemy. The armed forces of every country have *censors* who read the letters written and received by servicemen and servicewomen. The censors snip out or blot out any information that might be valuable to the enemy.

The military also may withhold information from the press for security reasons. In Canada, the United States, and some other countries, the press, radio, and TV voluntarily censor themselves during wartime. Most nations have some military censorship during peacetime as well.

Political censorship is used by governments that fear the free expression of criticism and opposing ideas. It is common in nondemocratic countries, where unapproved forms of expression are forbidden.

Democracies do not officially permit political censorship. But many democratic governments try to discourage the expression of certain radical ideas. In the United States, various laws prohibit speeches or writings that might lead to violence. During wartime, many democratic governments carry on political censorship. They believe that criticism of the government or opposition to the war could aid the enemy.

Religious censorship occurs in some nations where the government is close to one religion or where religious feelings run high. Those in power may censor the ideas and practices of other religions. Throughout much of its history, Spain, almost all of whose people are Roman Catholics, did not allow Protestants or Jews to hold public religious services. The Spanish government dropped this ban in 1967.

Censorship methods. There are two main kinds of censorship methods, *formal* and *informal.* Formal censorship occurs when government officials follow the law to control free expression. Informal censorship takes place if no specific law covers an offense.

Officials may act informally because of pressure from a private group to censor something the group dislikes. Some groups also pressure various companies by threatening not to buy their products. A number of businesses, including the motion-picture and television industries, censor themselves in an effort to avoid public disapproval. But standards have loosened since the 1950's.

Censorship can occur before or after something is released to the public. In checking material before release, officials may approve it, reject it, or approve it with certain changes. Censors may also act against a book, magazine, or motion picture after its release, although they rarely succeed in doing so in the United States. The U.S. Postal Service may refuse to deliver objectionable mail, and the United States Customs Service may prevent the importation of certain materials.   Jethro K. Lieberman

Additional resources

Foerstel, Herbert N. *Free Expression and Censorship in America.*
    Greenwood, 1997.
Hull, Mary E. *Censorship in America.* ABC-Clio, 1999.
Riley, Gail B. *Censorship.* Facts on File, 1998.
Steffens, Bradley. *Censorship.* Lucent Bks., 1995.

Civil rights are the freedoms and rights that a person may have as a member of a community, state, or nation. Civil rights include freedom of speech, of the press, and of religion. Among others are the right to own property and to receive fair and equal treatment from government, other persons, and private groups.

In democratic countries, a person's civil rights are protected by law and custom. The constitutions of many democracies have *bills of rights* that describe basic liberties and rights. Courts of law decide whether a person's civil rights have been violated. The courts also determine the limits of civil rights, so that people do not use their freedoms to violate the rights of others.

In many nondemocratic countries, the government

claims to respect and guarantee civil rights. But in most of these countries, such claims differ greatly from the actual conditions. In some Communist countries, for example, the people are denied such basic rights as freedom of speech and of the press. Yet their constitutions guarantee these rights.

Some people draw sharp distinctions between *civil liberties* and *civil rights*. These people distinguish between *freedom from* certain actions and *freedom to* be treated in certain ways. They regard civil liberties as guarantees that a person will enjoy *freedom from* government interference. They think of civil rights as guarantees that all people will have the *freedom to* be treated equally. For example, civil liberties would include freedom from government interference with a person's right to free speech. Civil rights would include everyone's freedom to receive equal protection of the law. In this article, the term *civil rights* refers to both civil liberties and civil rights.

Limits of civil rights

All civil rights have limits, even in democratic countries. For example, a person may be denied freedom of speech in a democracy if it can be shown that his or her speech might lead to the overthrow of the government. A person may not use civil rights to justify actions that might seriously harm the health, welfare, safety, or morals of others. In 1919, U.S. Supreme Court Justice Oliver Wendell Holmes, Jr., wrote: "The most stringent protection of free speech would not protect a man in falsely shouting fire in a theatre and causing a panic."

A person may be denied a civil right if that right is used to violate other people's rights. Freedom of expression, for example, does not permit a person to tell lies that ruin another person's reputation. Property owners have the right to do what they choose with their property. However, this right may not allow a person legally to refuse to sell property to a person of a certain race or religion. This is because the property owner would be denying the other person equal freedom of choice.

The specific limits of civil rights vary with the times. In time of war, a government may restrict personal freedoms to safeguard the country. Changing social and economic conditions also cause changes in the importance that people give certain rights. During the late 1800's, most people in the United States valued property rights more than personal freedoms. But since the late 1930's, most Americans have shown greater concern for personal freedoms and equality of opportunity.

Civil rights in the United States

The United States Constitution describes the basic civil rights of American citizens. The first 10 amendments to the Constitution are usually regarded as the U.S. Bill of Rights. However, civil rights are also mentioned in the main body of the Constitution and in later amendments. Each state constitution also has a bill or declaration of rights. Since the mid-1950's, the federal, state, and local governments have passed several civil rights laws. But the courts—especially the Supreme Court—have probably done the most to define civil rights. When Americans raise questions about the extent and limits of civil rights, they turn to the Supreme Court's decisions for the answers. The court often defines the limits of a right by balancing the right of the individual against the rights of society in general.

The First Amendment is the basis of the democratic process in the United States. The First Amendment forbids Congress to pass laws restricting freedom of speech, of the press, of peaceful assembly, or of petition. Many people consider freedom of speech the most important freedom and the foundation of all other freedoms. The First Amendment also forbids Congress to pass laws establishing a state religion or restricting religious freedom. The Supreme Court has ruled that the 14th Amendment makes the guarantees of the 1st Amendment apply to the state governments.

Due process. Many parts of the Constitution, congressional and state laws, and court decisions require the government to treat individuals fairly. These requirements reflect a basic principle in the American legal system called *due process*. The 5th and 14th amendments forbid the government to deprive a person of life, liberty, or property "without due process of law."

Various statements in the Constitution guarantee due process. For example, the Constitution forbids the government to suspend the *writ of habeas corpus* except during an invasion or rebellion. This right protects citizens against arrest and detention without good reason. Neither Congress nor the states may pass *bills of attainder*. Such bills declare a person guilty of a crime and take away the person's property and civil rights without a trial. The Constitution also prohibits *ex post facto laws*. Such laws make a particular act a crime and punish people who committed the act before it was a crime.

Due process of law also includes court procedures that protect individuals accused of wrongdoing. For example, a person may not be tried for a major federal crime unless a grand jury has first decided that enough evidence exists against the individual. Persons accused of a crime also must be informed of their constitutional rights and of the charges against them. They may demand a jury trial, which must be held soon after the charges are filed. Persons on trial may cross-examine their accusers and may force witnesses to testify.

Other constitutional guarantees. The Constitution also guarantees that accused persons may not be tried twice for the same crime, and they may not be forced to testify against themselves. If they cannot afford a lawyer and want one, the government must provide one. Persons accused of crimes must not be required to pay excessive bail. In addition, those convicted of crimes must not be fined excessively nor made to suffer cruel or unusual punishment.

The Constitution also provides for the security of people and their property. The government may not conduct "unreasonable searches and seizures" of persons or property. It may not take a person's property without due process of law. If it takes private property for public use, it must pay the owner a fair price.

The Constitution forbids the states to pass laws interfering with contracts made between persons or groups. Each state must recognize the legislative acts, public records, and court decisions of other states. A state must extend its legal protections to the citizens of any other state while they are within its jurisdiction.

Protecting the rights of minorities. The United States has many minority groups. These minorities include African Americans, Jews, Asian Americans, European immigrants, Hispanic Americans, American Indians, homosexuals, and people with handicaps. Members of these groups often have not had an equal chance for economic, political, or social advancement. Members of some minorities have been denied the right to vote. Many persons have been discriminated against in housing, education, and employment, and have been denied equal access to restaurants, hotels, and other public accommodations and facilities. A main goal has been to end such discrimination and guarantee equal rights and opportunities for all people.

The struggle for the rights of African Americans. African Americans, who make up one of the largest minority groups in the United States, have been denied their full civil rights more than any other minority group.

African Americans made significant gains in their struggle for equal rights during *Reconstruction,* the 12-year period after the American Civil War. The 13th Amendment, adopted in 1865, abolished slavery in the United States. In 1868, the 14th Amendment made the former slaves citizens. It also provided that the states must grant all people within their jurisdiction "equal protection of the laws." The 15th Amendment, which became law in 1870, prohibited the states from denying people the right to vote because of their race. During Reconstruction, Congress passed several laws to protect blacks' civil rights.

During the late 1870's, white Americans increasingly disregarded the newly won rights of black Americans. The government itself contributed greatly to denying blacks their rights. In 1883, the Supreme Court ruled that congressional acts to prevent racial discrimination by private individuals were unconstitutional. In 1896, in the case of *Plessy v. Ferguson,* the Supreme Court upheld a Louisiana law requiring separate but equal accommodations for blacks and whites in railroad cars. For over 50 years, many Southern states used the "separate but equal" rule established in this case to segregate the races in public schools, and in transportation, recreation, and such public establishments as hotels and restaurants. Many states also used literacy tests, poll taxes, and other means to deprive blacks of their voting rights.

Since the 1930's, blacks have had fairer hearings on civil rights cases in the federal courts. The high point came in 1954 in *Brown v. Board of Education of Topeka.* In this case, the Supreme Court ruled that segregation in public schools is unconstitutional. In time, this decision broke down the "separate but equal" principle.

In 1955, the Supreme Court ordered that public school desegregation be carried out "with all deliberate speed." But many Southern school districts continued to have segregated schools. In 1969, the court departed from its "all deliberate speed" doctrine and ordered the integration of all school systems "at once." By the 1980's, public schools in the South were more integrated than those in many Northern and Western states.

In 1957, Congress passed the first federal civil rights law since Reconstruction. The Civil Rights Act of 1957 set up the Commission on Civil Rights to investigate charges of denial of civil rights. It also created the Civil Rights Division in the Department of Justice to enforce federal civil rights laws and regulations.

During the 1960's, African Americans' voting rights received increased protection. The Civil Rights Act of 1960 provided for the appointment of referees to help blacks register to vote. The 24th Amendment, adopted in 1964, barred poll taxes in federal elections. The Voting Rights Act of 1965 outlawed literacy tests in many Southern states. A 1970 law made literacy tests illegal in all the states. In 1966, the Supreme Court prohibited poll taxes in state and local elections.

The Civil Rights Act of 1964 was one of the strongest civil rights bills in U.S. history. It ordered restaurants, hotels, and other businesses that serve the general public to serve all people without regard to race, color, religion, or national origin. It also barred discrimination by employers and unions, and established the Equal Employment Opportunity Commission to enforce fair employment practices. In addition, the act provided for a cutoff of federal funds from any program or activity that allowed racial discrimination.

The Civil Rights Act of 1968 aimed chiefly at ending discrimination in the sale or rental of housing. Also in 1968, the Supreme Court ruled that the federal government had the power to enforce housing-discrimination laws even in cases involving only private individuals. Before the court's ruling, such laws had been applied only to cases that involved government agencies.

The struggle for women's rights in the United States at first concentrated on gaining the right to vote. A proposed constitutional amendment granting women the vote was introduced in every session of Congress from 1878 to 1919. In 1920, it finally became law as the 19th Amendment to the Constitution.

During the mid-1900's, women gained increased protection against job discrimination. In the 1940's, the U.S. government established a policy of equal pay for equal work. Under this policy, the government forbade businesses with federal contracts to pay a woman less than a man for the same job. Title VII of the Civil Rights Act of 1964 prohibited job discrimination on the basis of sex. In 1972, Congress approved the Equal Rights Amendment. It failed to become law because only 35 of the necessary 38 states approved it by the deadline of June 30, 1982. The amendment would have guaranteed equal rights for all citizens, regardless of sex.

Major changes in the field of civil rights occurred during the 1970's. Earlier civil rights efforts had involved lawsuits and other attempts to protect individual rights. In the 1970's, the emphasis shifted from individual rights to group rights.

The federal government began to enact laws designed to assure rights for groups that formerly had suffered discrimination. For example, the government began a program of *affirmative action.* Affirmative action consists of efforts to counteract past discrimination by giving special help to disadvantaged groups. Typical measures included recruiting drives among women and minority groups, and special training for minority workers. The government required such plans to be set up by businesses that had government contracts, by other employers, and by schools receiving federal funds.

Efforts to help groups that had suffered discrimination raised a number of new civil rights issues. Many people felt the government violated the principle of equality under the law by giving preference to certain groups at the

Topic for study

The American Civil Liberties Union (ACLU) is an organization that defends civil rights in the United States. Examine some recent issues in which the ACLU was active and explain why you agree or disagree with its position on each issue.

expense of others. Some white men complained of *reverse discrimination,* saying they were treated unfairly because of their race and sex. Other individuals believed such efforts were necessary to help the disadvantaged overcome past discrimination and eventually compete on an equal basis with white males.

In 1995, the Supreme Court ruled that a federal program requiring preference based on a person's race is unconstitutional unless the preference is designed to make up for specific instances of past discrimination. This meant that affirmative action could no longer be used to counteract racial discrimination by society as a whole. In 1989, the court had made a similar decision regarding state and local programs.

In 1990, Congress passed the Americans with Disabilities Act to protect handicapped people from discrimination by private employers. The law also requires that public buildings and mass transportation systems be accessible to disabled people. In addition, the act orders telephone companies to provide telephone relay services that enable people with speech or hearing disorders to make and receive calls.

In 1996, the Supreme Court struck down an amendment to the Colorado Constitution that forbade laws protecting homosexuals from discrimination. Several Colorado cities had adopted such laws. The constitutional amendment was approved by a majority of Colorado's voters in 1992. In 1986, the Supreme Court had ruled that states could outlaw homosexual conduct.

Civil rights in Canada

The Canadian and U.S. governments apply the same broad principles in dealing with civil rights. Generally, Canadian courts have protected individual liberties, and most of the provinces have civil rights laws similar to those in the United States. In 1960, Canada's Parliament passed an act establishing the Canadian Bill of Rights. An expanded version of the bill, called the Canadian Charter of Rights and Freedoms, became part of Canada's constitution in 1982. The charter is similar to the U.S. Bill of Rights. It guarantees the same basic freedoms and most of the same protections.

As in the United States, the main civil rights problems in Canada involve assuring equal rights for members of minority groups. In the past, Canadian Inuit (formerly called Eskimos) and Indians were sometimes denied their full civil rights. French Canadians of the province of Quebec have long struggled against what they consider discrimination by Canada's English-speaking majority. Many French Canadians claim they have been denied jobs because they speak French rather than English.

Development of civil rights

Natural law. The idea that people have certain rights that cannot be taken away probably began thousands of years ago with the theory of natural law. This theory states that a natural order exists in the universe because all things are created by nature, or God. Everything has its own qualities and is subject to the rules of nature to achieve its full potential. According to this theory, anything that detracts from a person's human qualities, or prevents their full achievement, violates natural law.

The ancient Greek philosophers and the writers of the Old Testament stressed that there is a higher law than human law. In the first century B.C., the Roman philosopher Cicero insisted that this higher (natural) law is universal and can be discovered through human reason. This idea led to the belief that governmental power has limits, and that people and governments everywhere are bound by natural law.

Some of the most historic English legal documents are based on natural law. The earliest and most famous was Magna Carta, which the king approved against his will in 1215. The document placed the king himself under the law. In 1628, the English Parliament drew up a Petition of Right. The petition claimed that certain actions of the king, such as levying taxes without the consent of Parliament, were unconstitutional.

Natural rights. Natural law had always stressed the duties over the rights of government and individuals. But in the late 1600's, natural law began to emphasize natural rights. This change was brought about largely by the writings of the English philosopher John Locke.

Locke argued that governmental authority depends on the people's consent. According to Locke, people originally lived in a state of nature with no restrictions on their freedom. Then they came to realize that confusion would result if each person enforced his or her own rights. People agreed to live under a common government, but not to surrender their "rights of nature" to the government. Instead, they expected the government to protect these rights, especially the rights of life, liberty, and property. Locke's ideas of limited government and natural rights became part of the English Bill of Rights (1689), the French Declaration of the Rights of Man (1789), and the U.S. Bill of Rights (1791).

Today, many scholars reject the natural law and natural rights theories. They believe that all laws—including those guaranteeing civil rights—are simply devices that people find convenient or useful at a particular time. Nevertheless, nearly all civil rights laws have resulted from the theories of natural law and natural rights.

Civil rights today. Civil rights have long been protected in the constitutional democracies of Western Europe. These nations include France, the United Kingdom, Switzerland, and the Scandinavian countries. Personal liberties are also secure in such newer democracies as Australia, New Zealand, Canada, and the United States. Many new nations of Africa and Asia have adopted constitutions that guarantee basic civil rights. But in many of these countries, unstable governments and inexperience with self-rule have often led to political arrests, censorship, and other denials of civil rights.

Most nondemocratic governments claim to protect civil rights. But in practice, they grant civil rights only when they find it politically convenient to do so. China's Constitution, for example, guarantees the right to vote and assures freedom of speech, of the press, and of assembly. But China's Communist Party completely controls the government, and the people may be punished if they publicly criticize the party. The Chinese government controls the newspapers and other forms of communication.

The United Nations General Assembly adopted a Universal Declaration of Human Rights in 1948. It states that all people are born free and are equal in dignity and rights. Many experts in international law believe that the declaration lacks legal authority, but most agree that it has high moral authority. Bruce Allen Murphy

Additional resources

Level I

Lucas, Eileen. *Civil Rights.* Enslow, 1996.
Quiri, Patricia R. *The Bill of Rights.* Children's Pr., 1998.
Rochelle, Belinda. *Witnesses to Freedom: Young People Who Fought for Civil Rights.* Lodestar, 1993.

Level II

Engelbert, Phillis. *American Civil Rights: Biographies.* UXL, 1999.
Fairclough, Adam. *Better Day Coming: Blacks and Equality, 1890-2000.* Viking, 2001.
Meltzer, Milton. *There Comes a Time: The Struggle for Civil Rights.* Random Hse., 2001.

Web site

Universal Declaration of Human Rights
http://www.un.org/Overview/rights.html
Text of the Universal Declaration of Human Rights, adopted by the United Nations in 1948.

Due process of law is a basic principle in the American legal system that requires fairness in the government's dealing with persons. The term *due process of law* appears in the 5th and 14th amendments to the Constitution of the United States. These amendments forbid federal, state, and local governments from depriving a person of "life, liberty, or property, without due process of law." The Supreme Court of the United States has never clearly defined these words, and has applied them to a number of widely different situations.

The idea of due process of law dates from England's Magna Carta of 1215. One article in this document promises that no one shall be deprived of life, liberty, or property, except "by the lawful judgment of his peers or by the law of the land." Some early English *writs* (written legal orders) were designed to bring the government under a rule of law. For example, a writ of *habeas corpus* requires that the government show just cause before it can hold a person in custody.

Through law and custom, various safeguards have been developed in the United States to assure that persons accused of wrongdoing will be treated fairly. These safeguards are sometimes called *procedural due process.* Procedural due process includes the following requirements: (1) The law must be administered fairly. (2) People must be informed of the charges against them and must be given the opportunity for a fair hearing. (3) The person bringing the charges must not be allowed to judge the case. (4) Criminal laws must be clearly worded so that they give adequate warning of the action prohibited. Procedural due process concepts apply to civil and criminal cases.

Courts have also used the "due process" clauses of the 5th and 14th amendments to limit the content of laws, even though there was no procedural unfairness. For example, they have declared unconstitutional some laws restricting personal freedoms and business, on the ground that the laws violate due process of law. This practice involves the *substance* of public policy and is called *substantive due process.* Sherman L. Cohn

Freedom is the ability to make choices and to carry them out. The words *freedom* and *liberty* mean much the same thing. For people to have complete freedom, there must be no restrictions on how they think, speak, or act. They must be aware of what their choices are, and they must have the power to decide among those choices. They also must have the means and the opportunity to think, speak, and act without being controlled by anyone else. However, no organized society can actually provide all these conditions at all times.

From a legal point of view, people are free if society imposes no unjust, unnecessary, or unreasonable limits on them. Society must also protect their rights—that is, their basic liberties, powers, and privileges. A free society tries to distribute the conditions of freedom equally among the people.

Today, many societies put a high value on legal freedom. But people have not always considered it so desirable. Through the centuries, for example, many men and women—and even whole societies—have set goals of self-fulfillment or self-perfection. They have believed that achieving those goals would do more to make people "free" than would the legal protection of their rights in society. Many societies have thought it natural and desirable for a few people to restrict the liberty of all others. This article discusses the ways that governments and laws both protect and restrict freedom.

Kinds of freedom

Most legal freedoms can be divided into three main groups: (1) political freedom, (2) social freedom, and (3) economic freedom.

Political freedom gives people a voice in government and an opportunity to take part in its decisions. This freedom includes the right to vote, to choose between rival candidates for public office, and to run for office oneself. Political freedom also includes the right to criticize government policies, which is part of free speech. People who are politically free can also form and join political parties and organizations. This right is part of the freedom of assembly.

In the past, many people considered political freedom the most important freedom. They believed that men and women who were politically free could vote all other freedoms for themselves. But most people now realize that political liberty means little unless economic and social freedom support it. For example, the right to vote does not have much value if people lack the information to vote in their own best interests.

Social freedom includes freedom of speech, of the press, and of religion; freedom of assembly; academic freedom; and the right to due process of law.

Freedom of speech is the right to speak out publicly or privately. Political liberty depends on this right. People need to hold free discussions and to exchange ideas so they can decide wisely on political issues. Free speech also contributes to political freedom by making government officials aware of public opinion.

Freedom of the press is the right to publish facts, ideas, and opinions without interference from the government or private groups. This right extends to radio, television, and motion pictures as well as to printed material. Freedom of the press may be considered a special type of freedom of speech, and it is important for the same reasons.

Freedom of religion means the right to believe in and to practice the faith of one's choice. It also includes the right to have no religion at all.

Freedom of assembly is the right to meet together and to form groups with others of similar interests. It also means that people may associate with anyone they wish. On the other hand, no one may be forced to join an association against his or her will.

Academic freedom is a group of freedoms claimed by teachers and students. It includes the right to teach, discuss, research, write, and publish without interference. It promotes the exchange of ideas and the spread of knowledge.

Due process of law is a group of legal requirements that must be met before a person accused of a crime can be punished. By protecting an individual against unjust imprisonment, due process serves as a safeguard of personal freedom. Due process includes people's right to know the charges against them. The law also guarantees the right to obtain a legal order called a *writ of habeas corpus*. This writ orders the police to free a prisoner if no legal charge can be placed against the person. It protects people from being imprisoned unjustly.

Economic freedom enables people to make their own economic decisions. This freedom includes the right to own property, to use it, and to profit from it. Workers are free to choose and change jobs. People have the freedom to save money and invest it as they wish. Such freedoms form the basis of an economic system called *capitalism.*

The basic principle of capitalism is the policy of *laissez faire,* which states that government should not interfere in most economic affairs. According to laissez faire, everyone would be best off if allowed to pursue his or her own economic interests without restriction or special treatment from government.

Since the 1930's, economic freedom has come to mean that everyone has the right to a satisfactory standard of living. This concept of economic freedom, sometimes called "freedom from want," often conflicts with the principle of laissez faire. For example, government has imposed minimum-wage laws that limit the smallest amount of money per hour an employer can pay. Laws also protect workers' rights to reasonable hours, holidays with pay, and safe working conditions. And if people cannot earn a living because of disability, old age, or unemployment, they receive special aid.

Limits on freedom

The laws of every organized society form a complicated pattern of balanced freedoms and restrictions. Some people think of laws as the natural enemies of freedom. In fact, people called *anarchists* believe that all systems of government and laws destroy liberty. Actually, the law both limits and protects the freedom of an individual. For example, it forbids people to hit others. But it also guarantees that people will be free from being hit.

Reasons for limits on freedom. The major reason for restricting freedom is to prevent harm to others. To achieve the goal of equal freedom for everyone, a government may have to restrict the liberty of certain individuals or groups to act in certain ways. In the United States, for example, restaurant owners no longer have the freedom to refuse to serve people because of race.

Society also limits personal freedom in order to maintain order and keep things running smoothly. When two cars cannot cross an intersection at the same time without colliding, traffic regulations specify which should go first.

Also, every person must accept certain duties and responsibilities to maintain and protect society. Many of these duties limit freedom. For example, a citizen has the duty to pay taxes and to serve on a jury. The idea of personal freedom has nearly always carried with it some amount of duty to society.

Limits on political freedom. Democracies divide political power among the branches of government, between government and the citizens, and between the majority and minority parties. These divisions of power restrict various liberties. For example, citizens have the right to vote. As a result, elected officials must respect voter opinion. They are not free to govern as they please. A system called the *separation of powers* divides authority among the three branches of government—executive, legislative, and judicial. Each branch is limited by the others' power. Majority rule does not give the majority party the liberty to do whatever it wants. No matter how large the majority, it can never take away certain rights and freedoms of the minority.

Limits on social freedom prevent people from using their liberty in ways that would harm the health, safety, or welfare of others. For example, free speech does not include the right to shout "Fire!" in a crowded theater if there is no fire. Freedom of speech and of the press do not allow a person to tell lies that damage another's reputation. Such statements are called *slander* if spoken and *libel* if written.

The law also prohibits speeches or publications that would endanger the nation's peace or security. Under certain conditions, it forbids speeches that call on people to riot. It also outlaws *sedition* (calling for rebellion).

In addition, many governments limit freedom of speech and of the press to protect public morals. For example, many states of the United States have laws against *pornography* (indecent pictures and writings).

The government limits freedom of religion by forbidding certain religious practices. For example, it prohibits human sacrifice. It also bans *polygamy* (marriage to more than one person at a time), though Islam and other religions permit the practice.

Most other social freedoms can be restricted or set aside to protect other people or to safeguard the nation. For example, people may not use freedom of assembly to disturb the peace or to block public streets or sidewalks. The writ of habeas corpus may be suspended during a rebellion or an invasion.

Limits on economic freedom. In the past, most governments put few limits on economic freedom. They followed a policy of not interfering in economic affairs.

But since the 1800's, the development of large-scale capitalism has concentrated wealth in the hands of relatively few people. This development has convinced many people that government must intervene to protect underprivileged groups and promote equality of economic opportunity. Such beliefs have led to increased restrictions on big business and other powerful economic groups. For example, the Supreme Court of the United States once ruled that minimum-wage laws violated the "freedom of contract" between employer and employee. But today, laws regulate wages, hours, and working conditions; forbid child labor; and even guarantee unemployment insurance. Most people believe these laws protect economic freedom rather than violate it.

Economic freedom is also limited when it conflicts with other people's rights or welfare. For example, no one is free to cheat others. The right of hotelkeepers to do what they choose with their property does not allow them to refuse a room to people of a certain race or religion. The freedom of manufacturers to run their factories as they wish does not allow them to dump industrial wastes into other people's drinking water.

History

In ancient Greece and Rome, only the highest classes had much freedom. By about 500 B.C., Athens and several other Greek city-states had democratic governments. Citizens could vote and hold office, but they made up a minority of the population. Women, slaves, and foreigners did not have these rights.

For many years, the lower classes could not hold public office or marry into upper-class families. Lowest of all were the slaves, who, as a form of property, had no legal rights.

The Middle Ages produced a political and economic system called *feudalism*. Under feudalism, the peasants known as *serfs* had little freedom, but nobles had much. Lower-ranking noblemen furnished troops and paid taxes to a higher-ranking nobleman called their *lord*. The lower-ranking noblemen were known as the lord's *vassals*. Vassals had many important rights. For example, a lord had to call his vassals together and get their permission before he could collect extra taxes. Another custom called for disputes between a vassal and his lord to be settled by a court of the vassal's *peers*—men of the same rank as he.

In 1215, King John of England approved a document called Magna Carta. This document made laws of many customary feudal liberties. For example, it confirmed the tradition that the king could raise no special tax without the consent of his nobles. This provision brought about the development of Parliament. The document also stated that no freeman could be imprisoned, exiled, or deprived of property, except as provided by law. The ideas of due process of law and trial by jury developed from this concept. Most importantly, Magna Carta established the principle that even the king had to obey the law.

In the Middle Ages, the Christian church restricted freedom of thought in Europe. The church persecuted Jews, Muslims, and others who disagreed with its beliefs. It restricted writings it considered contrary to church teachings. But church teachings also acted as a check on the unreasonable use of political power.

The Renaissance and the Reformation emphasized the importance of the individual. As a result, people began to demand greater personal freedom. Anabaptists and other Protestant groups elected their own ministers and held free and open discussions. These practices carried over into politics and contributed to the growth of

democracy and political freedom. In 1620, for example, the Pilgrims who settled in Massachusetts signed a document called the Mayflower Compact, in which they agreed to obey "just and equal laws."

During the Age of Reason, many people began to regard freedom as a natural right. Parliament passed the English Bill of Rights in 1689. This bill eliminated many powers of the king and guaranteed the basic rights and liberties of the English people.

At the same time, the English philosopher John Locke declared that every person is born with natural rights that cannot be taken away. These rights include the right to life and to own property; and freedom of opinion, religion, and speech. Locke's book *Two Treatises of Government* (1690) argued that the chief purpose of government was to protect these rights. If a government did not adequately protect the citizens' liberty, they had the right to revolt.

In 1776, the American colonists used many of Locke's ideas in the Declaration of Independence. For example, the declaration stated that people had God-given rights to "Life, Liberty and the pursuit of Happiness."

As the Industrial Revolution spread during the 1700's, the free enterprise system became firmly established. The Scottish economist Adam Smith argued for the laissez faire policy in his book *The Wealth of Nations* (1776).

During the 1700's, three important French philosophers—Montesquieu, Jean-Jacques Rousseau, and Voltaire—spoke out for individual rights and freedoms. Montesquieu's book *The Spirit of the Laws* (1748) called for representative government with separation of powers into executive, legislative, and judicial branches. Rousseau declared in his book *The Social Contract* (1762) that government draws its powers from the consent of the people who are governed. Voltaire's many writings opposed government interference with individual rights.

The writings of these three men helped cause the French Revolution, which began in 1789. The revolution was devoted to liberty and equality. It did not succeed in making France a democracy. But it did wipe out many abuses and limit the king's powers.

The Revolutionary War in America (1775-1783) won the colonies independence from Britain. In 1788, the Constitution of the United States established a democratic government with powers divided among the president, Congress, and the federal courts. The first 10 amendments to the Constitution took effect in 1791. These amendments, now known as the Bill of Rights, guaranteed such basic liberties as freedom of speech, press, and religion; and the right to trial by jury.

The 1800's brought into practice many beliefs about freedom that had developed during the Age of Reason. In 1830, and again in 1848, revolutionary movements swept over much of Europe. Many European monarchs lost most of their powers. By 1848, the citizens of many nations had won basic civil liberties and at least the beginnings of democratic government. These nations included Belgium, Denmark, and the Netherlands.

Most European nations also ended slavery during the 1800's. In 1865, the 13th Amendment to the Constitution abolished slavery in the United States. The 15th Amendment, adopted in 1870, gave former slaves the right to vote.

Workers also gained many important rights during the 1800's. Many nations, including Britain and the United States, passed laws that regulated working conditions in factories. Workers in several countries won the right to form labor unions.

The 1900's. After World War I ended in 1918, many European nations established representative democracies. A number of them also gave women the right to vote. The United States did so in 1920 with the 19th Amendment. By 1932, 16 European nations had become republics governed by elected representatives.

By the 1930's, many people no longer believed that the simple absence of restrictions could make them free. Instead, the idea of freedom expanded to include employment, health, and adequate food and housing. In 1941, President Franklin D. Roosevelt reflected this broad view in his "four freedoms" message. He called for four freedoms—freedom of speech, freedom of religion, freedom from want, and freedom from fear—to be spread throughout the world.

In 1948, the United Nations General Assembly adopted the Universal Declaration of Human Rights. This declaration listed rights and freedoms that the UN thought should be the goals of all nations.

In the 1960's, the civil rights struggle by blacks resulted in much important legislation in the United States. The 24th Amendment to the Constitution, adopted in 1964, banned poll taxes in federal elections. The Civil Rights Act of 1964 forbade employers and unions to discriminate on the basis of color, national origin, race, religion, or sex. The act also prohibited hotels and restaurants from such discrimination in serving customers.

In 1972, Congress passed the Equal Rights Amendment to the Constitution. The amendment would have guaranteed equality of rights under the law to all persons regardless of sex. However, it never took effect because it failed to win ratification from the states.

Critically reviewed by William C. Havard, Jr.

Additional resources

Farish, Leah. *The First Amendment.* Enslow, 1998.
Foner, Eric. *The Story of American Freedom.* Norton, 1998.
Ingelhart, Louis E., comp. *Press and Speech Freedoms in the World, from Antiquity Until 1998.* Greenwood, 1998.
Jones, Howard. *Abraham Lincoln and a New Birth of Freedom.* Univ. of Neb. Pr., 1999.
Karatnycky, Adrian, ed. *Freedom in the World.* Transaction Pubs., published annually.
Treadgold, Donald W. *Freedom: A History.* N. Y. Univ. Pr., 1990.

Freedom of assembly is the right of people to gather peacefully to exchange ideas or to protest social, economic, or political conditions and demand reform. Constitutions and the traditions of democracies throughout the world respect the right of freedom of assembly. But no country, including the United States, claims the right as absolute.

In the United States, the First Amendment to the Constitution guarantees the right of freedom of assembly. It says that the government may make no law that diminishes "the right of the people peaceably to assemble." Almost all state constitutions also ensure freedom of assembly.

Most public gatherings in the United States proceed without active interference by police or other officials. But sometimes law enforcement officers make arrests

when political demonstrations are large or controversial, or when the demonstrations threaten to turn violent. Later, courts may be asked to determine whether the police violated the people's right to assemble.

In 1937, the Supreme Court of the United States struck down an attempt by the state of Oregon to limit freedom of assembly. A speaker at a Communist Party rally was convicted under a state law. The law said that citizens of Oregon could not participate in organizations that advocated the violent overthrow of the government. The meeting itself was peaceful. The speaker did not urge anyone to act violently or to commit a crime. The Supreme Court reversed the speaker's conviction. The court ruled that peaceful assembly for lawful discussion could not be made a crime. It also said that those who help conduct such meetings could not be considered criminals.

People do not have an absolute right to gather wherever or whenever they please. A town, city, or county may reasonably regulate the time, place, and manner of assembling. For example, a city might restrict large, noisy demonstrations to a particular area or to certain times of the day. The Supreme Court has ruled that protesters cannot be denied access to public places traditionally open to gatherings, such as parks and public sidewalks. But the government may refuse entrance to other places, such as military bases and prisons, that have traditionally been off limits to demonstrations.

Although the government may regulate gatherings, it may not do so unreasonably. Most cities and towns require demonstrators, strikers, and marchers to obtain a permit before assembling. The Supreme Court has struck down permit systems that give officials absolute authority to deny people the opportunity to meet. In 1939, in the first such case, the court voided a permit plan in Jersey City, New Jersey. This plan had given absolute power to the director of public safety to decide who could assemble in public places and who could not. The court said that no city official may deny the right to assemble because of a personal whim. It said laws regulating permits for the use of public property should be based only on safety standards that all groups could know in advance.

In other countries. All democratic governments recognize some form of freedom of assembly. But none of them uphold it to the degree established by the U.S. Constitution. The United Kingdom generally permits peaceful assemblies. But the British police have considerable power to prohibit or disband large gatherings as they think necessary. In several instances in the 1900's, the British government exercised emergency powers to suppress public meetings, even on private premises. For example, the government prevented fascists and others from meeting during World War II (1939-1945). In Canada, the 1982 Charter of Rights and Freedoms specifically guarantees the right of peaceful assembly.

International organizations recognize freedom of assembly as a fundamental human right. The Universal Declaration of Human Rights, adopted in 1948, proclaims that "everyone has the right to freedom of peaceful assembly." The International Labor Organization, a specialized agency of the United Nations, calls for permitting workers to meet and organize free of government interference.

Not every society, however, endorses freedom of assembly. In 1989, the Chinese government brutally disbanded a large, peaceful assembly of students and other citizens in Beijing's Tiananmen Square. Soldiers fired into the crowd and killed many demonstrators. The protesters were calling for more democracy in China and an end to corruption in government.

A mass protest led to a much different outcome in the Soviet Union. In 1991, a huge crowd gathered in Moscow's Red Square. The group defied tanks and troops to protest the temporary imprisonment of Soviet President Mikhail S. Gorbachev by a group of conservative officials of the Communist Party. The coup against Gorbachev eventually failed, and the Soviet Union soon dissolved.

History. Freedom of assembly has been fully recognized only since the late 1600's. Ancient democracies endorsed a more limited right to assemble. At various times in the history of Greece and Rome, a small part of the total population could meet in citizen assemblies to help make government decisions. But the majority of the people could not protest government actions.

In England, people traditionally assembled mainly for the purpose of *petitioning* (making a formal request of) the government. England first recognized this as a right in Magna Carta, a historic charter of liberties, in 1215. A later act stated that if more than 10 people gathered to present a signed appeal to the king or Parliament, even respectfully requesting a change in the law, they were guilty of the crime of "tumultuous petitioning." The English Bill of Rights of 1689 finally recognized an absolute right to petition the king. But assembly still carried risks. In 1715, a statute called the Riot Act banned "riotous assemblies." The act required groups of 12 or more to disband when a government authority told them to do so. The phrase *to read the riot act,* which means *to order a disturbance to stop,* refers to this law.

In the American Colonies, the First Continental Congress, in 1774, demanded a broader right of the people "peaceably to assemble, consider of their grievances, and petition the King." State constitutions and the First Amendment finally incorporated the specific rights of petition and assembly.   Jethro K. Lieberman

Additional resources

King, David C. *Freedom of Assembly.* Millbrook, 1997. Younger readers.
Soifer, Aviam. *Law and the Company We Keep.* Harvard Univ. Pr., 1995.

Freedom of religion is the right of a person to believe in and practice whatever faith he or she chooses. It also includes the right of an individual to have no religious beliefs at all.

Like most rights, freedom of religion is not absolute. Most countries prohibit religious practices that injure people or that are thought to threaten to destroy society. For example, most governments forbid human sacrifice and *polygamy,* the practice of having more than one wife or husband at the same time.

Throughout most of history, many people have been persecuted for their religious beliefs. The denial of religious liberty probably stems from two major sources—personal and political. Religion touches the deepest feelings of many people. Strong religious views have

led to intolerance among various faiths. Some governments have close ties to one religion and consider people of other faiths to be a threat to political authority. A government also may regard religion as politically dangerous because religions may place allegiance to God above obedience to the state.

The question of morality has caused many conflicts between church and state. Both religion and government are concerned with morality. They work together if the moral goals desired by the state are the same as those sought by the church. But discord may result if they have different views about morality. An example is the disagreement of many religious people with governments that allow abortion.

In the United States. The desire for religious freedom was a major reason Europeans settled in America. The Puritans and many other groups came to the New World to escape religious persecution in Europe.

The First Amendment of the U.S. Constitution guarantees that "Congress shall make no law respecting an establishment of religion, or prohibiting the free exercise thereof . . . ." This provision originally protected religious groups from unfair treatment by the federal government only. Until the mid-1800's, New Hampshire and other states had laws that prohibited non-Protestants from holding public office. Several states, including Connecticut and Massachusetts, even had official churches. Since the 1940's, however, the Supreme Court of the United States has ruled that all the states must uphold the First Amendment's guarantees of religious freedom.

Today, freedom of religion remains an issue in the United States. Various court rulings have interpreted the First Amendment to mean that the government may not promote or give special treatment to any religion. Judges have struck down plans that called for the government to give financial aid to religious schools. The courts have also ruled unconstitutional a number of programs to teach the Bible or recite prayers in public schools. These rulings are highly controversial.

But church and state are not completely separated in the United States. The nation's motto is *In God We Trust.* Sessions of Congress open with prayers, and court witnesses swear oaths on the Bible. Several court decisions support such practices.

Christian moral views have had a predominant influence on U.S. laws because most of the nation's people are Christians. In 1878, for example, the Supreme Court upheld a federal law against polygamy, even though this law restricted the religious freedom of one Christian group, the Mormons. At that time, the Mormon faith included belief in polygamy. But the laws and the courts agreed with the view of most Americans that polygamy is harmful to society.

In other countries. Religion has been discouraged or even forbidden in countries ruled by dictators. Before the 1980's, for example, the Communist governments of the Soviet Union and Eastern European countries persecuted religion on a large scale. A person's highest allegiance, they believed, belonged to Communism, not to a Supreme Being. Although they did not forbid religion entirely, they made it difficult for people to practice any faith. Beginning in 1989, the Communist governments of many Eastern European countries were replaced with reform governments that permitted more religious free-

Topic for study

Among the rights guaranteed by the First Amendment to the U.S. Constitution is freedom of religion. Why did the framers of the Constitution want to prohibit an official state church? Cite a recent case involving the principle of separation of church and state.

dom. In 1990, Soviet leaders passed a law that restored religious freedom in the Soviet Union. In 1991, the Communist Party lost control of the Soviet government, and later that year the Soviet Union was dissolved.

In some countries that have an official state church, or where most of the people belong to one church, other faiths do not have religious freedom. For example, many Muslim nations discriminate against Christians and Jews.

Other countries, including Denmark and Norway, have state churches. But the governments of these nations grant freedom of worship to other religious groups. In some countries, the government provides equal support for all religions.

History. Many ancient peoples permitted broad religious freedom. These peoples worshiped a large number of gods and readily accepted groups with new gods. Jews and, later, Christians could not do so because they worshiped only one God. In addition, they believed that allegiance to God was higher than allegiance to any ruler or state. Some ancient peoples did not accept these beliefs, and they persecuted Christians and Jews.

During the Middle Ages, from about the A.D. 400's through the 1400's, the Roman Catholic Church dominated Europe and permitted little religious freedom. The Catholic Church persecuted Jews and Muslims. The church also punished people for any serious disagreement with its teachings. In 1415, the Bohemian religious reformer John Hus was burned at the stake for challenging the authority of the pope.

The Reformation, a religious movement of the 1500's, gave birth to Protestantism. The Catholic Church and Catholic rulers persecuted Protestant groups. Many Protestant denominations persecuted Catholics and other Protestant groups as well.

However, by the 1700's and 1800's the variety of religions that resulted from the Reformation had led to increased tolerance in many countries. These countries included the United Kingdom, the Netherlands, and the United States. But intolerance remained strong in some countries. Poland and Russia, for example, severely persecuted Jews. One of the most savage religious persecutions in history occurred in the 1930's and 1940's, when Nazi Germany killed about 6 million Jews.

Richard E. Morgan

Additional resources

Eastland, Terry, ed. *Religious Liberty in the Supreme Court: The Cases That Define the Debate Over Church and State.* Eerdmans, 1993.

Gay, Kathlyn. *Church and State: Government and Religion in the United States.* Millbrook, 1992.

Hirst, Mike. *Freedom of Belief.* Watts, 1997. Younger readers.

Sherrow, Victoria. *Freedom of Worship.* Millbrook, 1997. Younger readers.

Web site

Baylor University Church-State Studies
http://www.baylor.edu/~Church_State/church-state_links.htm
A page of links to church-state resources on the Internet from the J. M. Dawson Institute of Church-State Studies at Baylor University. Includes links to primary source materials as well as links to current issues. Covers various points of view on the political and philosophical debates involved in church-state issues.

Freedom of speech is the right to speak out publicly or privately. The term covers all forms of expression, including books, newspapers, magazines, radio, television, motion pictures, and electronic documents on computer networks. Many scholars consider freedom of speech a natural right.

In a democracy, freedom of speech is a necessity. Democratic constitutions guarantee people the right to express their opinions freely because democracy is government of, by, and for the people. The people need information to help them determine the best political and social policies. Democratic governments need to know what most people believe and want. The governments also need to know the opinions of various minorities.

Most nondemocratic nations deny freedom of speech to their people. The governments of these countries operate under the theory that the ruler or governing party "knows best" what is good for the people. Such governments believe that freedom of speech would interfere with the conduct of public affairs and would create disorder.

Limitations. All societies, including democratic ones, put various limitations on what people may say. They prohibit certain types of speech that they believe might harm the government or the people. But drawing a line between dangerous and harmless speech can be extremely difficult.

Most democratic nations have four major restrictions on free expression. (1) Laws covering *libel* and *slander* prohibit speech or publication that harms a person's reputation. (2) Some laws forbid speech that offends public decency by using obscenities or by encouraging people to commit acts considered immoral. (3) Laws against spying, treason, and urging violence prohibit speech that endangers life, property, or national security. (4) Other laws forbid speech that invades the right of people not to listen to it. For example, a city ordinance might limit the times when people may use loudspeakers on public streets.

In the United States. Freedom of speech was one of the goals of the American colonists that led to the Revolutionary War in America (1775-1783). Since 1791, the First Amendment to the United States Constitution has protected freedom of speech from interference by the federal government.

Since 1925, the Supreme Court of the United States has protected free speech against interference by state or local governments. The court has done this by using the *due process* clause of the 14th Amendment.

The government restricts some speech considered dangerous or immoral. The first major federal law that limited speech was the Sedition Act of 1798. It provided punishment for speaking or writing against the government. The law expired in 1801 and was not renewed.

Topic for study

The United States, like all democratic nations, places certain limitations on freedom of speech. List the principal kinds of expression that are not protected by the First Amendment to the U.S. Constitution and explain why they are not protected. Do you agree that freedom of speech must be limited in certain ways? If you disagree, explain why you think there should be no such limitations.

In the late 1800's, Congress passed several laws against obscenity. But during the 1900's, court decisions generally eased such restrictions. For example, judges lifted the bans on such famous books as *Ulysses* by James Joyce, in 1933, and *Lady Chatterley's Lover* by D. H. Lawrence, in 1960.

The Espionage Act of 1917 and the Sedition Act of 1918, passed during World War I, forbade speeches and publications that interfered with the war effort. Since 1919, the Supreme Court has suggested that speech presenting "a clear and present danger" to the nation may be restricted. In 1940, Congress passed the Smith Act, which made it a crime to urge the violent overthrow of the United States government.

Most periods of increased restrictions on speech occur when threats to individuals, national security, or social morality seem grave. During such times of stress, the courts have provided little protection for individual freedom. In the early 1950's, for example, fear of Communism was strong in the United States because of the Korean War and the conviction of several Americans as Soviet spies. In 1951, the Supreme Court upheld the Smith Act in the case of 11 leaders of the Communist Party convicted for advocating the overthrow of the government. Since the mid-1950's, however, the courts have become more concerned about personal rights and have provided greater protection for freedom of expression. In 1989, for example, the Supreme Court ruled that the government cannot punish a person for burning the American flag as a form of political protest. In 2000, the court ruled that the government could not require cable systems to limit sexually explicit channels to late-night hours.

In other countries. The development of freedom of speech in most Western European countries and English-speaking nations has resembled that in the United States. In various other countries, this freedom has grown more slowly or not at all.

France and the United Kingdom have long traditions of protecting free speech. But like the United States, these countries place certain restrictions on free expression in the interests of national security. Smaller Western European countries, such as Denmark and Switzerland, generally have fewer restrictions on free speech. Ireland bases some of its controls over freedom of expression on the moral teachings of the Roman Catholic Church, to which about 95 percent of the Irish people belong.

The rulers of some countries have simply ignored or have taken away constitutional guarantees of freedom of speech. For example, the rulers of China and North Korea severely limit freedom of speech. These dictators believe they alone hold the truth. Therefore, they say, any opposition must be based on falsehood and regarded as dangerous.

History. Throughout history, people have fought for freedom of speech. In the 400's B.C., the city-state of Athens in ancient Greece gave its citizens considerable freedom of expression. Later, freedom of speech became linked with struggles for political and religious freedom. These struggles took place in the Middle Ages, from about the A.D. 400's through the 1400's. They also played an important part in the Reformation, a religious movement of the 1500's that gave rise to Protestantism.

In the 1600's and 1700's, a period called the Age of Reason, many people began to regard freedom of speech as a natural right. Such philosophers as John Locke of England and Voltaire of France based this idea on their belief in the importance of the individual. Every person, they declared, has a right to speak freely and to have a voice in the government. Thomas Jefferson expressed this idea in the Declaration of Independence.

During the 1800's, democratic ideas grew and increasing numbers of people gained freedom of speech. At the same time, however, the growth of cities and industry required more and more people to live and work in large groups. To some people, such as the German philosopher Karl Marx, the interests of society became more important than those of the individual. They thought nations could operate best under an intelligent central authority, rather than with democracy and individual freedom.

In the 1900's, a number of nations came under such totalitarian forms of government as Communism and fascism. These nations abolished or put heavy curbs on freedom of speech. By the late 1980's, however, many of these nations had begun to ease the restrictions.

Technological advances have helped create a centralization of both power and communications in many industrial nations. In such nations, a government can use this power to restrict speech, so that the ordinary person with an idea to express may find it difficult to reach an audience. On the other hand, the same technological advances have produced new methods of communication. These new methods could lead to increased freedom of speech.   Jethro K. Lieberman

Additional resources

Foerstel, Herbert N. *Free Expression and Censorship in America: An Encyclopedia.* Greenwood, 1997.
King, David C. *The Right to Speak Out.* Millbrook, 1997. Younger readers.

Freedom of the press is the right to publish facts, ideas, and opinions without interference from the government or from private groups. This right applies to the printed media, including books and newspapers, and to the electronic media, including radio, television, and computer networks.

Freedom of the press has been disputed since modern printing began in the 1400's, because words have great power to influence people. Today, this power is greater than ever because of the many modern methods of communication. A number of governments place limits on the press because they believe the power of words would be used to oppose them. Many governments have taken control of the press to use it in their own interests. Most publishers and writers, on the other hand, fight for as much freedom as possible.

Democratic constitutions grant freedom of the press to encourage the exchange of ideas and to check the power of the government. Citizens of democracies need information to help them decide whether to support the policies of their national and local governments. In a democracy, freedom of the press applies not only to political and social issues but also to business, cultural, religious, and scientific matters.

Most democratic governments limit freedom of the press in three major types of cases. In such cases, these governments believe that press freedom could endanger individuals, national security, or social morality. (1) Laws against *libel* and *invasion of privacy* protect people from writings that could threaten their reputation or privacy. (2) Laws against *sedition* (urging revolution) and treason work to prevent publication of material that could harm a nation's security. (3) Laws against *obscenity* (offensive language) aim at the protection of the morals of the people.

Dictatorships do not allow freedom of the press. Dictators believe they alone hold the truth—and that opposition to them endangers the nation.

In the United States, freedom of the press is guaranteed by the First Amendment to the Constitution. All state constitutions also include protection for press freedom. Court decisions help make clear both the extent and the limits of this freedom. In general, the First Amendment prohibits censorship by the government before publication.

The U.S. press regulates itself to a great extent. For example, most publishers do not print material that they know is false or that could lead to crime, riot, or revolution. They also avoid publishing libelous material, obscenities, and other matter that might offend a large number of readers. In addition, because the press in the United States depends heavily on advertising income, it sometimes does not publish material that would displease its advertisers.

Freedom of the press was one goal of the American Colonies in their struggle for independence from the United Kingdom. The libel trial of John Peter Zenger in 1735 became a major step in the fight for this freedom. Zenger was the publisher of the *New-York Weekly Journal,* which criticized the British government. A jury found Zenger innocent after his attorney argued that Zenger had printed the truth and that truth is not libelous.

The severest restrictions on the press in the United States—and in all other countries—are imposed during times of stress, especially wartime. During World War II (1939-1945), for example, Congress passed laws banning the publication of any material that could interfere with the war effort or harm national security.

During the late 1960's and early 1970's, criticism by the U.S. press of the nation's involvement in Vietnam became increasingly widespread. This criticism helped broaden public opposition to the Vietnam War and probably influenced the government's change in policy toward the war. In 1971, the government tried to stop *The New York Times* and *The Washington Post* from publishing parts of a secret study of the war. The government claimed that publication of the so-called *Penta-*

gon Papers could harm national security. But the Supreme Court of the United States blocked the government's action.

Also in the 1960's and 1970's, many judges issued rulings frequently referred to as *gag orders.* The orders forbade the press to publish information that judges thought might violate a defendant's right to a fair trial. Such information might include confessions made by defendants or facts about their past. The press argued that gag orders violated the First Amendment. In 1976, the Nebraska Press Association challenged a Nebraska gag order before the Supreme Court. The court ruled that such orders are unconstitutional, except in extraordinary circumstances.

In other countries. Freedom of the press exists largely in the Western European countries, the English-speaking nations, and Japan. It is present to a limited extent in some Latin-American countries.

Press restrictions vary greatly from country to country. In Italy, the press restricts itself on what it prints about the pope. Such nations as Australia and Ireland have strict obscenity laws. However, the obscenity laws in such countries as Norway and Sweden are not strict. Denmark dropped all its obscenity laws during the 1960's.

The governments of many countries have strict overall controls on the press. A number of nations in Asia, Latin America, and the Middle East have censorship boards that check all publications. The censorship boards make sure newspapers and other publications follow government guidelines and that they agree with official policy.

The governments of China and certain other Communist nations own and operate the press themselves. The Communist Party makes sure that the press follows the policies of the party.

History. Rulers and church leaders restricted the writing and distribution of certain material even before there was a press. In those days, when everything was written by hand, books considered offensive were banned or burned. Since the A.D. 400's, the Roman Catholic Church has restricted material that it considers contrary to church teachings.

Early printers had to obtain a license from the government or from some religious group for any material they wanted to publish. In 1644, the English poet and political writer John Milton criticized such licensing in his pamphlet *Areopagitica.* This essay was one of the earliest arguments for freedom of the press. In time, the United Kingdom and other nations ended the licensing system. By the 1800's, the press of many countries had considerable freedom.

Freedom of the press led to some abuses. In the late 1800's, for example, some U.S. newspapers published false and sensational material to attract readers. Some people favored government regulation to stop such abuses by the so-called "yellow press." In most cases, however, such regulation would have been unconstitutional.

During the 1900's, the U.S. press grew to accept its responsibility to the public. Journalists and other media professionals became far more careful and conscientious in checking facts and reporting the news. In many other countries, however, the press lost its freedom. For example, the Fascists in Italy and the Nazis in Germany destroyed press freedom before and during World War II and used the press for their own purposes. Civilian or military dictatorships ruled many countries in the middle and late 1900's. All these governments censored the press heavily.　Jethro K. Lieberman

Additional resources

Flink, Stanley E. *Sentinel Under Siege: The Triumphs and Troubles of America's Free Press.* Westview, 1997.
Ingelhart, Louis E., comp. *Press and Speech Freedoms in America, 1619-1995: A Chronology.* Greenwood, 1997.

Privacy, Right of, is the right claimed by individuals to control the disclosure of personal information about themselves. It also covers people's freedom to make their own decisions about their private lives in the face of government attempts to regulate behavior.

The Constitution of the United States guarantees a number of privacy rights. The Fifth Amendment, for example, upholds the right to refuse to testify against oneself in a criminal case. The Fourth Amendment protects a person against unreasonable searches and seizures by government officials. The Supreme Court of the United States has ruled that the Constitution also protects privacy in certain matters relating to marriage, reproduction, birth control, family relationships, and child rearing and education.

Privacy is also protected by a branch of civil law called *tort law.* Under tort law, one person can sue another for violation of privacy in any of four categories: (1) disclosing private facts that are not newsworthy; (2) portraying a person in a false light; (3) using a person's image or personal facts for profit without the person's permission; and (4) intruding into a person's private physical space.

But federal law permits a number of activities that might be considered violations of privacy. For example, a person may intercept or record a conversation between two or more other persons with the consent of only one of those persons. Law enforcement officials, with a court order or other form of approval, may intercept calls without the consent of any party to the conversation. In most cases, employers may legally monitor employees' telephone conversations, e-mail (electronic mail), and voice mail.

Computer systems enable many organizations, including government agencies, financial institutions, and health care providers, to collect information on a person without the individual's knowledge. Such information, as well as e-mail and digital photographs of individuals, can be circulated worldwide on the Internet.

Organizations collect information on individuals to investigate or prevent crime, to manage vast service programs, or to determine a person's eligibility for—or interest in—credit, insurance, education, or other services. Since the 1970's, however, Congress and the states have passed laws that restrict disclosure of personal information and give individuals the right to challenge the accuracy of information about themselves. These laws cover federal agencies, school records, credit reports, and telephone solicitation. In addition, the law holds that most privileged conversations with lawyers, spouses, clergy, and others are confidential.　Robert Ellis Smith

Racial profiling is the act of targeting a person for criminal investigation primarily because of racial or ethnic characteristics. This practice is based on an assump-

tion that people of color or ethnic minorities are more likely to commit crimes. This assumption is common among people with racially prejudiced beliefs. However, racial profiling, also known as *ethnic profiling,* is generally considered to be a violation of the civil rights of minority groups. Charges of racial profiling commonly involve automobile stops by law enforcement officers. But people have also claimed to be targets of racial profiling at other times—for example, while walking on city streets or while shopping in stores or malls.

In the United States, many legal experts regard racial profiling to be a violation of certain constitutional protections, including the prohibition against unreasonable searches and seizures. The U.S. Supreme Court has limited the degree to which police officers may use racial profiles. According to the court, the police must demonstrate that the racial profile, along with other information, justifies a reasonable suspicion that the person is engaged in criminal activity.

In 2001, terrorists destroyed the World Trade Center in New York City and part of the Pentagon Building near Washington, D.C. Because the terrorists involved were believed to be Arab Muslims, the investigation focused on individuals of that background. Many critics argued that U.S. investigators and law enforcement officers engaged in racial profiling in the months following the attack. The U.S. Department of Justice said that it did not tolerate racial profiling against Arab Americans.
　Kenneth B. Nunn

Search warrant is a document issued by a court to permit a police officer to search a house, automobile, locker, or any other specified place. It is issued if there is reasonable cause to believe that illegal materials, such as gambling devices, burglar tools, or illegal drugs, are hidden there. A search warrant may also be issued to search for people.

In the Constitution of the United States, Amendment 4 states that no unreasonable searches or seizures may be made. The cause of search must be supported by oath. The search warrant must describe the place to be searched and what is to be seized in the search. The United States Supreme Court, however, allows some exceptions. In 1982, the court ruled that police do not need a search warrant to accompany an arrested person into the person's home or to seize any possible criminal evidence in sight there. In 1984, the court declared that evidence obtained with a search warrant later ruled to be defective may be used in court if the police reasonably believed they followed proper procedures in obtaining the search warrant.

Before 1760, search warrants in England and America were issued only to locate concealed stolen goods. In England, searches and seizures became so great an issue, and were finally so restricted, that it led to the saying that "every man's home is his castle."
　James O. Finckenauer

Warrant, *WAHR uhnt,* is a document authorizing a person to do something. A search warrant authorizes a law officer to search a house or other premises for goods held illegally. A bench warrant authorizes a law officer to arrest and bring before the court a person charged with a crime, misdemeanor, or contempt of court. Other warrants certify or guarantee the quality and validity of things.　George T. Felkenes

Focus on
TERRORISM

Terrorism: Past and Present

The word *terrorism* first appeared in the 1700's during a period of
the French Revolution known as the Reign of Terror. However,
acts that we would now consider terrorist in nature occurred long
before then. Since ancient times, individuals, rebel groups, and
governments have used violence to eliminate enemies, spread fear
and alarm, and attract attention for political or religious causes. This
section looks at terrorism from a historical and global perspective.

The French Revolution, which lasted from 1789 to 1799, marked the earliest use of the word *terrorism.* During one period of the revolution, the revolutionary government sentenced thousands of people to be beheaded by guillotine. The period became known as the Reign of Terror.

Granger Collection

Terrorism: Past and Present

The September 11 attacks on the World Trade Center in New York City and the Pentagon Building near Washington, D.C., were unlike any previous terrorist act in the United States. The intentional crashing of hijacked airplanes into buildings represented a new method of terrorist mass murder, and the planning of the attacks illustrated like never before the alarming reach of global terrorist networks. The attacks forced the United States and the world to confront a new kind of enemy threat—one that operated in secret and without a defined geographic base. As a result, the U.S.-led campaign against terrorist groups in Afghanistan and elsewhere lacked many traditional features of warfare between nations. In many ways, the September 11 attacks opened a new chapter in the history of violent conflict.

The word *terrorism* first appeared in the late 1700's. However, the use of terror is as old as civilization itself. From ancient times to the present, individuals, rebel groups, and governments have used violence to eliminate enemies, to spread fear and alarm, and to attract attention for political or religious causes. This article provides a brief history of terrorism from ancient times to today.

Early terrorism

Although historical evidence is incomplete, experts believe that early states practiced terrorism long before rebel groups did. Examples of state terrorism and brutality in ancient times are numerous.

Empire builders of ancient times often maintained control over conquered peoples through intimidation.

They frequently used brutality to frighten large populations, to discourage resistance and revolt, and to achieve political goals. For example, the Assyrians of the 700's B.C. treated conquered people especially cruelly. They impaled their victims on stakes or removed their skin while they were still alive.

The Romans were among the most powerful empire builders in history, and they too made use of terror to warn subjects of the consequences of revolt. In 71 B.C., for instance, the Roman general Crassus crushed a revolt of the gladiator Spartacus and publicly crucified the captured rebels. In A.D. 70, in response to a revolt by Jews in the province of Judea (now southern Israel), the Romans captured Jerusalem and destroyed the Temple. By eliminating the Temple, which the Romans considered the focus of Jewish worship and nationalism, the conquerors hoped to prevent further problems in the rebellious province.

The decline and fall of the Roman Empire in the 300's and 400's ushered in several centuries of violent upheaval. During this time, groups of invaders used gruesome methods to frighten enemies. Huns swept through Europe with enemy heads adorning their spears, and Anglo-Saxons nailed the hides of Viking raiders to church doors.

Peasant uprisings. As powerful kingdoms and large baronial estates emerged in the 1300's and 1400's, new threats to authority came not from foreign enemies, but from rebellious peasants. In 1381, a peasants' revolt in England produced widespread violence, much of which would now be considered terrorist in nature. Serfs murdered their lords, executed the Archbishop of Canterbury, and looted the palace of one of the king's principal advisers. A similar uprising, called the Jacquerie, occurred in northern France in 1358. Peasants, joined by

Tom Mockaitis, the contributor of this article, is Professor of History at DePaul University.

the lower middle classes, attacked nobles and looted their manors. The peasants ultimately faced defeat at the hands of trained soldiers, and the authorities responded with brutality and intimidation. The authorities hanged serfs from trees and from the door frames of their own cottages.

A similar pattern of violence persisted throughout the Renaissance and Reformation. Peasants and the urban lower classes could cause widespread damage, but they lacked the resources and organization to overthrow their rulers. They could commit acts of terror, but states could more effectively use terror as an instrument of intimidation and repression.

The beginnings of modern terrorism

During the Revolutionary War in America (1775-1783), both sides at times used tactics that today might be considered acts of terrorism. Patriots in the Southern Colonies engaged in guerrilla warfare against British troops. The patriots staged ambushes and sudden raids against the British and the Americans who supported them. The British conducted attacks against civilians, destroying property and murdering captured patriots.

The word *terrorism* was first used during the French Revolution (1789-1799). During one period of the revolution, the government declared a policy of terror against rebels and others who publicly disagreed with official policy. Thousands of suspected opponents of the revolution were executed by guillotine in what became known as the Reign of Terror.

By the early 1800's, the use of terrorism had become a fixture of rebellion and warfare. One noteworthy example involved efforts by the French emperor Napoleon I to hold Spain. Spanish guerrillas, supported by British army troops, resisted and attacked French supply lines and outposts. The guerrillas wore no uniforms and hid among sympathetic civilians. In response, French forces conducted attacks against the general population in areas where incidents occurred.

Terrorism in the 1900's

Terrorist acts in the early and middle 1900's had, for the most part, a decidedly local focus. Terrorists typically aimed to assassinate government officials, bomb government facilities, and murder people who opposed them or who supported the established social and political system. They usually chose prominent, often symbolic targets to create the impression that they could strike whenever and wherever they chose.

Assassinations. The 1900's began with one of the most dramatic terrorist acts in U.S. history. In Buffalo, New York, on Sept. 6, 1901, an anarchist shot President William McKinley. McKinley died on September 14. Another major assassination took place in 1914, when Archduke Franz Ferdinand, heir to the throne of Austria-Hungary, was shot while visiting Sarajevo, Bosnia. The murderer belonged to a Serbian terrorist organization known as the Black Hand. The assassination led to the start of World War I (1914-1918).

Rebellions and state terror. In March 1917, the people of Russia revolted. Later that year, revolutionaries formed a new government headed by the Communist leader V. I. Lenin. In 1918, revolutionaries shot the czar and his family to death. For the next two years, a bloody civil war raged between the Communists and anti-Communists. The Communists won the war and established the Soviet Union.

In the 1930's, the dictators Adolf Hitler of Germany, Benito Mussolini of Italy, and Joseph Stalin of the Soviet Union used terrorism and brutality to discourage opposition to their governments. Hitler alone had tens of thousands of his opponents executed and hundreds of thousands thrown into jail.

Many revolutionary movements in Africa, Asia, and elsewhere that sought to end colonial rule or to promote a particular ideology, such as Communism, adopted terrorist tactics. Many governments made use of state terrorism to suppress the rebellions or to intimidate citizens. In Algeria, for example, an organization called the *Front de Liberation Nationale* (FLN), or National Liberation Front, led the fight for independence from France. In 1954, the FLN began carrying out ambushes, assassinations, and bombing raids against European settlers and the French forces in Algeria. In response, the French army destroyed orchards and cropland belonging to native Algerians, forced millions of native Algerians into concentration camps, and tortured rebel leaders. Algeria finally became independent in 1962.

Domestic groups. Numerous terrorist groups have sought the destruction of the social, political, and economic systems in their home countries. These groups have included the Red Brigades in Italy, which was active until the late 1980's, and the Red Army Faction, also known as the Baader-Meinhof Gang, in West Germany, active until the early 1990's. The Red Brigades assassinated former Italian Prime Minister Aldo Moro in 1978. Since the 1960's, Spain has faced terrorist attacks by members of the Basque separatist group *Euzkadita Azkatasuna* (Basque Fatherland and Liberty), also known as ETA. This group seeks the establishment of an independent Basque state.

Since the 1980's, Peru has faced attacks by leftist terrorist groups called Shining Path and the Tupac Amaru Revolutionary Movement. In 1992, Abimael Guzmán Reynoso, the leader of Shining Path, and 10 other group leaders were convicted of high treason for terrorist crimes and sentenced to life in prison.

Northern Ireland has a long history of violence between Protestant *unionists,* who want Northern Ireland to remain in the United Kingdom, and Roman Catholic *nationalists,* who want Northern Ireland to become part of the Republic of Ireland. The dispute has led to riots, bombings, and other forms of terrorism. At various times during the 1900's, attacks by pro-Catholic militant groups such as the Irish Republican Army led to violent responses by Protestant terrorist groups.

Since the late 1800's, an American group, the Ku Klux Klan, has used violence to intimidate African Americans, Jews, and others based on the ideology of white supremacy. Other white supremacist organizations, such as the Aryan Nations, have also supported terrorist campaigns. In addition, a number of other American groups have used bombings, arson, and other terrorist tactics. For example, a radical group called the Weather Underground or Weathermen, which opposed U.S. involvement in the Vietnam War (1957-1975), sometimes used violence to bring attention to its cause.

Terrorism in the Middle East. Before the independence of Israel in 1948, Jewish organizations such as Irgun Zvai Leumi and the Stern Gang used violence to speed the end of British rule in Palestine. Because the groups hoped to gain international support for their cause, they focused on destroying property and made attempts to avoid civilian casualties. In July 1946, for instance, the Irgun bombed Jerusalem's King David Hotel, the site of the British military command in Palestine. However, the group had issued warnings prior to bombing so that some people could be evacuated.

The use of terrorism became more widespread during the lengthy Arab-Israeli conflict that followed the British withdrawal. In 1948, the armies of five neighboring Arab states attacked Israel. In an effort to create a unified state with defendable borders, Israeli forces expelled Palestinians from villages through the calculated use of violence. The Irgun's 1948 massacre of more than 100 civilians at the village of Deir Yassir spread panic among the Palestinians. Arab soldiers, in turn, sometimes brutalized Jewish prisoners and civilians.

In the 1960's, the Palestine Liberation Organization (PLO) organized guerrilla groups dedicated to defeating Israel. In response to PLO attacks, Israeli forces assassinated PLO leaders and attacked Palestinian refugee camps in Jordan and Lebanon. Palestinian terrorists also attacked Israelis abroad. In 1972, members of the Black September movement murdered two Israeli athletes and took nine others hostage at the Summer Olympic Games in Munich. All the hostages were killed during a failed rescue attempt by the West German police.

Since the 1970's, Palestinian groups such as Hamas and Hezbollah have continued to carry out campaigns of terrorism aimed at defeating Israel and establishing an independent Palestinian state. For example, Hamas spearheaded the Palestinian suicide bombing campaign of the early 2000's. Israel, in turn, has assassinated Palestinian leaders suspected of terrorism and conducted reprisals that have taken civilian lives.

The changing face of terrorism

Around the 1970's, many terrorist groups began forming networks, found state sponsors, and operated on an increasingly global scale. Since the 1990's, fears that weapons of mass destruction could fall into the hands of terrorists have increased significantly. In addition, many terrorist groups, particularly in the Middle East, have developed a deep hatred for the United States in particular or the West in general.

Factors contributing to change. A number of major world developments and technological advances have influenced the growth of terrorism since the late 1900's. The breakup of the Soviet Union in 1991 flooded illegal markets with surplus weapons and unemployed scientists willing to sell their services. In the years following the Soviet breakup, the possibility that terrorists might obtain dangerous biological, chemical, and nuclear materials became a matter of growing concern. The concern intensified in 1995, when members of a Japanese religious cult released sarin, a nerve gas, into the Tokyo subway system. The attack killed 12 people.

Advances in communications technology have also affected the impact and strategies of terrorism. The increased use of computers and the Internet has provided

© Corbis/Agence France-Presse

Abimael Guzmán Reynoso, leader of the terrorist group Shining Path, sought to overthrow the government in Peru. He was convicted of high treason and sentenced to life in prison in 1992.

terrorist networks with fast and anonymous ways of communicating with one another. Some Web sites have been used to spread terrorist propaganda or to offer detailed instructions for making bombs.

Attacks on the United States. Because of its global influence and support for Israel, the United States has become a central target for terrorist groups based in the Middle East. The most famous and far-reaching of these groups has been al-Qa'ida, the network formed by the Saudi-born millionaire and radical Muslim leader Osama bin Laden. In 1998, terrorists linked to bin Laden bombed U.S. embassies in Kenya and Tanzania. Bin Laden was also suspected in the 2000 bombing of the U.S. Navy warship *Cole* in a harbor in Yemen and the Sept. 11, 2001, terrorist attacks in the United States.

The United States has also faced terrorist attacks from individuals and groups within its own borders. In 1995, for instance, a bomb exploded in front of the Alfred P. Murrah Federal Building in Oklahoma City. The building was destroyed, and 168 people were killed. The terrorists, Timothy J. McVeigh and Terry L. Nichols, were reportedly motivated by an extreme hatred for the U.S. government.

A new emphasis on counterterrorism

The hijackings of Sept. 11, 2001, marked the beginning of a new era in the world's approach to terrorism. Since the attacks, *counterterrorism*—that is, efforts to prevent or fight terrorism—has become a top priority for governments and law enforcement agencies throughout the world. Features of counterterrorism include widespread intelligence-gathering efforts, increased security at airports and other potential targets, the use of economic restrictions against countries that support terror, and military action against terrorist groups and nations that harbor them.   Tom Mockaitis

Index